Communicating GLOBALLY

Intercultural Communication and International Business

Wallace V. Schmidt, *Rollins College*
Roger N. Conaway, *University of Texas at Tyler*
Susan S. Easton, *Rollins College*
William J. Wardrope, *University of Central Oklahoma*

SAGE Publications
Los Angeles • London • New Delhi • Singapore

For Ed Bonneau and Bryan Fulwider, and the counselors of peace

For information:

Sage Publications, Inc.
2455 Teller Road
Thousand Oaks, California 91320
E-mail: order@sagepub.com

Sage Publications Ltd.
1 Oliver's Yard
55 City Road
London EC1Y 1SP
United Kingdom

Sage Publications India Pvt. Ltd.
B-42, Panchsheel Enclave
Post Box 4109
New Delhi 110 017 India

Printed in the United States of America

Library of Congress Cataloging-in-Publication Data

Communicating globally : intercultural communication and international
business / Wallace V. Schmidt . . . [et al.].
  p. cm.
Includes bibliographical references and index.
ISBN 978-1-4129-1317-1 (pbk.)
  1. Business communication—Cross-cultural studies.
2. Intercultural communication. 3. International business enterprises.
4. Cross-cultural orientation. I. Schmidt, Wallace V., 1946-

HF5718.C624 2007
658.4'5—dc22   2006028039

This book is printed on acid-free paper.

11   10   9   8   7   6   5   4   3

Acquiring Editor:	Todd R. Armstrong
Editorial Assistant:	Katie Grim
Project Editor:	Astrid Virding
Copyeditor:	Cheryl Rivard
Typesetter:	C&M Digitals (P) Ltd.
Proofreader:	Word Wise Webb
Indexer:	Will Ragsdale

Brief Contents

Contents

Preface

We began this project with two intentions and one question. Our first intention was to write a modest-sized book about a massive subject. Our second intention concerned the ongoing scholarship that has given us a keener understanding of culture, communication, and international business. Issues that were formerly in the background have now been moved to the foreground—contrasting cultural orientations, culture shock, differing communication patterns, cosmopolitan complexity, conflict management and global negotiating, synergistic and virtual teams, varying business and social customs, and universal systems, to name a few. The primary question driving our exploration was how could we become effective cosmopolitan leaders capable of benefiting from the cultural synergy of others in order to create successful global enterprises?

Communicating Globally: Intercultural Communication and International Business recognizes our multinational and multicultural world and focuses on developing culturally sensitive cosmopolitan leaders—effective intercultural communicators capable of creating cultural synergy and leading cultural change in organizations. This type of leader is currently in demand and includes everyone whose responsibilities require them to deal with other people and their learned cultures. It provides a cultural general awareness of diverse worldviews, valuable insights on understanding and overcoming cultural differences, and a path to international business success that draws on the cultural synergy of all involved. It is intended to augment existing communication or business courses as well as serve as a supplemental guide for new graduates entering a cosmopolitan environment, senior managers in multinational organizations, and anyone who plans to conduct business overseas. We must all be prepared for an incredibly diverse global business community.

For organizations to flourish, let alone survive in the decades ahead, their perspective must be global. We must become more culturally sensitive and cosmopolitan, learning to move beyond mere coping with cultural differences among the earth's inhabitants to creating mutually benefiting synergy among them. We operate in a world market that demands an integration of intercultural communication skills and international business competence. Successful college graduates, corporate managers, and business professionals must be able to adapt to varying cultures and be capable of stepping outside their own box.

Significant Features of the Book

Communicating Globally: Intercultural Communication and International Business is distinctively different from other texts in the area. Many current texts assume a strictly anthropological/sociological perspective with a communication orientation. Other popular texts in the marketplace are intercultural readers, which present a variety of essays focusing on cultural diversity with the intent of increasing cultural awareness and sensitivity. There are also those texts that emphasize international business and issues of organizational management. We integrate intercultural communication theory with the practice of international business as applied to the emerging global setting. Theoretical perspectives serve to build practical skills and abilities that strengthen one's personal competencies and international business acumen. This distinctive orientation focuses on the process of creating meaningful intercultural dialogue and organizing relationships with others to create strong multinational organizations and visionary work teams capable of coping with the chaos of global change. It provides a valuable framework for helping undergraduate and graduate students, professional managers and consultants, and corporate enterprises achieve a multicultural outlook and forge a cosmopolitan perspective. It offers readers a philosophy and practice of how to galvanize a global vision and develop a spirit of cultural synergy.

Additionally, we offer readers a number of ways to begin thinking critically about intercultural communication and international business. This textbook

- Provides readers an integrated framework for understanding intercultural communication and international business by focusing on essential principles and practices.

- Draws on a variety of sources and familiarizes readers with important intercultural and organizational theories that they are likely to encounter in the communication and business disciplines.

- Provides readers with an innovative perspective on cosmopolitan communication, global leadership, cultural synergy, and the dynamic processes affecting international business and globalism.

- Includes a balanced treatment of theory and practice by assuming an action orientation. Emphasis is placed on relating research findings to personal experiences and real-life contexts. Grounded on established principles and tested procedures, attention is directed to what readers can or should *do*.

- Introduces readers to different ways of conducting business around the world and prepares them to enter the global marketplace and world bazaar.

- Facilitates and supports individual research interests by including regional resource guides and supplemental data sources.

We hope that readers will not just thumb through the pages, reading words, nodding to themselves when they encounter things they like and then moving on to the next chapter. Rather, we encourage readers to reflect and respond actively to what they read. The concepts discussed do not lend themselves to passivity but require active participation.

Overview of the Book

We've made a deliberate effort to write a reader-friendly text that presents its ideas coherently and lucidly. The ideas are tied together to maintain a consistent focus on the vital importance of effective intercultural communication in a dynamic international business arena.

Unit One explains the key concepts and describes the forces, technologies, and trends at play in the global business setting. Chapter 1 defines international business and the nature of globalism and outlines the challenges of living in a changing global business environment. Chapter 2 discusses differing research approaches to the study of culture, describes the interdependent nature of culture, communication, and international business, and defines cosmopolitan leadership in an emerging world culture. Chapter 3 defines the concept of cultural synergy and outlines the essential variables influencing global organizations.

Unit Two develops knowledge, skills, and intercultural competence at an individual level. It examines the cognitive, social, and personal skills needed by cosmopolitan leaders and defines intercultural competence. Specifically, it explores relational building, the ability to communicate effectively with others, and constructively coping with intercultural conflict along with the necessary traits of flexibility, adaptability, and mindfulness. Chapter 4 examines the dialectics of intercultural relationships, cultural transitions, adaptation, and the effects of culture shock. It identifies intercultural effectiveness and cross-cultural competencies. Chapter 5 explores the interdependence of language, thought, and culture and specifically looks at the intercultural dimensions of verbal and nonverbal communication. Chapter 6 addresses intercultural communication and conflict management, noting how face-saving and conflict-handling strategies and styles influence our conflict negotiations with others. It further explores the alternative dispute resolution methods of mediation and arbitration.

Unit Three builds on this individual level and its conceptual framework by focusing on intercultural-related business theory, strategy, and the organizational level. It directly applies the key concept of cultural synergy to the areas of decision-making, problem-solving, conflict management, and organizational innovation and change. It also examines leadership, working effectively in groups, and a commitment to innovativeness. Chapter 7 deals with cosmopolitan leadership, teams, problem-solving, and the global workforce. Chapter 8 deals with the effects of chaos and the strategies needed for innovation and change when taking a long view.

Unit Four concludes the book by providing specific regional overviews profiling cultural themes and patterns, socioeconomic and political factors, business conduct and characteristics, and emerging trends. It also includes respective resource guides useful for more intense culture-specific study. The final chapters discuss doing business in various regions of the world: North America in Chapter 9, the Caribbean and Latin America in Chapter 10, Asia and the Pacific Rim in Chapter 11, Western Europe and Eastern Europe in Chapter 12, and the Middle East and Africa in Chapter 13.

Finally, in the epilogue, we examine the road ahead and offer suggestions regarding the direction of intercultural communication and international business. We speculate on the evolving nature of this global arena and draw tentative conclusions based on societal and business trends.

This new postmodern millennium is shaping up to be a wild frontier. The organizations that will succeed and thrive will be those led by culturally cosmopolitan leaders who understand how to animate people and seize opportunities. Globalism represents changing from a national to an international understanding of business activity and responding in interculturally appropriate ways to international opportunities and challenges.

We *do not* necessarily provide answers to the challenges ahead. We provide a framework that can alter the way you think about issues, help you define things in ways that are more understandable and acceptable to others, and begin a development process that can lead to new skills and competencies. We supply insight based on research and application that can permit you to make the necessary choices and important decisions.

Acknowledgments

Any book owes its existence to efforts made by others in addition to the listed authors. *Communicating Globally: Intercultural Communication and International Business* could not have been possible without the encouragement, generous support, and participation of a number of people. We would like to thank all those who have helped us as we worked our way through this project.

We are grateful that Dr. Robert Moore and Dr. Wenxian Zhang, Asian specialists in the Department of Anthropology at Rollins College, and Dr. Ilan Alon, an International Business specialist in the Crummer School of Business, agreed to jointly collaborate on writing Chapter 11: Doing Business in East Asia and the Pacific Rim. Their combined expertise and personal experiences led to an insightful chapter that helps explain the complexities of this region.

We are indebted to Samuel J. Wolff for contributing Chapter 13: Doing Business in Africa and the Middle East. Sam has a background in Islamic studies and served as a pastor and missionary to Kenya and Tanzania for 20 years. His knowledge, experience, and personal insights helped lift the curtain on this little-known and often-misunderstood region to reveal the available opportunities and many challenges. Thanks also to Karen Tollefson Roemer, who assisted in reviewing and editing the chapter. She has been active in German and Swiss business concerns and currently teaches courses in cross-cultural awareness in Frankfurt, Germany.

We thank Gary and Kathy Randel for permitting us to include portions of their expatriate journal in Chapter 4: Cultural Contact and Interfacing With Others. Their experiences in Singapore helped to illustrate the joys and frustrations accompanying an overseas assignment.

Thanks also to Roger Schmidt, whose tales of international business and accounts of intercultural encounters helped to inspire this project. His experiences further confirmed the need to integrate intercultural communication with international business.

We appreciate Kim K. Johnson for assisting in developing the Resource Guides that accompany our discussion of doing business in the various regions. Her dedicated research and high energy contributed to producing a list of resources that expands the understanding of each region.

We certainly wish to thank Rollins College, the Hamilton Holt School, The University of Texas at Tyler, Texas State University–San Marcos, and the University of Central Oklahoma for offering supportive climates that allowed us to finish this project in a timely manner. We thank our colleagues for their support and encouragement along the way and thank our students who have contributed to this book in both direct and indirect ways.

We sincerely express our thanks to Jeffrey C. Ady at the University of Hawai'i at Manoa, Cecile W. Garmon at Western Kentucky University, Beth Hoger at Western Michigan University, Wenshan Jia at Chapman University, and Melody van Lidth de Jeude at the University of North Carolina at Chapel Hill, who reviewed early or late drafts of the manuscript and gave their time and expertise to keep us on track. We benefited from their careful reading and insightful suggestions that expanded and clarified our thinking in many ways and greatly contributed to a much-improved final manuscript.

We also would like to thank the people at SAGE who worked hard to transform an exciting idea into a book. We particularly appreciate the support and backing from Todd Armstrong and the tireless assistance of Deya Saoud, Camille Herrera, and Sarah Quesenberry. Their confidence, encouragement, and continued faith in the project helped keep us going.

Special and unprecedented thanks must be given to Dr. Dunn, Dr. Sombeck, Dr. Ho, Dr. Straker, Dr. Boyce, Dr. Padhya, Melissa Czapla, and Dr. Yang for helping Wally survive cancer and regain his health so we could finish this project. It is quite appropriate that this was a multicultural and international team of outstanding medical specialists.

Finally, and most importantly, we treasure the support and love of our families because writing is intensely irksome work and a lonely business most of the time. For urging us forward, for patience, and for sustenance, we cannot thank them enough. For enduring our vacant stares and tolerating us during the weekends and late nights of writing, we are greatly appreciative. For listening to us read early drafts and for being by our side through each stage of the manuscript, we are grateful. Special thanks, then, to Susan, Phyllis, Matthew, Stephanie, Scott, Grant, Justin, Darcy, Cori, Jeff and Katie for their contributions both large and small.

Unit One

Key Concepts

We could learn a lot from crayons . . . some are sharp, some are pretty, some are dull, some have weird names, and all are different colors . . . but they all have to learn to live in the same box.

—Anonymous

We bind our hands together with the sacred thread of unity. Muslims, Sikhs, Hindus alike—come all and work together for peace, friendship, and unity. Together we work to overcome our difficulties and dream of charming days ahead.

—Howrah Women's Association Motto, India

1

The Concept of International Business and a Global Marketplace

- 100,000 U.S. firms are engaged in overseas ventures valued at over $1 trillion.
- Foreign investment in the U.S. has now surpassed the $2 trillion mark.
- Financial markets are open 24 hours a day around the world.
- $1 trillion of business is done on the Internet.
- The Pacific Rim will influence our future—Asia is a $3 trillion a year market growing at $3 billion per week.

When Magellan, Columbus, Marco Polo, and the other early adventurers set out on their explorations, few people had any concept of the size or shape of the earth. Many ardently believed that sea serpents and other fiendish monsters would threaten them and possibly devour their crews. Today, although some still believe in a Loch Ness monster, we are able to measure the earth's circumference to within inches, physically relocate personnel or transport goods to anywhere on its surface within hours, and communicate worldwide in a fraction of a second. "Global" has been turned into more than a geometric construct; it has become a socioeconomic concept that recognizes that most—if not all—human activity happening around the world is interconnected and interdependent (Friedman, 2005). This has prompted one CEO to propose that globalism "means a complete revolution in the thought process, a kind of Copernican revolution in business thinking" (Benveniste, 1994, p. 85).

This chapter advances reasons for studying global communication and international business. It defines international business, introduces certain key concepts, and examines the growth of globalization. It also addresses selected political, economic, and technological influences affecting the global business setting. Finally, it looks at the training challenges a complex intercultural world poses for a changing global business environment.

Why Study Global Communication and International Business?

The growing number of international corporations and the globalization of the economy have made intercultural business communication a current area of important concern. Moreover, forward-thinking corporations expect to send more professionals abroad and want entry-level candidates with cross-cultural competence. This increasing interest in a multicultural orientation and the incredible global opportunities available obviously serve to motivate a study of global communication and international business.

Communication is uniquely suited to study the global workplace. A communication focus concentrates on the dynamic unfolding relations among people and their organizations. The study of communication also underscores structure, process, and interpretation and is sensitive to diverse cultural environments. Communication "is the substance of global organizing," and the ability to navigate the treacherous waters of intercultural conflict and the level of skill and tact necessary to coax high-quality decisions out of multicultural teams require effective communication (Stohl, 2001, p. 335).

Globalization is inevitable. Dramatic changes in transportation, technology, and trade have altered the way people communicate and relate to others around the world. Improvements in the speed of transportation have increased our mobility. Affordable and accessible transportation has reduced the barrier of distance and bridged our cultures. Additionally, fundamental changes in technology have been a driving force in globalization. Conrad and Poole (2002) emphasize that today's globalization is unique because "technological developments have fundamentally changed the way that information and expertise is [sic] disseminated around the globe" (p. 391).

Dramatic changes in speed and access with the Internet have significantly influenced international business and contact with other cultures. A company Web page gives its customers worldwide access to products or services at any hour of the day. Users can "opt in" to a Web page of a large international company and receive e-mail updates on new products or services. Customers purchasing computers on Dell's Web site can do so in their own language. Such customers are given instant access to pricing information and product availability, which reduces costs and improves service for Dell. The Internet also benefits many users through improved competition. Most hotels and airlines now offer their best prices online. These fundamental changes affect each one of us individually and have created a global matrix where cultures and individuals are increasingly connected.

There is a massive relocation of people around the world. Today there is a global repositioning of people that includes legal and illegal immigrants, temporary workers, retirees, and visitors. At least 60 million people were living outside their country of birth or citizenship in 2000, an increase of about 25 percent since 1990 (Martin & Widgren, 2002). The three main reasons people voluntarily migrate are political asylum, family reunification, and economics (Featherstone, 2002), with power struggles or internal ethnic strife accounting for the involuntary migration (Martin & Nakayama, 2003). This relocation has resulted in all contemporary societies becoming culturally pluralistic.

Global corporations are increasingly reaching across borders to find the skills they need. The need for knowledgeable workers has caused industrialized nations to reconsider their protectionist immigration policies as they come to rely on, and compete for, foreign-born workers. Moreover, nations having slow-growing workforces but rapid growth in service-sector jobs are becoming magnets for immigrants. Additionally, nations whose educational systems produce prospective workers faster than their economies can absorb them are exporting people and their skills. The result is a major redefinition of labor markets and a workplace that is increasingly multicultural, at both the unskilled and skilled levels (Benveniste, 1994). Thus, the combination of a global workforce and multinational organizations means that managers and employees must be able to work effectively with more and more people with differing cultures, customs, values, beliefs, and practices.

There is a widespread increase in free trade agreements and bilateral investment treaties. This trend in "open borders" means greater opportunities for international business and possibly a gradual standardization of labor practices around the world in such areas as vacation time, workplace safety, and employee rights (Benveniste, 1994). Trade agreements specifically spell out to participating countries certain areas of conformity for products covered under the agreement and explicitly state areas of cooperative activity. The North American Free Trade Agreement (NAFTA) is an agreement among Canada, the United States, and Mexico that seeks to ease border restrictions between the three countries on goods and services. The European Union (EU) was formed among selected European countries, creating a new central currency called the Euro and opening markets to international business and travel. Mercosur was formed in an effort to establish a common market among selected Latin American countries, and the Central American Free Trade Agreement (CAFTA) was established between Costa Rica, El Salvador, Guatemala, Honduras, and Nicaragua. This liberalization or opening of borders to the free flow of products and services continues as a significant trend in globalization.

Finally, studying global communication and international business can assist us in developing self-awareness and building a vigorous trading community keenly committed to the promotion of peace. Studying other cultures and their business practices can help us better understand our own cultural identity and background. Our cultural identities are negotiated, co-created, reinforced, and challenged through communication with others. Peter Adler (1975) observes that such a study may begin as a journey into another culture and reality but end as a journey into one's own culture. We acquire a respect for other points of view while becoming acutely aware of our own choices and actions. We come to accept others and deal with others fairly and civilly (Branden, 1997). Civility and tolerance of plurality and diversity are essential values necessary for building community, and community is critical to peace and economic harmony (Peck, 1987, 1993; Tinder, 1980). Catherine R. Stimpson (1994) believes "that people can talk about, through, across, and around their differences and that these exchanges will help us live together justly" (p. B1). A spirited market community and world at peace will require considerable effort and hard work but without it "there may be very little future to think about at all" (Bellah, Madsen, Sullivan, Swindler, & Tipton, 1985, p. 286).

International Business, Globalism, and the Nature of Global Communication

Daniels, Radebaugh, and Sullivan (2004) define international business as "all commercial transactions—private and governmental—between two or more countries" (p. 3). Private companies are engaged in international business to increase profit in sales or distribution of services or to develop another country's resources. Government agencies and nongovernmental organizations (NGOs) work to influence political or economic policies or provide aid to people or groups through international volunteer or faith-based agencies. Many scholars today assert that all employees, whether domestic or abroad, inevitably engage in international business activities because all business is international (Kotabe & Aulakh, 2002).

6

Chaney and Martin (2004) define business globalization as "the ability of a corporation to take a product and market it in other countries" (p. 4). Globalism, however, is more than simply doing business in another country. As one American CEO observed, "We used to be an American company operating overseas. Now we're trying to become a global company, and there's a big difference in how you think about doing business" (Harris & Moran, 1991, p. 27). Global organizations must become an integral part of the countries and local people where they choose to do business, exhibiting diplomacy and cooperative behavior. For example, Proctor & Gamble recast itself into a number of global business units with responsibility for profits, new business, product development, manufacturing, and marketing when it went global. This maximized the business potential of the entire product portfolio by developing both local and regional marketing strategies and strategic alliances. Senior management was recast to promote functional knowledge and transfer best practices. Ericsson, the Swedish telephone maker, also decentralized when it went global. They regionalized their operations in China to better service network operators and suppliers—the fastest growing market segment. As a result, the China division became Ericsson's largest source of annual sales (Forteza & Neilson, 1999). Choosing the right people for a global enterprise is also critical. Global managers must be accommodating to the tapestry of cultures and sensibilities that are tied to success in a variety of countries. They must be able to mediate between disparate factions and manage a complexity of human issues. Consequently, in all aspects, the growth of international business hinges on the effectiveness of global communication.

Varner (2002) states that "research over the past few years has increasingly shown that the best theories and models in the areas of management, marketing, finance, and production can be transformed into successful operations only through effective business communication" (p. ix). People in business create and manage meanings to build profitable relationships and accomplish specific goals. Intercultural communication adds to the dynamics of business communication by mixing diversity of languages and culture. In Chapter 2, we will more fully define intercultural communication and related terms. Further contributing to this mix is intercultural business communication or "communication within and between businesses that involves peoples from more than one culture" (Chaney & Martin, 2004, p. 2). Here, the organizational context and the environment of the interaction shape messages, influence relationships, and affect outcomes.

Globalism is no longer a concept but a reality, and intercultural communication and international business form the essential supporting pillars for successful global communication. Global communication operates in a worldwide context and includes all the complexities, barriers, and diversities of interpersonal and intercultural business communication. Today, business dealings that were once confined primarily to local economies have given way to an extensively integrated world economy (Appadwal, 1996). This international pattern of "world-wide connectedness" (Held & McGrew, 2000, p. 54) means "events and developments in far-away distant places can have an impact on local happenings and events, just as forces and structures of local places can influence and enable events with rather significant global effects" (Shome & Hegde, 2002, p. 174).

Moran and Riesenberger (1997) help us understand the current state of globalization when they delineate three phases that illustrate the market shifts that have emerged over the past 65 years. Phase one refers to the 30 years following World War II (1945–1975), when high demand and growth led to a focus on economy of scale and a rising standard of living. The emphasis was on raw materials, quantity, capital, and efficient use of labor. Phase two (1975–1985) witnessed increased production that in turn led to an eventual surplus in many industries. Quality became the new focus, along with an emphasis on low cost and technical advances. Governments provided lower tariffs and tax incentives to encourage global companies to build new factories in their countries. During phase three (1985–2000), strategic alliances increased whereby regional trading blocs offered economic advantages for those states that are members. This has created volatile change as globalism has come to dominate international business. Just as Condoleezza Rice wants to lead the reshaping of America's role in the world through "transformational diplomacy," American business wants to reassert its leadership role in international business and give direction to this ever-increasing globalism (Chollet, 2005, p. G1).

In response to increasing globalism, we contend that cosmopolitanism and cultural synergy need to become distinguishing characteristics of the new emerging work culture and key concepts affecting the interactional dynamics of multicultural organizations. The complexity and shrinking of today's world literally force international business to understand cultural differences and to capitalize on those differences. Cosmopolitan communicators understand the impact of cultural factors when interacting with others, especially with persons from foreign cultures, and are willing to revise and expand their views as part of personal growth. Such individuals seek to get into the "world" of the receiver and improve their intercultural communication skills. This concept further promotes sensitive, innovative, and participative leaders capable of operating comfortably in a global or pluralistic environment. These are multinational, interculturally oriented people who can manage accelerating change and differences in their own lives. Culturally alert cosmopolitan leaders are open and flexible in approaching others, can cope with situations and people quite different from their own background, and are willing to alter personal attitudes and perspectives. Such leaders acquire knowledge about cultural influences on behavior, cultural patterns, themes, or universals and integrate this understanding of macrocultures and microcultures with international business experiences.

Cultural synergy builds on the varying differences in the world's people for mutual growth and accomplishment through cooperation. For such aggregate action to occur, cosmopolitan leaders must effectively adjust and adapt to cultural differences and avoid the barriers posed by stereotyping, prejudice, and ethnocentrism. This concept further entails understanding that a homogenization process is underway and a unique world culture is emerging. Advances in mass media, transportation, and technology are breaking down the traditional obstacles among groups of peoples and their differing cultures, permitting international business to develop transnational strategies for serving the needs and markets of this evolving world economy. In Chapters 2 and 3, we further develop the concepts of cosmopolitanism and cultural synergy.

This new era of globalization is not simply an ephemeral fad, but a new international system. This new international system emphasizes flexibility and speed and open markets. International business leaders need to be aware of acceptable, universal business principles and procedures and be sophisticated enough to appreciate the effect of global differences on standard business practices. Being able to cope with the interdependence of business activity throughout the world requires a basic understanding of the political, economic, and technological issues affecting the global marketplace.

Political Issues and Globalization

A number of political issues affect global communication. These often intertwine with business issues in the macro-environment of country relationships. Political actions are not peripheral to international business activity but integrally influence an interdependent world economy and shape the world bazaar. They raise questions about the roles of a superpowers and market-dominant minorities (MDM) in a "retribalized" world.

A particularly significant political issue influencing globalization and transcending national boundaries is the homogenization or polarization of countries (Kotabe & Aulakh, 2002). Homogenization refers to the global trend where Western products such as Coca-Cola, McDonald's, or Wal-Mart are being promoted around the world and are exposing other societies to Western values and practices (Conrad & Poole, 2002; Georgi-Findley, 2002). Most scholars agree that the news media from around the world, including MTV and Hollywood movies, have clearly influenced the rest of the world. One popular

U.S. television show, *Baywatch*, was viewed in 103 countries around the globe. The Walt Disney Company, one of the largest media and entertainment corporations in the world, has established Disneyland, Disneyland Paris, Tokyo Disneyland, Hong Kong Disneyland, and Disney World. Despite some legitimate concerns, there are benefits to this Western homogenization. Jagdish Bhagwati (2004), former economic adviser to the United Nations, sees globalization as the best way to raise incomes and speed up the long-term development of the world's poorest economies. He identifies a number of benefits that can be derived from this increased globalization:

> Wages and labor standards are improved.
> Poverty is diminished and individuals have greater opportunities for success.
> Child labor is reduced and gender discrimination is reduced.
> Democracy is promoted and cultures are enriched.
> Global interdependence promotes intercultural cooperation that advances the cause of peace.
> Globalization can tie us together and create a connectedness among cultures in a way the world has never experienced before (Wolff, 2004).

However, for some there is too much homogenization. Polarization or "Balkanization" is a critical response to globalization where peoples or groups reject outside influence and see it as undermining their values and endangering their cultural legacy (Conrad & Poole, 2002). Many countries have reacted with anger and alienation to the cultural influence of the United States and a leveling of culture in general. Mexico and France as well as a number of other countries have limited the importation of U.S. television programming and films. They hope to develop a media industry that will promote their own cultural values. Moreover, instead of adopting wholesale the ways of Western culture, some Middle Eastern and Asian societies are resisting the perceived corruption and immoral influences emanating from the West.

Venezuela serves as an example of a developing country resisting the outside effects of international competition and regional trading blocs and the potential implications for the global marketplace. Venezuela's government, led by president Hugo Chavez, developed a state-run plan designed for economic self-sufficiency (Cordoba, 2004). The Venezuelan government has poured billions of dollars into new social welfare programs focused primarily on healthcare education and job training for the poor. The policy sought to develop Venezuela from within by using its own country's resources, materials, and leaders. It effectively erected a "wall" against international competition. Believing the Venezuelan people should "eschew Pepsis and Big Macs for sugar-cane juice and Venezuelan-style pancakes called cachapas" (Cordoba, 2004, p. 1), Venezuela's indigenous economic model relies on the state-run government to end economic oppression by creating new societal structures. Such an economic model has experienced some popularity with Latin countries, but most rejected it as unworkable in the 1990s (Cordoba, 2004). Venezuela ranks as the world's fifth-largest oil exporter. If the indigenous policies collapse, the result could have a significant impact on global oil markets and international business.

Economic Issues and Globalization

Globalization has also raised a number of economic issues regarding international business, such as the growth and influence of multinational organizations, the development of world trade organizations, and the increasing interdependence of the world economy. During the 1980s and 1990s, multinational organizations extended their overseas operations at an accelerated rate. Multinational organizations (MNOs) are companies with an established presence in both domestic and international markets that export or import merchandise or invest in international locations through joint ventures, contracts, and agreements.

MNOs primarily operate through foreign direct investments (Daniels et al., 2004). Foreign direct investments (FDI) refer to the amount of funds an MNO invests in its manufacturing or service operations in another country. For example, Japanese auto manufacturers may decide to build a solely owned subsidiary plant in the United States, or General Motors may invest in an auto manufacturing plant in Tokyo where it owns 10 to 25 percent of the voting stock. Such international connectedness has often been used as a key measure of globalization in international business, although other economic, cultural, demographic, and technological factors are also involved. Overall, the rate of FDI worldwide has increased tenfold over the last 20 years, according to the Global Policy Forum (www.globalpolicy.org), a nonprofit group that monitors policy making at the United Nations and provides information and education to the public on global issues. According to one globalization index, Ireland ranks as the most global nation because of its economic integration, technological connectivity, personal contact, and political engagement (Kearney, 2004). China still remains the world's most popular destination for FDI because of its size, and investors believe its economy will remain strong.

A multinational organization's decision to make a foreign direct investment is based on economic and political factors. The business may seek to assess the economic stability of the foreign country's market and currency. Whether the currency is currently falling or rising may determine if the company believes the investment to be a timely one. Low labor costs or less costly materials may attract an investor. Developing market share may attract an MNO to a different country. An MNO may also find that developing closer political ties with another country provides certain benefits in a globalized economy. Industrialized or developed countries are particularly attractive to investors because of their natural resources and political stability. Conversely, political instability in many developing countries makes the risk of doing business in them very high.

Besides FDI activities (i.e., wholly owned investments and joint investments), companies have available other private avenues for conducting international business such as exporting, licensing and franchising, contract manufacturing, and turnkey agreements. Exporting involves the manufacturing of a product in one country and its sale to another country. Licensing provides a fee structure for the use of a product or service by another country for a specified period of time, whereas franchising additionally provides the technological and management know-how and the capital necessary for the construction and operation of the franchise. Two well-known and visible examples of worldwide franchises are Domino's Pizza and McDonald's restaurants. When you look at the textile label on a piece of apparel or the tag on appliances, you can see where the product was manufactured. By law, this is required to be displayed. Finally, turnkey agreements involve the construction of new plants using a company's technology for another country. For example, the constructions of hydroelectric dams, oil refineries, or communication systems are eventually turned over to the government of another country to operate.

Complicating all these transactions is determining the monetary currency to be used in a contract, because developing country currencies are more volatile in terms of their exchange rate than those of developed countries. Consequently, companies may engage in bartering with the developing country, where the seller receives goods or services in payment for goods or services sold. One well-known and rather interesting barter agreement was made between PepsiCo and the former Soviet Union in the 1970s when vodka was accepted as payment for Pepsi syrup and bottling equipment. A business relationship between PepsiCo and Russia still exits today—more than 30 years later.

World trade organizations have significantly influenced the evolution of globalization. The World Trade Organization (WTO) began officially in 1995 as a successor to the General Agreement on Tariffs and Trade (GATT). The WTO is designed to govern international economic affairs. Specifically, this multilateral organization is charged with liberalizing trade and lowering tariffs and nontariff barriers so as to increase international trade. According to

Sampson (2003), the WTO is "undeniably a major player in the field of global governance, and its rules and process will profoundly affect the future economic and political orientation of its 139 member countries as well as the 30 countries in the process of joining" (p. 1). Recently, critics of the WTO have alleged that its current practices benefit trade with rich countries but only continue the "race to the bottom" for poor countries and NGOs.

Two sister organizations of the WTO also wield tremendous economic leverage worldwide. First, the International Monetary Fund (IMF), also known as "the Fund," is based in Washington, DC., and lends money to governments to help stabilize their currencies. It was established by the United Nations in July 1944 and "is an organization of 184 countries, working to foster global monetary cooperation, secure financial stability, facilitate international trade, promote high employment and sustainable economic growth, and reduce poverty" (International Monetary Fund, 2005, www.imf.org). The second institution is the World Bank (WB), which provides loans, policy advice, and technical assistance to improve the living standards of people in developing countries. The World Bank, located in Washington, DC., focuses on allocating resources to development projects for emerging countries and investigates fraud and corruption in projects funded by the development bank. Critics contend that the mission of both the IMF and the WB differs from what actually happens, believing that those who actually benefit from economic policies are the richer, stronger traders who increase their dominance over the poorer traders.

Globalization has met with some protest around the world because public regulatory institutions have forgotten that economics is a social science and must also concern itself with the welfare of the people, not just international corporations. The main institutions that govern globalization—the WTO, the IMF, and the WB—can reform their one-size-fits all economic policies that sometimes damage rather than help countries with unique financial, governmental, and social institutions. They can also become more transparent and responsive to their constituents. Globalization can be a positive force around the world, particularly for the poor. It can help to eradicate poverty and promote economic growth. It can address the issues of education, health, welfare, the environment, and the redistribution of income and opportunity in the "developed" and "developing" worlds (Stiglitz, 2003).

The rise of MNOs and increasingly open borders has helped promote "outsourcing." Outsourcing occurs when an organization opts to move some of its operations overseas and invest in businesses with established vendors in a foreign country. Instead of buying land or building its own facilities, the organization will outsource its operations by seeking foreign vendors who provide lower labor costs or cheaper resources for their products. Many developing countries have untapped natural resources or excess labor pools that organizations can draw on. India is the fastest growing white-collar workforce for outsourcing. When an organization outsources its jobs overseas, it may receive many benefits including higher company profits and lower prices for consumers. On the other hand, workers who lose their jobs to foreign vendors because of outsourcing experience the loss personally for themselves and their families.

Opinions differ regarding outsourcing, but the fact remains that it has become a major issue in our global economy. Both the scope and breadth of outsourcing continue to grow. Many economists have estimated that approximately 300,000 U.S. jobs were outsourced overseas during 2004. John McCarthy (2004), a researcher at Forrester Research, Inc., in Cambridge, Massachusetts, predicts that the number of outsourced jobs in the United States will rise to 3.3 million by 2015, but more conservative economists believe the number will reach only 600,000 jobs by the year 2010. International competition places pressure on industries to outsource their operations, and major U.S. firms typify this trend. The Web-search company Google led the way in outsourcing when it created an engineering center in Bangalore, India, which has since become a thriving global technological servicing hub. Moreover, Northwest Airlines cut its operating costs by over a billion dollars by outsourcing heavy maintenance overseas and reducing the number of mechanics and flight attendants.

Multinational organizations engaged in overseas ventures and outsourcing must consider managing their financial risk. When companies outsource abroad, risk management increases and must be considered when reviewing business strategies and operations. When Levi Strauss chooses to establish textile operations in Mexico, the market offers potentially lower production costs and higher returns but adds risks beyond what the company normally experiences in San Francisco. Day-to-day business risks are increased in the globalization of markets and can be identified in a number of ways (Poole-Robb & Bailey, 2002). First, political factors increase risk for a company's normal business operations when a country's government becomes unstable, a military coup occurs, or other political circumstances create challenges for business operations. Second, economic factors increase risks when the host country's currency inflates dramatically or an international financial market drops suddenly. Third, unique security risks exist in the internal and external environment for MNOs as they do business in international markets. Personnel security becomes extremely important when executives face physical harm from car bombing, kidnapping, or other forms of violent behavior. A less secure work environment also increases security risks for all employees. Today, all U.S. multinational organizations must enact enterprise risk management (ERM) at all levels of their operations as a result of the Sarbanes-Oxley Act enacted on July 30, 2002. They need to be able to estimate consequences when creating planned change.

Technological Issues and Globalism

Regardless of the range of perspectives regarding globalization, it will inevitably move forward because of the dramatic changes in technology and transportation that have forever altered the landscape of communication and international business. Today, people and organizations are connected—via answering machines, faxes, e-mail, electronic bulletin boards, and the Internet—to other people and organizations around the world. This technology has significantly altered how we do business and our patterns of communication (Gergen, 1991). The marketplace now consists of human beings connected to each other and engaged in an open, unregulated conversation.

Through their electronic office systems, companies can communicate with their markets directly, but they also need to come down from their "ivory towers" and talk to the people with whom they hope to create relationships. To speak with a human voice, companies must share the concerns of the communities they serve. This requires belonging to a community and being an active, concerned participant. Companies that do not belong to a community of discourse will die (Levine, Locke, Searls, & Weinberger, 2000). Consequently, in the midst of our technological capabilities we need to think high touch as well and remember the human element (O'Brian, 1993). This is particularly true for multinational companies transitioning into new societies and attempting to bridge the differences. In Chapters 7 and 8, we further examine the changes in how multinational organizations operate and the need to proactively anticipate and plan change.

Marshall McLuhan (1962; also see McLuhan & Fiore, 1968) coined the term "global village" to characterize our shrinking world resulting from emerging communication technologies and the rapid expansion of worldwide transportation. Although it is popularly used, a growing number of scholars see it as a metaphor that conceals more than it reveals. People in villages know one another; they do not merely know *about* one another. There is an atmosphere of intimacy where people's lives are intertwined and all know their relationships to others. Despite the rapid increases in the speed of travel and the growing complexity of communication systems, McLuhan's vision of a re-tribalized village of global proportions remains as distant as ever (Benge, 1972; Pleydell-Bouverie, 1991). The Internet has not resulted in a global village as is so often stated, because only individuals with similar interests usually seek one another out (Wallace, 1999). Rather, the Internet has led to as much differentiation as integration and possibly more differentiation (Chua, 2003). However, ours is a "world of international interdependence" (Gudykunst & Kim, 2003, p. 3), and perhaps what has actually been created is a global metropolis. Unlike the idealized village, "people living together in a metropolis may know little of one another's affairs [and] some groups in the metropolis will be better known than others [therefore] intimacy is thus restricted and often artificial" (Fortner, 1993, p. 24). This altered metaphor still captures the notion of cultures in motion as well as the uneven and heterogeneous workings and effects of globalization. However, it better focuses our attention on the "dis-location" of culture in our postmodern society, where culture has "become more abstract and imploded . . . what looks the same may already be different and what is already different may still look the same" (Ackbar, 1997, p. 205).

Globalization is the manifestation of a now-constant flow of changing technology inducing permanent, long-term economic change. It will be a troubling and unsettling period as local customs, habits, laws, and even languages experience the stress of rapid change. And international business will have to realize that it cannot go global without making some concessions to local interests in host countries (Friedman, 2000).

Training Challenges of a Complex Intercultural World for International Business

As multinational organizations expand into international markets, they are challenged to train employees how to communicate within new environments and with new people. A small number of public and private concerns have developed to assist in transitioning business people and their families into new cultures (Bennett, 1986). This is done to help ensure the successful completion of their overseas assignments. The variety of intercultural training programs may be grouped as follows.

The intellectual model is a culture-specific classroom model. Participants are given facts about the host country, using a variety of instructional methods such as lecture and discussion and videotapes. This frequently used model emphasizes cognitive understanding and learned knowledge.

The area-training model is a culture-specific approach that emphasizes experiential processes. Participants engage in selected simulations and role-play experiences that emphasize flexible thinking, problem solving, and attitudinal adjustment given a particular culture. Critics of this approach argue that the simulations and role-play experiences may be dissimilar from what one will actually encounter abroad. There is also a lack of specific knowledge and formal learning.

The cultural awareness model is a culture-general approach that stresses affective goals and emphasizes cultural insights and awareness. Participants go from recognizing their own cultural values to contrasting their values with those of other cultures, using a variety of techniques including realistic simulations and role-playing. Additionally, participants may interact with people visiting from other cultures or expatriates who have been on overseas assignments. This approach more nearly approximates interactions participants would experience in new cultures but does not provide extensive knowledge of any specific culture, nor does it develop particular business skills or address international business issues.

The multidimensional model attempts to combine cognitive, affective, and behavioral aspects of training. This highly ambitious integrative approach seeks to balance content with process, affective learning with cognitive, and culture-specific knowledge with culture-general. Critics agree that such an approach may better prepare participants for a successful overseas assignment, but it may be somewhat overwhelming. In this text, the early chapters assume a culture-general approach, and the later chapters examine in more detail specific regions and provide a resource guide for your own explorations.

The technological model uses global videoconferencing and computer-aided learning to train employees and their families for overseas assignments. Global educational networks with various universities are being developed to train people for going international. Moreover, computer-aided training is used to cut across traditional language barriers and encourage one-to-one learning. Cognitive, affective, and behavioral dimensions of training are included in these culture-specific or culture-general programs. Research indicates that such instruction can save 30 percent more time than traditional methods (Chaney & Martin, 2004).

The aim of these organizational training programs is to develop people who will do well in a multicultural, international business environment. Harvey (1985) suggests that it is essential that such individuals absolutely understand their own culturally derived values and be attentive and aware of the values of the other culture. They need to develop contacts with counterparts in the foreign culture and cooperatively work with others. This requires being open to the opinions of others and making an effort to understand and appreciate differences. They also need to be patient when dealing with problems and resilient when faced with adverse situations. Finally, success in this globally multicultural environment requires new skills and competencies that permit flexibility and adaptability, careful planning and organization, and personal empowerment. Still, there is no substitute for actually living in another culture. Chapters 4, 5, and 6 more fully develop the ability to transition into another culture and effectively interact with others.

Things are changing—it's a different ballgame now—and the status quo won't work. Given our global economy, there is a heightened need to understand the role of culture in interpersonal communication and our relational development with others in an international marketplace (Lustig & Koester, 2003). As the 21st century unfolds and the global marketplace continues to expand, nothing less than a commitment to global leadership, cosmopolitan competence, and cultural synergy will suffice.

Summary

This chapter has addressed the concept of international business and the global marketplace. Globalization is no longer simply a concept, but a reality. Political, economic, and technological issues are globally intertwined. Consequently, this becomes an important area to study because multinational organizations will come to depend upon competent communicators who can bridge cultural differences and achieve the desired international objectives. As one CEO has observed, "Tomorrow's executive must possess a broad understanding of history, of culture, of technology, and of human relations. They must be as comfortable with management, as with history, anthropology, sociology, and with the physical and natural sciences" (Harris & Moran, 1991, p. 7). Therefore, consider this chapter as a starting point for your journey toward acquiring a global perspective. We challenge you as you read the remaining chapters to adopt an international view and develop the mindset and skills of a global communicator. We hope that you will become an active force in this lively, spirited, and growing global marketplace.

2

The Concept of Intercultural
Communication and the
Cosmopolitan Leader

The various cultures of the world are far more accessible than ever before, and people are more mobile and more likely to traverse into cultures different than their own. In the past, most people were born, lived, and died within a very limited geographical area; this is no longer the case. A visit to any major city such as Vancouver, New York, Mexico City, London, Frankfurt, Amsterdam, Singapore, or Tokyo, with its multicultural population, demonstrates that the movement of people from one country and culture to another has become commonplace and that business is an international affair.

The purpose of this chapter is to provide conceptual tools needed to understand culture, communication, and cosmopolitan leadership in a world economy. The chapter explores varying approaches to culture and explains how culture and communication are intertwined in the process of communicating with people from different cultures. It also examines some barriers to intercultural communication and identifies the essential characteristics cosmopolitan leaders need to effectively cope with an emerging world culture and to compete in an international arena. Such knowledge is necessary if we are to fully understand the complex nature of intercultural communication and hope to comprehend the essential interface between international commerce, culture, communication, synergy, and the global organization.

Defining Culture and Cultural Patterns

What is culture? The late British writer Raymond Williams (1983) wrote that culture "is one of the two or three most complicated words in the English language" (p. 89). Edward T. Hall (1959), a pioneer in the study of culture and intercultural communication, observes that much of the difficulty is that "culture controls behavior in deep and persisting ways, many of which are outside of awareness and therefore beyond conscious control of the individual" (p. 35). Perhaps the song "Tradition" from the musical *Fiddler on the Roof* best extols the intricate composition of culture: "Because of our traditions, we keep our sanity . . . Tradition tells us how to sleep, how to work, how to wear clothes . . . How did it get started? I don't know—it's tradition . . . Because of our traditions, everyone knows who he is and what God expects of him." Traditions express a particular culture, provide people with a mindset, and give them a sense of belonging and uniqueness. As Hall (1976) notes, "Culture is man's medium; there is not one aspect of human life that is not touched and altered by culture" (p. 16). Therefore, it can be valuable to explore how others have defined this medium and related terms.

CULTURE AND RELATED TERMS

A primary characteristic distinguishing humans from other animals is our development of culture, which many think of as a place—the South American culture of Brazil, the Western European culture of France, the Middle East culture of Saudi Arabia, and the Far East culture of China. Culture may certainly include geography as well as material objects and artifacts (Herskovits, 1955) but Clifford Geertz (1973) perceives culture more importantly to be the means by which people "communicate, perpetuate, and develop their knowledge about and attitudes towards life. Culture is the fabric of meaning in terms of which human beings interpret their experience and guide their action" (p. 24). Keesing (1974) suggests that our cultures provide us with "internal models of reality" (p. 89) and implicit theories of the "games being played" in our societies, whereas Olsen (1978) points out that "as people communicate the meanings of their actions to each other and work out shared interpretations of activities and definitions of situations, they develop a common culture that is shared by the participants . . . providing them with interpretations of social life, role expectations, common definitions of situations, and social norms" (p. 107). We are not born with the genetic imprint of a particular culture, but rather learn about our culture through interactions with parents, extended family members, friends, teachers, and others who are part of the culture. Moreover, television and other electronic media convey many of the day-to-day norms and expectations of our culture (Gerbner, Gross, Morgan, & Signorielli, 1980). The mutually shared beliefs, values, and norms that characterize culture give each of us guidelines about what things mean, what is important, and what should be done. Philip Harris and Robert Moran (1991) observe that "culture gives people a sense of who they are, of belonging, of how they should behave, and what they should be doing" (p. 12). Consequently, "culture is not one thing, but many" (Hall, 1959, p. 169). Culture is the luggage we carry with us in our daily lives and when we travel abroad. It is a set of objective and subjective elements that shape perception and define our worldview.

Besides culture, there are other related terms that require definition if we are to properly put in perspective the relationship between culture and international business. These terms are often used interchangeably with culture or referred to in conjunction with culture—nation, ethnicity, race, subculture, counterculture, enculturation, acculturation, and popular culture.

- *Nation* is a political term referring to the formal governmental and legal apparatus that structurally binds a geographic region together (e.g., the United States, Mexico, France, Egypt, or Japan) and regulates how leaders are selected, the way diplomatic relations are conducted, and what social, political, economic, and educational institutions should do to serve the greater community.

- *Ethnic group* refers to a wide variety of groups who might share a language, historical origin, religion, or home culture (e.g., African Americans, Irish Americans, Asian Americans, Polish Americans, Italian Americans, or Mexican Americans).

- *Race*, although biological in nature, is more a political and legal construction referring to certain physical similarities (e.g., skin color or eye shape) that are shared by a group of people and used to justify economic and social distinctions.

- *Subcultures* or *co-cultures* are groups of people compatibly co-existing within a larger culture, yet possessing a conscious identity that distinguishes them from others within the larger society. Subculture or co-culture is often used to refer to ethnic and racial groups that share both a common national boundary with the larger collectivity as well as many of the other aspects of the prevailing macroculture. However, we can also identify and talk about other types of subcultures or co-cultures that share many common cultural ideas with the larger culture while still possessing some that are unique (e.g., an urban subculture, homeless subculture, rural subculture, family subculture, legal subculture, or

21

business/organizational subculture). These subcultures of identification are often defined by class, education, age, religion, wealth, residence, work, family, or gender and assume significance depending upon their saliency for any particular individual.

• *Countercultures* are groups that engage in behavior that is distinctively different from and in opposition to that of the dominant culture. Members of these groups not only reject the values of the larger culture but also actively confront society and work against the traditionally recognized values (e.g., organized crime and drug dealers).

• *Enculturation* is the socialization process we go through to adapt to our larger society.

• *Acculturation* is the process of adjusting and adapting to a new and different culture.

• *Popular culture* refers to those "systems or artifacts that most people share and that most people know about" such as television, music, videos, and popular books or magazines (Brummett, 1994, p. 21). Popular culture is ubiquitous and distinct from folk culture. It is produced by culture industries and bears the "interests of the people" so it serves a variety of social functions (Fiske, 1989, p. 23). Popular culture may transmit values, may serve to entertain, and is a frequent forum for the development of our ideas about other people and places. We may choose, however, to consume or resist the messages of popular culture. A great deal of popular culture is produced in the United States and circulated, raising concerns from other countries about "cultural imperialism."

LEVELS OF CULTURE

Culture is often compared to an iceberg—much of it lies beneath the surface, out of our immediate awareness. We generally respond to the surface values that we can sense; however, to truly understand a culture, we must also explore the behaviors below the waterline. This is a useful metaphor for examining the technical, formal, and informal levels of culture (Hall, 1959):

• The *technical level* is the explicitly clear and visible portion of our cultural iceberg and includes the artistic, technological, and materialistic components of a culture as well as its institutional systems. We generally find the fewest intercultural misunderstandings or problems at this level. Still, changes at this level can dramatically alter the balance of forces that maintain a culture. For example, the introduction of snowmobiles into the nomadic reindeer herding tribes of Greenland transformed some small family enter-prises into large business conglomerates that monopolized the herding activ-ity and dispossessed other tribal members.

• The *formal level* of our cultural iceberg rests at sea level, partially above and slightly below the surface. The formal level includes the norms, rules, roles, traditions, rituals, customs, and communication patterns of a group. Norms provide a guide for how group members *should* behave, and rules clarify what is mutually considered "right" and "wrong" by a group. Roles define and explain expected or actual performance in relationships or social situations, whereas traditions, rituals, and customs describe regular practices within a culture. The communication patterns of a group denote how members communicate with others as well as their associations—who communicates with whom about what.

• The *informal level* of our cultural iceberg extends far below sea level and includes the cultural history and core values and beliefs that shape a culture's worldview and influence cultural identity. Cultural history, or the origin and background of a culture, can generate insight into the norms of a group and assist us in understanding a culture's identity. Cultural identity is our sense of who we think we are, and because we participate in many cultural systems and belong to various groups, we develop multiple identities that come into play at different times depending on the circum-stances and context (e.g., gender identity, age identity, racial identity, eth-nic identity, religious identity, class identity, national identity, regional identity, personal identity). Cultural identities commonly emerge through daily social practices (Carbaugh, 1990; Collier, 1998; Collier & Thomas, 1988) and reflect the values and worldview of the culture. Values form the core of a culture and convey what is good and bad as well as express what is proper and improper or what is normal and abnormal behavior (Feather, 1990, 1995). A culture's worldview is its "set of more or less sys-tematized beliefs and values in terms of which [it] evaluates and attaches meaning to the reality that surrounds it" (Kraft, 1978, p. 407).

Worldviews are unconsciously accepted as the way things are.

A knowledge of these cultural levels can help us identify the principal elements and coordinating systems composing a culture as well as recognize its salient features. Understanding these various levels can also alert us to the dominant norms, rules, and values inherent in the culture and assist us in deter-mining the *structural tightness* of the culture. In "tight" cultures, the norms and rules of the culture tend to be clear, whereas in "loose" cultures, the norms and rules are more ambiguous, permitting greater deviation and more flexibility

(Pelto, 1968). Cultural homogeneity tends to contribute to cultural tightness, whereas cultural heterogeneity tends to lead to cultural looseness because the differences among group members make it difficult to agree on what behavior is correct in a particular situation. The degree to which there is a need for coordinated action also influences the degree of structural tightness. The greater the need for coordinated action, the tighter the culture; the less the need for coordinated action, the looser the culture (Triandis, 1994). Japan is an example of a tight culture, and the United States is an example of a loose culture.

International business seeks to create a "single marketplace," so understanding the way people live will be important because, when operating beyond our own borders, the best strategies and plans can easily go astray if one ignores the cultural differences and fails to recognize and grasp opportunities for cultural synergy. Moreover, multinational organizations and world corporations will have to be well enculturated, understanding their own cultural, business, and organizational values, and capable of adapting and seeking a collaborative working relationship with the world as a whole (Terpstra & David, 1985). This means, in the language of Edward T. Hall (1976), "that if one is to prosper in this new world without being unexpectedly battered, one must transcend one's own system" (p. 51). To do so entails acknowledging cultural alternatives, exploring the multiple levels of these cultures, and identifying their elements, characteristics, and coordinating institutional systems. Therefore, a familiarization with the different approaches researchers have taken toward culture can be helpful in understanding the fundamental constructs of cultures.

APPROACHES TO CULTURE

The approaches to culture and conceptual taxonomies presented here provide frames of reference that allow us to use culture-specific knowledge to improve our intercultural awareness and competence. As you study these approaches to cultural patterns, we encourage you to keep in mind that individual members of a culture may vary greatly from the pattern that is typical of that culture. Martin and Nakayama (2001) note that an underlying problem with cultural taxonomies is the tendency to "essentialize" people. In other words, "people tend to assume that a particular group characteristic is the essential characteristic of given group members at all times and in all contexts . . . this ignores the heterogeneity within any population . . . [or] the contexts when interacting" (p. 36).

Hall's Low- and High-Context Cultures

Hall (1976) contends that cultures differ on a continuum that ranges from low to high context. Information and rules are explicit in low-context cultures that use linear logic and a direct style of communication. In contrast, information and rules are implicit in high-context cultures that draw upon intuition and utilize an indirect style of communication. People using high-context communication tend to be extremely reserved, with much more being taken for granted and assumed to be shared, thus permitting an emphasis on understatement and nonverbal codes (Gudykunst & Ting-Toomey, 1988).

Hall (1976) notes that in high-context cultures, the commitment between people is very strong and responsibility to others takes precedence over responsibility to oneself. In low-context cultures, the emphasis is placed on the individual, with the bonds between people being more tenuous and the extent of involvement and commitment to long-term relationships being lower. Thus, in high-context cultures meaning is couched in the nature of situations and relationships are very important, whereas in low-context cultures meaning is explicit and dependent on verbal codes and group memberships change rapidly with individualism being valued. Examples of high-context cultures include Asian, Latin American, and African countries, whereas low-context cultures include the United States and Western European countries.

Hofstede's Dimensions of Cultural Variability

Geert Hofstede's (1979, 1980, 1983, 1991, 2001) studies of cultural differences in value orientations offer another approach to understanding the range of cultural differences. Using empirical methods of analysis, Hofstede initially developed four dimensions of cultural variability that he labeled individualism-collectivism, masculinity-femininity, power distance, and uncertainty avoidance. Subsequent research extended his investigations and theorizing to incorporate time orientation as a dimension along which cultures can be ordered (see McSweeney, 2005, for a country-by-country breakdown of the dimensions):

- The *individualism-collectivism* dimension assesses a culture's tendency to encourage people to be unique and independent or conforming and interdependent. In individualistic cultures, the autonomy of the individual is paramount, with personal motivation and personal goals taking precedence over group or collective concerns and interests. Decisions are based on what is good or desirable for the individual rather than the collectivity. Collectivistic cultures require an absolute loyalty to the group, and groups to which a person belongs are the most important social units. Decisions that juxtapose the benefits to the individual and the benefits to the group are always based on what is best for the group. In turn, the group is expected to look out for and take care of its individual members. Members of collectivistic cultures also rank-order the importance of their group memberships—the company is often considered the primary group in Japan, whereas the family is the primary group in Latin America and the community is the primary group in most of Africa. Collectivistic cultures clearly distinguish between those who are members of their group and those who are not, whereas members of individualistic cultures do not create a large chasm between in-group and out-group members, applying the same standards to all people and permitting greater possibilities for connecting and becoming involved (Kim, 1995). Thus, the emphasis in individualistic cultures is on individual initiative and achievement, whereas the emphasis in collectivistic societies is on fitting in or belonging. A number of scholars and researchers believe that the individualism-collectivism dimension is the most important attribute that distinguishes one culture from another (Gudykunst & Kim, 2003; Hui & Triandis, 1986; Triandis, 1972, 1984, 1988, 1990, 1995).

• The *masculinity-femininity* dimension refers to the degree to which gender-specific roles are valued and the degree to which a cultural group values "masculine" (achievement, ambition, acquisition of material goods) or "feminine" (quality of life, service to others, nurturance) values. Cultural systems high in masculinity clearly distinguish between social gender roles (e.g., men are supposed to be assertive and focused on professional success whereas women are supposed to be modest, tender, and caring) and emphasize achievement, personal wealth, and ambition. Cultures high in femininity prefer equality between the sexes and less prescriptive role behaviors associated with gender roles, valuing service to others and quality of life (Hofstede, 1998). The United States, Austria, Italy, Japan, and Mexico score high on the masculinity index, viewing work, recognition, and advancement as particularly important. Chile, Portugal, Sweden, Norway, Denmark, and Thailand display a feminine orientation, where personal intrinsic balance and the importance of life choices that improve society are important.

• The *power distance* dimension focuses on the appropriateness or importance of status differences and social hierarchies. People from high power distance cultures accept a particular social order or hierarchy and believe that recognized authorities should not be challenged or questioned and that those with preferred social status have a right to use their power for whatever purposes or in whatever ways they deem desirable. In contrast, people in low power distance cultures believe in the importance of social equality—reducing hierarchical structures, minimizing social or class inequities, questioning or challenging authority figures, and using power only for legitimate purposes. Canada, Ireland, Israel, and the United

States represent low power distance cultures favoring high egalitarianism. The Arab countries, Guatemala, Egypt, Ghana, Malaysia, and Venezuela represent high power distance cultures that presume that each person has a rightful and protected place in the social order. It should be noted that high power distance cultures tend to be collectivist, whereas low power distance cultures tend to be individualistic.

- The *uncertainty avoidance* dimension deals with how cultures adapt to change and cope with uncertainties. People in high uncertainty avoidance cultures demand consensus and do not tolerate dissent or allow deviation in the behaviors of members. Rather, they try to ensure certainty and security through an extensive set of rules, regulations, and rituals; they resist change and have higher levels of anxiety as well as intolerance for ambiguity. Conversely, people in low uncertainty avoidance cultures live day-to-day, regarding the uncertainties of life as natural, and they are more willing to accept change and take risks. Hofstede (1991) characterizes the view of people in low uncertainty avoidance cultures as "what is different, is curious" (p. 119) and the view of people in high uncertainty avoidance cultures as "what is different, is dangerous" (p. 119). Canada, Denmark, England, India, Jamaica, Singapore, South Africa, and the United States all score low in uncertainty avoidance, being willing to accept dissent, tolerate deviance, and try new things. Spain, Egypt, Venezuela, Greece, Japan, and Ukraine regard the uncertainties of life as a continuous threat and therefore do not tolerate dissent or allow deviation in the behavior of cultural members.

- The *time* dimension or *long-term orientation* (Hofstede, 2001) draws on the work of the Chinese Culture Connection (1987) and refers to a person's point of reference about life and work. Long-term orientation cultures admire persistence, thriftiness, humility, and deferred gratification of needs. They also recognize status differences in interpersonal relationships and look forward to a satisfying old age. They believe good and evil depends on the circumstances and opposites complement each other. Short-term orientation cultures have a deep appreciation for tradition, personal steadfastness, maintaining the "face" of self and others, giving and receiving gifts and favors, and an expectation for quick results. They believe in absolute guidelines about good and evil, the need for cognitive consistency, and the use of probabilistic and analytic thinking. Cultures that tend to have long-term orientations include China, Taiwan, Japan, Brazil, India, Thailand, Singapore, and the Netherlands. Cultures that tend to have short-term orientations include Pakistan, Nigeria, the Philippines, Canada, Great Britain, New Zealand, Australia, Germany, Poland, Sweden, and the United States.

Hofstede's dimensions of cultural patterns and range of social behaviors continue to provide reasonable descriptions of the predominant tendencies in the cultures studied (Fernandez, Carlson, Stepina, & Nicholson, 1997; Merritt, 2000; Oudenhoven, 2001). Critics, however, argue that Hofstede's national cultural descriptions are invalid and misleading because of flawed research assumptions and faulty methods (S. Schwartz, 1994). Brenden McSweeney (2002) contends that Hofstede's "reductive, closed, single-cause analysis," which relied on questionnaires, is deficient compared to action theories that can cope with "change, power, variety, and multiple influences" (p. 118). Still, Hofstede's findings provide a powerful explanation for understanding cultural similarities and differences while describing important cultural expectations for a wide range of social behaviors that leaders and managers of multinational organizations should understand. Moreover, his study determined that managers had to adjust the corporate management philosophy to fit the beliefs, values, and behaviors of the country in which they were working if they hoped to be successful in a complex global arena.

Currently, a group of researchers are engaged in a long-term study of culture, leadership, and organizations that significantly extends Hofstede's studies. The Global Leadership and Organizational Behavior Effectiveness (GLOBE) research program is designed to conceptualize, operationalize, test, and validate a cross-level integrated theory of the relationship between culture and societal, organizational, and leadership effectiveness (House, Hanges, Javidan, Dorfman, & Gupta, 2004). A team of 170 scholars has worked together since 1994 to study societal culture, organizational culture, and attributes of effective leadership in 62 cultures. GLOBE is a truly cross-cultural research program with the constructs being defined, conceptualized, and operationalized by a multicultural team of researchers and the data in each country being collected by investigators who were either natives of the cultures studied or had extensive knowledge and experience in that culture. Their approach addresses some of the concerns raised by Hofstede's critics, so their results should be of particular interest to leaders of multinational organizations and managers active in the international business arena.

Kluckhohn and Strodtbeck's Value Orientation

The value orientations identified by Florence Kluckhohn and Fred Strodtbeck (1961) are deeply held beliefs about the way the world should be, and not necessarily the way it is.

- The *human nature orientation* focuses on the innate character of human nature and whether human beings should be seen as good, evil, or a mixture of both. It further asks whether human beings are capable of change (mutable) or not able to change (immutable).

• The *person-nature orientation* examines the potential types of relations between humans and nature—mastery over nature, harmony with nature, or subjugation to nature. The United States attempts to dominate nature, whereas many Native American groups and the Japanese believe in the value of humans living in harmony with nature.

• The *relational orientation* identifies three potential ways whereby humans might define their relationships with others—individualism, lineality, and collaterality. Individualism is characterized by autonomy and a preference for individual goals and objectives over group goals and objectives. Lineality focuses on the group and group goals; however, the crucial issue is the continuity of the group through time. An example of this are the aristocracies found in many European countries. Finally, collaterality focuses on the value of the group, group membership, and group goals but not the group extended through time.

• The *activity orientation* focuses on three types of human activity—doing, being, and being-in-becoming or growing. A doing orientation emphasizes productivity and tangible outcomes. This orientation is prevalent in the United States. The being orientation is characterized by a sense of spontaneity, emotional gratification, and personal balance. This orientation can be found in Central and South America, and in Greek and Spanish cultural groups. The final activity orientation, being-in-becoming or growing, is concerned with who we are and places importance on personal and spiritual development. Japan, for example, emphasizes doing as well as growing personally and spiritually.

• The *time orientation* examines how cultures come to terms with the past, the present, and the future. The past orientation predominates in cultures placing a high value on tradition and emphasizing ancestors and strong family ties. Many European and Asian societies place a relatively strong emphasis on the past, believing that history has something to contribute to an understanding of contemporary life. The present orientation predominates where people see only the here and now as real—the past is seen as unimportant and the future is seen as vague and unpredictable. Spain, Greece, and Mexico seem to emphasize the importance of the present, recognizing the value of living in the here and now and the potential of the current moment. Finally, the future orientation highly values change and progress. This orientation predominates in the United States, where it is optimistically accepted that the future will be "new and improved."

One culture can be distinguished from another by the arrangement of the specific solutions it selects for each set of problem situations and how it gives meaning to the different orientations.

Parsons's Pattern Variables

Parsons's (1951) concept of pattern variables is another view of cultural variability. The six pattern variables identified are mutually exclusive orientations individuals consciously and/or unconsciously make and can therefore be used to analyze cultural differences (Parsons & Shils, 1951). They describe ways people have learned to meaningfully organize their experiences and perceive phenomena around them in a coherent and orderly fashion.

- The *self-collective orientation* is identical to individualism-collectivism, where people emphasize both personal achievement and responsibility or group achievement and joint responsibility.

- The *affectivity-affective neutrality orientation* is concerned with the extent to which people look for immediate gratification or delayed gratification and show their feelings plainly by laughing, smiling, grimacing, and gesturing or keep them carefully controlled and subdued. Members of Latin American cultures with an affectivity orientation are more likely to base decisions on emotional responses, whereas people from the affectively neutral United States are more likely to base decisions on cognitive information.

- The *universalism-particularism orientation* is concerned with treating all people equally or responding to people on their specific merits. People from cultures in which a universalistic orientation predominates strive for consistency and focus more on rules than relationships, whereas people from cultures in which a particularistic orientation predominates focus more on relationships and building informal networks with others and creating private understandings. Individualistic cultures like the United States are characterized by a universalistic orientation. A particularistic orientation characterizes collectivistic cultures like those in Asia.

- The *diffuseness-specificity orientation* refers to our perceptions of public versus private space and how we respond to people. In diffuse cultures everything is connected to everything, whereas specific cultures rigorously separate out private and public life. In Germany or Japan, one's standing and reputation cross over into every space or relationship, whereas in the United States a title such as CEO or doctor is a specific label for a specific job in a specific place. Members of specific cultures often say, "Do not take this personally," but this can be interpreted as offensive by members of diffuse cultures where their ideas are not separated from themselves and are an extension of their personal honor.

- The *ascription-achievement orientation* focuses on whether societies ascribe status to people by virtue of age, class, gender, education, race, or ethnic group, or accord recognition to people on the basis of what they have achieved through their own efforts or personal accomplishments.

- The *instrumental-expressive orientation* is concerned with whether relational interactions with others are principally viewed as a means to other goals or are valued as an end in and of themselves. People from cultures in which an expressive orientation predominates tend to value friendships for their own sake more than do people from cultures in which an instrumental orientation predominates. The instrumental orientation is the predominant pattern in the United States, whereas the expressive orientation predominates in many Arab, Latin American, and Asian cultures.

Philipsen's Speech Code Theory

Gerry Philipsen (1992) describes culture as "a socially constructed and historically transmitted pattern of symbols, meanings, premises, and rules" (p. 7). He proposes three general propositions regarding speech code theory: (1) a speech code involves a culturally distinctive psychology, sociology, and rhetoric; (2) the terms, rules, and premises of a speech code are inextricably woven into speaking itself; and (3) the artful use of a shared speech code is a sufficient condition for predicting, explaining, and controlling the form of discourse about the intelligibility, prudence, and morality of communication conduct (Philipsen, 1989, 1997, 2001). Philipsen presents us with an interesting perspective to explain and even predict the discourse within a language community. Chapter 5 further elaborates on Philipsen's speech code theory.

The Interface of International Business, Culture, and Communication

Alfred G. Smith (1966) says that "the way people communicate is the way they live. It is their culture. Who talks with whom? How? And about what? These are questions of communication and culture" (p. 1). Clearly, culture and communication are inseparable.

INTERCULTURAL COMMUNICATION AND RELATED TERMS

Given the interface between culture and communication, we are ready to present a working definition of intercultural communication. *Intercultural communication* is a symbolic, interpretive, transactional, contextual process whereby people from different cultures negotiate, at varying levels of awareness, shared meanings. What distinguishes intercultural communication from other types of communication is that we are interacting with *people from different cultures*—people perceived as "different from us" (Gudykunst & Nishida, 1989). This perceived cultural variability and diversity might include differences in communication and social style, worldview, customs, traditions, norms, rules, roles, and expectations. It is this medley of people from diverse cultures that prompts our study and requires international business to adjust, accommodate, and appeal to commonality—to exercise cultural sensitivity and employ intercultural coping skills.

Several related terms commonly applied to the intercultural communication arena also require definition.

- *Intracultural communication* refers to communication between and among members of the same culture—people who share the same beliefs, values, and constructs.

- *Interethnic communication* is communication between people from different ethnic groups.

- *Interracial communication* is communication between people from different races.

- *Cross-cultural communication* technically implies a comparison of specific interpersonal variables such as conversational distance or conflict management styles across two or more different cultures, but it is often used as a synonym for intercultural communication.

SITUATING INTERCULTURAL COMMUNICATION

W. Barnett Pearce (1989), in his book *Communication and the Human Condition*, develops a communication perspective that can help us situate intercultural communication and understand the role of the cosmopolitan communicator. His notion of how communication works focuses on three terms: coordination, coherence, and mystery.

- *Coordination* involves meshing one's messages and actions with those of another and exists when the parties feel that the sequence of messages and actions seem logical or appropriate. Because people enter conversations with a variety of abilities and competencies, achieving coordination can be difficult at times (Pearce, 1989).

- *Coherence* refers to the process by which we attempt to interpret the world around us and our place in it. It is the effort by which "persons invent, test, and tell themselves and others stories that make intelligible the world around them, tame the terrors of history, make familiar the unknowns that go thump in the night, and give acceptable accounts for their success and failures in coordinating with other persons" (Pearce, 1989, p. 67).

- *Mystery* "is a reminder of what is beyond the immediate, present moment" (Pearce, 1989, p. 23). It is the sense of wonder and recognition that there could be a range of stories or interpretations.

An examination of coordinated management of meaning (CMM) theory can illustrate the challenges confronting a cosmopolitan communicator and help explain the difficulties of coordination between people from different cultures (Cronen, Chen, & Pearce, 1988).

COORDINATED MANAGEMENT OF MEANING

Coordinated management of meaning is a comprehensive communication theory that states that people interpret and act on the basis of rules that allow them to coordinate their meanings when interacting with others (Cronen, Pearce, & Harris, 1982). *Constitutive rules* help us understand or interpret an event or message; they tell us what certain actions constitute or mean. For example, in some cultures preparing a detailed agenda and assertively guiding discussion count as leadership, whereas in other cultures indirectness and subtlety constitute effective leadership. *Regulative rules* are essentially rules of action that tell us when it's appropriate to do certain things and how to respond or behave in an interaction. For example, in some cultures heated business discussions where individuals promote a personal position is appropriate business conduct, but in other cultures the maintenance of harmony and the sense of group regulates business behavior. When constitutive and regulative rules are understood and coordinated, interactions tend to run smoothly and comfortably. But friction and misunderstandings often result when individuals operate according to different constitutive and regulative rules. Rules tell us what interpretations and actions are logical or appropriate in a given situation and are tied to our overall hierarchy of meanings (Cronen & Pearce, 1981).

Pearce and Cronen (1980) further develop a *nestled hierarchy* in which one context is embedded within another and each context is itself part of a larger context. They identify six contexts or levels of meaning in their hierarchy, but are quick to note that there may be additional contexts or levels of meaning that have not yet been recognized.

- The *content* level represents the raw sensory data—the denotative meaning of words and what we see and hear. To construct the meaning of this content, we have to refer to higher levels of meaning in the hierarchy.

- *Speech acts* communicate the intention of the speaker, and the relationship embedded in speech acts indicates how the content should be taken.

- *Episodes* are recurring communication routines that have definite rules and boundaries—definable beginnings, middles, and endings. Various cultures and speech communities have developed different episodes, some of which are functionally similar and some of which are not. Consequently, episodes are larger frames for interpreting speech acts.

- *Relationships* include mutually scripted expectations among group members and reflect how we interact with others (Shailor, 1994).

- *Autobiographies,* originally labeled "life-scripts," represent an individual's view of himself or herself that both shapes and is shaped by communication. Think of autobiographies as clusters of past and present speech acts and episodes that define your sense of self. Autobiographies reveal a person's overall pattern of communicating, responding, and acting in the world. It's important to note that our autobiographies are not fixed or static, but constantly evolving and changing.

- *Cultural patterns* or archetypes can be described as "very broad images of world order and [a person's] relationship to that order" (Cronen & Pearce, 1981, p. 21). They are the overriding cultural rules that coordinate our personal interpretations with others; however, different speech communities may have different worldviews and distinctive ways of interpreting experiences that affect how groups construct meanings or rhetorical visions (see Bormann, 1972, 1982, 1985, 1990; Bormann, Cragan, & Shields, 1996).

Thus, from a CMM and intercultural communication perspective, "the human condition is that of being *variably enmeshed in multiple symbolic systems, each with its own logic of meaning and action*" (Pearce, 1989, p. 86).

Because different social groups develop distinct cultural patterns, communication between cultures is often laced with misunderstandings and plagued with confusion and misinterpretations. Moreover, particular barriers or obstacles often jeopardize intercultural contact and impede effective intercultural communication.

BARRIERS TO INTERCULTURAL COMMUNICATION

As international managers in expanding world corporations, you will be exposed daily to a bewildering variety of value systems that challenge your intercultural communication competencies and skills. You will need to see the world as a whole and recognize the importance of constructively managing stereotypes, controlling prejudice, avoiding discrimination, and reducing ethnocentrism. You will need to place a premium on effective intercultural communication and make every effort to become more cosmopolitan or one who can function "effectively *anywhere* in the world" (Harris & Moran, 1991, p. 6).

STEREOTYPES

Journalist Walter Lippman (1922) first introduced the term stereotyping and referred to stereotypes as "pictures in our heads," suggesting that they have both a cognitive component and an affective component. Stereotyping is a selection process that we use to organize and simplify perceptions of others, and stereotypes are our mental representations of others. The content of our stereotypes reveals our "constellation of beliefs about members of social groups" (Operario & Fiske, 2001, p. 23). Our stereotypes also create expectations regarding how members of other groups will behave, and we unconsciously try to confirm our expectations when we communicate with others and tend to process information that is consistent with our stereotypes (Snyder & Haugen, 1995). Consequently, the stereotypes we hold directly influence our communication with others, and our initial predictions about others are based on the stereotypes we have about their culture, race, or ethnic group. However, stereotypes are often inaccurate, and they do not work well with individuals who have worked in international business or who have lived or studied abroad because they will display increased differences from their national cultures (M. Lewis, 2000).

So, how can we more constructively manage our customary tendency to stereotype? Richards and Hewstone (2001) point to subtyping and subgrouping as constructive and positive stereotype control strategies. One way we can deal with those who do not fit our original stereotypes is to put them in a "subtype" that includes members of other groups who are "exceptions to the rule." Another way we can deal with those who do not fit our stereotypes is to put members of the group who are alike in some ways and different in others into one "subgroup" while placing those who fit the stereotype in another subgroup. Subgrouping leads to new categories and may better facilitate stereotype change. Stereotypes are a problem when you tend to see only that information that supports your stereotyped belief rather than information that runs counter to it. However, by creating subtypes or developing more accurate subgroupings, you can make more precise cultural and sociocultural predictions about others.

Prejudice

Whereas a stereotype is a belief or conviction that something is probably true or that something exists, a prejudice is an attitude or an evaluation. Prejudice, then, may be defined as a positive or negative attitude toward a group or its individual members. Most people, however, think of it as negative. Allport (1954) defines negative ethnic prejudice as "an antipathy based on a faulty and inflexible generalization . . . expressed . . . toward a group as a whole, or toward an individual . . . member of that group" (p. 7). Racism, for example, is a tendency to categorize people who are culturally different in terms of their physical traits. Prejudice is often thought of in terms of a dichotomy; however, it is more accurate to think of prejudice as varying along a continuum from low to high (E. Smith, 1994). This suggests that we are all prejudiced to some degree or another.

Discrimination

Prejudice should not be confused with its behavioral counterpart, discrimination. Discrimination can be thought of as prejudice "in action." Essentially, discrimination involves behaving in such a way that members of outgroups are treated disadvantageously (R. M. Williams, 1947). This disadvantaged treatment can range from segregation to biases in the availability of housing, employment, education, legal protection, and other resources. In sum, certain individuals are treated unequally solely because of their membership in a particular group.

A contemporary aspect of prejudice and discrimination that needs to be addressed is hate speech. Hate speech can range from "speech attacks based on race, religion or sexual orientation to any offensive expression directed toward women, discrete minorities, and ethnic, religious, and racial groups" (Ruscher, 2001, p. 194). Words become weapons of animosity and loathing that foster hostile intergroup relations and often physical violence (I. Allen, 1990).

Ethnocentrism

Ruhly (1982) defines ethnocentrism as "the tendency to interpret or to judge all other groups, their environments, and their communication according to the categories and values of our own culture" (p. 28). Ethnocentrism, then, is a belief in cultural superiority where people perceive their nation as the center of the world and believe that the values of their culture are natural and correct and that people from other cultures who do things differently are wrong. Everyone is ethnocentric to some degree, and ethnocentrism exists in all cultures (Triandis, 1994). Fisher (1997) refers to ethnocentrism as learned mindsets. The opposite of ethnocentrism is cultural relativism, which involves trying to understand others' behavior in the context of the cultures or groups of people engaging in the behavior (Herskovits, 1973). Cultural relativism can be developed and is necessary to engage in effective intercultural communication and for conducting international business.

Willis Harmon (1988) of the Stanford Research Institute argues that we can no longer view our world or culture in terms of industrial-age paradigms that have influenced our past perceptions, values, and behavior. Today's business leaders are challenged to create new models of management systems and organizations that are better suited to our increasingly complex geocentric stage of development. For this to happen, they must become more innovative and cosmopolitan. A cosmopolitan leader is a "citizen of the world" who interacts comfortably with people who come from diverse backgrounds, hold different values, and express discrepant beliefs (Pearce & Pearce, 2000).

Cosmopolitan Leadership and an Emerging World Culture

To perform well in this increasingly intercultural world requires a special kind of personal orientation where the different cultural elements are internalized and one is open to further intercultural growth. The cosmopolitan communicator or "universal person" is not owned by his or her culture but "is capable of negotiating ever new formations of reality . . . [and] lives on the boundary" (Adler, 1987, p. 39). Cosmopolitan or "transcultural" communicators show respect for all cultures; demonstrate an understanding of what individuals in other cultures think, feel, and believe; and appreciate the differences among cultures (Walsh, 1973, 1979; Y. Kim, 1988, 2001). They possess a mental outlook that exhibits greater cognitive differentiation, permitting them to step into and "participate in the other's world view" (Bennett, 1977, p. 49).

COSMOPOLITAN COMMUNICATORS
AND COSMOPOLITAN COMMUNICATION

Cosmopolitan communicators possess a number of specific qualities: (1) the cognitive complexity necessary to perceive and consider alternative explanations of phenomena, (2) the mindfulness needed for active information processing, and (3) the rhetorical sensitivity required for adapting messages to diverse audiences. Cosmopolitan communicators with highly developed interpretive schemes can make more discriminations than those who see the world simplistically, thus they can make more sophisticated distinctions in a situation than can cognitively uncomplicated people (Burleson & Caplan, 1998; Delia, O'Keefe, & O'Keefe, 1982). They are astute observers of the human scene, capable of picturing people using a vast range of colors, shades, and hues (Burlson & Waltman, 1988). Moreover, they have a greater capacity to create person-centered messages and employ a rhetorical message design logic that seeks to accomplish multiple goals (O'Keefe, 1988, 1996).

Mindfulness is a "state of alertness and lively awareness" characterized by actively processing information, analyzing it, categorizing it, and considering how and why distinctions may exist (Langer, 1989b, p. 138). Cosmopolitan communicators are mindful in that they are open to new information and recognize that there is more than one perspective that can be used to understand or explain our interactions with others (Langer, 1989a). This results in their being able to "negotiate potentially problematic social interactions more effectively" than "mindless" individuals who engage in the menial processing of information that is only relevant to their current tasks (Devine, Evett, & Vasquez-Suson, 1996, p. 444). Situations that are characterized by ambiguity or uncertainty necessitate mindfulness as communicators consider their behavior in relation to the circumstances (Burgoon & Langer, 1996).

Cosmopolitan communicators are rhetorically adaptive individuals who avoid rigidity in communicating with others and attempt to balance self-interests with the interests of others. They try to adjust what they say to the level, mood, and beliefs of the other person. They do not forsake their own values, but they realize that they can communicate those values in a variety of ways (Hart & Burks, 1972). Cosmopolitan communication champions tentativeness over rigidity and appreciates the complexity of social exchange (Hart, Carlson, & Eadie, 1980).

COSMOPOLITAN LEADERS AND AN EMERGING WORLD CULTURE

Cosmopolitan leaders are sensitive, innovative, and participative leaders, capable of operating comfortably in a global or pluralistic environment (Harris & Moran, 1991). These multinational and multicultural representatives are open and flexible when approaching others, can cope with situations and people quite different from their background, and are willing to adjust personal attitudes and perceptions. Cosmopolitan leaders strive to create cultural synergy by seeking the widest input and combining the best in varied cultures while managing accelerating change. They are knowledgeable about cultural influences and build on the very differences in the world's people for mutual growth and accomplishment by cooperation.

As we become increasingly cosmopolitan, we gain new perspectives and outlooks that reflect an integrative "third-culture" perspective (Casmir, 1999). We are better able to reconcile seemingly contradictory elements of peoples and cultures and transform them into a complementary system. Gudykunst and Kim (2003) note that "becoming intercultural is a gradual process of liberating ourselves from our limited and exclusive interests and viewpoints and striving to attain a perspective in which we see ourselves as a part of a larger, more inclusive whole" (p. 385).

Recent research has also linked cosmopolitan leadership with a concept called "emotional intelligence" (Gardner & Stough, 2002; Sivanathan & Fekken, 2002). Where traditional notions of intelligence emphasize knowledge, training, and expertise in a particular field, the qualities associated with emotional intelligence are (1) self-awareness, (2) self-regulation, (3) motivation, (4) empathy, and (5) social skill (Goleman, 1998; Palmer, Walls, Burgess, & Stough, 2001). Specifically, emotionally intelligent individuals display self-confidence, comfort with ambiguity, openness to change, optimism, commitment, and people-centeredness that manifests itself in cooperative relationships. The cosmopolitan leader is active instead of reactive, shaping ideas instead of responding to them. Cosmopolitan leadership will be further outlined in Chapter 3, which addresses the concept of cultural synergy, and more fully developed in Chapter 7, which examines leadership, teams, and the global workforce.

The globalization of the economy, coupled with advances in mass media and transportation, is breaking down the traditional barriers among groups of peoples and their differing cultures. A homogenization process is underway that is contributing to the emergence of a world culture. A *world culture* is the idea that, as conventional impediments of differing cultures decline and the commonality of human needs is emphasized, one culture will emerge—a new culture to which all people will adhere (Chaney & Martin, 2004). This world culture demands more culturally sensitive leaders who are alert to serving the commonality of human needs and markets with strategies that are transnational. It requires cosmopolitan leaders who can transcend their own culture.

Summary

Those in international business are exposed daily to a bewildering variety of value systems and differing business practices. To communicate effectively in this hectic business environment requires an understanding of other cultures, an awareness of the interdependence of nations, and the need to break interfering cultural barriers in order to find productive ways to work constructively with people of all cultures.

Today, the changing nature of business and the increasing amount of commerce conducted by global organizations require a fundamentally different kind of leader. Cosmopolitan leaders are familiar with their own culture as well as those that make up the world bazaar. They see in these multiple cultural orientations a vast array of opportunities and are willing to accept a degree of predictable risk to achieve their goals. They are technologically savvy but not prone to getting lost in details or overlooking the personal touch; entrepreneurial and passionate about what they do as well as rhetorically sensitive to others; and inspirational and inclusive rather than independent or autocratic. Being flexible, open-minded, and person-centered, they are willing to initiate communication and cooperatively pursue their objectives. For them, the international business terrain is a dynamic and active milieu.

3

The Concept of Cultural Synergy and the Global Organization

We live in an organized society, and organizations are an accepted part of life. Today, many organizations are becoming multinational global alliances with advanced telecommunications and data processing and a diverse, multicultural, mobile workforce. These growing international business concerns and the cultural synergy they create present exciting yet daunting challenges to study and understand. However, as the world becomes more interdependent, it is difficult to find an industry or segment of a country's economy that is insulated from the decisions of global managers and global organizations.

The purpose of this chapter is to explore the impact of cultural variability on global organizations and the resulting cultural synergy. We survey the emerging global landscape, highlighting shifts in the marketplace as businesses become more global. We examine various corporate cultural models to discover emerging structures and patterns as businesses form strategic alliances and transition into an international environment. We consider the growing number of virtual workplaces, as well as the technology and mediated communication needed to maintain them. The chapter concludes by acknowledging the global challenge of creating unifying visions as we continue to move our business mindset away from the mantra of "think globally and act locally" to "think both locally and globally, and respond as appropriate" (Moran & Riesenberger, 1997).

The Emerging Global Landscape

Scholars looking at the emerging global landscape suggest that the driving forces are the current shifts in society, technology, economics, politics, and the environment (Moran & Riesenberger, 1997; Pascale, Millemann, & Gioja, 2000; Trompenaars & Hampden-Turner, 1998). These shifts have seriously affected the U.S. dominance of business, as evidenced by the declining survival rate of many successful companies and the loss of market share in many industries. To illustrate, here are some examples:

- Production of automobiles and trucks decreased 60 percent from 1960 to 1990.

- Computer production decreased 19 percent from 1980 to 1989, while in Asian countries it increased 35 percent and European countries' computer production increased 18 percent.

- Although the United States holds 75 percent of the world's manufacturing of aerospace products, current projections suggest that this dominance will erode as the European Airbus consortium grows even stronger (Gongloff, 2003).

The impact of these trends is significant in both domestic and global scenarios as large corporations and small businesses go international (Rossant et al., 2004). The end result is that many cultures around the world are experiencing significant change. For example, Europe has experienced economic reform with the introduction of the Euro, and in Japan the promise of lifetime employment with companies has been abandoned and traditional consensus-building techniques to preserve social harmony are being rendered obsolete in an era of rapid change (Baker, 2005, p. G1). Terpstra and Kenneth (1992) observe that "as the macro culture shifts, so does the micro culture of institutions [with] organizational cultures within these societies . . . experiencing profound transformations" (p. 91). These global factors are demanding a restructuring of organizations and a convergence of core competencies for managers and workers alike.

The Reconfigurable Organization and Globalism

At the beginning of the 20th century, scientific management prevailed. The organization was conceived as a well-functioning machine that was carefully designed to achieve well-understood goals. Today, we realize the organization is composed of people and success is often tied to the articulation of the work of many in organizations. Globalism and new, more porous conceptions of the organization characterize this new postmodern millennium (Schmidt & Gardner, 1995). The organization per se is less important, as workers create and recreate new organizations, invent new products and services, and adapt to an evolving environment. In this redefined organizational context, trust will matter much more because the informal dimensions of the organization will be where the action is (Froggatt, 2001). To succeed, we will have to develop new mindsets and work habits for a radically changing world. We need to be prepared for almost anything and be willing to give up some of the attitudes and postures that have limited our thinking and constricted our behavior. In *Future Shock*, Alvin Toffler (1970) keenly observed that "never before has the future so rapidly become the past [and] we need to open our minds to more distant futures, both probable and possible" (p. 27).

The current organizational restructuring frequently seen in downsizing and the establishment of network organizations are only the starting point for the many newly reconfigured organizations preparing to launch global operations. Several major corporations have delayered, outsourced, and created business-to-business supply-chain partnerships and ad hoc project teams that have emerged to address the task at hand. Jack Welch, former CEO of General Electric, coined the term "boundarylessness" to describe these new organizational structures that seek to remove typical communication barriers to the traditional hierarchy. However, this term has taken on new meaning and has expanded beyond just communication barriers. Tung (1997) argues that the four essential boundaries to be spanned to achieve increased organizational speed, flexibility, integration, and innovation are "vertical (hierarchical levels), horizontal (specialization and compartmentalization), internal/external, and geographical/cultural" (p. 166). She further suggests that "specialization and compartmentalization, which were characteristic of efficient organizations in the past, will prove dysfunctional in the future" (p. 182). Moran and Riesenberger (1997) also confirm these observations when they note that this new paradigm shift "requires organizations and managers to continuously be a part of a seemingly endless adaptive process involving both functional and cross-functional expertise" (p. 14).

These transformed and reconfigured organizations still continue to struggle with the timeless issue of centralization versus decentralization as they seek to become global players. This is one of the most difficult dilemmas to resolve for those who hope to manage across cultures. Sullivan (1996) refers to this as "the art of being local worldwide." Peter Schwartz (1991) notes more specifically that multinational organizations must possess the ability to coordinate and control their operations while responding to local needs and maximizing organizational learning. Centralization does impose rules and procedures that might challenge local cultures, and decentralization brings issues of consistency and core values into question. Still, the advantages for decentralization include maximizing economies of scale, flexibly competing at a global level, and reducing transportation and communication costs for products produced locally. However, the challenges are also greater—protectionism, trade barriers, local competitors, local distribution concerns, and cultural differences. Stan Shin (1998), founder and CEO of the Acer Group, explains two productive strategies they use for directing and managing a global business. One strategy is referred to as "global brand, local touch." It develops local shareholder majorities around the world as well as local management teams. The second strategy he labels the "fast-food business model." Similar to a franchise, each unit of the company in every location is independent and has different shareholders. In this way, the entire company is both virtual *and* networked. These strategies have proven beneficial to the Acer Group as they attempt to balance centralization and decentralization and cope with the challenges of globalism. Stan Shin would quickly note, however, that each corporation must discover and design its own international business plan.

Although most would agree in theory on the need for independence at the local level, it is often more difficult in practice. Frequently, tensions arise from divided loyalties split between local managers and their objectives and the global organizational goals. Additionally, alternative objectives and subgoals with changing priorities for each manager can emerge, causing employees to be puzzled and confused. McDonough and Kahn (1996) call attention to a multinational company where considerable cultural diversity existed and positions varied significantly within the organizational hierarchy. Tension was created when the European division's top priority was to implement a telecommunications inventory management system, whereas at the corporate headquarters the focus was on converting existing databases. Production managers were fighting for increased throughput and shorter cycle times, but application engineers wanted additional time for systems integration and development standards. Employees caught in the middle were baffled and perplexed. Although conflict is typical within any large organization, it can become a complicated contest when managing conversations virtually across language boundaries and cultural constraints. The definite need for coordination and an understanding of cultural differences becomes obvious in this archetypical scenario of global business planning and communicating globally. It is increasingly difficult for companies to adhere to a mentality fueled by the geographic location of the home office and still remain globally competitive. Maznevski and Peterson (1997) suggest that "the days are passing when major multinational corporations such as General Electric or Matsushita could operate complex, dynamic industries from the unambiguous cultural base of a home country" (p. 61).

Successful global organizations need to assess their own distinctive corporate postures and strategically locate themselves along the power continuum of centralization/decentralization. Peter Schwartz (1991) states that "just as power is universally less centralized, so are information and culture" (p. 94). Decentralization is easier for some organizations and cultures than others. Trompenaars and Hampden-Turner (1998) note that organizations with a clear task and high context orientation are better equipped to delegate effectively, resulting in specific responses. Certainly, there is no master plan and no one organizational structure that can solve all the problems. What is clear is that over-centralizing or over-decentralizing can lead to failure (Lawrence & Lorsch, 1967). Therefore, each multinational organization must locate itself on this influence scale on the basis of how best to meet its own unique global strategic vision.

Corporate Cultural Models and Critical Cultural Factors

Businesses are reconfiguring in ways that create new corporate cultures shaped not only by technologies and markets but also by the cultural preferences of their leaders and the interaction of their employees as they respond to change. Galbraith (1997) proposes that, instead of merely responding to change, global organizations should be designed for change. Drucker (1997) reiterates this sentiment and suggests that it is not about replacing the current organizational designs, but that new designs are "being superimposed on them" (p. 4). He continues by noting that organizational design must incorporate "different purposes, different people, and different cultures" (p. 5). Pascale et al. (2000) use a compelling organic metaphor to describe the emerging global businesses based on the principles of self-organization. Their "life science model" suggests that organizations today develop like a new species by "creating an ecological niche— innovate . . . proliferate . . . aggregate" (p. 3). It is this rapid response sequence that successful multinational organizations need to emulate in order to remain competitive and to thrive in today's brisk international business environment.

Odenwald (1996) explores contrasting corporate cultures and differing corporate values within three Japanese companies. Matsushita is very policy oriented, with a strong emphasis on customer satisfaction while maintaining a focus on its contribution to society to coexist and co-prosper. Its concern for individuals results in a lower sense of risk-taking as a company. Sony's culture, on the other hand, is liberal, with a focus on internationalism and a high tolerance for risk and change. Then there is Mitsubishi's culture that focuses on fair play in business, with an orientation toward employee satisfaction to ensure high morale. Minoru Makihara (1998), president of Mitsubishi Corporation, states that leadership should be strategically focused on relationships in which they "lead through global trust networks" (p. 18). In the United States private, for-profit enterprises such as Stanley Home Products, Mary Kay, and Tupperware as well as volunteer, nonprofit groups like Greenpeace, The Sierra Club, and MADD illustrate how organizations can tie into the strength of the independent individual worker for collective success. Moreover, the organization is sustained by the combined effort of its members who are imbued with a clear vision and outcome. The companies that "seize the high ground . . . by inspiring front line workers to operate as independent agents, pursuing their own solutions with little central control" will succeed and thrive in this volatile global bazaar (Pascale et al., 2000, p. 12). This networking has prompted some scholars to describe the new emerging organizational design as a web, particularly given our wired society (Drucker, 1997; Galbraith, 1997; Pascale et al., 2000).

Trompenaars and Hampden-Turner (1998) propose four corporate cultural models that can help define and clarify the emerging organizational structures. Their models are based on the relationship between employees and their organization, the vertical or hierarchical system of authority, and the employees' view of the organization's mission and vision. The models are differentiated one from another on the basis of two primary dimensions—people versus tasks and the egalitarian versus hierarchical nature of the organization.

The *Eiffel Tower* culture corresponds to a formal bureaucracy in which the structure strongly defines one's legitimate role and place in the organization. Status and power are explicitly allocated to the position, and decision making reflects a depersonalized, rational-legal system that adheres to strict rules that ultimately uphold the hierarchy itself. In the Eiffel Tower culture, task and accomplishment far outweigh any concern for relationship. Examples of the Eiffel Tower model can be found in Australia, France, Hungary, and Venezuela.

The *Guided Missile* culture is also task oriented but has an egalitarian perspective that is "ends oriented" rather than "means driven." People are considered important to achieving ends; consequently, the use of self-directed teams and the matrix management of projects create a cybernetic culture that continually renews itself through feedback and open systems. Change is embraced as teams dissolve and emerge again on the basis of required tasks. In Guided Missile cultures, employees generally have greater loyalty to the project and their professions than to the organization itself. The organization per se is simply a place to get work done through the coordinated and combined efforts of others who share in decision-making and problem-solving. The Guided Missile model can be found in Ireland, Norway, and the United States.

The *Family* culture reflects the established power structure often seen in the traditional home, with a strong parent figure who cares for the family unit and has ultimate decision-making power that is accepted by the other family members. The dominant force is the sense of loyalty and high context that allows a great amount of information to be assumed and taken for granted. Relationships tend to be diffuse, such that the leader is influential and unchallenged in all situations (i.e., work, family, and community). The Family model is typical in Belgium, Greece, Spain, India, and South Korea.

Finally, the *Incubator* culture serves the self-expression and self-fulfillment of its employees. This culture is managed from a strong egalitarian perspective and performs best within an intensely emotional environment. The driving purpose of these organizations is personal development. The culture provides a sounding board for revolutionary thinking and the unleashing of inventive creativity. The structure is very loose, with few constraints, so as to encourage the "bootlegging" of time on other projects and to promote brainstorming and the entrepreneurial development of pioneering ideas. Employees are dutifully devoted to the organization but are individually loyal to their profession and committed to their self-interest (i.e., "I"-Incorporated). Consequently, they "may take a free ride until their eggs are close to hatching [and] larger organizations [can] find themselves successively undermined" (Trompenaars & Hampden-Turner, 1998, p. 180). For this reason, some suggest that these organizations are dependent on an individualistic culture and may be viewed as transitional rather than permanent. Examples of these types of organizations include the many start-up firms in the computer industry, whether it is Silicon Valley in the United States or Silicon Glen in Scotland. The Incubator model can also be commonly found in Canada, Denmark, and Switzerland.

Alignment throughout independent systems is required so that the selected corporate model and its purposes are synchronized with the culture and its values and worldview. Terpstra and Kenneth (1992) have identified five critical factors that multicultural corporations should consider when developing a corporate cultural model and/or choosing to expand into a new global area:

1. *Cultural variability* refers to the conditions of stability within the organization. The more unstable an organization is, the more it needs strong internal structures to manage rapid change, open communication channels, and decentralized decision-making with local experts to provide responses.

2. Cultural complexity relates to high- and low-context cultures and concerns itself with the need to match the degree of context with the appropriate communication content, style, and quantity.

3. Cultural hostility is the degree to which local conditions appear threatening to employees and organizational values. It reflects the perception of the local or host culture toward the multinational corporation itself. The greater the degree of hostility, the more difficult it is to establish trust and build relationships between the host culture and the organization.

4. Cultural heterogeneity is the degree to which the organizational culture is similar to or different from the local or national culture. When cultures are very diverse or heterogeneous, it is more difficult to coordinate the behavior of local subsidiaries and their employees, thereby requiring management to be more differentiated and to decentralize communication and policy. The greater the similarities or increased homophily, the easier it is to purposefully communicate mission and vision.

5. Cultural interdependence refers to the economic dependence the organization has with other interacting cultures to obtain resources such as raw materials, equipment, technological support, and critical institutional and infrastructure processes. The more independent the organization is, the less need for strategic alliances and host culture support.

These critical cultural factors are helpful in gaining a global perspective and developing specific strategic objectives. Alldregde and Nilan (2000) studied 3M's leadership style to determine those characteristics of strong multinational corporations that respect and leverage other customs, cultures, and values to better understand and grow the total business. They found that it is highly important to optimize and integrate resources on a global basis, including manufacturing, research and development, and information technology. John R. Fulkerson, Vice-President of Organization and Management Development for PepsiCo Foods and Beverages International, concurs and describes the organization of the future as "global, competency based, virtual/fluid, empowered, decentralized, and connected" (Odenwald, 1996, p. 94). The global organization has the potential for exponential growth and financial success if the integration of cultures can be harnessed and aligned with the strategic goals of the corporation.

Globalism and Cultural Synergy

Several perspectives drive current research on the impact of globalization and cultural variability on multicultural organizations. Should organizations adapt to external cultural conditions or should their structural, process, and interpretive distinctions be retained despite cultural pressures? Stohl (2001) states that "environmental and technological pressures on contemporary organizations to become more and more similar clash with the proprietary pull of cultural identifications, traditional values, and conventional practices of social life" (p. 326). Barber (1992) would refer to this clash as the political forces of "Jihad vs. McWorld." Those who assume a perspective of cultural convergence would encourage organizations to mutually accommodate to the external environment. Others who maintain a perspective of cultural divergence would warn against losing distinctive corporate characteristics and important corporate values (Stohl, 2001).

A third alternative perspective also exists that shifts the focus from a specific demographic or geographic culture to understanding how multinational organizations can jointly with the host country develop a "third culture." For example, General Electric is rooted in a North American culture and Siemens is rooted in a German culture, but both are seeking an international mix as they go global. Although they are strongly influenced by their respective geographic and political worldviews, as they become increasingly international they combine their workforces to produce their products or services and jointly blend their respective views. The ultimate success for these organizations is when they can transform themselves and essentially metamorphose into a "third culture" in which they mutually share decision-making and capitalize on the synergistic output. Trompenaars and Hampden-Turner (1998) suggest that when two cultures blend, they dance with each other to "manage cultural polarities and value dimensions that self-organize in systems to generate new meanings" (p. 27). The resulting synergy allows global businesses to better manage their diverse components and create a stronger, more flexible and adaptive organization ready to compete in the world market.

SYNERGY DEFINED

Synergy is cooperative or combined action that can occur when diverse or disparate groups of people with varying viewpoints work together. The objective is to increase effectiveness by sharing perceptions, insights, and knowledge. But synergy is more than simply working together toward the mutual achievement of certain goals. The power of synergy rests in the reality that "when solving problems, groups are often smarter than the smartest people within them" (Surowiecki, 2004, p. G1). Consequently, when ordinary people using available resources are allowed to freely exchange opinions and argue points of view, extraordinary results can occur.

Synergy is also vital in solving complex international business problems. When a European conglomerate purchases the controlling rights of a U.S.

rubber manufacturer or Common Market partners join together in a joint venture to produce an innovative airplane, synergistic skills are required. Differences in organizational cultures in these instances can either undermine the intended actions or can be used to enhance goal achievement. Synergy is needed to pool resources, talent, and capital for a successful operation. The very complexities of our super-industrial and postmodern society demand such collaboration, particularly in large-scale enterprises such as space exploration and research.

SYSTEMS THEORY, COMPLEXITY SCIENCE, AND THE NATURE OF SYNERGY

MIT professor Norbert Wiener (1967) coined the term cybernetics to describe the field of artificial intelligence and then went on to pioneer the study of information processing, feedback, and control in communication systems. Karl Weick (1979, 1989, 2001) applied information and general systems theory to organizational contexts, declaring that organizations only survive in hostile environments by managing to reduce equivocality or uncertainty through retrospective sensemaking. He urged leaders to continually discredit much of what they think they know—to doubt, argue, contradict, disbelieve, challenge, question, and actively listen—in other words, to be synergistic. Complexity science represents a quantum leap forward, advancing information and general systems theory beyond their linear dimensions and causal constraints (Pascale et al., 2000). So, to facilitate understanding the nature of synergy, it is necessary to discuss several pivotal principles of systems theory and complexity science:

- *The principle of interdependence* suggests that systems consist of a network of relationships among interacting parts. Consequently, the functioning of one component relies on the other component. Synergistic group members understand the need to work together if they are to take advantage of available opportunities and achieve mutually desired objectives.

- *The principle of permeability* implies that information and materials freely flow in and out. This principle connotes a seamless quality to organizations that permits a higher order of sharing and distribution of human assets, important data, and capital. Trust is the fuel that makes permeability work. Synergistic groups need timely access to all available information and resources to solve the problem.

- *The principle of requisite variety* states that a system's survival depends on its ability to cultivate variety in its internal structure in order to cope successfully with variations introduced from external sources. Openness permits diversity, and an organization must be as diverse as the environment in which it exists. Variety brings richness, depth, and artistry to any endeavor.

- *The principle of feedback* proposes that corrective or negative feedback serves to keep the system on course, and growth or positive feedback serves to transform or change a system. Synergistic leaders and managers understand that communication and feedback are at the heart of "the great game of business" (Kouzes & Posner, 1993, p. 171).

- *The principle of balance or equilibrium* asserts that systems tend to resist deviation and maintain a steady course. This can be hazardous because the environment in which organizations are embedded is always in flux, and prolonged equilibrium can dull an organization's senses and sap its ability to rouse itself in the face of change. Danny Miller (1990) notes that the higher the reliance on past practices, especially successful ones, the greater the organizational risk because it fails to anticipate the future. He labels this phenomenon the "Icarus Paradox," where organizations extend and amplify the strategies to which they credit their success until tunnel vision rules and flexibility is lost. In order for organizations to remain competitive, they must learn to master these "perils of excellence" and "unlearn the past by questioning world views, opening up cultures, and disassembling structures" (Miller, 1990, p. 204). Organizations have to unfreeze before they can renew themselves.

- *The principle of adaptation* gives emphasis to the view that systems must change to survive in a dynamic environment. Complex systems become more vulnerable as they become more homogeneous, thereby revealing the importance of adapting to the greater cultural diversity.

- *The principle of connection* contends that systems must connect to one another and are always part of other systems. Global businesses need to increase the effectiveness and number of connections to which they can share and solicit information. Charles Handy (1998) refers to the core periphery model as one way to define these connections. There are people working in the core, while others work outside the core. In this way, power is distributed and membership communities are formed at various locations, resulting in distributed intelligence and better solutions.

- *The principle of negative entropy* suggests that openness permits systems to sustain themselves and grow rather than run down and deteriorate. John Kao (1998) uses the term "jamming" to describe the needed spontaneity and openness of synergistic organizations. He is referring to the improvisation of jazz where success depends on the need for everybody to perform as individuals and as a group.

- *The principle of equifinality* involves multiple approaches to any system outcome. Synergistic organizations and groups realize that there are many pathways for accomplishing goals. Consequently they seek competent, curious, obstreperous people who agree on values and priorities, but who might think differently about how to get there.

- *The principle of holism* states that a system is more than the sum of its parts. We are all holographic images of the organizations we work for and the groups to which we belong. Each of us is important to the success of the organization or the effectiveness of the group. Everyone counts.

Complexity science is concerned with nonlinear effects where very small perturbations, such as the flutter of a butterfly's wings, may lead to a tsunami. For those in complexity science, the world is constantly changing beyond our powers of precise prediction. The challenge for organizations is being alert to both large and small changes and attempting to understand the world landscape as it unfolds. This may seem unnerving because it is comparable to walking on a trampoline, but that is the nature of reality—it is constantly new. Collins and Porras (1994) note in their bestseller *Built to Last* that the companies that have prospered the longest are those that preserve core values and skills while engaged in self-renewal and making creative use of their changing environments to stimulate progress.

SYNERGY AND CROSS-CULTURAL COMMUNICATION COMPETENCE

Cultural synergy in today's global economy requires that individuals within multinational organizations be culturally aware and competent in cross-cultural communication. Extensive research indicates that cross-cultural competence impacts the effectiveness of global corporations (Cox, Lobel, & McLeod, 1991; Matveev & Nelson, 2004; Townsend, DeMarie, & Hendrickson, 1996; Triandis & Singelis, 1998; Wheelen & Hunger, 1998). The culturally diverse workforce offers a variety of perspectives, skills, and attitudes (Maznevski, 1994) and outperforms homogeneous groups in identifying problems and generating more creative solutions (Marquardt & Horvath, 2001; McLeod & Lobel, 1992; Watson, Pitt, Cunningham, & Nel, 1993). In their study of Russian and American managers, Matveev and Nelson (2004) found that "cross cultural competence accounted for 20% of the variance in the performance level of multicultural teams" (p. 33). Ng and Tung (1998) found that multicultural divisions reported higher levels of productivity and financial profitability than their homogeneous counterparts within a multibranch financial services organization. Those organizations that have realized the benefits of diversity have learned how to maximize its strengths while mitigating the costs and are able to incorporate positive and winning communication skills.

Today we are transitioning into a new high-synergy postmodern society in which leadership fosters win-win and all triumph. It is an open system of connected people that emphasizes cooperation for mutual advantage. Social institutions promote individual and group development and utilize community resources and talents for the commonwealth. Successfully transitioning into the emerging postmodern era requires acceptance of this new high-synergy society that can provide new energy for international business practices. Synergy takes on increasing importance as multinational organizations, non-profit agencies, and governmental activities become more global in scope, more complex in practice, and more sophisticated in technology. Charles Handy (1995) declares that "the world is up for re-invention [and] we cannot wait for great visions from great people, for they are in short supply. It is up to us to light our own small fire in the darkness" (p. 286).

The Virtual Organization, Cultural Synergy, and the Global Marketplace

With today's technology, time and distance are collapsed. Anyone can access anyone and anything through groupware, intranets, and expert systems. This technological mobility, along with increased globalism, has given rise to organizations becoming virtual—harnessing each other's strengths via alliances, subcontracts, partnerships, and co-contracts. As global organizations become increasingly virtual, people in alliances and partnerships will jointly locate and integrate opportunities, ventures, and resources. In the virtual, real-time world, the line between organizational and national boundaries will blur.

DEFINING VIRTUAL ORGANIZATIONS AND WORK GROUPS

Ahuja and Carley (1999) define a virtual organization as "a geographically distributed organization whose members are bound by a long-term common interest or goal, and who communicate and coordinate their work through information technology" (p. 743). Some scholars use the term "virtual" to denote those organizations and teams whose members never meet face-to-face (Jarvenpaa & Leidner, 1998; Kristof, Brown, Sims, & Smith, 1995). However, most define a workplace as "virtual" when the majority of communication is mediated by technology (Maznevski & Chudoba, 2000; Townsend et al., 1996; M. Young, 1998).

In general, virtual work groups create the structural mechanism for mitigating the increased travel, time, coordination, and costs associated with physically bringing people together. Many researchers are even considering "virtualness" a characteristic of all teams and are shifting studies away from comparisons between virtual teams and those that meet face-to-face (Griffith & Neale, 2001; Martins, Gilson, & Maynard, 2004). Griffith and Neale (2001) propose that teams exist on a continuum between purely face-to-face and purely virtual, resulting from the interplay between "the structures and capabilities provided by the technology, the demands of the task, and the structures that emerge" (p. 386). For example, organizations like Sun, IBM, and Caterpillar have created "collaboratories" of scientists and engineers in separate locales, who work in real time together on product development and design via televiewers, videoconferencing, shared computer displays or whiteboards, networked electronic notebooks, and synchronized Web browsers. These organizations also use electronic connections (EDI, shared databases, extranets) with vendors, suppliers, distributors, customers, sales forces, and subsidiaries around the world to transcend boundaries and ensure real-time responses (Bell & Harari, 2000). Netscape's Marc Andreessen believes "we are seeing the networking of the world as the interconnecting of all businesses and a growing number of individuals creates a seamless electronic web" (Bell & Harari, 2000, p. 92).

GLOBAL ORGANIZATIONS, TEAMS, AND THE NATURE OF VIRTUAL COMMUNICATION

Global organizations operate in the midst of language and cultural diversity and consequently must surmount certain obstacles when using virtual communication. Orasanu, Fisher, and Davison (1997) identify three distinct ways that computer-mediated communication can go seriously wrong. First, messages may encounter transmission problems, prohibiting information from reaching its destination. Second, errors can occur when messages are transmitted so their original meaning is not conveyed as intended. Finally, messages may be accurately sent and received, but a shared understanding of the situation does not exist between the parties.

When the primary communication between members is mediated by either voice or computer and groups are multicultural, they are unable to make assumptions that would be typical within homogeneous groups on the basis of similar culture and nonverbal cues (Barczak & McDonough, 2003; Maznevski & DeStefano, 2000). People of different backgrounds know how to best communicate with those who are similar as a result of "built-in characteristics in their language which facilitates [sic] the conveyance of ideas to their own kind [and] they . . . [are] only vaguely aware of the dependence on these linguistic traits which make their job easier" (R. Lewis, 1999, p. 83). In the same manner, those who use technology are rarely aware of the traits and protocols that have become ingrained in their usage but that can facilitate or inhibit communication with others who may not be aware of these nuances. Examples include the use of acronyms (JIT, MRP, ROI), shortcuts (BTW, FYI, IMHO), and pacing behaviors as well as the frequency of how often one responds to e-mail. Orasanu et al. (1997) investigated a number of international airline disasters between 1972 and 1990 that claimed over 700 lives, and discovered in every instance a variety of communication failures due to a lack of cultural or linguistic awareness.

The reduced access to social cues resulting from the absence of proxemics, kinesics, and paralanguage can also prove challenging to effective virtual communication. Bordia (1997) observes that a "preoccupation with receiving, composing, and sending messages leads to a lack of awareness of social context" (p. 108) and often depersonalizes the communication itself. The absence of proximity often results in a loss of casual conversations that enable members to expand contacts that support their formal work or provide needed feedback and constructive support that helps to build rapport and smooth future conversations (Hage, 1974; March & Savon, 1984; Sarbaugh-Thompson & Feldman, 1998). When anonymity is involved, it may increase participation, but it also increases the potential for inappropriate behavior such as "flaming, excessive self-disclosure, [and] manipulation of other group members through violation of group behavioral norms" (Haythornthwaite, Wellman, & Garton, 1998, p. 210). Researchers have also found that technology-mediated communication requires more time and effort than face-to-face communication to exchange social information and uncover "situated knowledge" within teams (Sole & Edmondson, 2002).

Maznevski and Chudoba (2000) report that "effective global virtual team outcomes are a function of appropriate interaction incidents and the structuring of those incidents into a temporal rhythm" (p. 489). Their analysis included structural characteristics of media selection based on the characteristics proposed by Straub and Karahanna (1998): (1) richness, (2) social presence, (3) accessibility, and (4) recipient availability. Their results regarding media choices were consistent with the theories of media richness that contend that all organizational communication channels can be arrayed along a continuum. The "rich" end of this continuum (high in data) is anchored by face-to-face communication with instant feedback and multiple verbal and nonverbal cues, whereas the other end of the spectrum (low in data) makes use of impersonal static media such as bulletins and generalized computer reports. In between we find electronic mail, personal written communication, letters, and memos. Maznevski and Chudoba (2000) found that media choice was a function of the required decision process and complexity of the message, and "function followed form—the higher the level of decision process and/or the more complex the message, the more rich the communication medium used" (p. 484). They further reported that in effective teams, if a rich medium is not required, members will select the medium that is most accessible and "if an incident serves multiple functions or messages, its medium and duration will be shaped by the highest function and the most complexity" (p. 485). That is, when dealing with highly ambiguous and complex tasks, teams will choose to use a rich communication medium, but when dealing with a communication message low in ambiguity and complexity, teams will opt for a lean communication medium. For example, when a team needs to make a decision that requires extensive conversation because of strong feelings and opinions versus a clear factual discourse, effective teams will use a telephone conference over an e-mail exchange.

Many researchers indicate that virtual communications technology is a factor of the team's task, its context, and its timing (DeSanctis & Jackson, 1994; Fulk, 1993; Hiltz, Johnson, & Turoff, 1991; Hinds & Kiesler, 1995; Turoff, Hiltz, Bahgat, & Rama, 1993; Zack, 1993). Tasks requiring greater levels of interdependence, for instance, require more complex modes of communication support and more frequent interaction (Maznevski & Chudoba, 2000; Mintzberg, 1989; Turoff et al., 1993). Social context also affects media choices, and "messages that cross boundaries are inherently more complex, but can be made simpler if members build a shared view of their task and strong trusting relationships among each other" (Maznevski & Chudoba, 2000, p. 486). Consequently, the greater the cultural and professional differences among team members, the more complex the team's messages will be, whereas the stronger the shared views and relationships among virtual team members, the less complex the team's messages will be.

CHALLENGES TO WORKING IN VIRTUAL ORGANIZATIONS

McDonough and Cedrone (2000) point out three primary challenges to working in a virtual global environment: (1) motivation, (2) creating a "safe" environment, and (3) managing the process of communication. Motivation requires that all members have a compelling reason and clear understanding of why they need to communicate with others and the benefits of collaboration regarding business outcomes.

A psychologically safe environment depends on trust and mutual respect often built from open information exchanges and meeting agreed-on deadlines. To facilitate this, many virtual groups have access to each others' work products or an "electronic workplace" such as a bulletin board to post documented minutes and notes that can provide incremental exposure. Some work groups find it easier to start with simplified linear work that is objective or task driven (schedules, budgets, task prioritization) and then move toward nonlinear work requiring agreements, judgment calls, and innovation, where trust is indispensable.

The challenge of managing the process of communication includes being sensitive to technology selection and understanding the complexities of various media. Fulk and Collin-Jarvis (2001) suggest the following six criteria to determine the potential effectiveness of various media: (1) equality of participation, (2) socioemotional expression, (3) encourages consensus, (4) efficiency, (5) decision quality, and (6) satisfaction. In addition to media selection, Maznevski and Chudoba (2000) found that the temporal rhythm of communication was critical to the interaction process because "the rhythm prevented inadvertent transitions from happening and maintained effective interaction equilibrium patterns" (p. 488).

Allwood and Schroeder (2000) studied the virtual communication patterns of an international online community and identified five important skill sets used for communication management. The first is a summons that refers to catching the attention of a potential receiver, often through the use of a name or greeting. The second is providing feedback to let others know the message has been received and understood. Third is turn management used as a way to share the "virtual floor" with others. The fourth skill identified for online conversations is sequencing and understanding when one thing must precede the other. Sequencing is often a challenge in the online environment and is affected by technology and processing delays that often lead to redundancy in the form of repetition or paraphrasing. Finally, one must own communication management. This involves the need to choose the right expressions or change your contribution for various reasons, such as errors in content, clarification, or a change of mind. In some cases, communication management also includes the process of soliciting feedback to ensure that the receiver has interpreted the message as intended.

A final challenge confronting virtual organizations concerns the political nature of communicating in this environment where access seems endlessly open. Previous research had proposed that virtual organizations were less hierarchical and that role and status effects were reduced (Beyerlein & Johnson, 1994; Camillus, 1993; Goldman, Nagel, & Preiss, 1995; Sproull & Kessler, 1986). Several studies concluded that participation would ultimately become more egalitarian when compared to face-to-face groups (Bikson & Eveland, 1990; Straus, 1996), and electronic communication was believed to help increase participation while lowering distinctions among members (Dubrovsky,

Kiesler, & Sethna, 1991). More recently, however, scholars have discovered that virtual groups tend to recreate hierarchies and remain somewhat centralized (Owens, Neale, & Sutton, 2000). Ahuja and Carley (1999) assert that "the reason for this rests in the communicative efficiency and robustness of the hierarchical form and in the benefits of role" (p. 20) to manage work processes. The opportunity to excel may rest with the organization's ability to balance control with the need for innovative thinking and open collaboration.

VIRTUAL FREEDOM AND TECHNOLOGY-MEDIATED COMMUNICATION

The spirit of freedom has the potential to thrive in the virtual organization. Freedom is the act of liberating employees from organizational rules and structures that suppress speed, agility, and imagination. This freedom is definitely evidenced in Buckman Laboratories (Harvard Business School case study number N9-899-175) located in Memphis, Tennessee (Buckman, 1997, 2000; Meek, 1999). When Robert H. Buckman inherited the company in 1978, it had about 500 employees and provided specialty chemicals to a variety of industries in seven countries. He made up his mind to change the organization so that customers could be served better and faster. Buckman replaced the old command-and-control model with open information sharing, and technology was made available to the general managers and salespeople that allowed them to share information electronically. Then he linked all employees or associates to a variety of databases and online forums that allowed them to exchange knowledge that was constantly being updated. Buckman Laboratories now sells to customers in 90 countries, business is conducted in 15 languages, and half of the associates are outside the United States. The tremendous progress and significant rewards achieved by Bob Buckman were not without conflict, resistance, and frustration, but today Buckman Laboratories attests to the value of the virtual workplace and dramatically illustrates that, when the potential of the individual is optimized, the power of the organization is maximized.

Technology-mediated communication is integral to the virtual workplace and often creates the structure for conversations in global organizations. Computers and computer-related technologies are stimulating and supporting a virtual revolution in the workplace that is turning international business and global markets upside down. The new business model is predicated on anticipating the customers' constantly changing business needs and quickly responding. Tom Peters (1992) describes the emerging marketplace as one populated by "ephemeral organizations, joined in ephemeral combinations to produce ephemeral products for ephemeral markets . . . FAST" (p. 18).

Summary

The emerging global landscape is in flux, and many multinational organizations are struggling with creating inclusive worldwide mission statements and visions that foster cultural alignment. As they seek solutions to the complicated issues globalism presents, many organizations are reconfiguring themselves. New and more elastic corporate cultural models are being adopted to address the critical cultural factors influencing today's international business environment. Increasingly, these models hope to capitalize on cultural synergy and the diversity within the workplace.

Cultural synergy, through collaboration, emphasizes similarities and common concerns to integrate differences and enrich human activities and organizational systems. It requires looking at the challenges and opportunities together, accessing whatever information is needed together, and finally taking bold and imaginative action together. Constantly changing market concerns, sociopolitical issues, and technology urgently require a resilient, resourceful workforce that can take advantage of cultural synergy.

As the global marketplace expands and changes, so does the way multinational organizations structure themselves and conduct business. Increasingly, more are becoming virtual organizations and emerging as trusted guides and a helpful channel to what is new. Disney has expanded its domain to become a reliable medium to family entertainment. Dell has become more than a manufacturer: it is a portal for computers and electronic solutions to problems. Harvard University has expanded beyond being an excellent degree-granting institution to becoming the world's preeminent brand-portal for learning. Brandeis University professor and former Secretary of Labor Robert Reich (2000) puts it well when he says that in this new global economy, "economic value comes not from assets . . . but from the domain of trust [and winning companies] stand not for specific products, but for continuing solutions" (p. 37).

We cannot ignore these changes and the new order of doing business if we hope to remain globally competitive. Cosmopolitan leaders need to accept the changes and embrace the global opportunities presented.

Unit Two

Developing New Skills and Intercultural Competencies

There is very little difference between one [person] and another; but what little there is, is very important. This distinction seems to me to go to the root of the matter.

—William James, in "The Will to Believe"

If we seek to understand a people we have to put ourselves, as far as we can, in that particular historical and cultural background . . . One has to recognize that countries and people differ in their approach and their ways, in their approach to life and their ways of living and thinking. In order to understand them we have to understand their way of life and approach. If we wish to convince them, we have to use their language as far as we can, not language in the narrow sense of the word, but the language of the mind.

—Jawaharlal Nehru

4

Cultural Contact and Interfacing With Others

C ommunication with others is an integral aspect of international business and is vital to achieving the multinational objectives for which these businesses were formed. Yet, communication is perhaps the most complex structure we engage in, and relating to others can be a seemingly puzzling process. Our desire to communicate and interface with people from other cultures depends on how we deal with anxiety, stress, and pressure as well as our ability to build and maintain satisfying intercultural relationships (Hammer, Gudykunst, & Wiseman, 1978).

The purpose of this chapter is to explore dimensions of cultural contact and examine the relational nature of intercultural communication and international business. It looks into the dialectical forces or tensions that influence the building of intercultural relationships and further complicate the international business equation. It defines and explains the effects of culture shock and considers varying approaches to intercultural transitions and adaptation. Finally, it identifies cross-cultural competencies essential to intercultural effectiveness. Such knowledge acquaints us with the basic cognitive, social, and personal skills needed to compete in an international business arena.

Relational Dialectics and Cultural Contact

The dialectical perspective provides a fundamental framework within which to consider the dynamics involved when communicating with others and helps us better understand the perplexing relational problems that arise when making contact and interfacing with others. We selected it here because it identifies the complex variety of forces that influence our relationships with others. The dialectical model proposed by Baxter (1992) and Montgomery (1993) contends that relationships are messy and always in flux; they are characterized by "contradictions, contingencies, non-rationalities, and multiple realities" (p. 330). Four primary assumptions guide a dialectical approach to relationship: praxis, change, contradiction, and totality (Baxter & Montgomery, 1996):

- Praxis suggests that relational trajectories are neither linear nor repetitive but rather spiral forward in time, transforming reality for the participants as they act and react.
- Change is the only guarantee in a relationship, thus relationships cannot be "maintained," only "sustained."
- The notion of contradictions asserts that in any relationship there are inherent tensions between contradictory impulses or dialectics (e.g., autonomy/connectedness or open/closed).
- Totality emphasizes the essential interdependence between relational partners for a relationship to exist. Thus, a dialectical tension experienced by one partner will ultimately affect the other and vice versa, contributing to relational change.

Dialectics or contradictory tensions or forces influence both our internal and external relationships. Internally or within their private relationship, people must decide how connected or autonomous, how predictable or novel, and how open or closed their relational behavior will be. Externally vis-à-vis their public networks, they must also decide who to include in their social circle and who to exclude, how conventional or unique their relationship will appear, and what to reveal to or conceal from outsiders. Moreover, each of the relational forces identified is drawn in tension with every other pole. However, dialectical moments represent brief momentary periods of equilibrium between opposing dialectics in the larger pattern of continuous change that marks relationships (Baxter & Simon, 1993). This messy view of relationships and chaotic jumble of contradictions is far removed from the more ideal notions of communication as persuasion or shared meaning or increasing certainty.

A dialectical approach emphasizes the processual, relational, and contradictory nature of intercultural communication as evidenced in international business (Martin & Nakayama, 2003). With regard to the processual nature of intercultural communication, it is important to remember that cultures change, as do individuals. The dialectical perspective further emphasizes the importance of relationships among the various aspects of intercultural communication and the importance of viewing these holistically rather than in isolation. Finally, the dialectical perspective transcends dichotomous thinking and highlights the necessity of holding contradictory ideas simultaneously. Thinking dialectically forces us to move beyond our familiar categories and opens us up to new possibilities.

The notion of dialectical tensions can further be extended to encompass intercultural communication and the entire relational sphere. Some specific dialectical tensions associated with intercultural communication and international business have been identified (Martin & Nakayama, 2003; Montgomery, 1992; Rawlins, 1992):

- *Similarities-difference dialectic.* We are similar to and different from others as a result of culture. In that people are simultaneously similar to and different from each other with regard to values, language, nonverbal behavior, conflict management, and so on, building intercultural relationships can become a knotty business. Emphasizing only similarities can cause us to ignore important cultural variations, whereas emphasizing only differences can make established stereotypes and learned prejudices all too inviting.

- *Cultural-individual dialectic.* We share certain patterns of thinking and behavior with members of the culture to which we belong. However, some patterns are completely idiosyncratic or particular to us as individuals and no one else.

- *Personal-contextual dialectic.* We communicate as individuals on a personal level with others; however, the context or situation is also important. Interactional dialectics refers to the relationship tensions between persons, whereas contextual dialectics refers to the relationship tensions between the personal and the cultural.

- *Privilege-disadvantage dialectic.* We all possess some resources that may privilege us in certain contexts, but by the same token we may be disadvantaged in other instances. For example, we may have significant cognitive understanding of a work project but be unable to speak the local language. Nationality, gender, age, race, socioeconomic status, and other identities may provide certain privileges or disadvantages.

- *Affection-instrumentality dialectic.* We may like someone for him- or herself or alternatively enact strategies for some payoff or reward. Instrumentality regards people as a means to an end rather than an end in itself as affection.

- *Judgment-acceptance dialectic.* Our intercultural contacts with others can lead to closing judgments regarding the encounter or unconditional acceptance of the other party. This dialectic considers the evaluative quality of our communication and encounters with others.

- *Past-present-future dialectic.* We need to be aware of contemporary forces and realities that shape interactions of people from different cultural groups while simultaneously recognizing past influences and future expectations. Various peoples and cultures deal with time differently.

- *Ideal-real dialectic.* Ideals tend to arise from cultural expectations, whereas the "real" is that which actually occurs. Ideals often go unstated and may even remain out of our awareness, yet they can still damage a relationship when the ideals are unrealistic.

- *Static-dynamic dialectic.* Intercultural communication tends to be both static and dynamic at the same time. Some cultural and communication patterns remain relatively constant, whereas other aspects of cultures are more dynamic and shift over time.

- *Confidence/certainty-anxiety/uncertainty dialectic.* We communicate with relative confidence and certainty with those with whom we are familiar, but we find anxiety and uncertainty inhibiting our communication with someone from an unfamiliar culture. Our ability to communicate effectively is based, at least in part, on our ability to manage our anxiety and uncertainty (Gudykunst, 1995).

Anxiety and uncertainty are powerful dialectical forces and together are the basic causes of most communication failures in intercultural situations (Gudykunst, 1988). Anxiety is the feeling of being tense, worried, or apprehensive about what might happen. It is born out of fear of negative consequences when interacting with people from other cultures (Crocker, Major, & Steele, 1998; Hoyle, Pinkley, & Insko, 1989; Stephan & Stephan, 1985). We may fear performing poorly or worry "about feeling incompetent, confused, and not in control" (Stephan & Stephan, 1985, p. 159). We may feel that others will exploit or take advantage of us. Or, we may fear rejection, ridicule, or disapproval by those of the host culture and negative evaluations from members of our own culture. Uncertainty pertains to our inability to understand the feelings, beliefs, or values of others and in turn to explain their behavior (Berger & Calabrese, 1975). We prefer being able to project what will happen in a particular situation and to state why something occurred. The problem is that our life experiences, cultural values, and social memberships that influence our interpretations differ from those of other cultures (Berger, Gardner, Parks, Schulman, & Miller, 1976). Thus, to successfully transition into another culture and effectively communicate with others requires minimizing our anxiety and misunderstandings. However, this is not to imply that we want to totally reduce or eliminate our anxiety and uncertainty when interculturally engaged. An optimal level of anxiety can lead to adaptive processes and some degree of uncertainty can lead to creativity, permitting us to move beyond relying on simple social categorizations (Csikszentmihalyi, 1990; Janis, 1971; Weick, 1979).

Many factors influence the amount of anxiety and uncertainty we experience when communicating with people from other cultures (Gudykunst, 1988). If we perceive others to be similar to us, we are less anxious and have more confidence in our ability to predict their behavior, although we may perceive similarities when we are actually very different. Moreover, the more typical our social identities tend to be and the degree to which we share acquaintances and memberships along common social networks will decrease anxiety and uncertainty (Gudykunst & Hammer, 1988). Also, the more we understand and can speak another's language and the more knowledge we have of his or her culture, the more our anxiety and uncertainty will be reduced. Generally, as we get to know people from other cultures, the anxiety and uncertainty we initially experience in interacting with them tends to decrease (Hubbert, Gudykunst, & Guerrero, 1999). However, unexpected events may occur in our established relationships that could increase anxiety and uncertainty, such as being taken advantage of or deceived (Planalp, Rutherford, & Honeycutt, 1988). Thus, anxiety and uncertainty may fluctuate over time.

The various dialectical tensions require constant attention and negotiation by the relational partners who must continually recalibrate and reaffirm the influence of such pressures (Baxter & Montgomery, 1997; Montgomery & Baxter, 1998). To successfully manage dialectical pressures in relationships is to remain open and responsive to the emerging present, which is itself in dialectical tension with the past and the future. This is the challenge as we attempt to transition into another culture and build intercultural relationships.

Adaptation and Building Intercultural Relationships

Cultural adaptation is principally the long-term process of adjusting to and finally feeling comfortable in a new environment. Brislin (1981) notes that frequently during short cross-cultural encounters, no effort is made to adapt to the host culture, or sometimes individuals simply substitute or add some culturally appropriate behaviors when convenient. In the long-term, a synthesis or integration of the cultures must occur.

ADAPTATION AND ACCULTURATION

Environmental and personal factors influence how individuals will respond to a new culture. The overall similarity or difference and compatibility or incompatibility with the host society will largely determine the degree to which potential barriers may impede adaptation (Y. Kim, 1979, 1988). The larger the disparity between the two cultures, the more difficulty individuals are likely to face. Language differences, distinct speech patterns, and physical characteristics play a salient role in determining compatibility and subsequent communication with host nationals. Additional differences to be spanned in the adaptation process include verbal and nonverbal behaviors, rules and norms of social engagement, economic and political ideology, and religious beliefs, ceremonies, and rituals. Essentially, individuals readily accept what promises to be rewarding and reject what seems to be unworkable or disadvantageous. The environment further influences the adaptation process by being receptive or hostile toward outsiders. Receptivity refers to an attitude of openness and acceptance by the host culture as well as providing opportunities for intercultural engagement (Y. Kim, Lujan, & Dixon, 1998). The attitudes of the native population toward a specific group may be due to contemporary economic or political conditions or longstanding historical issues. Mass media also plays a particularly important role in shaping the emotional mood of the host society toward other cultural groups (Y. Kim, 1995). Still, the extent to which the host culture expects others to conform to its existing cultural norms and values varies from society to society. Relatively freer and more pluralistic societies such as the United States permit a greater latitude or tolerance for cultural differences. The degree to which a given host environment extends receptivity to and exerts conformity pressure on others is influenced strongly by how favorably the group is viewed by the host environment at large (Y. Kim, 2001).

The adaptation process is influenced not only by the conditions existing or developing in the host society but also by personal factors such as age, education, and personality. The older someone is, the greater difficulties they experience in adapting to a new culture and the slower they are in acquiring new cultural patterns (Rogler, Cooney, & Ortiz, 1980; Searle & Ward, 1990; Szapocznik & Kurtines, 1980; Szapocznik, Kurtines, & Fernandez, 1980). We tend to become more rigid and increasingly dogmatic as we grow older. Education, regardless of its cultural context, expands our mental capacity for new learning and for the challenges of life in general (Y. Kim, 1980; Yum, 1982). Finally, along with age and education, personality plays an important role in adaptation. Everyone possesses a personality—a unique set of dispositions that are enduring but also adaptive. Those personality attributes associated with adaptation include tolerance for ambiguity and risk taking, sociability, resilience, and an internal sense of control or responsibility (Bradburn, 1969; Fiske & Maddi, 1961; J. Johnson & Sarason, 1978; Quisumbing, 1982; Yum, 1988). Y. Kim (1988) has consolidated these related personality attributes into three higher level constructs of openness, strength, and positivity. Openness refers to flexibility and open-mindedness; strength represents tolerance for ambiguity, persistence, and resourcefulness; and positivity correlates to an affirmative and optimistic outlook.

Adaptive potential increases dramatically for those who prepare themselves for the new environment (Brabant, Palmer, & Grambling, 1990; Brislin & Yoshida, 1994; Landis & Brislin, 1983). Many enter new cultures with unrealistic expectations and little knowledge. Cross-cultural training and host orientation programs can increase cultural awareness, heighten cultural understanding, and assist in language acquisition. Everyone entering a new culture undergoes a process of adaptation that improves the odds for successful acculturation and makes functioning in the new environment possible. Still, acculturative change and adaptation is a slow process normally involving a struggle between the desire to retain old customs and the desire to adopt new ways (Boekestijn, 1988; Brim & Wheeler, 1966). Adaptation is usually a continuous effort, and most people fall on a continuum ranging from minimally adapted to maximally adapted.

BUILDING INTERCULTURAL RELATIONSHIPS

Communication between outsiders and hosts is successful to the extent that cohesive functional relationships are developed and mutual enjoyment and productivity are derived through shared experiences. This requires possessing basic language skills, job skills, and other practical or technical skills as well as necessary social skills that permit the initiation of conversations and the ability to adjust to different interaction patterns (Taft, 1977). Such skills increase the likelihood of success in intercultural encounters.

An awareness of the importance of both similarities and differences is at the heart of building intercultural relationships. We are attracted to and tend to like people who are similar to us; however, similarity is based not on whether people actually are similar, but on the perceived recognition or discovery of similar traits. When people think they're similar, they have higher expectations about future interactions. Therefore, this process of discovery is crucial in developing relationships (Duck & Barnes, 1992). Irwin Altman and Dalmas Taylor (Altman & Taylor, 1973, Taylor & Altman, 1987) argue that interpersonal closeness proceeds in a gradual and orderly fashion from superficial to intimate levels of exchange. Only by allowing one to penetrate well below the surface can a trusting relationship be established. The depth and breadth of self-disclosure contributes to a lasting relationship. Contributing further to this relationship is the fact that each finds it rewarding. We find satisfaction in those intercultural relationships where the benefits outweigh the costs (Taylor & Altman, 1975). Kelley and Thibaut (1978) advance a social exchange theory that suggests that people act to maximize their benefits and minimize their costs when choosing to build relationships with others.

It should be noted that although similarities are important to the building of relationships, at other times we might seek out people who have different personality traits and therefore provide balance in a relationship. Some individuals are attracted to people simply because they have different cultural backgrounds. Intercultural relationships can present intriguing opportunities for new experiences and to learn new ways of looking at the world (LaGaipa, 1987).

The health and well being of those entering a new culture are directly related to their ability to communicate and build meaningful intercultural relationships with host nationals. The lack of communication competence accounts for many of the problems and difficulties associated with maladaptation, including low self-esteem, low morale, social isolation, and dissatisfaction with life in the host culture that contributes to continuous frustration (Berry, 1990; Dyal & Dyal, 1981). Smoothly and effectively dealing with those of another culture is dependent on one's social communication activities, particularly the ability to build and establish a network of relationships. In short, an individual's functional fitness in a new environment depends on their intercultural effectiveness and cross-cultural competencies. This is most evident when experiencing culture shock and attempting to grow into a new kind of person at a higher level of accommodation and integration.

ACCOMMODATING CULTURE SHOCK

The term culture shock was first introduced by anthropologist Kalervo Oberg (1960) in connection with "the problems of adjustment to new cultural environments" (p. 170). Entering an unfamiliar culture is stressful; in fact, transitions of any type are both psychologically and physically demanding. Taft (1977) has identified a number of common reactions, including (1) irritability, insomnia, and other psychosomatic disorders; (2) a sense of loss arising from being uprooted from one's familiar surroundings; (3) rejection of the individual by members of the new environment; and (4) a feeling of impotence from being unable to deal competently with the environmental unfamiliarity. Culture shock can be costly to international business because it often results in the premature return of businesspeople working overseas. Research shows that employees sent to work in foreign countries fail not because they lack technical or professional competence but because they lack the ability to understand and adapt to another culture's way of life (Ferraro, 1990).

A special kind of cultural shock experienced by U.S. travelers and businesspeople has been identified by Engholm (1991) as AsiaShock. Limited cultural knowledge, limited intercultural experience, and personal rigidity contribute to AsiaShock. There is frustration with the language, the food, and the local customs, with all Asians being unflatteringly labeled together. Unwilling to understand the rationale behind the local ways, U.S. travelers and international businesspeople tend to form their own clubs at which they commiserate about the difficulty of doing business in Asia rather than intermingling with the people of the culture.

The U-curve and W-curve provide two popular explanations of culture shock and adaptation. The U-curve depicts culture shock as a "cycle of readjustment" marked by a progression of phases or stages (Chaney & Martin, 2004; Copeland & Griggs, 1985; S. Deutsch & Won, 1963; Lysgaard, 1955). In the beginning, individuals experience a euphoric period sometimes referred to as a "tourist phase" or "honeymoon stage." During this period, they are excited about the move, and their enthusiasm for the new culture causes them to overlook minor problems such as having to drink bottled water and the absence of central heating or air conditioning. Soon the elements of the new culture begin to intrude and the initial enchantment is replaced with irritation, impatience, frustration, anger, and depression. During this "disenchantment phase" or "everything is awful stage," differences are accentuated and problems with transportation, unfamiliar foods, and people who do not speak English seem overwhelming. People cope with this crisis period differently. Some become hostile and fight back, making disparaging remarks about the culture. Others deal with this stage by fleeing—they simply leave. Estimates on early return of U.S. expatriate managers range from 45 to 85 percent (Ferraro, 1990). However, when companies implement training programs to combat culture shock, the early return rate drops to less than 2 percent (Chaney & Martin, 2004). Some who choose to remain during this phase withdraw from people in the culture and refuse to learn the language or develop coping behaviors. Others who remain "go native" and actually deny differences and speak in glowing terms of the new culture. Those who are flexible eventually experience an "adjustment phase" or "recovery stage." They begin feeling comfortable in the new cultural environment. They make adjustments in their behavior and begin to accept local ways. Self-confidence returns and they feel less isolated and more at ease. This positive momentum leads to a final "adaptation phase" or "acceptance stage." Anxiety is largely gone and new customs are accepted and enjoyed. Individuals feel at home in the new culture and cultivate friendships among the nationals as well as becoming involved in cultural activities. They feel comfortable in social situations with people from the host culture and truly enjoy the country and culture. The W-curve extends the U-curve

71

pattern of adaptive change with the addition of a re-entry or return-home phase (Gullahorn & Gullahorn, 1963; Trifonovitch, 1977). Re-entry shock is the emotional and physiological difficulties an individual may experience on returning home from an overseas assignment. Re-entry shock can be almost as traumatic as the initial adjustment to the new culture, particularly after an extended stay abroad. However, most expatriates eventually adjust and again become comfortable with the mores of their home culture (Dodd, 1998; Klopf, 1991).

Despite the popularity of the U-curve and W-curve patterns of adaptive change, they may not be applicable to all intercultural experiences. Church (1982) notes that support for the U-curve hypothesis is somewhat inconclusive, and even those studies supporting the hypothesis show marked differences in the time parameters of the curve, making the U-curve description less than precise in its ability to predict cross-cultural adaptation (Ward, Okura, Kennedy, & Kojima, 1998). Moreover, Kealey (1989) found that the U-curve was an accurate description of the adaptation process for only about 10 percent of the individuals he studied and consequently should not be viewed as a single "package" of related features that all follow. Y. Kim (2001) provides a more contemporary model that presents adaptation as a process of acculturation or learning and deculturation or unlearning. She argues that experiences of stress prompt adaptation because, when the environment threatens individuals, they reflexively respond by employing a new set of creative coping abilities. They work out new ways of handling problems and thereby experience cultural growth. This interdependence of stress, adaptation, and subsequent internal transformation is referred to by Kim as the stress-adaptation-growth dynamic. From this point of view, intercultural learning and growth are emphasized and at the heart of successful intercultural adaptation. The intercultural experience is one of transformation, a "movement from a state of low self- and cultural awareness to a state of high self- and cultural awareness" (Adler, 1987, p. 15). The stress that produces culture shock permits individuals to confront the physiological, psychological, social, and philosophical differences between themselves and the host culture (Kealey, 1989). Therefore, the stress and pressure of culture shock are natural consequences of transitioning into a new and changed environment whereby we develop essential cross-cultural competencies and an increased cultural awareness (Bennett, 1977).

Intercultural Effectiveness and Cross-Cultural Competencies

G. Gardner (1962) labels people who are effective at intercultural communication as being "universal communicators" (p. 248). He describes these cosmopolitan communicators as being stable, confident, sensitive, and outgoing. They look for common ground among cultures, exhibit universal values, and show respect for all. Additionally, cosmopolitan communicators assume that people are basically good, value other cultures as well as their own, and speak with hopefulness and candor. They are people-oriented and feel comfortable in a variety of different situations and circumstances in which cultural differences prevail (Kleinjans, 1972).

Cross-cultural competence is broadly considered behavior that is perceived by others to be appropriate and effective in a given context (Gudykunst, 1991; Kim, 1991; Spitzberg, 1988, 2000). Cross-culturally competent communicators are motivated to communicate with others and integrate a wide array of culture-general knowledge into their behavioral repertoires, thus being able to skillfully apply that knowledge to the specific cultures with which they interact (Lustig & Koester, 2003; Spitzberg & Cupach, 1984). Moreover, they have typically had extensive intercultural communication experiences and have learned to adjust to alternative patterns of thinking and behaving. Howell (1982) identifies four levels of cross-cultural communication competence:

1. *Unconscious incompetence* refers to individuals who are unaware of any cultural differences, fail to appropriately adapt to the new milieu, and are perceived to be ineffective and inept.

2. *Conscious incompetence* refers to individuals who realize that things may not be going well in their interactions with others but cannot determine why and are unsure what to do about it.

3. *Conscious competent* individuals have moved beyond their original cultural conditioning to incorporate other cultural realities—a process labeled intercultural transformation (Y. Kim & Ruben, 1988)—and can analyze the encounter and apply their thinking and learning to the situation.

4. *Unconscious competence* is the level at which communication goes smoothly without conscious thought and individuals move in "sync" together without disrupting others around them (Hall, 1976).

Ultimately, however, competence in any encounter is contingent on all parties to the interaction. Consider, for example, the trait of assertiveness in Japan and in the United States (Singhal & Nagao, 1993). In the United States, people who are assertive are viewed as highly competent, whereas people who are more reticent are perceived as less competent. In contrast, the Japanese perceive as more competent people who are reticent, whereas people who are assertive are regarded as incompetent. Therefore, our motivation, knowledge, and skills do not necessarily ensure that we will be perceived as competent in any particular interaction. Our skills, however, do increase the likelihood that we are able to adapt our behavior so that others will see us as competent (Wiemann & Bradac, 1989).

Certain specific cross-cultural competencies are necessary to communicate appropriately and effectively with people from another culture. They help us manage our uncertainty and anxiety as well as surmount group stereotypes, social prejudices, and our own ethnocentrism so that we can make more accurate interpretations and predictions of another's behavior (Hwang, Chase, & Kelly, 1980). The following competencies help promote cosmopolitan communication:

- *Being mindful of others* involves negotiating meaning through dialogue with people from the host culture. We must focus on understanding another's perspectives (Burgoon, Berger, & Waldron, 2000; Gass & Varonis, 1985).

- *Ability to empathize* involves being sensitive to the needs of others and understanding their point of view (Bell, 1987). Bennett (1979) strongly suggests that the "Golden Rule"—"Do unto others as you would have them do unto you"—should be replaced by the "Platinum Rule"—"Do unto others as they would have you do unto them"—which is a more empathetic response.

- *Active listening* is a process of thinking with people. It is a "complex, innate and learned human process of sensing, interpreting, evaluating, storing, and responding to messages" (Steil & Bommelje, 2004, p. 31).

- *Tolerance for change* encourages calm when confronting the unknown and facing new, untested alternatives so we are not overwhelmed by the unfamiliar or mysterious.

- *Tolerance for ambiguity* implies the ability to deal successfully with novel situations and with people who do not comply with the norm (Furnham & Ribchester, 1995).

- *Ability to flexibly adapt our behavior* means the ability to be flexible and accommodate our behavior to people from other cultures. We create appropriate options given the circumstances in which we find ourselves (Langer, 1997).

- *Language skills* are definitely essential if we plan to spend a year or more in another country (Copeland & Griggs, 1985). It is simply not true that most people around the world speak English. Outside the major cities, the average person does not necessarily speak English. Furthermore, a growing number of foreign nations are now insisting that government contracts and negotiations be conducted solely in the local language (e.g., Germany, Belgium, Spain, Thailand, India, Pakistan, Sri Lanka). Consequently, a good oral interpreter and written translator may be needed. A good interpreter can take on the personality of the speaker and adjust to the cultural context, turning American idiom into a foreign version with the same message. Translators make sure the locals understand your style and vocabulary.

• *Body language* is not universal, and we must be aware of the messages our gestures, facial expressions, and other nonverbal cues convey to members of the host culture (Bosrock, 1994). Chapter 5 will more thoroughly explore the nature of language and nonverbal communication.

• *Professional qualifications* include knowledge of business practices in the host culture and technical competence (Tung, 1981). Women in international business need to be aware that often times they are crossing traditional barriers in many countries and consequently they may be both pioneers and models for the culture (Copeland & Griggs, 1985).

• *Making accurate predictions and explanations* is a crucial competency for reducing anxiety and uncertainty and understanding people of another culture. Being able to describe people's behavior and accurately interpret their messages contributes to successful adaptation and acculturation (Gudykunst & Kim, 2003).

These competencies can contribute to feelings of communication satisfaction—whether communication meets or fails to meet our expectations (Hecht, 1978). The more communication in intercultural relationships is personalized and synchronized and the less difficulty people experience in communicating with others, the more satisfied they are with their communication (Gudykunst, Nishida, & Chua, 1986, 1987). This satisfaction encourages further contact and intercultural communication.

An Expatriate's Journal: A Three-Year Sojourn in Singapore

To illustrate the concepts discussed in this chapter, let's look at the personal experiences of a Florida couple who became expatriates in Southeast Asia. Gary and Kathy Randel live in Orlando. Gary worked for Lucent Technologies and in 1998 agreed to move to Singapore for three years to work on a joint venture. The following are selected journal entries documenting their expatriate experience:

Dear Diary: (Kathy)

Gary has such a sense of humor. He came home from work today and said that somebody asked him if he would consider working in Singapore for a couple of years! All I know about Singapore is that it is in Southeast Asia somewhere, and it has a drink named after it (Singapore Sling). Well, we laughed about it.

Dear Diary: (Kathy)

We have decided to move to Singapore! Gary and I talked it over and decided to go for it. He is looking forward to working for SMP (a joint venture between Lucent and Chartered Semiconductor) and they are looking forward to getting him over there. I'm ready for a change and this move should fill the bill. We have told our families and friends that we are going to do this. I get the feeling some of them think we have lost our minds and they may be right, but you only go around once in life. We might as well make the most of it. We have a lot of things to do in order to be ready to move. Things to do before moving to Singapore:

1. Get house ready to sell

2. Decide what to take, what to store, what to sell, and what to donate to charity

3. Get in touch with moving and storage company and change mailing address

4. Pick up medical and dental records

5. Get vaccinations

6. Contact lawyer and meet with Orlando banker

7. Find new home for turtle

8. Go shopping for bedding, cleaning items, underwear, etc. to ship to Singapore

9. Sell my Buick and Gary's Camaro

10. Have utility companies turn everything off and cancel car insurance

11. Check to make sure we have airline tickets, passports, and pack bags

12. WE'RE OUT OF HERE!

Dear Diary: (Gary)

Things to do—Make a trip to New Jersey to meet with Lucent accountants and lawyers regarding opening a bank account in Singapore as well as taxes, benefits, relocation allowance, interim living expenses, vouchers, etc.; Go through an orientation program; Make two-week trip to Singapore without Kathy to get job started up; Return and help Kathy finish preparing for the move. We're on our way—FINALLY!

Dear Diary: (Kathy)

We are in the air—on our way to Singapore—what a thrill! Thirty hours after leaving Orlando we finally landed at Changi Airport in Singapore. What an airport—I read that it was rated number one in the world. We're staying at the Westin Stamford Hotel—the tallest hotel in the world—around 70 stories. The view is great—on a clear day you can see Malaysia and some of the Indonesian islands. It is also attached to the Raffles City shopping center with lots of stores and restaurants as well as museums within walking distance.

We went to the Raffles Hotel—the oldest hotel in Singapore—and had Singapore Slings at the Long Bar. This is where the drink was invented. I think this must have been what Singapore was like when Somerset Maugham, Joseph Conrad, and Noel Coward stayed here. Lots of verandas, courtyards, paddle fans, and rattan furniture. Talk about atmosphere. Hmm, this might not be so bad after all.

Dear Diary: (Kathy)

We went to look at apartments. None of the apartments had the air conditioning on, so they were very hot as well as being pretty miserable looking. They were small, in out-of-the-way areas and I discovered that most have two kitchens. There is a not-so-great regular kitchen and a "wet" kitchen. The "wet" kitchen is shut off from the rest of the apartment because they do all of the wok cooking in it. The window is opened so all the odors (fish, cabbage, etc.) go outside instead of into the apartment. I don't think it always works that way. At lunch, I was hot and discouraged—if these are the types of apartments that are available, FORGET IT! Later we looked at additional apartments that were great and fit within our housing allowance. They were very big (2800 square feet) with lots of windows and some had balconies. This is more like it.

Dear Diary: (Kathy)

I'm slowly getting the apartment the way I want it. After our things came, I realized I needed to pick up a lot of items to make it feel more like home. We had furniture in every room but we needed some area rugs, plants, things for the walls, furniture for the balcony, bedspreads, decorative items, etc. This is taking time but a lot of fun—I'm learning my way around. Gary bought a VCR to tape football games shown on ESPN while he was at work, only to discover that they weren't shown after all. American football is not very popular here—they prefer rugby, soccer, bowling, and golf. Someone I know could go into severe withdrawal.

Decided to catch up on laundry—the washer and dryer are very small. The air conditioner in our bedroom is not working the way it should—will have to get a repairman to come out. Our landlords are very nice—Steve and Anne Lee—and have helped familiarize us with the culture.

Dear Diary: (Gary)

I got my driver's license. Passed the test the first time. It is a little tricky driving on the left side of the road, but you get used to it. Kathy has decided to walk, take a taxi, or use the MRT. Went to see the plant and was impressed with the facilities at SMP (Silicon Manufacturing Partners). It is located in an area called the Woodlands, and is right across from Malaysia! In fact, I can drive across the Causeway and be in Malaysia in minutes. This is a very nice location.

Dear Diary: (Kathy)

I'm starting to feel at home. Everything I need is within walking distance. It is hard adjusting to buying only what I can carry home. I'm used to driving all over and loading up the trunk. I stop by the grocery store every day. It is fun to walk around the store to see what they have. Besides American products, you can find biscuits (cookies) from England, meat from Australia and New Zealand and lots of Japanese products. This is durian season. Durian is a fruit that smells quite a bit like natural gas and you're not allowed to carry them on a bus, airplane, or MRT since everybody would need a gas mask. I tried a durian and liked it— you just hold your breath at first but, once you get used to it, it is very tasty—a creamy, tangy, butterscotch flavor. Durian pudding and durian cream puffs are also very good. Other interesting fruits are rambutan, mangosteens, soursop, and pomelo.

At first trying to understand people, particularly when talking on the telephone, is difficult. Everybody speaks English but with a heavy accent—I'm sure they have trouble understanding me too. I have gotten better and have learned to listen carefully and watch them when they talk to me. As I deal with the same people, it gets easier.

Singapore currency still looks like Monopoly money to me. When we get a telephone bill or credit card bill a postage-paid envelope is included— isn't that nice? Hand phones (cell phones) are everywhere—everybody has one and talks on it all the time—in restaurants, on the MRT, in shops, on the street, in movie theaters. TV isn't too great, so I read a lot.

I enjoy taking lunch or a snack at one of the food stalls. My favorite is dry beef noodle (a big bowl of noodles with beef gravy and thin-sliced beef). I use chopsticks and can slurp my noodles with the best of them. My favorite dessert is ice kachang—a mound of shaved ice topped with fruit-flavored syrups. Under the ice are some red beans, corn, and little cubes of jelly. Evaporated milk is poured over the whole thing to finish it off—it's great!

Dear Diary: (Gary)

Now comes the easy part—I go to work, leaving Kathy to deal with the apartment and getting to know Singapore. At work the first problem I recognized was the work ethic. I had been used to working $5\frac{1}{2}$ days per week and 50–70 hours. My people were used to working 40 hours and then going home. Fortunately, they also didn't want to work less than their boss, so they slowly started working on my schedule. I also had to learn and observe their customs and rituals.

They were used to feeling their job was done when they reported a problem. I had always worked under the assumption that my job wasn't finished until I could also report the solution to a problem. Being an engineer, I have always believed that the data would not only help identify the problem but would also confirm the solution. My first experience with the pace of work occurred shortly after arriving in Singapore. A problem was identified and a solution was proposed. I accepted the solution, but asked for a confirming experiment. I was used to having these experiments conducted quickly, so when several days went by with no word on the results I called a meeting. At the meeting the engineer responsible presented the data and the proposed solution. When asked when the confirming data would be available, he said in a couple of weeks. This wasn't acceptable to me, so I took charge of the meeting and asked the group to help design the experiment and then put a timetable on getting the results with the goal of having the data the next day. Much to the group's surprise, not only were they able to put together a plan to accomplish this, but they also were able to execute the plan. I bought lunch for the team the next week. Also, my whole lunch routine has changed. Instead of having a cheeseburger and French fries, I now go with colleagues to one of the food courts and have fish, rice, and vegetables served on a banana leaf which I eat with chopsticks.

Dear Diary: (Kathy)

I enjoy exploring. I walked over to Ft. Canning Park, part of which is a European cemetery. I have also gone hiking at Bukit Timah Nature Reserve which is what Singapore was like 200 years ago. A tropical forest with monkeys, lots of hanging vines, and lizards—hot and steamy. It is something different and lets me get away from Orchard Road and the shops. Life is truly bizarre, I leave a cosmopolitan city to go crashing through the jungle, but it's great.

Dear Diary: (Gary)

Everyone will tell you that as an expatriate you will be asked to work at a higher level than you were used to in the States. Let me confirm this. As the senior assignee, I am not only expected to make the normal decisions associated with my level, but also to set the tone for the whole organization. This includes reviewing all presentations of others as well as making my own presentations to the Board of Directors for the company.

The time zone differences have created both opportunities and problems. I can fire off an e-mail at the end of the day and expect a response when I come in the next day. This is terrific. Then there are the conference calls, where I either have to get up very early or stay late to participate. These are scheduled two to three times a week unless there are problems and then they may be more frequent. The upshot of all this is that I am at work from 7:00 a.m. to at least 6:00 p.m. and frequently until nine or ten at night. This leaves Kathy with a lot of time on her hands, but she has dealt with it well. Some of the expat wives have had problems with this.

Dear Diary: (Kathy)

We experienced Chinese New Year—the biggest holiday of the year in Asia—the Year of the Rabbit. The festivities go on for days. Chinese families have reunions and dinners, and relatives come from all over to celebrate. A major housecleaning takes place. Old items are tossed out (chipped dishes, torn clothes), all debts are paid, old arguments are forgotten, ancestors are worshipped, and new clothes are worn. The New Year represents a new beginning. It is fun to be out in the streets because there are decorations everywhere with the predominant colors being red and gold since they are considered joyous colors. This is when Chinese Lion dancers rule—they perform at shopping malls, in parades, and at special events. We even had a special Lion dance performance at our apartment complex on New Year's Day.

Dear Diary: (Kathy)

We decided we need to travel more. Our first stop is Bali. Bali is a beautiful place with wonderful people and temples everywhere. I used up about a dozen rolls of film. Our next trip will be to Bintan—a resort in the middle of a rain forest right on the South China Sea. Gary enjoys the scuba diving and I love to sit on the beach and read. From now on whenever I need to decompress and Gary needs a break we're going to travel—it's perfect for relaxing.

Dear Diary: (Kathy)

We finally decided to join the American Club. They have a nice big pool with a snack bar where you can get sandwiches and pizza, plus an ice cream parlor. They also have bowling, a travel desk, gift shop, computer lab, concierge desk, courier service, dry cleaning, gym, slot machines, a library, photo developing, scuba diving, video rental, and two good restaurants—one specializing in Western food and other in Chinese. And, the Union Bar where you can watch football, eat a ground beef hamburger, and drink the cheapest gin and tonics in town. I also joined the AWA (American Women's Association). They are very helpful if someone is having trouble settling in, needs help with anything, or just wants to get together with other women. Most expat communities have this organization. I'm glad we didn't join the first year we lived here—it would have been too easy to spend all of our time here, instead of discovering Singapore. Also, we might have assumed an arrogant sense of importance as displayed by some members toward host nationals who work in the Club.

Dear Diary: (Kathy)

The AWA had a meeting about volunteering and I signed up with SINDA (Singapore Indian Development Association). My assignment is to read to a child once a week. The best part is that I get to go to his home and get to meet his family. Mohd Ashiq is in kindergarten and his schoolwork was suffering—he needed some help. I got to know his mother and his siblings and I felt like I was a part of the community not just an expatriate. I will keep in touch with Ashiq and his family.

Dear Diary: (Kathy)

It has been three years, and we will now be returning to the States. We have over the three years briefly returned on several occasions to visit family and friends and for Gary to meet with senior people in the company. We feel prepared for this trip back home but regret leaving our new friends behind. We've gotten to know the people and learn the culture. I am a whole new person with much more confidence and a clearer sense of where I am going. I am certain this growth would not have occurred without the experiences gained while abroad.

For Gary and Kathy Randel, the overseas assignment was a wonderful, life-changing adventure. Lucent Technologies had wisely sent them to Singapore on a short visit to determine whether they would want to move there. Once they agreed to the assignment, Gary went through an orientation program and Kathy prepared for the move as well. Reading and talking to other expatriates helped acquaint them with Singapore. Together they settled their affairs at home and, before moving, spent time with friends and family. These early steps helped to reduce some of the uncertainty and anxiety associated with the move. Individuals and organizations should seek to minimize the dysfunctional effects and maximize the opportunities of the cultural experience.

Singapore is a modern, cosmopolitan city that reflects a global influence. When confronted with this new culture, Gary and Kathy demonstrated the necessary competencies and abilities to successfully cope with the stress of culture shock. They were open minded and flexible, possessing a tolerance for change. They had previously traveled abroad and were somewhat accustomed to ambiguous situations. Moreover, Gary was an avid scuba diver, an activity requiring the ability to adapt to an alien environment that could be potentially friendly or hostile. Certainly they noticed the differences, which at times could prove difficult—shopping daily for groceries, the air conditioning, the strange foods, and the variety of dialects and accents. Gary had to assert his leadership role to contend with a different work ethic and sense of job responsibility. He also had to adapt to new workplace customs and rituals and treat these cultural differences as a resource. They asked questions, actively listened, and were patient, realizing that accomplishing their goals in this new environment may take more time and effort. By taking the responsibility to make contact, by being mindful of others, by empathizing with others, and by learning the basics of the language, Gary and Kathy were able to build lasting relationships with host nationals and adapt to this new culture.

Gary and Kathy traveled and explored the surrounding area. They did not spend all their time in the American Club, but preferred to live in the culture and try new things. Kathy volunteered to help young Mohd Ashiq learn to read, and he went on to become a model student in the program who taught others to read as well. The Randels not only lived and worked in Singapore for three years, but also affected the lives of those they touched. Their constructive and caring influence contributed in a small way to bridging international differences and building positive intercultural relations. They unknowingly heeded the words of Aristotle: "Where your talents and the needs of the world cross, there lies your mission." Multinational organizations with their international ventures do more than simply add to the economic development of a country. All expatriates have the potential to leave a positive and enduring legacy.

Although it was difficult to leave acquired friends, Gary and Kathy had maintained personal and organizational ties that assisted in their repatriation. Occasional trips to the United States helped them maintain a broader perspective and keep in touch with their home culture. Organizations are realizing that re-entry shock is a natural part of culture shock, and forward-thinking multinational corporations continually work to ensure that the transition back to the home culture is a favorable experience.

Gary and Kathy Randel displayed a positive, cosmopolitan attitude and maintained a sense of humor throughout their Singapore sojourn. Even today, they keep in contact with many of the host nationals they met, including Mohd Ashiq, Kathy's former student. Moreover, their Orlando home reflects both Asian and U.S. influences, making for a culturally integrated interior design.

International business assignments can have a profound and significant impact on those who are positively committed and choose to become interculturally involved.

Summary

Making contact and interfacing with others from another culture can be stressful and lead to culture shock. By managing our uncertainty and anxiety, we can constructively cope with the differences and begin to build relationships with others in the culture. Furthermore, successful adaptation requires certain competencies that can help sustain relationships with others. Therefore, careful selection of persons for overseas assignments is important for a profitable sojourn.

Personal qualifications needed when working in an unfamiliar culture include adaptability, flexibility, empathy, and tolerance. Good interpersonal skills and high self-esteem have also been found to be important. The ability to react to different and often unpredictable situations with little apparent irritation shows a tolerance for ambiguity. Ambiguities are inherent in intercultural communication, and maintaining a high degree of tolerance and flexibility is essential. International work inflicts stress; consequently, individuals must be emotionally secure and possess a strong sense of self. The foundation for successful interaction with people anywhere in the world is sincere respect for and interest in others—in other words, positive regard for others. In sum, to succeed abroad, one needs to maintain a sense of humor and be like an inquisitive child.

5

The Nature of Language and Nonverbal Communication

Carlos and Roberto, the two Argentine agricultural co-op representatives, smile widely as they greet the senior John Deere agri-products dealer arriving from the United States. Using broad gestures and animated delivery they convey their warm regards, "Bienvenidos! Hemos estado esperando por tu regreso a nuestro país." ("Welcome back! We have been looking forward to your return to our country!") Their enthusiastic Latin greeting continues with strong shoulder hugs and extended dialogue about the nature of the flight, family, and friends. They all talk on a personal level for some time and renew their old friendship. The conversation then turns to translation problems the Argentine co-op representatives are experiencing with several parts manuals and the accompanying visual drawings. They all agree that the translations are confusing and can be further clarified during the weeklong visit. The conversation then segues to chatting about lighter topics—weather and sports—as they head for the airport baggage claim area. This is a typical cross-cultural conversational exchange between individuals renewing a business friendship, and it illustrates many of the complexities of language and nonverbal communication encountered when communicating globally.

Now, assume for a moment that you are talking with a close friend from your own culture with whom you have many similarities. Your friend is of the same gender, grew up in the same geographical area, works in the same occupation, and has many of the same beliefs and values as you. During an ordinary conversation, you say, "I'm gonna run by that new restaurant after work. Wanna go?" Your friend understands the colloquial "gonna" to mean "going to" and "wanna" to mean, "would you like to." This is a straightforward, though rather unsophisticated, interpersonal exchange in your own culture that also illustrates the complexities of language. Finding a translation for the word run, for instance, may be difficult. The word has many different definitions in modern dictionaries and can be used in different contexts: a John Deere tractor runs well, a factory runs smoothly, an athlete might run a marathon, water runs down a hill, and there can be a run in a woman's hosiery. Yet, your friend correctly interpreted your use of the word "run" to know that you plan to drive your car (not physically run) to the restaurant, that you plan to stop and eat (not merely drive past the building), and that you want him or her to join you (not simply ride in the car with you). Although your friend intuitively understood your message, we know that such accurate interpretations do not automatically happen when we use language interculturally. Someone whose native language is different from ours may easily misinterpret our use of slang expressions. Obviously, language differences and diverse symbolic codes magnify communication problems when we go global.

Language is a tool "with which we make sense of the world and share that sense with others" (Beebe & Masterson, 1982, p. 27). It provides us with verbal vehicles for transmitting information, creating messages with others, and sharing meaning. Although language may be dulled by incorrect usage and often not readily at hand, it is a principal medium by which we make ourselves understood by other people. Certainly, the various levels of linguistic abstraction, along with the complexities of nonverbal communication, can create challenges when communicating with others, and intercultural factors further compound them in the international business arena.

In this chapter, we explore selected characteristics of language and look at our use of symbols, abstractions, and perceptions in shaping language. We discuss the Sapir-Whorf hypothesis, the Bernstein hypothesis, and Philipsen's speech codes. We discover the rules that govern our language use and identify the functions that language serves in global communication. Because language and words cannot be separated from their nonverbal components, we also address several dimensions of nonverbal communication and nonverbal messages. Understanding verbal and nonverbal message sending is critical to becoming a competent global communicator.

Characteristics of Language

Language involves accents, dialects, pronunciation, rules, and other communication behaviors such as style or rate of speaking. Our ability to talk with one another, understand vague terms, and fill in the gaps when someone is being abstract is truly a unique ability. As you communicate in your native language, your individual speech behaviors take on distinct variations. Competent global communicators are aware of these differences and understand the value of using speech patterns that conform to standard linguistic norms.

A dialect is the unique pronunciation, grammar, and vocabulary we use when speaking. Our dialect or ethnolinguistic variation identifies us with a certain country or region of a country (Giles, 1973). Furthermore, our distinctive dialect can directly influence another person's perception of us; we can be stereotyped on the basis of our dialect. We may be viewed as urbane or primitive, pleasant sounding or harsh, educated or unlearned because of our particular pronunciation, grammar, and vocabulary. French Canadians view European-style French as more sophisticated and intelligent, and Spanish speakers in Barcelona tend to view their unique dialect as superior.

Accents, jargon, and argot represent additional variations in language. An accent is a more specific mode of personal discourse characterized by how people articulate certain words using a unique inflection or tone. Students in the United States, for example, may be able to identify an eastern accent, southern accent, or general American accent. Similarly, Hindi speakers from Delhi, India, who travel south to Bhopal will be quickly identified by their accent from the north, although they still speak the common language of Hindi. Again, speakers may be negatively stereotyped by their accent. Speaking with an accent may create negative impressions with the listener when the speaker's accent differs significantly from that of the dominant group.

Jargon refers to a type of code or specialized vocabulary that is shared among knowledgeable in-group members. Consider the terminology of doctors, lawyers, professors, and business people who have a shorthand way of speaking among themselves based on professional training and mutual experiences. Their specialized vocabulary contains rich meaning, is efficient, and saves time for the speakers as they go about their tasks. It can also be confusing to outsiders.

Argot refers to a secret or covert vocabulary developed by an in-group to keep outsiders from understanding their messages. Mob-speak, gang-speak, or drug-speak represents argot where in-group members are seeking to conceal their messages from others. Other examples might include the restricted codes of fraternal organizations and teen slang that are known only by members inside the group.

The dynamic of multilanguage speakers frequently switching back and forth between languages is called code-switching, and some find this behavior disconcerting and difficult to follow (Auer, 1995, 1998). There are, however, a number of reasons why code-switching occurs. First, the "decision to use one language over another is often related to the setting in which the interaction occurs—a social, public, and formal setting versus a personal, private, and informal one" (Lustig & Koester, 2003, p. 232). Second, the topic of conversation is an important factor affecting code-switching. A technical topic, for instance, requiring a specialized vocabulary may require the speaker to switch to his or her stronger language in search of a correct term. Finally, a person's conversational partner is another important factor in code-switching. A person often switches back and forth when learning a new language but frequently uses profanity only in his or her native language.

LANGUAGE IS SYMBOLIC

The verbal symbolic world is one of words that allow us to describe the real world, and therein lies the problem with any language system. Symbols are arbitrary and ambiguous constructs used to stand for or represent something else, and the same word often means different things to different people. Consider that there are currently about 600,000 words in the English language, with educated adults using about 2,000 words in daily conversation. For the 500 most frequently used words, there are some 14,000 dictionary meanings. Alfred Korzybski (1948), the founder of general semantics, used the analogy of distinguishing between a map and the territory to clarify the importance of differentiating between verbal symbols and structural reality: (1) the map is not the territory (the symbol is not the thing symbolized); (2) the map does not represent all the territory (symbols cannot say all there is to be said about a thing); and (3) the ideal map would have to include a map of itself (symbols are self-reflective). These abstract symbolic "maps of reality" represent the shared or agreed-on meanings that are communicated within a particular culture and may vary from culture to culture.

LANGUAGE IS ABSTRACT

Abstraction is a process of selecting some details and omitting others. Any use of language involves some abstraction because words don't have meaning—people provide meaning. Meaning is a human creation accomplished when human beings interpret symbols. Ogden and Richards (1923) developed a semantic triangle that illustrates the interrelationships among symbols, thoughts, and referents. Communication begins with a thought. You might think of an object and then select what you consider to be an appropriate symbol to represent that object. The thought, object, and symbol form the points of the triangle. The important relationships are these: A direct relationship exists between thought and object and between thought and symbol; an inferred relationship exists between object and symbol. In other words, the object of communication can be precise and the symbol of communication can be specifically selected, but we can only hope that others will perceive a similar relationship between object and symbol and come to a similar understanding of the thought being conveyed. Communication is not easy because our language is limited, and we abstract and categorize. Consequently, effective communication requires "the ability and willingness of an individual to participate responsibly in a transaction in such a way as to maximize the outcomes of shared meanings" (Littlejohn & Jabusch, 1982, p. 32). The value of being precise and the need for clarification are obvious in intercultural situations.

LANGUAGE SHAPES PERCEPTION

We interpret the symbolic behaviors of others and assign significance to some of those behaviors in order to try to create a meaningful account of their actions (Watzlawick, Beavin, & Jackson, 1967). However, many intercultural misunderstandings are due to the behaviors of a person from one culture being incorrectly perceived, interpreted, and reacted to by a person from another culture. Nierenberg and Calero (1974) suggest that communication exists on at least three levels of meaning: (1) what the speaker says; (2) what the speaker thinks is said; and (3) what the listener thinks the speaker said. The language system we learn from our culture has a profound influence on how we interpret another's behavior and the world.

Edward Sapir (1921) and Benjamin Lee Whorf (1956) developed the Sapir-Whorf hypothesis, which ties language to culture and refers to the way language affects our perception of reality and influences our thought processes. They suggest that language functions not simply as a device for reporting experience but, more significantly, as a way of defining experience for its users. Their hypothesis is composed of two constituent parts: linguistic relativity and linguistic determinism. Linguistic relativity refers to how language shapes our thinking regarding what is important in our culture and defines how we perceive reality. Linguistic determinism refers to the notion that language determines cognition or actually shapes our thinking. The Sapir-Whorf hypothesis is important because it suggests that there is a connection between one's language and behavior.

In the United States, we are highly competitive, and words and phrases from athletics are incorporated into our business speech (e.g., the ball is in your court; three strikes and you're out; take the ball and run with it). This also contributes to our linear way of thinking and being direct and to the point. By contrast, many

European and Latin American countries emphasize relationships with many words and phrases used to characterize the nature of those associations and define the appropriate interaction. This further contributes to distinctive thinking patterns that incorporate relational loops that are more circuitous and meandering. When individuals conduct business in relationship-intensive cultures, much of what the listener thinks the speaker said is dependent on the previous relationship. Finally, this connection between language, thought, and behavior can also be illustrated in how advertisers use language to shape our perception of products. Lexicon Branding, Inc., is a naming consultant firm that evaluates the benefits and liabilities of product names through their GlobalTalk service. They use semantic associations to name companies, automobiles, and pharmaceuticals. For example, Viagra rhymes with Niagara, Prozac connotes speed of recovery, and ExxonMobil was named Humble Oil before it became a worldwide organization in 1965 (Begley, 2002). Effective global communicators must be aware of the dynamic relationships between thinking, language, culture, and behavior. John Carroll (1956) humorously notes that we have all been tricked by "the structure of language into a certain way of perceiving reality" (p. 27).

LANGUAGE IS A CONTEXTUAL CODE

Language defines our social context and helps us develop and maintain relationships within a group that in turn affect the type of speech used by the group. The structure of language employed in everyday talk reflects and shapes the assumptions of social groups, with people learning their place in the world by virtue of the language codes they employ. The Bernstein hypothesis is an important sociolinguistic theory that establishes a connection between social groupings or classifications of people and their different ways of speaking. It assumes that relationships established in a social group affect the type of speech used by the group. Basil Bernstein (1971) focuses on two types of codes— elaborated and restricted.

Elaborated codes are explicit and complex and allow individuals an opportunity to negotiate meaning. They are appropriate in groups in which perspectives are not shared and people are required to expand on what they mean. Elaborated codes are more empowering because they provide greater opportunities for adapting to a wide range of audiences and enable speakers to appeal to widely different types of persons (Bernstein, 1966).

Restricted codes are "shorthand" messages high in prediction with a narrower range of options. They are appropriate in groups in which there is a strongly shared set of assumptions and little need to elaborate on what is meant. They are oriented toward social groups in which everybody has a common understanding of who people are and how they should behave. Restricted codes possess a "vast potential of meanings, of delicacy, subtlety and diversity of cultural forms" (Bernstein, 1971, p. 186). Pluralistic societies that value individuality tend to promote elaborated codes, whereas narrower societies promote restricted ones (Bernstein, 2000). Bernstein's work illustrates that our interactions shape language but language in turn shapes our interactions.

Gerry Philipsen (1989) furthers our understanding of language codes and culture when he isolates four basic assumptions underlying the ethnography of communication: (1) cultural participants create meaning through the use of commonly shared codes; (2) communicators in any cultural group must coordinate their actions; (3) meanings and actions are particular to individual groups and may differ from culture to culture; and (4) not only are patterns of behavior and codes different from group to group, but each cultural group has its own ways of understanding certain codes and actions. He then draws on ethnographic research to develop his speech code theory—that wherever there is a distinctive culture, there are to be found distinctive codes of communication conduct (Philipsen, 1997). Speech codes are unique to the history, people, and language of each individual culture. They permit us to identify with others and adapt to our world as well as shape the world around us (Philipsen, 1975, 1976). Every culture exhibits a distinctive speech code, and communicators within any culture create and interpret meaning according to the rules they use. Although Philipsen's theory is controversial and his conclusions have been criticized (Carbaugh, 1995; West, 1993), he is regarded by many as the "first ethnographer of communication in our discipline" (Griffin, 2003, p. 458).

The work of Bernstein and Philipsen helps explain why we communicate at varying levels of awareness and differing degrees of competency. We usually rely on our learned communication codes and taken-for-granted assumptions about communication in everyday situations (Abelson, 1976; Berger & Bradac, 1982; Langer, 1978, 1989a). We employ our implicit theories of communication "about social reality . . . [and] about how other people will communicate with us" (Wegner & Vallacher, 1977, p. 21). Our predictions about other people's behavior are based on the cultures in which we were raised, our ethnic backgrounds, our gender, our classes, and our unique individual experiences. Our learned speech codes and implicit theories further influence how we structure or punctuate the communication process (Watzlawick et al., 1967) and affect the various communication strategies we might choose when communicating with others (G. Miller & Steinberg, 1975). Edward T. Hall and Mildred Hall (1987) observe in *Hidden Differences* that "communication underlies everything [and] cultures can be likened to an enormous, subtle, extraordinarily complex computer. It programs the actions and responses of every person, and these programs can be mastered by anyone wishing to make the system work" (p. 15). We become more consciously aware of our communication behavior and speech codes when we encounter new or novel situations such as communicating with people from other cultures (Turner, 1988). Cosmopolitan communicators are able to flexibly respond to these new international business situations and competently bridge communication differences.

LANGUAGE IS RULE BASED

Language influences the way a linguistic system develops and is transmitted. As a set of signs, symbols, and signals, language has a grammar associated with it. All languages have a set of codified rules and their own unique organizational patterns (DeSaussure, 1960). Rules refer to commonly agreed-on structural properties underlying the foundation of a language system. We depend on others to follow these phonological, morphological, syntactic, semantic, and pragmatic rules:

- *Phonology* refers to the rules by which sounds are organized and used. Every language specifies the way vowels, consonants, or clusters of vowels and consonants interact with each other. Chinese and other Asian languages rely heavily on tonal sounds and pitch to add meaning to certain words, and some African and Arabic languages add tongue clicks or lip smacks to spoken words. Thus, actively listening to the sounds of words is critical to understanding another language and negotiating a shared meaning.

- *Morphology* refers rules that govern the internal structure of words. For instance, a present-tense verb will have a suffix added to it to make it past-tense, such as -ed or -ido. Or a prefix such as dis- or un- may be added before the verb to change the meaning.

- *Semantics* refers to the way meaning is culturally created. Dictionaries are often mistakenly regarded as the "defining source" pertaining to the definition of a word. Yet, dictionaries merely record significant word usages commonly employed by an educated populace within a particular cultural context, and word meanings may change over time (Winchester, 1998).

- *Denotative meaning* refers to the actual or agreed-on meaning or meanings of a word. This meaning is frequently referred to as the literal or "dictionary" meaning. Dictionaries are created to provide us with the "accepted" standard definitions of words, but one's personal, private meanings ultimately determine any response to certain symbols.

- *Connotative meaning* refers to subjective associations—the personal and emotional attachments that people associate with a word or symbol. This meaning contains all of the judgments and evaluations that people have for a word or symbol. Competent global communicators distinguish between denotative and connotative meanings of words.

- *Syntax* governs the way words form phrases, clauses, or sentences. Every language has grammatical or syntactical rules that govern the way nouns, verbs, adjectives, or objects must be arranged when spoken or written. French and Spanish usually place the object pronoun before the subject and verb, in contrast to English, which places the direct object following the subject and verb. Knowledge of syntax is critical for effective communication.

- *Pragmatics* pertains to the meanings applied to words given the relational associations of the parties and the social or environmental context. Watzlawick et al. (1967) note that "every communication has a content and relationship aspect such that the latter classifies the former" (p. 54). The pragmatic approach to conversational coherence assumes that conversations are practical, rule-governed acts that achieve meaningful goals for the parties involved (Heritage, 1989). Pragmatic rules operate at different levels during conversational discourse, permitting the parties to create and construct their own social environment (Cronen et al., 1988; Cronen, Pearce, & Harris, 1979; Pearce & Cronen, 1980). We display greater intercultural competence and reveal ourselves to be cosmopolitan communicators when we learn the pragmatic interpretations of idiomatic expressions unique to a country, reveal an understanding of their language structure, and demonstrate an awareness of the conversational rules that pertain to the host culture.

LANGUAGE IS FUNCTIONAL

Words are tools and become important only when they are used. W. Charles Readding (1972) suggests three general functions of messages within the business and organizational arena: (1) task messages, which relate to products, services, and activities of specific concern to the organization such as improving sales or customer service; (2) maintenance messages, which help the organization to remain alive and perpetuate itself, such as policy and regulation messages; and (3) human messages, which are directed at people within the organization and affect their attitudes, morale, satisfaction, and self-fulfillment. To this list, Gerald Goldhaber (1993) would add innovative messages, or those messages that enable an organization to innovate and adapt to its changing environment.

The effective use of language facilitates the accommodation and adaptation to others and our environment. Stephen Littlejohn (2002) considers accommodation and adaptation part of a message-centered theory that focuses on behavioral traits instead of the social nature of communication. Most of us do not realize how frequently we adapt our communication behavior to others. Howard Giles and his colleagues (Giles, Mulac, Bradac, & Johnson, 1987; Giles, Henwood, Coupland, Harriman, & Coupland, 1992a; Giles, Mulac, Bradac, & Smith, 1992b) have developed an interesting body of research that reveals that we tend to accommodate others through our vocabulary, gestures, rate of talking, and placement of pauses, as well as volume, and level of politeness. When we adapt our communicative behavior to better identify with the other person or build solidarity, we are using a strategy of convergence. Researchers believe we choose to converge when we are attracted to the other person, or seek approval, or wish to increase mutual involvement. Accommodating can lead to increased social identity and stronger intercultural relationships (Beebe & Giles, 1984).

In contrast to convergence, we sometimes choose divergence, which is a language strategy of setting ourselves apart or creating distance between us and another person or group. Physicians use medical jargon or technical terms to maintain a professional distance between themselves and their patients. Counselors often choose to establish an emotional distance between themselves and their clients by adopting formal communication strategies. It is important to identify and be alert to our own convergence and divergence behaviors. As global communicators, we need to recognize when accommodation is mutually desirable and when divergence may be more professionally appropriate.

We learn our language and develop our effectiveness in communication through our culture and upbringing. Because we can represent our world through symbols, we have the ability to "foresee events, to reflect on past experiences, to plan, to make decisions, and to consciously control our own behavior" (Beebe & Masterson, 1982, p. 27). Language allows us to organize and accomplish tasks; it is the foundation on which we build international business and society.

Nonverbal Communication

Our language system is undeniably important when communicating with others, but equally important are the many nonverbal cues that accompany spoken messages. Indeed, some would argue that these cues are essentially more significant than verbal messages themselves. Dean C. Barnlund's (1968) early review of the literature on nonverbal communication led him to conclude that "many, and sometimes most, of the critical meanings generated in human encounters are elicited by touch, glance, vocal nuance, gesture, or facial expression with or without the aid of words" (p. 535). Barnlund's perceptive observations assume greater impact when we consider Birdwhistell's (1955) claim that during face-to-face communication only 35 percent of the meaning comes from words and 65 percent comes from the nonverbal messages. Albert Mehrabian (1968) raises this statistical estimate and contends that 93 percent of the emotional impact of a message comes from a nonverbal source and only 7 percent is verbal. Clearly, it is important to examine the functions nonverbal messages play in our interactions with people and to consider the array of nonverbal cues that influence our communication with others.

FUNCTIONS OF NONVERBAL MESSAGES

Our nonverbal behaviors are culturally acquired, and they perform many vital functions in the total communication process. These behaviors are particularly critical to relational development because many of the decisions we make about whether we like a person or about their status or responsiveness to us are based on these silent cues. We express emotions and convey attitudes nonverbally; we present ourselves and regulate our communication with others nonverbally.

Nonverbal behaviors are particularly effective in communicating our emotional state and expressing our attitudes. All people commonly express certain primary emotions facially: love, happiness, sadness, surprise, fear, anger, and disgust (Ekman, 2004; Ekman & Friesen, 1969). Additionally, Judee Burgoon and her colleagues (Burgoon, Buller, Hale, & deTurck, 1984; Burgoon & Hale, 1984) have discovered that some nonverbal behaviors particularly influence our relational perceptions of others. Proximity can be significant in communicating intimacy, attraction, trust, caring, dominance, persuasiveness, and aggressiveness. Smiling seems to communicate liking, composure, and formality. Touching communicates intimacy, and eye contact serves to intensify the effect of other nonverbal behaviors. Our attitudes can also be expressed nonverbally with our eyes, hands, physical movement, voice, and even silence (Knapp, 1980). These nonverbal behaviors, however, take on meaning only when viewed within the total context (Burgoon & Hale, 1988). Moreover, Mehrabian (1971) importantly notes that "when any nonverbal behavior contradicts speech, it is more likely to determine the total impact of the message" (p. 37).

Nonverbal communication serves as a principal means of self-presentation. Others come to know us by the nonverbal messages we send. Whether in casual conversations or business settings, our nonverbal behaviors reveal who we are (Feldman, 1991).

Finally, nonverbal behaviors serve a regulatory function in our communication with others. They can repeat, contradict, substitute, complement, underline or accent, and direct our verbal messages (Leathers, 1986). Nonverbal behaviors can initiate interactions, clarify relationships, direct turn-taking, guide emotional expression, and initiate leave-taking (Knapp & Hall, 2001). Moreover, the appropriateness of communication, conversational rules, and situational norms are conveyed nonverbally (Burgoon, Stern, & Dillman, 1995).

DIMENSIONS OF NONVERBAL BEHAVIOR

We send and receive a variety of nonverbal messages while communicating with others. Judee Burgoon (1994) has identified seven different nonverbal dimensions: (1) kinesics or body movements including facial expressions and eye contact; (2) vocalics or paralanguage that includes volume, rate, pitch, and timbre; (3) personal appearance; (4) our physical environment and the artifacts or objects that compose it; (5) proxemics or personal space; (6) haptics or touch; and (7) chronemics or time. To this list we would add signs or emblems.

Signs or emblems include all of those gestures that supplant words, numbers, and punctuation marks. They may vary from the monosyllabic gesture of a hitchhiker's prominent thumb to such complex systems as the American Sign Language for the deaf where nonverbal signals have a direct verbal translation. However, it should be emphasized that signs or emblems are culture specific. The thumb and forefinger gesture used to represent "A-Okay" in the United States assumes a derogatory and offensive interpretation in some Latin American countries. And, although most emblems are produced with our hands, such signals can be communicated in other ways. A nose-wrinkle may say, "I'm disgusted" or "Phew! It stinks!" A shrug of the shoulders may communicate helplessness or uncertainty. The number of signs or emblems used within a given culture may vary considerably—from fewer than 100 in the United States to more than 250 in Israel (Harrison, 1972). Even the deaf may sign somewhat differently from one geographic region to another.

Kinesics refers to body movement and includes facial expressions, hand and head gestures, crossing of arms and legs, posture, and eye contact. Birdwhistell (1970) has estimated that there are over 700,000 possible physical signs (head movements, facial expressions) that can be transmitted by body movement. More recently, Poyatos (2002) reviewed nonverbal communication internationally and included such behaviors as spitting, belching, and sighing. We use body language to communicate feelings and attitudes. Such commonly used expressions as "if looks could kill" or "it's all over your face" underscore the significance of body language.

The face has considerable communicative potential, mirroring both our intentions and our feelings. It is capable of making hundreds of distinct movements and communicating many emotional states with incredible speed. The feelings most easily identified are surprise, fear, anger, disgust, happiness, contempt, sadness, and interest (Ekman, Friesen, & Ellsworth, 1971; Leathers, 1976). McDaniel (2000) has reported that Japanese facial expressions reflect social balance and *gaman* or endurance, and their eye contact reflects the cultural themes of hierarchy, social balance, and humility. The face is a tremendously complicated channel of expression to interpret, but Dimitrius and Mazzarella (1999) believe that by sharpening and fine-tuning our powers of observation and deduction we can gather enough information to establish an overall pattern that can reveal personality and identify the meanings behind personal choices.

Eyes and eye movement, or oculesics, convey attitudes and communicate much information. Our eyes are a very expressive communication channel, and we are remarkably accurate in interpreting the messages being sent. Direct eye contact, particularly in Western cultures, is positively interpreted as a sign of trust and mutual attention and interest. Gazes during conversation also serve a regulatory function, indicating turn-taking. Even the pupils of the eyes can communicate excitement, interest, and surprise (Andersen, 1998). However, in Japan as well as some other cultures direct eye contact is considered threatening and disrespectful (McDaniel, 2000).

Vocalics or paralanguage refers to everything beyond or in addition to language itself. Such variables as tone, rate, volume, breathiness, nasality, and pitch offer a lot of information about a speaker's personality, attitude, status, and feelings. With information from the voice it is possible to predict physical characteristics, aptitudes and interests, personality traits, and overall personality (Kramer, 1963). We can correctly identify a speaker's ethnic group, education, and dialectical region (Nerbonne, 1967). There is also evidence that social status can be determined in large part by the signals we receive from the voice alone (Harms, 1961). And, we can identify certain emotions from vocal cues: anger, boredom, disgust, fear, joy, and sadness (Davitz, 1964). Paralinguistic cues are particularly important for understanding the highly tonal Spanish, Asian, African, and Arabic languages.

Personal appearance refers to clothing, jewelry, and personal hygiene as well as other symbols identifying the uniqueness of a person or environment. Our physical appearance, the clothing we wear, and the jewelry we display communicate something to others. For example, business attire reflects the unique corporate culture of an organization as well as communicating something about the individual. McDaniel and Quasha (2000) note how the Japanese business community tends to be conservative in dress and the dark blue, tailored suit represents the Japanese corporate salary man or *sariman.* Characteristics such as intelligence, sociability, trustworthiness, and success are initially determined by physical appearance. Status and prestige are also communicated by dress and appearance (Remland, 1981). Although these may be imprecise and unclear measures, they are important factors influencing our self-images and our relationships with others.

Our environment and the artifacts comprising our surroundings also say something about who we are and where we are. We encounter others in a limitless number of places—buses, subways, homes, apartments, elevators, restaurants, offices, parks, hotels, sports arenas, factories, libraries, movie theaters, classrooms, and so on. We evaluate these environments along selected dimensions, and both are influenced by and likewise influence our surroundings. One familiar dimension along which environments can be classified is a formal-informal continuum. Our determination of each may be based on the people present, the functions performed, or the objects in the room. Environments can also be judged as being private or public. Private environments are more enclosed, reduce distance, and encourage close, personal communication with others. Messages are less constrained, more candid, and self-disclosing. On the other hand, communication in public environments is impersonal, hesitant, guarded, and oftentimes superficial. Environments can encourage encounters and contribute to communication or prove counter-communicative. Moreover, our environments also comprise people who affect our behavior. These people may be perceived as active or passive participants, depending on the degree to which they are perceived as being involved. When others are perceived to be active ingredients in the environment, they may either facilitate or inhibit communication. Their presence may motivate us to interact with others or cause us to be cautious. The people who occupy space in our environment(s) influence what we say, how we say it, and who we say it to.

Proxemics is the study of how we use the space around us and the messages conveyed by distance. Each of us carries around a sort of invisible bubble of personal space that represents our established territory. How we regulate our space influences our communication with others and affects our personal orientations and experiences. In some fascinating research at MIT, Thomas Allen (1967) reported that people working more than 10 meters apart have only 8 to 9 percent probability of communicating at least once a week, versus a 25 percent chance at five meters. Distance further defines our relationships and determines the nature and function of our communication with others. Hall (1959) has identified four distances ranging from public to intimate that affect our communication with others. Public distance (6–20 feet) involves messages intended for and sent to large groups. Social distance (20 inches to 6 feet) involves messages more suitable for casual conversations and business discussions. Personal distance (12–20 inches) represents something more than casual conversation but still keeps others at arm's length. Intimate distance (3–12 inches) is close and private and reserved for those with whom we are emotionally and relationally close. These informal spatial dimensions may vary according to the nature of the situation and the particular culture. Our sense of personal space, business etiquette, and office design can clearly create barriers or bridges to communication (Ornstein, 1989; Schmidt & Dorsey, 1986).

Haptics or touch is a potent nonverbal message cue and may represent our most basic communication code because we all need the warmth, tenderness, and security that only touching provides (Knapp, 1980). Heslin and Alper (1983) suggest five functions that touch serves in nonverbal communication. Functional-professional touch is impersonal and is exemplified by the many professional/client relationships that exist. Social-polite touch is part of the greeting behaviors of a culture and includes handshaking, hugging, and kissing. Friendship-warmth touch involves maintaining and reinforcing close bonds with others and may be expressed by hugging and holding. Love-intimacy touch is also reinforcing but the relationship is deep and personal, requiring gentle touches and caresses to communicate mutual feelings. Sexual-arousal touch is highly intimate and functions to satisfy primary needs. Touch, however, is highly influenced by our respective cultures. The United States, for instance, is basically a nontactile, low-contact culture as compared to Latin American and Arabic cultures, which are high-contact. People who live in San Juan, Puerto Rico, for example, touch an average of 180 times per conversation, whereas people from Gainesville, Florida, touch an average of two times per conversation (Wade & Jarvis, 1987). Touch can effectively communicate strong emotional meanings, power, and status within specific contexts and from particular cultural perspectives (Leathers, 1986).

Chronemics or time is a particularly important dimension of nonverbal communication. We are constantly reminded of its importance by such everyday expressions as "time flies," "it's about time," and "don't waste time." In the United States, we are particularly serious, if not neurotic, about time and are quick to attribute messages and attitudes to people on the basis of their "time" behavior. Cultural expectations and personality, however, influence how time is perceived. Punctuality is interpreted differently in Latin American and other high-context cultures—promptness with appointments and schedules are viewed casually, with family matters and people issues taking precedence over punctuality. Hall (1976) identified varying cultural orientations toward time that he labeled as monochronic and polychronic. In low-context monochronic cultures, time is highly organized, whereas in high-context polychronic cultures time is less structured, more flexible, and responsive to the immediate needs of people. Thus, monochronic or M-time involves linear, sequential thinking and doing one thing at a time whereas polychronic or P-time is holistic and involves doing a number of things simultaneously.

Personality further determines how time functions for different people. Researchers have identified four basic personality types, each of which experiences time in unique ways that affect their communication with others (Mann, Siegler, & Osmond, 1972). The thinking types perceive time as being linear. They enjoy planning, logically plotting issues out through time, and discovering principles and processes for a problem. The feeling types view the present through past experiences, and this strong association with the past makes change difficult. The sensation types perceive time mainly in terms of the present. They are realists who cannot tolerate delay and are more action oriented. They are particularly competent in dealing with crises and making immediate decisions. Finally, the intuitive types view time primarily in terms of the future. Intuitives feel they must change the world to realize their visions of the future. This sense of mission, when combined with a vision of what could be, represents their most outstanding talent.

Time can also reflect status and power (Remland, 1981). Higher status people act in ways that control the time of others. Superiors, for instance, typically establish the agenda for meetings and determine the amount of time spent in committees, conferences, and other business situations. Additionally, greater status may excuse the abuse of time while still expecting rigid adherence by others. Time communicates in many clear and forceful ways.

Nonverbal cues serve a variety of functions in communication and influence how we interact with others. Understanding nonverbal communication helps unlock people to each other and is crucial for successful intercultural encounters. Amiso George (2003) reminds us that "people in high-context cultures are more attentive to the subliminal messages embedded in nonverbal behavior than their counterparts in low-context cultures. So to avoid cross-cultural misunderstandings, messages should be tailored to mirror cultural context and differences between the sender and audience" (p. 103).

Summary

Verbal and nonverbal messages convey content and define relationships. Through the use of verbal symbols, words, and language, we relay information, opinions, and attitudes in an effort to influence the behavior of others.

Language, however, is a complex and at times troublesome vehicle affecting both the cultures and the people involved in meaningful exchange. Especially bothersome is the arbitrary and often abstract relationship among words, objects, and thoughts. Our examination of Ogden and Richards's semantic triangle and discussion of the Sapir-Whorf hypothesis help explain the nature of language, thought, and meaning. Bernstein's hypothesis and Philipsen's speech codes reveal additional characteristics about language and the dynamics involved with accommodation and adaptation. Language serves a variety of functions and is a critical part of the hectic and active international business arena.

Nonverbal messages are outside of spoken and written languages, but they also transmit a great deal of meaning. Where words usually convey ideas, nonverbal cues express emotions, attitudes, and self and serve certain regulatory functions. Nonverbally, we communicate through signs or emblems, body movement or kinesics, vocalics or paralanguage, personal appearance, artifacts and objects, space and territory or proxemics, touch or haptics, and chronemics or time. The quantity of nonverbal stimuli that exists indicates how important it is to the total process of communication. Although large portions of the meaning of our messages are carried nonverbally, these cues are culturally influenced, and overreactions to nonverbal behaviors can create misunderstandings, particularly in intercultural contexts. However, an awareness of nonverbal communication cues can help reveal and explain different cultural orientations. For example, those of us in low-context cultures can better appreciate why some individuals in high-context cultures may perceive wristwatches as "mental handcuffs," and those in high-context cultures can gain an understanding regarding our "strange hurry" (O'Connell, 1990). Martin and Colburn (1972) observe that "we have to understand [communication] as thoroughly as we can, and we need the faith to believe that it can, in crucial ways, make us one people" (p. 19).

6

Intercultural Communication
and Conflict Management

One of the more challenging problems confronting individuals and multinational organizations is handling conflict. Communication plays an intimate role in conflict and conflict management. It is pivotal in conceptualizing the controversy and in choosing ways to handle disputes. It shapes the formation of issues, the emotional climate of conflicts, and the cyclical development of interaction. Linda Putnam (1988) observes that "since communication permeates every aspect of conflict, it is more than a variable, it constitutes the essence of conflict" (p. 295).

In this chapter we define intercultural conflict and discuss the essential characteristics and types of intercultural conflict. We also investigate such intercultural dimensions as face negotiation and styles of conflict management. Finally, we examine the stages of intercultural conflict management and address conflict negotiation and international mediation and arbitration.

Defining Intercultural Conflict

When the terms "conflict" and "global communication" are mentioned together, we often think of ongoing international disputes between nations that threaten one another with mass destruction. However, our focus on intercultural conflict refers to less volatile contexts in which interdependent parties with cultural differences perceive incompatible goals. Stella Ting-Toomey and John Oetzel (2001) assert that intercultural conflict derives from the existence of parties of different cultural communities involved in interaction and having an "experience of emotional frustration in conjunction with perceived incompatibility [of goals]" (p. 17). The more divergent the differences in group membership, the wider the conflict gap between the two cultures will grow. Emotional frustration may stem from the cultural differences, expectancy violations, role and status differences, misplaced formality or informality, or communication avoidance.

Intercultural conflicts occur in a variety of contexts, and various classifications have been suggested for describing these contexts. Social psychologist Morton Deutsch (1973) notes that essentially "conflict can occur in a cooperative or competitive context" (p. 157). Conflicts occurring within cooperative contexts reveal open, free-flowing, and honest communication. Disagreements are settled through lively and open discussion, with the personal needs and concerns of the involved parties being considered and respected. Solutions sought are acceptable and beneficial to everyone and further solidify close and supportive relationships. However, conflicts in contexts characterized by competition exhibit a contest-like striving where participants contend against each other. Certainly there are varying levels of conflict intensity, but the outcome is predictable—there is a winner and a loser.

Intercultural conflicts are caused by a wide variety of complex psychological, social, and situational factors, but there is general agreement pertaining to the types of conflict. Affective conflict occurs when feelings and emotions are incompatible. Value conflict occurs when people differ in ideologies on specific issues. Cognitive conflict occurs when thought processes or perceptions are incongruent. Goal conflict occurs over disagreement about preferred outcomes (Folger, Poole, & Stutman, 1993).

A closer look at some essential qualities of intercultural conflict can help us more positively manage cross-cultural disputes:

- Conflict is an integral part of our international social fabric. Conflict is a pervasive activity that is often mistakenly viewed as abnormal or destructive. Yet, the presence of conflict is evidence of the resiliency and fundamental strength of our varied social systems. Conflict suggests both the need for and the possible directions of necessary change. From this perspective, conflict may be viewed as an activator or energy source for constructive dialogue that can transform the ordinary into the extraordinary (Kellett & Dalton, 2001). Conflict need not be overwhelming or debilitating if it is approached intelligently, honestly, and confidently (Semlak, 1982).

- Conflict may result in either positive or negative outcomes. Louis Pondy (1967) observed that "conflict may be functional as well as dysfunctional for the individual and organization" (p. 298). Adler, Rosenfeld, and Proctor (2004) identify a number of characteristics that distinguish between functional and dysfunctional conflict. Conflict that tends toward greater polarization between parties, such as an "us" versus "them" mentality, reflects dysfunctional conflict, whereas those interactions leaning toward integration reflect functional conflict. Those interactions characterized by coercion, including manipulation, hidden agendas, or misused power, will experience dysfunctional outcomes, whereas conflicts actively working toward cooperative agreements will experience functional results including greater trust, stronger relationships, mutual commitment, and positive outcomes more satisfactory to all parties. Thus, far from representing breakdowns in communication, conflicts may be the very stimuli that prompt us to communicate with others and to sustain communicative relationships (Isenhart & Spangle, 2000).

• Conflicts can be satisfactorily managed. Although we would like to believe that all conflicts are resolvable through some means, experience and common sense suggest a far different reality. Some are so deeply ingrained, so fundamental, and perhaps so necessary that they consistently defy resolution. However, conflicts can be constructively managed (Wilmot & Hocker, 2001). These struggles may be defused and mediated or arbitrated so that those with opposing goals, values, and philosophies can respect each other and learn to coexist while retaining their differing points of view (Borisoff & Victor, 1989).

Clarke and Lipp (1998) describe a cross-cultural business scenario between a U.S. sales manager working for a large Japanese manufacturing firm based in the United States and its Japanese representatives based at the firm's headquarters in Tokyo. The U.S. sales manager had sold a multimillion-dollar order, and to meet deadlines she worked diligently to ensure that the order would be filled to specifications on time. She established strategic planning sessions with key division managers and carefully balanced representation on the planning sessions with equal numbers of managers from the United States and Tokyo. However, the U.S. division managers tended to dominate the discussion, with the Japanese representatives generally remaining quiet. During the strategy meetings, the U.S. sales manager expressed concern about the Japanese managers' lack of participation and silence but moved forward with processing the customer's order. She e-mailed the Japanese managers her recommendations and faxed her specifications and timeline to the Tokyo office. However, she was troubled when there was no response and repeated attempts failed until she finally heard that Tokyo was having difficulty meeting her order and the customer would have to be patient. When the extended deadlines were not met, the customer contracted with another supplier and the sales manager missed her bonus and lost the division's profit margin. She learned later that Tokyo refused her order because it had committed its output to another customer for the next few months.

This example is typical of the kind of conflict and misunderstanding of values and norms between cultural groups that can occur in multinational organizations. The U.S. sales manager believed the Japanese were slow to respond and indifferent to e-mail and written messages and was unaware of their information network. The Japanese managers believed she was impatient, treated everything with unnecessary urgency, and relied too much on formal communication. Such negative experiences can be avoided when conflict is managed competently and effective intercultural communication skills are applied to the situation. However, Dudley Weeks (1994) notes that "we have spent far more energy and resources on our material technologies than we have in developing the people skills to deal effectively with our differences and with building mutually enriching relationships [but] devoting some time and energy to developing effective resolution skills is now an essential need" (pp. xiii–xiv).

Phases of Intercultural Conflict

Intercultural conflict may be viewed as a series of five interlocking phases or stages that mutually interact with one another and influence the outcome of any conflict situation: (1) latent conflict, (2) perceived conflict, (3) felt conflict, (4) manifest conflict, and (5) conflict aftermath (Pondy, 1967). Latent conflict refers to the underlying conditions that can trigger a conflict. Inherent differences between values, norms, and beliefs may be a source of conflict, as can a scarcity of resources and incompatible goals or a desire for autonomy. Perceived conflict occurs when the involved parties become aware of their differences and consequently begin to experience significant frustration. Felt conflict is the phase when the participants become ego-involved and begin to assess their individual motives, the motives of others, and the importance of the problem. It represents the merger of their perceptions and emotional reactions. Manifest conflict is that phase when actual conflict behaviors are exhibited—open aggression, verbal displays, overpowering competition, making of threats, silence, withdrawal, or agreeing to solutions are some of the possibilities. It is the stage when participants readily recognize conflict and use their communication skills and peacemaking abilities to manage it. Finally, conflict aftermath, resulting from the complex interactions of the previous phases, is that point when outcomes are evaluated as being productive or counterproductive. Each phase of conflict leaves an aftermath that affects the course of future interactions. These five phases are helpful in visualizing conflict as a process and can be useful when selecting appropriate communication styles and conflict-handling strategies for constructive intervention management.

Characteristics of Intercultural Conflict

Communication scholars are only beginning to address intercultural conflict and assume an international focus. Some early research has been given to our Western perspective, and we are only now starting to examine Eastern communication theory and non-Western conflict management and resolution (Chen & Ma, 2001; Jia, Lu, & Heisey, 2002). Those scholars who have explored intercultural conflict have identified three particularly prominent and interrelated characteristics that significantly influence outcomes—face-negotiation, styles of conflict management, and conflict-handling strategies (Ting-Toomey & Oetzel, 2001).

FACE-NEGOTIATION

Erving Goffman (1959) conducted extensive research in interpersonal relationships and found that we strategically present a social "front" or impression "which regularly functions in a general and fixed fashion to define the situation for those who observe the performance" (p. 22). On the basis of this finding, Goffman (1967) explored the unique concept of "face" in shaping our individual identity. He views each human interaction as a "performance" and believes we seek to present consistent impressions to others regarding our desired goals in any interaction. Thus, the concept of face refers to a socially approved identity we seek when we interact with others. Facework refers to those verbal and nonverbal efforts we use to strategically construct and maintain our identities during an interaction. Several characteristics of face and facework can be identified that exist in all cultures:

- Face concerns are both public and private. Our private face can be described best by how we act when we are alone. This private self typically contrasts with the public self we present to others, even when we are among our closest friends.

- We maintain multiple faces in our interactions. These multiple faces serve as a way to maintain an identity with others and with ourselves given the various social roles we choose to assume.

- Our facework in establishing an identity is mutually influenced by each participant to the interaction. Each exchange is shaped by the preceding episode, and our ability to maintain or establish social identities across cultures is a mark of our communication competence.

Researchers believe that face-negotiation theory applies universally across cultures (P. Brown & Levinson, 1987; Oetzel & Ting-Toomey, 2003). Although individual verbal and nonverbal behaviors vary widely between cultures, face-negotiation still exists as cultural members engage in presenting and maintaining impressions during their interactions. Lustig and Koester (2003) identify three universal face needs among cultures: (1) control, (2) approval, and (3) admiration or respect. Oetzel and Ting-Toomey (2003) further note that facework becomes especially important in cultural situations when we experience embarrassment, encounter threats, become excessively polite, or express apologies. They astutely observe that numerous factors influence face-negotiation, whether a person engages in self-oriented face restoration or other-oriented facegiving. In other words, what may be an appropriate and acceptable face-negotiation strategy in one culture may not be in another.

Face concerns become particularly important during interactions between members of individualistic low-context cultures and collectivist high-context cultures. The former tend to give more importance to face restoration or safeguarding their own face, whereas the latter tend to engage in facegiving or protecting another's face. According to Stella Ting-Toomey (1988), face can be negotiated along two different dimensions. The first dimension plots on a horizontal axis and ranges from self-face concerns on the left to other-face concerns on the right. The second dimension plots on a vertical axis and ranges from positive-face need on the top to negative-face need on the bottom. An individual who approaches conflict with positive face builds inclusion in the relationship and tends to communicate respect, approval, and appreciation to the other party. Approaching the conflict with negative face refers to exclusion and claiming basic rights of privacy and noninterference. Collectivistic, high-context cultures tend toward positive-face/other-face concerns, and individualistic, low-context cultures tend toward self-face concern/negative-face needs. Thus, relationship orientation and indirectness characterize collectivist high-context cultures, whereas directness and open expression reflect individualistic low-context cultures.

A U.S. company had a contract from a German buyer to sell bicycles produced in China. When the first shipment was ready, there was a problem: The bikes rattled. The U.S. buyer did not want to accept the shipment because the rattle would not be acceptable to the German client, whose high-end market niche was dominated by bikes that were whisper-quiet. In the United States, the normal approach would be to tell the manufacturer that the rattling bikes were unacceptable and that the problem had to be fixed. However, in the Chinese culture, such a direct confrontation would be extremely rude and cause much loss of face. Knowing this, the U.S. manager, with remarkable insight, went to the Chinese plant, inspected the bicycles, rode a few, and asked about the rattle. "Is this rattle normal? Do all the bikes rattle? Do you think the German buyer will think there is something wrong with the bike if it rattles?" Then he left. The next shipment of bikes had no rattles (Brett, 2001, p. 10). Our ability to handle face concerns in intercultural relationships often determines whether we are able to reach successful and positive conflict outcomes (Oetzel et al., 2001).

CONFLICT STYLES

Oetzel and Ting-Toomey (2003) contend that face-negotiation theory also serves as an explanatory framework for one's communicator style and the different cross-cultural conflict management styles used. An individual's communicator style can be described as the way one verbally and nonverbally interacts with others to interpret, filter, or understand how literal meaning should be taken during the interaction (Norton, 1978). Conflict style refers to a "characteristic mode or habitual way that a person handles a dispute" (Putnam & Poole, 1987, p. 556). An individual may adopt different styles according to each situation, but one style typically emerges as a consistent default orientation toward facing conflict. The outcome of conflict appears to depend on individual communicator style and the conflict management style that communicators choose (Weeks, 1994).

Conflict styles frequently are described as five fundamental orientations based on the balance between satisfying individual needs and goals and satisfying the needs and goals of others in the conflict. The five stylistic choices generally identified are (1) avoidance or withdrawal, (2) competition or dominating, (3) compromise or conceding, (4) accommodation or yielding, and (5) collaboration or integration (Blake & Mouton, 1964; C. Brown, Yelsmer, & Keller, 1981; L. Brown, 1983; Canary & Cupach, 1988; Fogg, 1985; Heitler, 1990; Hime, 1980; Putnam & Folger, 1988; Ting-Toomey, 1985; Weiman & Daly, 1990).

Avoidance (or *withdrawal*) is a style characterized by denying the conflict, or being noncommittal, and withdrawing from the situation. Although avoiders may have a genuine concern for goals and relationships, they refrain from either psychologically or physically participating in conflict situations. This style may be useful when the issue is trivial or when others can manage the conflict without direct involvement, but avoidance frequently permits conflict to simmer and heat up unnecessarily instead of opening an avenue for resolution. It usually preserves the conflict and sets the stage for a later, more violent explosion.

Competition (or *dominating*) is a style characterized by assertive or aggressive behavior and overt disagreement. Competitive people often conceptualize conflict as win-lose and prefer to view themselves as winners. Competition can be useful in situations in which the involved parties recognize competitive behavior as a sign of strength and treat it as a natural response, such as in games and sports or litigation. It may also be used to demonstrate personal interest and commitment regarding the conflicting issues. In other circumstances, such a dominating style can damage relationships, lock participants into destructive attack/counterattack sequences, and prevent participants from seeking cooperative solutions to their problems. The Navajo Indians believe that if one ends a dispute by having a winner and a loser, one dispute may have ended but another dispute surely will have started, because harmony will not have been restored (Isenhart & Spangle, 2000). Alfie Kohn (1976) is convinced that any competition is dysfunctional; there is no such thing as "healthy" competition. However, Hamilton and Parker (1997) contend that a competitive conflict style may work successfully if individuals must make timely decisions and expect and value such behavior.

Compromising (or *conceding*) is a style preferred by those who seek to balance *people concerns* with *task issues* and often approach conflict with a give-and-take attitude that contributes to negotiation. Compromise is a useful style for restoring harmony when the conflicting participants are willing to make some concessions to achieve a mutually satisfying agreement. However, if the parties are pressured or coerced into compromising or believe they are conceding important values, the conflict will likely surface again. In such a case, compromise may provide only a temporary respite rather than a productive and positive solution.

Accommodating (or *yielding*) is a style characterized by the sacrifice of personal goals in order to resolve conflict and maintain relationships. People who seek connections, have high affiliative needs, and genuinely are concerned about relational associations often prefer an accommodating or yielding approach to conflict. Often mistakenly perceived as an abandonment style, it may be useful when disputed issues seem personally unimportant or trivial. Accommodating individuals under such circumstances might indebt you to them, which can be capitalized upon at a later date. However, this style becomes problematic if consistently employed or used when issues, goals, or tasks are regarded as personally significant. Then, accommodation may generate feelings of victimization and exploitation.

Collaborating (or *integrating*) is a style that recognizes the productive potential of conflict and encourages people to engage in dialogue and thoughtfully work toward accomplishing common goals or objectives (Anderson, Baxter, & Cissna, 2003; Ellinor & Gerard, 1998; Muldoon, 1996). Collaboration assumes a mutually exploratory problem-solving orientation and works well when one wants to find an integrative solution that will satisfy all parties. It is an active affirmation of the importance of relationship and content goals, and thus builds a team or partner approach to conflict management. However, collaboration is a difficult, emotionally intense, time-consuming style, and people can only behave collaboratively when others are also willing to assume a collaborative orientation. Moreover, collaboration can be difficult to maintain when the specific interests of the parties collide or clash.

Conflict management styles and stylistic choices are intimately linked with cross-cultural themes and patterns (Oetzel & Ting-Toomey, 2006). Members of individualistic cultures tend to use more dominating conflict strategies and work toward more integrating strategies. They are less inclined to avoid conflict than members of collectivistic cultures. In contrast, individuals from collectivistic cultures tend toward avoiding or obliging conflict strategies and seek to develop cooperating or compromising conflict strategies. Research also shows that individualistic, small power distance cultures use more dominating or forcing conflict strategies than members of collectivistic large power distance cultures (Oetzel et al., 2001).

Understanding the differences among cultures helps us select the best ways to manage intercultural conflict (Ting-Toomey & Chung, 2005). Individualistic countries like the United States tend to use a more competitive style when faced with conflict than do collectivistic countries like Japan. The Japanese consider conflict disruptive to their society and a threat to group cohesion. Thus, the Japanese will rely on personal contacts and small group discussions to reach consensus and agreement. In contrast, those from the United States value openness, and those who are articulate and can argue their points in a clear and rational manner are esteemed. These contrasting attitudes and approaches toward conflict management can result in a broad range of culturally based misunderstandings and disagreements (McDaniel & Quasha, 2000). It is, therefore, crucial to select a conflict-handling strategy suitable to the particular cultural context.

CONFLICT-HANDLING STRATEGIES

Putnam and Wilson's Organizational Communication Conflict Instrument (OCCI) and Jay Hall's (1986) Conflict Management Survey identify deep-seated conflict-handling strategies or "lines of action for pursuing and coordinating goals within a specific situation" (Wilson & Waltman, 1988, p. 368). The three categories of conflict strategies include (1) nonconfrontational or yield-lose strategies, (2) solution-oriented or win-win strategies, and (3) control or win-lose strategies. Nonconfrontational strategies approach conflict indirectly, either by physically avoiding disagreements or by downplaying controversy and sidestepping volatile issues because relationships carry more importance than personal goals and must be maintained even at the high cost to personal ambitions. Solution-oriented strategies manage conflict by both making compromises and searching for creative, integrative solutions. These strategies attempt to make trades between personal and relationship goals or synergistically seek solutions that favorably affect both the relationship and personal goals. Control strategies deal with conflict by arguing persistently for previously established positions and using nonverbal messages to emphasize demands. These win-lose strategies emphasize personal goals to the exclusion of relationships. These two instruments can further assess our verbal and nonverbal tactics as they influence our conflict management behaviors. Consequently, individuals have opportunities to choose from a set of essential communication strategies and tactics as they relate to their goals and the particular cultural situation or context. Only by being sensitive to and strategically working within the parameters of the particular cultural environment can we positively manage intercultural conflict.

Many participants are dissatisfied with conflict outcomes because of unrealistic expectations, ignorance, and a failure to adapt communication to the existing cultural differences. Productive conflicts leave participants satisfied and feeling that they have gained something: the problem is solved, the relationship is enhanced, and a new reason for working together in the future is developed (Samovar, Porter, & McDaniel, 2006).

Steps in Constructive Intercultural Conflict Management

Constructive intercultural conflict management and intervention require methodically examining the nature of the conflict, assessing the pattern of relationships between the parties, and determining which approach or communication style will prove most constructive. Borisoff and Victor (1989) present a concise and useful model consisting of five steps that can help a cosmopolitan communicator constructively contend with intercultural conflict: (1) assessment, (2) acknowledgement, (3) attitude, (4) action, and (5) analysis.

Assessment is an important initial step in managing differences and requires that we carefully consider the following five aspects of the communication environment: (1) the individual traits of the participants and the nature of the relationship; (2) the nature and cause of the conflict; (3) the clarification of each party's personal agenda, goals, and objectives; (4) an examination of the prevailing communication climate; and (5) a preliminary determination of an appropriate conflict-handling style.

Acknowledging the other party's involvement and constructively dealing with the perceptual differences are fundamental to effective conflict management. It is incumbent on the participants to appreciate the diversity that may exist and nonjudgmentally recognize the cultural, ideological, value, gender, experiential, and communicative differences.

A positive *attitude* that generates trust and cooperation is mandatory for productive conflict management. Demonstrating conciliation, compassion, concern, and a willingness to assume responsibility for one's actions is crucial for satisfactorily managing differences.

Ultimately, direct, deliberate, positive *action* must be taken toward managing conflict. Integrating the information gathered from the previous steps should be useful in selecting and applying productive communication techniques that will actively move the participants toward a mutually satisfying solution. Certainly one's actions should be conducive to, rather than inhibitive of, interpersonal exchange. Koester and Olebe (1988) have developed a Behavioral Assessment Scale for Intercultural Competence (BASIC) that focuses on important categories of communication behavior necessary to achieving productive intercultural conflict management outcomes. These dimensions include the following:

- *Display of respect* or demonstrating positive regard for another person
- *Orientation to knowledge* or understanding the terms people use to explain themselves and their world
- *Empathy* or understanding the world as another sees it
- *Interaction management* or being skillful at regulating conversations
- *Task role behavior* or being able to initiate group problem-solving ideas
- *Relational role behavior* or behaving with interpersonal harmony
- *Tolerance for ambiguity* or being able to adjust to new situations with little discomfort
- *Interaction posture* or having the ability to respond to others in a descriptive, nonevaluative manner

Cosmopolitan communicators, competent in these valuable behaviors, will be able to confidently approach intercultural conflict and positively respond to the conflict styles of others.

Analysis is the final essential step in this conflict management model. Decisions should be reviewed and evaluated with an eye to the future impact on the participants—their goals and relationship. Thus, it is important to consider if (1) the concerns of all parties have been met as adequately as possible, (2) the decisions can be implemented swiftly and/or effectively, (3) the short- or long-term effects of the solution are viable, and (4) the relationship between the conflicting parties has been modified productively. Applying this model can result in both a heightened awareness of the dimensions of inter-cultural conflict and a greater ability to use appropriate conflict-handling behavior. It can further contribute to a lasting and mutually satisfying out-come. Intercultural conflict management is an activity that depends on people being sensitive to the concerns of others and open to diverse ways of approach-ing this difficult process.

Interestingly, the Elastic Rebound theory, which focuses on the movement of tectonic plates to explain the cause of earthquakes, can be usefully applied to our understanding of intercultural conflict without too much stretch of the imagination. The celebrated geologist Harry Fielding Reid basically proposed that the earth was elastic: "tighten it and it changes; over tighten it and it breaks" (Winchester, 2005). Similarly, multinational organizations and their global representatives who are involved in cross-cultural interactions are under considerable pressure to accomplish joint business ends and maintain produc-tive relationships with others as their culturally diverse "plates" slip, slide, and bump into each other. The factors composing the cross-cultural context by necessity influence the perspectives of the respective parties who must flexibly respond to one another. However, the tensions can build and erupt into inter-cultural conflict that may threaten the mutual goals of the involved parties unless they can maintain their balance and synergistic harmony.

The comparison of railway cars in a marshaling yard is used to explain the movement of the North American and Pacific tectonic plates, which influence the active San Andreas Fault (Winchester, 2005). A similar analogy can be help-ful in understanding intercultural conflict. Think of a line of railway freight cars all on a slope that makes them want to move downhill headfirst, as one. However, the wheels of the cars at the head of the line are rusted solid, as are those of the cars at the distant end, with only the cars in the middle having well-oiled wheels, which permits them to ever so slightly move downhill under the force of gravity. Enormous stresses thus build up in the clasps binding the cars together, with those at the front being pressed tightly together and those at the rear being stretched beyond endurance. Eventually the compounded weight of the cars in the midsection becomes simply too much for the rust holding fast the wheels of the locked cars, and under this terrible mounting pressure the rust gives way and the cars shoot forward, releasing kinetic energy. The pressure from the midsection of the cars suddenly eases for a while, but day by day the middle cars begin to move once more, and after a while the intolerable stress will again cause the cars to dramatically shift. The parties to intercultural interactions are often locked into their respective worldviews and learned cultural behaviors much like the rust-bound railway freight cars at the front and end of the line. It is the prospect of a successful business venture that brings the parties together, and it is the common concerns of commerce that provides the momentum for the interaction, much like the rail cars in the middle with their well-oiled wheels. Business and investment interests place considerable pressure on the parties to be pliable, to flexibly adjust, and to cooperatively work together despite their cultural differences. Still, the dialogical tensions of culture can build and suddenly give way to intercultural conflict requiring the parties to perhaps make some dramatic shifts before all the energy of the moment is dispelled. Such "shudders" can shake cognitive consistency and upset behavioral uniformity and turn stalled transactions around. The pressure eases for a while but will slowly begin to build until it again becomes overwhelming. The danger is that next time this release of energy might produce such violent discord that relationships are ruptured and the business transaction shattered. Rummel (1976) describes the development of conflict as passing through a similar sequence of events: cultural attitudes and business objectives (latent phase of conflict) become triggered (initiation) by an event; confrontational, nonconfrontational, or solution-oriented strategies are used (attempts to negotiate face and balance power) as parties confront the issue(s); parties may reach a level of resolution (balance of power) until another event triggers further confrontation (disruption), and the next time the conflict might be insurmountable (war). It seems apparent that culture is the epicenter of conflict management and global negotiation; it is that point where the seismic energy of the parties begins to radiate outward.

Conflict Negotiation, Mediation, and Arbitration

The growing globalization in international business necessitates an understanding of conflict negotiation and alternative dispute resolution (Spangle & Isenhart, 2002). Effective conflict negotiation has become a requirement when conducting international business, and mediation and arbitration are increasingly becoming third-party alternatives to dispute resolution.

Successful conflict negotiation requires taking the other party's needs into account while satisfying our needs through others. Negotiation refers to "a special form of social interaction or decision-making that (a) involves more than one party; (b) who hold potentially conflicting interests, as well as common interests or interdependence to motivate each to remain within the relationship or complete the exchange; and (c) requires a reciprocal exchange of information" (Schmidt & Conaway, 1999, p. 221). Conflict negotiation is a process, not an event.

Bertram Spector, a senior research associate in the Policy Sciences division of the research firm CACI, Inc., in Arlington, Virginia, has developed a three-phase conflict negotiation model that incorporates many of the complex factors present in intercultural contexts (Schmidt & Conaway, 1999). First is the background phase, which refers to all the essential planning for the negotiation session. It includes phrasing your exact purpose and analyzing your own position. You will identify your interests and determine your priorities, goals, and strategies. The fit between a negotiator's priorities and interests is what generates the potential for an integrative agreement (Edelman & Crain, 1993). Goal-setting also requires developing the Best Alternative to a Negotiated Agreement (BATNA), which means the negotiator must at least consider an alternative should negotiation fail (R. Fisher & Ury, 1991). In this initial phase, you will also want to acquire an understanding of the other party or parties. Understanding the mindset, personality attributes, roles, perceptions, and expectations of the other negotiator(s), including differing cultural values, norms, and beliefs, is essential to successful conflict negotiation (G. Fisher, 1980). Although developing specific background knowledge about the other party is important, there is a risk of knowing too much about the other party and their culture. Not all members of a culture behave like the cultural prototype, and cultural profiles overlap. Moreover, cultural norms for negotiation may be cued more strongly in some situations than others (E. Hall & Hall, 1990). Finally, during the background phase you will want to also select an appropriate negotiation setting and determine the role of translators and interpreters if there are any language differences (Chaney & Martin, 2004).

Second is the process phase, which refers to the actual give-and-take and competitive or collaborative engagement of the parties themselves. During this phase, each party interacts in an intercultural context and shapes the ongoing negotiation according to their unique backgrounds, styles, and personalities. A distinctive relationship typically forms between the parties based on their selected strategies and tactics. Two specific negotiation styles tend to emerge during this process phase: (1) distributive or positional negotiation, which makes use of competitive strategies, and (2) integrative or principled negotiation, which utilizes collaborative strategies to achieve mutually satisfying ends. Positional negotiation promotes one's own goals and outcomes without regard to the other party. Negotiators using this style concern themselves only with winning and personally achieving as much as possible from the interaction. This highly intense win-lose style of negotiation may contribute to destructive outcomes and losses in other arenas. It is best suited to isolated business situations in which ongoing relationships are irrelevant and future interactions unlikely.

Principled negotiation is grounded in a win-win attitude, meaning that negotiators seek goals and work toward mutual interests and solutions for all parties. It values others and focuses on joint interests in order to achieve joint gains. Trust and credibility are critical to principled negotiation (Kouzes & Posner, 1993; Thompson, 1998). As trust and credibility grow, negotiators reciprocally share more information and improve their joint agreement. The principled style of negotiation is best suited where long-term relationships are important.

The process stage of negotiation also involves applying selected strategies and tactics. Strategies are the overall "game plan," and tactics are the specific methods used during the negotiation process. Researchers have identified numerous strategies and tactics used in conflict negotiation and designed to gain compliance from the other party (Bazerman & Neale, 1992; Nierenberg, 1973; Pruitt, 1981). Reward-based strategies, punishment-based strategies, altruism-based strategies, and rationale-based strategies are combined with such compliance-gaining tactics as promises, threats, liking, self-feeling, and moral appeal to bluff, force, and intimidate or work toward mutual gains (Marwell & Schmitt, 1967; G. Miller, Bosster, Roloff, & Siebold, 1977; M. Williams & Cooper, 1992). Individualistic low-context cultures generally use fairness, rules, procedures, logical force, and argumentative appeals, whereas collectivistic high-context cultures more often employ precedent, status, relational appeals, and the moral imperative to achieve their goals (Brett, 2001). However, effective conflict negotiators proceed slowly, testing their assumptions about what strategies will be effective with the other party and demonstrate a willingness to adjust their strategies to achieve their goals.

Finally, the outcome phase concludes the complex set of events and communication behaviors composing the conflict negotiation process. Sometimes expectations will have been surpassed, whereas other times the results will fall short of predetermined goals. Negotiating in bad faith or lacking the authority to conclude the negotiations account for some of the reasons for breakdowns and failure (Rapoport, 1967). Winning or losing, the possibility for trade-offs and compromises, or agreeing to disagree frames this phase. The outcome phase largely determines whether future interactions will occur and whether relationships will endure.

In today's global environment, conflict negotiators who understand cultural differences and negotiation fundamentals have a decided advantage at bridging cultural boundaries and resolving intercultural disputes. The value of becoming a better global negotiator can be measured by the relationships preserved, the collective interests served, and the flexibility retained by managing conflict rather than becoming a captive of it.

Negotiating across cultures is never easy, and dispute resolution negotiations can break down despite our central premise that the involved parties should responsibly manage their own conflicts. At such times, third-party intervention by a mediator or arbitrator may be advisable because there is no culturally common or culturally neutral legal system to turn to in a global environment. Mediators work to help the parties themselves resolve the dispute through creative problem solving, whereas arbitrators evaluate the merits of each party's position and render a judgment (Littlejohn & Domenici, 2001; C. Moore, 1996; Yarborough & Wilmot, 1995).

Mediation is one of the oldest and most ubiquitous forms of conflict "reconciliation." As long as people have had disputes with each other, mediators have counseled the use of reason over arms and the benefits of compromise over lethal competition (Kolb, 1994). Mediation is generally understood as a process in which a neutral third party with no power to impose a resolution helps the disputing parties try to reach a mutually acceptable settlement through dialogue (Bush & Folger, 1994; Duffy, Grosch, & Olczak, 1991). The parties, having reached a stalemate or crisis, have voluntarily agreed to accept an impartial mediator who will assist them in reframing their conflict and working collaboratively toward a jointly constructive future. By facilitating the dialogue between the parties, the mediator works to break the attack/defend communication cycles that have created the stalemate and build trust and cooperation. Maintaining objectivity, the mediator encourages the parties to advance solutions and make reciprocally beneficial commitments. Mediation can replace the negative story of confusion with the positive story of empowerment and order; it can replace the negative story of "being stuck" with the positive story of "moving forward."

Arbitration is also a voluntary dispute resolution alternative that "conflict stalled" parties might choose. The arbitrator is a neutral, objective third-party who will resolve the conflict solely on the content presented by the immediate parties themselves. Unlike mediation, arbitration leads to a timely resolution by the arbitrator. Although the roles of mediation and arbitration are well established, only in the last 10 to 15 years have they become a formal complement to dispute resolution in a wide array of international settings and global arenas.

Summary

The 2005 Nobel Prize in economic sciences went to Robert Aumann at the Hebrew University of Jerusalem and Thomas C. Schelling at the University of Maryland for "having enhanced our understanding of conflict and cooperation through game-theory analysis" (Henderson, 2005, p. A16). The central tenet underlying all their theories is that we must put ourselves in the shoes of the person with whom we are interacting (Schelling, 1960). This is axiomatic to constructive intercultural conflict management and productive conflict negotiation.

Markets are becoming global at an astonishing rate as suppliers look for new outlets with less competition and buyers look for variety in quality and price. All this market activity inevitably produces disagreements that necessitate conflict negotiation across cultural boundaries. Cosmopolitan communicators and global leaders must have a repertoire of styles and strategies that permit them to navigate the treacherous waters of intercultural conflict management where direct confrontation is not always the norm and face-negotiation is imperative.

Those negotiating conflict outcomes can avoid potential pitfalls by understanding the conflict negotiation process and learning how culture affects the path to distributive outcomes and integrative agreements. The challenge to effectively negotiating across cultures is to understand negotiators' interests and exercising strategic flexibility. Culturally sensitive conflict negotiation skills are increasingly necessary if multinational organizations hope to avoid cultural misunderstandings that may sabotage even the simplest negotiation. Moreover, conflict-savvy communicators who understand the nature and substance of international mediation and arbitration will have a marked advantage in constructively coping with intercultural conflicts as they emerge in the global marketplace. Global leaders who are not intimidated by the mystery and potential peril of intercultural conflict will be able to capitalize on the synergistic opportunities afforded and reap personal and relational rewards.

Unit Three

Intercultural Communication and the New World of Business

Precision of communication is important, more important than ever, in our era of hair-trigger balances, when a false or misunderstood word may create as much disaster as a sudden thoughtless act.

—James Thurber

We [are] not just communicating to each other more than ever, we [are] now able to collaborate—to build coalitions, projects, and products together—more than ever.

—Joel Cawley

7

Cosmopolitan Leadership, Teams, and the Global Workforce

Globalization has increased workforce diversity in almost every industry around the world. More than ever, companies compete on the basis of how effectively they can integrate and synthesize the knowledge of their individual members, raising essential questions about ways to coordinate people of different backgrounds to promote organizational goals.

This chapter explores the necessary competencies and myriad of challenges facing a cosmopolitan leader or team member in complex global organizations. We address leadership strategies and competencies for managing projects and people and emphasize the important skills and knowledge required for an international environment. We define the various structural configurations that are emerging for global teams and discuss how they affect communication issues in the global workforce. We also look at some of the challenges embedded in the multicultural communication processes needed for problem-solving and decision-making. Finally, we examine some of the technologies designed to help virtual groups work more effectively.

Cosmopolitan Leadership and Leadership Competencies

As organizations become increasingly complex, leaders need to continually develop their personal and professional competencies. An effective cosmopolitan leader is one who can access the strengths of his or her employees while minimizing the weaknesses. Although this is true of any leader, the

123

cosmopolitan leader is often challenged with managing the complexities of a workforce rooted in various cultures. This is made even more difficult by the requirement of working through time, space, and technology.

LEADERSHIP CHALLENGES

Cosmopolitan leaders face challenges that are greater than those working with a homogeneous culture or those working locally. Most companies have found that the principal problems involve the failure to effectively manage their people issues (McDonough & Kahn, 1997). Challenges emerge from a variety of social contexts, such as the ambiguity that arises from differences manifested in stereotypes, the importance of face saving in various cultures, the use of nonverbal communication (including silence), and the disparate responses that result from the use of humor. These challenges must be addressed to thrive as a global leader.

One of the challenges is borne of the fact that managers develop their understanding of good leadership based on how it is defined in their native cultures. It is no surprise that they "often wield their power in conformity with the national set-up—for instance a confirmed democracy like Sweden produces low key democratic managers" (R. Lewis, 1999, p. 59). Still, problems often arise when the style of leadership encountered by subordinates does not match their expectations. Odenwald (1996) observes that "conflicting cultural values increase the risk of creating misunderstanding, lowering the morale of employees, and often alienating strategic global customers or business partners" (p. 65). Leaders and their employees are often puzzled by behaviors that are hard to interpret from their own paradigm (Brislin, 1993).

One's perspective of employee participation can also affect the working relationship. In many cultures, leaders are expected to be decisive without needing to check in with the team first, and leaders who ask for consensus may be seen as incompetent or weak. In other cultures, consensus and collaboration are the norm, and workers would expect to participate in decision-making or to have input on issues that affect their work and would negatively view leaders or micromanagers who did not consult them. Consequently, subordinates have differing expectations of leaders depending upon their cultural orientation (Brislin, 1993).

Another cross-cultural challenge for cosmopolitan leaders occurs when employees attribute meaning to the leaders' behavior or words based on their own perception of power distance. Responsibility taking and who initiates action are often impacted by one's sense of hierarchy and authority. Some workers may wait to be given explicit directions when the manager is expecting more assertive behavior. For individuals whose cultural values are in opposition to those used in their workplace, it is often one of the most difficult adjustments to make.

Often ambiguity arises from the continually changing demographics with which one has to operate. As one manager stated, "given the tri-cultural makeup of the county—I realized anyone could be offending $\frac{1}{3}$ of the population at any given point, resulting in a significant impact on attitude, communication, and productivity" (Dooley, 2003, p. 57). Jane Bloodworth (2005), Manager of General Services Printing, Graphics and Map Design, would agree. She has 38 nationalities and 18 languages reporting to her at the World Bank in Washington, DC. The cultures that report to her are also widely diverse (Nigerian, Philippine, Swiss, English, Barbados, United States, Japanese), which requires a skillful approach to leadership. Bloodworth noted in an interview that individual sensitivities manifest differently or more strongly in various cultures, yet she found that preconceptions about gender and age issues are the hardest to overcome. She also reflected on how she was more cautious and had to construct her messages more carefully to avoid offending some workers. With others she was able to be more informal and talk to them directly without needing to be overly concerned about cultural sensitivities. She summarized her experience by saying that "people are people . . . no matter what their cultural or national origin, they all bring their 'stuff' with them [and] it is often the 'stuff' that matters and needs to be handled carefully."

Cosmopolitan leadership or global management can often be more challenging for females, particularly if one is crossing traditional cultural barriers based on gender. One of the cultural differences defined by Hofstede (1980) is the degree of masculinity that is reinforced in a society. Those cultures with a high masculinity ranking typically experience a high degree of gender differentiation, such that males more frequently dominate positions of authority or power than females do. Therefore, female managers often find their authority and power tested by members of their workforce when the members are from a highly masculine orientation.

Bloodworth (2005) discussed her perception of those reporting to her from cultures with a highly masculine predominance. She noted that "the younger and more educated employees adjust most easily to adapting to having a woman leader, and perhaps this is based on their exposure to various others." As an illustration, she reflected on situations where male employees from highly masculine cultures tended to avoid taking instructions and feedback directly from her and preferred to hear from their own male supervisors. Additionally, when asking for compliance with required changes in the work, she found younger workers more adaptable and less resistant to the requests than older ones. She continued, "the bigger challenge is when you are in their country," and one is challenged by the norms of the larger community. Interestingly,

Baugh and Graen (1997) found that when gender and racial diversity in a team decreased, the team's perception of the team leader's competence decreased as well.

LEADERSHIP COMPETENCIES

Companies are recognizing the need to define the competencies of cosmopolitan leadership for global managers in order to improve recruitment and identify training needs. These competencies include strong personal characteristics, leadership skills, and cross-cultural knowledge. Leadership dimensions for the global manager involves understanding both the business itself and the global political scenarios in which the business is located. Researchers have identified several characteristics that constitute cross-cultural competence: interpersonal skills, communication skills, and interaction skills (Black & Gregersen, 1991; Earley & Mosakowski, 2000). Affective and behavioral skills such as empathy, charisma, and the ability to tolerate ambiguity and anxiety (Gudykunst, 1998; Spitzberg, 1991) have also been studied as critical components of cultural competence.

Learning how to assimilate the skills essential to cross-cultural competence follows a cyclical process of moving from ignorance to suspending judgment to adopting new behaviors based on greater understanding. Jo Lamb (2005), former Executive Development Manager at a major entertainment company, notes the importance of being able to "suspend and shift," to suspend one's initial reaction and think about the situation from multiple perspectives, and then shift one's response if appropriate. She considers suspending judgment to be a great first predictor of effective communication. It is important to reflect on your own experiences and build a learning framework around them.

Odenwald (1996) further calls attention to the sequence that teams must experience to progress through the initial phases of working across diverse backgrounds. First, all team members acknowledge their own cultures and perspectives. Second, they begin to understand the cultures of other team members. Finally, trust building ensues and members shift their focus to accomplishing team goals. Odenwald (1996) continues to describe several qualities of an effective cosmopolitan or global team member: (1) flexibility and adaptability, (2) strong interpersonal skills, (3) ability to think both globally and locally, (4) ability to work multiculturally, (5) linguistic skills, (6) listening skills, (7) strong commitment to product and corporate values, (8) initiative and enthusiasm, (9) ability to promote and/or achieve consensus, and (10) self-confidence. These same traits are equally important for cosmopolitan or global leaders and multicultural managers.

Rather than just learning to tolerate ambiguity, cosmopolitan leaders need to be able to manage it by being experts in learning through observation, reflection, and application. They also need skills to manage teams that work autonomously and communicate through technology (Barczak & McDonough, 2003; Maznevski & DiStefano, 2000; McDonough & Kahn, 1997). Moran and Riesenberger (1997) provide a comprehensive list of qualifications, stating that a cosmopolitan or global leader must (1) have a global mindset, (2) have a long-term orientation, (3) work as an equal with others from diverse backgrounds, (4) facilitate organizational change, (5) create internal learning systems, (6) negotiate and approach conflicts in a collaborative mode, (7) manage the for-eign development cycle skillfully, (8) accurately profile the organizational culture and national culture of others, (9) lead and participate effectively in multicul-tural teams, and (10) behave in a manner that demonstrates knowledge and respect for other countries.

PROFESSIONAL DEVELOPMENT STRATEGIES FOR BUILDING COSMOPOLITAN LEADERSHIP COMPETENCIES

Many organizations are beginning to focus on professional development and training for executives that specifically address these competencies. Alldredge and Nilan (2000) describe 3M's executive leadership and competency model and show how they delineate the transition in skills needed to move into the future. They list these as transitioning aptitudes: (1) from having the skills of "innovation" to "nurturing innovation"; (2) from understanding "how to grow the business" to understanding "how to assess business health and results"; (3) from "managing" systematic change to "integrating" change; (4) from effec-tively "analyzing" complex situations to "handling" multiple, complex, and paradoxical situations; and (5) from "giving feedback and reinforcement" to employees to "giving and seeking" open and authentic feedback (p. 138).

Being able to speak essential words and phrases in the language of the local workforce is critical, but knowing the language is even better. This skill lends credibility to the leader and also increases the trust and respect received from their employees. Hilton's (1992) work confirmed this concern and reported that Americans are often critical of non-English-speaking partici-pants in meetings and are impatient with mispronunciation and inadequate grammar, yet these same Americans are unwilling to learn the local language. Additionally, cosmopolitan or global leaders need to be sensitive to intercul-tural communication patterns and nonverbal cues for interaction.

Interestingly, some executives report that working overseas can create resentment and isolation upon their return (Lamb, 2005). Less than 2 percent of the U.S. managers surveyed rated the role of international experience as important for promotion or recruitment. Conversely, it was considered one of the top criteria by the European and Japanese managers in the same study (Tung & Miller, 1990). Tung and Miller (1990) assert "that if American corporations fail to integrate an international perspective into their human resources management policies and practices, their ability to compete successfully in the global marketplace will continue to be encumbered" (p. 13).

Cosmopolitan Leadership and Global Teams

Although cosmopolitan or global leaders are essential to the success of multinational organizations, teams do much of the decision-making in these companies. Therefore, one of the critical competencies of leadership is being able to lead a team. At the same time, it is estimated that over 30 million virtual teams are in existence (Scott, 2003), requiring new skills for leaders and team members. Today's cosmopolitan leaders must negotiate the complexities of multicultural, multinational teams located around the world whose primary communication is mediated via technology. This challenge includes managing cultural diversity, differences, and conflicts; handling geographic distances; dealing with coordination and control issues; maintaining communication richness over distances; and developing and maintaining a team identity among members.

GLOBAL TEAMS

Currently it is reported that more than 60 percent of professional employees work in virtual teams (Kelley, 2001). Barczak and McDonough (2003) cite several reasons to form global teams: (1) to address global market issues by identifying common product platforms, (2) to identify unique needs of local markets and offer customized products, (3) to create knowledge experts whose skills can be accessed from any country, and (4) to bring together dispersed resources.

Indeed, virtual teams are ubiquitous, yet the speed at which they are initiated often makes it difficult to understand the dynamics that emerge. Therefore, it is useful to define the various types of teams emerging in today's organizations. Lipnack and Stamps (1997) define a virtual team as "a group of people who work independently with shared purpose across space, time, and organizational boundaries using technology" (p. 18). Included in this definition are telecommuters who work from home offices and do most of their work via the computer, telephone, or fax. Others (Jarvenpaa & Leidner, 1999; Kristof et al., 1995) include cultural diversity and geographic dispersion in their definition of virtual teams, stating that virtual teams can be global, multicultural, local (across buildings), or any combination of these components. A global team specifically refers to groups of people who are working together across cultures and time zones for extended periods of time, and by nature of their geographic separation, they are also virtual teams (Lipnack & Stamps, 1997). According to this definition, a global team is multicultural, multinational, and virtual.

Stohl (2001) provides a matrix that further shows the different organizational structures for various teams. She includes the structure and management models evidenced in the five predominant team orientations: *domestic, multicultural, multinational, international,* and *global.* A domestic organization is hierarchical, using bureaucratic and matrix structures typically located in a central headquarters. The management model is monocultural, and cultural differences tend to be ignored or not recognized. A multicultural organization uses teamwork and is less hierarchical but also tends to have one centrally located headquarters. The management model typically has one culture that predominates, and differences are expected to be accommodated through assimilation with that dominant culture. The multinational organization is usually managed from a central location in essentially a hierarchical manner; however, national subsidiaries create miniature replicas of the core where teamwork is employed. It is centralized and globally scaled, and overseas operations implement parent company strategies. The management model recognizes cultural differences, and they are somewhat accepted, but the dominant culture is typically enacted in the task domain. The international organization uses a joint hierarchy in which international divisions integrate global activities and joint ventures. There is extensive teamwork with subsidiaries and some decentralized decision-making. The management model embraces cultural synergy, and members work together to try to build a third culture. Finally, the global organization incorporates decentralization of decision-making and sharing of responsibilities. The headquarters and subsidiaries see themselves as part of an organic worldwide entity with a strong global strategy and dominant global alliances. The management model promotes cultural integration that recognizes diverse cultures and business conditions. Cultural adaptation is experienced in the task realm, and cultural integrity is seen in the expressive realm.

At the most fluid end of the structural continuum, Weick and Van Orden (1990) propose that the global organization will exist without a central or specific location. Decision-making will be the result of "fields of activity and systems rather than a static hierarchical entity that continually redefine the task using ad hoc centers of authority located at critical but evolving locations" (p. 56). Lipnack and Stamps (1997) agree, proposing that traditional structures such as hierarchies are not complex enough to manage the multifaceted issues that emerge in a global workforce. They believe that "neither a hierarchical organization nor a hierarchy of concepts can handle a network of environmental problems ... without leaving many dangerous gaps through which unforeseen problems may emerge" (pp. 162–163). As information processing systems, organizations rely on the communication exchanges through formal and informal interactions. Over time these patterns often become rigidly institutionalized, thereby establishing and clarifying the team boundaries.

McCollom (1990) notes the clear lack of group boundaries for virtual teams as compared to those that characterize traditional teams (e.g., office location or reporting structures). These porous boundaries are often defined on the basis of the project status and organizational requirements. As a case in point, The Fusion Team at GE started with eight members chosen from research and development, computer design, and finance who were asked to develop a new software product in response to a unique market niche. Initially, several members were responsible for market analysis, but as a concrete product began to emerge, they dropped off the team and were replaced with a few software and hardware engineers. As the project approached beta testing, test engineers and customer service representatives joined the team, and those whose expertise was no longer needed dropped off the team. This continual reshaping of the team's membership illustrates how teams are essentially composed of patterns of relationships within a network.

Miles and Snow (1992) conclude that global networks are the ideal organizational form of the future and others propose that network structures offer better explanations of organizational behavior than formal organizational structures (Bacharach & Lawler, 1980; Krackhardt & Hanson, 1993). Across cultures, global organizations are expected to move from "centrally coordinated, multi-level hierarchies toward a variety of more flexible structures that loosely resemble networks rather than traditional pyramids" (Weick & Van Orden, 1990, p. 53). Networks are more flexible, allowing emergent communication structures and linkages easily supported by technology that many believe are needed in the complex and fluid organizations emerging today.

Still, hierarchies serve an important function in today's organizations. However, they often emerge in a unique fashion that combines the features of a matrix organization and those of adhocracy (Applegate, 1995). These hierarchical structures emerge naturally in organizations based on the need for order as organizations grow in size and complexity. Ahuja and Carley (1998) also studied the role of hierarchy in virtual teams and found that "virtual organizations may well be non-hierarchical and decentralized from an authority standpoint, however, from a communication standpoint they may still be hierarchical and somewhat centralized" (p. 20). They propose that managers should monitor and manage the communication structures just as carefully as they manage the formal reporting structures. They caution that "managers responsible for virtual project teams should not assume that non-hierarchical communication structures are necessarily more effective than hierarchical structures" (p. 23).

Thus, there are many strong business reasons for the emergence of global teams. Defining the variety of structures helps to identify critical aspects that describe the management models observed in each orientation. The team structure itself is often seen as a fluid composite of network links continually being shaped and defined by the formal and informal communication patterns established through the interaction of team members. Although hierarchies are somewhat diminished from an authoritarian perspective, they remain vigorous in that they define the communication network and influencing patterns. Managers need to monitor these communication patterns that characterize the team and affect productivity.

GLOBAL TEAM CHALLENGES

Eisenberg and Riley (2001) observe that "globalization is one of the drivers of growing workforce diversity in almost every industry, raising critical questions about ways to coordinate people of markedly different backgrounds to pro mote organizational and personal goals" (p. 315). All groups have some element of diversity, yet from a team perspective it becomes significant when it affects a group's performance. Maznevski (1994) identifies two different types of diversity: role-related and inherent (e.g., gender, nationality, cultural, personality). It is often these differences that allow a group to make decisions from a wider perspective. For example, if a company is marketing a product to women in France, having women and team members from France can assist the group in its advertising approach. Similarly, having team members from training, sales, and finance can help the group look holistically at various facets of the project and develop a comprehensive timeline for product release.

Although diversity in a team is valuable, the benefits of multiculturalism are not automatically positive or easily accomplished. In fact, more effort is usually required to establish the team's communication strategy and working relationships so that productivity is achieved. Parker (2003) perceptively observes that "the communication modes that make virtual group status possible are the same modes that make group interaction difficult" (p. 19).

Although several studies have shown that multicultural groups develop more and better alternatives to problems and offer more creativity than homogeneous groups (Ling, 1990; McLeod & Lobel, 1992), others report that the actual performance outcome of the groups was decreased (Kirchmeyer & Cohen, 1992; Kumar, Subramanian, & Nonis, 1991). Even the sense of

131

permanence affects the working relationship of team members. Walther (1994) found that communicating virtually as a team was perceived as more positive when team members believe the interaction would be extended over time. Maznevski (1994) concludes that the differentiating factor is the degree of integration of diversity itself. She states that "diversity led to higher performing groups only when members were able to understand each other, combine and build on each other's ideas" (p. 533).

Pothukuchi, Damanpour, Choi, Chen, and Park (2002) studied joint ventures and found that the outcome of cultural differences had both negative and positive results depending on whether the organizational members viewed national cultural differences as barriers or as opportunities. Keyton (2005) also observed that "if national cultural differences are perceived to be part of an international or multinational organizational culture and embraced positively, they can in turn create a challenging and stimulating work environment with organizational members developing an organizational culture to accommodate and bridge national cultural differences" (p. 117). In a similar study, Hobman, Bordia, and Gallois (2004) reported that "there was a negative relationship between dissimilarity and work group involvement when individuals perceived low group openness to diversity, whereas there was no relationship when individuals perceived high group openness to diversity" (p. 560). In their study of managers with an average of eight years of international experience, Hurn and Jenkins (2000) indicated that the managers' primary frustrations were (1) approaches to time which related to punctuality and keeping appointments and schedules, (2) decision-making—specifically knowing when a decision had been reached by the team, (3) managing the tension between the need to build personal relationships and the need for immediate action, (4) problems created by nonverbal communication (i.e., posture, gestures, and eye contact), (5) idiomatic phrases (i.e., "let's hook up so you can teach me because I'm new and pretty green"), (6) business practices for conducting meetings (e.g., unstructured versus structured or open versus closed), and (7) challenges with giving and receiving feedback. They also identified the following items as a "cultural minefield" for team members working across cultures: (1) greetings, (2) degree of politeness, (3) showing agreement or disagreement, (4) use of "small talk," (5) use of interpreters, (6) punctuality, (7) leave-taking, (8) gift giving, (9) status of women, and (10) body language.

Even the use of humor or teasing can be difficult to interpret when one is a member of a cross-cultural team. Dr. Jamie Murphy (2005), Business Professor at the University of Perth, Australia, recalled during an interview the challenges of understanding the role of teasing among coworkers that he encountered as an American working in an Australian culture. After several months of teasing, he asked a teammate to explain why people were frequently making sarcastic comments or continually using put-downs with colleagues. He was told that "we tease you to show you we accept you and like you, mate." However, without the cultural understanding, others might easily take offense or withdraw from communicating when the repartee is interpreted as negative or disrespectful.

Time issues often create challenges for global teams, including perceptions about past, present, and future scheduling of work projects and crossing time zones. For example, in the United States we try to do jobs faster, whereas the Japanese and Germans are more concerned with the overall synchronization of separate tasks. We analyze before we integrate, whereas Germans tend to integrate before they analyze and generally consider that part of the whole context. Even silence may cause misunderstandings. In one study conducted in Finland, Americans were offended at the gaps in conversation and the long periods of silence and mistook these as negative negotiation strategies. The Finns, however, have a high tolerance for silence and they were comfortable and considered this normal behavior (Hampden-Turner & Trompenaars, 2002).

Team coordination, specifically for synchronous meetings, can become a critical point of tension. For many global teams, the time that is scheduled for the meeting may privilege some members and disadvantage others. Carol Ellis (2005), a senior advisor for ExxonMobil, reflected during an interview that "for us in the United States it was 7:00 a.m. and in Singapore it was 7:00 p.m. It seemed that it was easier for Europeans . . . because they always got to work a 'normal' day." Time differences can not only disrupt family life but also often mean having less access to office resources needed to contribute to the dialogue or decisions being made.

Language skills also tend to favor some team members over others. Although teams may agree on a certain working language, those who are not as fluent in that language are disadvantaged (Bantz, 1993). Stohl (2001) pointedly states that "language not only directs what we say, but influences how we shape and frame experience, mediates the meanings we assign to action, helps define members of in- and out-groups, and confers status distinctions" (p. 354). It appears that the more linguistically skillful and articulate one is, "the greater the opportunity for the acquisition of resources, capital, information, and expertise" (p. 325).

Another issue that may create an advantage for some members and may potentially cause conflict is the choice of technology or software used for working together. Keyton (2005) has observed that "technology structures the work of organizations and, as a result, influences organizational culture, work activities, organizational members' work roles, and their work relationships" (p. 121). Consider the consequences when the leader wants every project to be monitored through a specific project management tool, yet some team members may not own or know how to use the program. Or, when individual members of the team have software skills to create more professional looking presentations—even if the content is the same—it may give an advantage in the decision-making process.

For most teams, e-mail is the primary communication medium, and members exchange messages asynchronously. When working asynchronously, interaction patterns change as one is not required to take turns and ideas are often shared without interruption. Ideas can be documented for retrieval, and the text is constructed with opportunities for revision and reflection. On the negative side, conversations may be discontinuous or disjointed, and it takes extra effort to reconstruct the threads of various comments to make them cohesive. Although time, language, and technology can make it challenging for global teams, many organizations are using strategies to offset these issues.

GLOBAL TEAM STRATEGIES FOR INCREASING EFFECTIVENESS

Learning to work together as a global team requires significant effort and should be included as part of the organizational strategy. While learning how to coordinate their interdependency to produce a product or service, team members also need to create a common level of understanding the cultural perspectives of other members of the team. Global communication "requires the ability to translate the cultural meaning behind the words and to anticipate the impact of spoken or written words" (Odenwald, 1996, p. 55) such that the collective outcomes are realized. Matveev and Nelson (2004) maintain that cross-cultural communication competence improves team performance by 20 percent.

Meeting in person is helpful to establish ground rules and begin to build relationships between team members. These sessions provide members with a personal connection to other team members and often serve as the reference point when potential conflict arises. Patterns that are established early in a group's life are often those that last throughout the team's lifecycle (Gersick, 1988; Jarvenpaa & Leidner, 1998). Once members have spent time together they are more likely to engage in dual perspective and ask for clarification instead of making assumptions. Some basic items should be addressed in the initial meetings, such as the team's goal(s) and agreement on team protocols. It is also essential for virtual teams to agree on the frequency of their meetings and expectations for each member's participation.

To address the issues with time, Oldenwald (1996) suggests developing a "team time culture" (p. 84). Montoya-Weiss, Massey, and Song (2001) state that having a pre-established communication plan can also help "address the

communication challenges facing virtual teams as it introduces temporal coordination mechanisms" (p. 1259). They also discovered that a rhythm of coordination mechanisms, such as a regularly scheduled team meeting, created
a structure that "mitigated the negative effects of avoidance and compromise"
(p. 1259).

Hurn and Jenkins (2000) cited one successful training program in which
the members of multicultural teams assembled and attended training classes
together to address issues and develop action plans for working together more
effectively. The group established concrete guidelines and had clear agreed-on
agendas going forward. They established a policy to use a skillful chairperson
to facilitate future meetings, frequently provide summaries of key points, and
use questions more effectively to elicit feedback from each other during the
meetings.

Working in a global team requires even more clarity about team protocols
for communicating. For groups to work together successfully, they must
negotiate their roles, norms, and behavior, as well as convey their various
approaches to information processing. To illustrate, one virtual team defined
what it meant to them when other members of the team did not respond to
their questions posted by e-mail. They agreed if a team member sent a question and did not receive a response within 24 hours, one should assume the
message was never received and the sender should re-send or use the telephone
depending on the urgency of the question. Another protocol they created was
to establish a priority code for their e-mail subject headings and voice mail
messages. They agreed that a "code 1" meant "this is a 'showstopper' . . . I can't
move forward until you respond"; "code 2" meant "this is the action I will take
unless I hear from you within 24 hours"; "code 3" indicated "this information
is For Your Information (FYI) only and does not require a response." In this
way, they were able to help each other organize their communication
exchanges and work more efficiently.

Maznevski and DiStefano (2000) describe three group processes for working with multiple cultures on a team: *mapping, bridging,* and *integrating.* They
define *mapping* as having an understanding of the team's "compositional differences and the corresponding implications for bringing to the team different
knowledge perspectives and approaches to relationship management" (p. 197).
Mapping requires suspending the assumption of similarity—believing that
"others think like I do." Useful maps create cognitive frameworks for understanding the preferences of others by providing a way to look at patterns
(e.g., Myers-Briggs Type Indicator or Hofstede's dimensions). However, caution must be taken to avoid the tendency of using quick labels and thereby
bypassing the need for deeper understanding. *Bridging* is the process of communicating across those differences to ensure that each member understands

the others. Bridging involves recentering, where team members find common perspectives and explore them to identify important definitions and goals. In this way, teams manage their norms so that everyone is involved and has an equal opportunity to be heard. *Integrating* is bringing the different perspectives and preferences together, resolving any differences among them, and building on these differences to generate innovation and quality in the team's work. The skills include managing participation, resolving disagreements, and constructively building new processes for the future.

Although the challenges are ever present, team members need to find a unifying goal that they have in common, focus on the issues rather than the personalities, and find ways to include everyone's perspective. Surfacing disagreements and articulating protocols builds the team so they can solve problems more effectively. Ultimately, work group performance and the individual members' attachment to the group itself are related (Kirchmeyer & Cohen, 1992). The success of a global team depends on the ability to create a shared team identity, to develop mutual respect and trust among team members, and to build supportive and collaborative personal relationships between team members. Goto's (1997) work reinforces this, affirming that "knowledge of the other culture [alone] is not effective. Rather [the] focus [should] be on encouraging perceptions of similarity, and opportunity for positive interactions" (p. 109). This foundation creates the culture of the team that emerges from the interaction of the individual members at work and communication exchanges between individuals themselves, not just between their respective cultures.

Decision-Making, Problem-Solving, and Global Teams

Effective decision-making often gives companies the competitive edge, especially when the playing field requires innovation and rapid solutions. Yet, working in a global environment creates new and complex challenges as members reach across cultures to solve problems through mediated technology. The research on the effectiveness of global teams is inconclusive and leads one to speculate about the best course of action.

DECISION-MAKING AND PROBLEM-SOLVING

Researchers have reported mixed and often conflicting results regarding the effects of working virtually on the quality of a team's decision-making. For instance, several scholars report that there is no difference in decision quality between teams who work virtually and those who work in person (Cappel & Windsor, 2000; Hiltz, Johnson, & Turoff, 1986; Straus & McGrath, 1994).

136

Others maintain that face-to-face teams outperform virtual ones (Andres, 2002; McDonough, Kahn, & Barczak, 2001), and some assert that virtual teams make better decisions than those working face-to-face (Hollingshead, 1996; Jarvenpaa & Leidner, 1998; Schmidt, Montoya-Weiss, & Massey, 2001). Some hypothesize that increased time and repeated exposure to team members enhances decision-making such that a virtual team may improve its ability to make decisions over time.

The same inconclusiveness is found in the literature about the performance outcomes of multicultural groups. Although previous research has shown that increased diversity on teams increases the innovation (Ancona & Caldwell, 1992; Cady & Valentine, 1999; W. Watson, Kuman, & Michaelson, 1993), Kirkman, Tesluk, and Rosen (2004) found that "team race heterogeneity was negatively related to team empowerment and to multiple indicators of team effectiveness" (p. 357). Further, they noted that "team members on more racially diverse teams reported experiencing less team empowerment than did team members on more racially homogeneous teams" (p. 358). At the same time, researchers found that empowerment was of greater importance for process improvement in teams that worked virtually (Kirkman, Rosen, Tesluk, & Gibson, 2004). Results like these are confusing for leaders and global teams, yet it is clear that there is a strong connection between message flow, participation, and quality of decision-making.

There is one point that most scholars and practitioners do agree on—communication, integration, and clarification are the keys to ensuring group performance. For groups to work together to make good decisions and solve problems, certain conditions must exist at both the individual and group level. It is critical that each member has (1) a clear understanding of his or her contribution to the task, (2) an ability to take the other's perspective long enough to consider input, (3) motivation to communicate and work together rather than independently, and (4) the ability to establish and maintain a sense of trust.

Crookes and Thomas (1998) compared Chinese managers and contrasted local managers with expatriates (who were more typically Western) to study how culture might correspond with approaches to problem-solving. Using adaptation-innovation theory (Kirton, 1987), they discovered a correlation between cultural stereotypes and preferences for either an adaptation style or innovation style. Adaptors tended to develop their ideas on the basis of preexisting definitions of the problem and tended to work within established guidelines and rules. They approached decision-making by "refining existing solutions to problems" (Crookes & Thomas, 1998, p. 587). Innovators tended to "reconstruct the problem separating it from the accepted definitions and frameworks, generated many ideas, and developed unusual solutions" (p. 587). They approached decision-making from the perspective of working outside traditional rules and constraints. Each approach carries its own level of risk. For the adaptor, however, risk is initially much lower because ideas are based on previously established precepts. Conversely, the "ideas of the innovator can be more strongly resisted and their originator treated with caution" (Crookes & Thomas, 1998, p. 588). It appears that both cultural value orientation and organizational culture influence one's predisposition to problem-solving. Large bureaucratic organizations may discourage risk-taking and encourage the adaptor style similar to those countries that value high power distance. This can affect how members themselves approach decision-making.

The effectiveness of decision-making in global teams is a factor of the decision process selected, the media used, and the complexity of the problem itself (E. Kelley, 2001). In effective teams, as task interdependence increased, so did interaction frequency; and as task complexity increased, so did message complexity, as the most effective teams selected richer media to match. For example, as the number of borders (cultural, professional, company, country) spanned within the group increased, they often used audio conference calls instead of e-mail and the "successful [team] focused specifically on building relationships to increase trust and develop shared views across these borders, while the ineffective team did not" (p. 132). The "effective teams exhibited a strong, repeating temporal pattern to their interaction incidents" that Kelley (2001) referred to as "a heartbeat rhythmically pumping new life into the team's processes" (p. 135) providing stability to the team.

Establishing a communication pattern in the early phase of a team's development is important for helping groups make decisions and solve problems. Social cognition theory (Bandura, 1986) reinforces the importance of strong communication patterns and suggests that empowerment is a socially constructed phenomenon requiring extensive communication, trust, and confidence in the skills of other team members. Roberto (2004) found that "groups attained greater efficiency and consensus if they made a series of small but critical choices during the process, rather than focusing entirely on the final selection of a course of action" (p. 639). He used the metaphor of "pruning a tree" in that successful groups systematically "pruned" member ideas, thoughts, and views, whereas the less effective teams tried to simultaneously analyze all views, which often proved to be cognitively overwhelming. "Pruning" makes the task more manageable and makes the evaluation process more transparent, enhancing members' perception of fairness in the process while gradually building momentum that is more sustainable.

Teams often experience the tension of finding the balance between efficiency in decision-making and the need to build consensus for smooth implementation. Previous research suggests that attempts to enhance efficiency inhibit the development of understanding and commitment (Roberto, 2004), so leaders must find ways to seek the balance between these seemingly oppo-site polarities. The process of working globally is still in its infancy, and research conducted only a few years ago may need to be confirmed or updated to include recent technologies and team members who have greater exposure to technology and working globally with multiple cultures.

TRUST AND TEAM PROBLEM-SOLVING

Trust has been identified as an essential ingredient by several scholars studying virtual teams (Grabowski & Roberts, 1998; Lipnack & Stamps, 1997; Jarvenpaa & Leidner, 1998). For many, trust implies an expectation that someone will do what they say they will do and that they are capable of doing it; however, trust is often undermined by a lack of clarity about purpose and goals or by a lack of understanding of individual roles and responsibilities. Social categorizing theory (Moreland, 1985) posits that people tend to sort one another into categories based on demographics and may attribute greater trust and confidence in other team members who are perceived to be more similar. Kirkman et al. (2004) state that "those who are recognizably different in terms of demographics may be more affected by in-group and out-group biases than those who are more similar" (p. 359). There are, however, certain communication behaviors that either encourage or discourage the building of trust.

Jarvenpaa and Leidner (1998) organized over 350 graduate students from different countries into virtual teams to study how trust was developed and maintained. They found that although all groups revealed sources of vulnerability, uncertainty, and expectations, how they responded to these challenges had a significant relationship to their final outcome. Specifically, they found that certain communication behaviors facilitated trust early in the team's lifecycle and other behaviors facilitated trust after the initial start-up phase. Communication behaviors that facilitated trust in the early stages of the team included the following:

- Developing a system for coping with technical and task uncertainty
- Individuals taking the initiative to make suggestions and respond
- Predictable and timely communication with a regular pattern for exchanges

Communication behaviors that facilitated trust after the initial start-up included the following:

- Leadership based on proven expertise and revealing a positive tone.
- Successful transitions from social to task focus with consistent expectations.

- Team members genuinely solicited input from others and did not judge responses.

Although trust is important to group cohesion and effective problem-solving, an individual's cultural values and cognitions affect their interactions. Trust, decision-making, and problem-solving occur "within intricately interwoven cultural tapestries that transcend individuals" (Stohl, 2001, p. 344). All studies concur that trust is essential to making good decisions and solving problems.

The Global Workforce and Technology

Since the use of the personal computer has become commonplace, there has been an increase in the use of mediated decision support software, and many teams are exploring the use of group decision support systems (GDSSs) and groupware. Groupware is defined by Bidgoli (1996) as "software systems that support a group of decision makers engaged in a common decision-making task by providing access to the same shared environment and information" (p. 59). He describes several levels of support—from software that automates file sharing allowing anonymous input for brainstorming, automatic summaries, and agenda, to advanced systems that structure input into PERT and Gantt charts or automatically suggests appropriate tools such as Delphi techniques or critical path analysis. Some groupware also includes electronic meeting systems that may use real-time computer conferencing, video conferencing, and/or desktop conferencing.

It's important to stress that teams with access to technology do not automatically become better groups. Technology does not guarantee team success. As wonderful as GDSSs might appear, it is obvious that their effective implementation is dependent on the training, protocols, and personal preferences of the members of the work group. As with any software tool, they have their advantages and disadvantages. Advantages may include (1) greater satisfaction with meeting outcomes thereby improving morale, (2) documentation in both electronic and hard copy format to serve as a team archives, and (3) enhanced collaboration. Disadvantages would include (1) it may be difficult to reward individuals for outstanding input, (2) those who traditionally have power may lose some influence as input is more democratic and difficult to dominate, and (3) it is harder to implement in an organization because of costs and potential training required. Ultimately, any system is only as useful as the members themselves determine it to be. It is easy to see how GDSSs have the potential to advantage those who are more technically competent and those whose cultural values are reinforced by working in an environment that reduces the need for the social and/or relationship aspects of collaboration.

The global workforce is constantly redefining itself, and there is an ongoing need to discover ways to maximize the performance of all employees. Previous research has shown that increased diversity on teams increases creativity and innovation (Ancona & Caldwell, 1992; Cady & Valentine, 1999; W. Watson et al., 1993), and today's global competition often rests on ingenuity and inventiveness.

Summary

This chapter has examined the competencies, challenges, and strategies for the cosmopolitan leader. The job of managing a global workforce has become more complex and difficult, as leaders must address a myriad of cross-cultural and technological issues. Teams are increasingly working autonomously, requiring more integration and clarification of their communication strategies. Although new technology holds promise for supporting their work, it may also disadvantage members of the workgroup and thereby offset some of the gains of the global team. Proactively anticipating the challenges of multicultural work teams and thoughtfully addressing the technological challenges are vitally important. Cosmopolitan leaders who do this effectively will be those who have positioned their global teams for great achievement.

8

Disturbing the Equilibrium and Creating Planned Change

Globalization and the accompanying organizational changes have increased the complexity of today's organizations. Peter Drucker (1994) affirms that no other century in recorded history has seen as many social or radical changes as the twentieth. Over the past three decades alone companies have responded to such profound changes as increased physical and technological mobility, environmentalism, civil rights, women's rights, personal computers, the Internet, and a wired world. Workplace changes are equally significant, including increased participatory management and team-based structures, inventory reduction, and customization. Finally, the marketplace itself has changed, with increased competition, more business-to-business approaches, and e-commerce.

Multinational organizations are reacting to this profound change, as are "tribes in Third World economies who must cope with rapid modernization, while former communists of the Second World countries must quickly abandon centralized planning to learn the intricacies of free market economies and entrepreneurship" (Harris & Moran, 1991, p. 81). However, individuals and organizations often miss important changes and their potential impact, as J. Barker (1992) illustrates with some famous business examples:

"The phonograph . . . is not of any commercial value."

(Thomas Edison, 1880)

"I think there is a world market for about five computers."

(Thomas Watson, chairman of IBM, 1943)

"There is no reason for any individual to have a computer in their home."

(Ken Olson, President of
Digital Equipment Corporation, 1977, p. 24)

Historically, the documented approach for change has been strikingly Anglo Saxon in its philosophy, perhaps because Western cultural values assume that change (and nature in general) can be managed. Several theories of change can assist in the planning stages, but international companies need to also consider the impact of change from a multicultural workforce perspective. All cultures convey mental constructs that provide "anchors" for how people create meaning and make sense of the information around them. Because various cultures hold different worldviews regarding change, the cosmopolitan leader needs to recognize and respond to these nuances when implementing new strategies in response to organizational needs.

This chapter explores how intercultural issues intensify the challenges of implementing change in global organizations. We examine the nature of chaos, change, and innovation and discuss why these are inherently a part of doing business. We further explore various models that can serve as a general framework for change and offer strategies for innovation and change. We also provide information on how to most effectively present and communicate organizational change using several case studies that illustrate both successes and challenges when implementing change in a multicultural workforce. Finally, we present a perspective on taking the long view that encourages cosmopolitan leaders to look into the future and to reflect before acting upon their culturally ingrained instincts. Planned change and innovation is a timely topic requiring continued research as we face uncharted territory on a worldwide scale.

Chaos, Change, and Innovation

Change is the adopting of something different; innovation is the adoption of something new (Daft & Becker, 1978; Naisbitt & Aburdene, 1985; Nora, Rogers, & Stramy, 1986). Trompenaars and Woolliams (2003) define change as the "changes in shared assumptions, values, and practices of organizational actors as they are stimulated by changes in the environment" (p. 362). Chaos, which is often considered a condition of great disorder or confusion, may actually be the starting point for breakthrough change and innovation. Several scholars (Pascale et al., 2000; Schwartz, 1991; Wheatley, 1999) reflect on the importance of embracing chaos as a way to move to higher levels of functioning and thinking about change. Leaders of international businesses are faced with the challenges of managing constant change in an environment where multiple cultural perspectives affect the communication and acceptance of change itself. A shift in thinking from destructive approaches to more thoughtful systems perspectives allows cosmopolitan leaders to incorporate the best of the past into a more cohesive future.

Although changes may be disruptive, from a systems perspective the absence of change is often a precursor to stagnation. The more complex a given system is, the faster its rate of change, and a system facing increasing complexity will either evolve toward a more connected and integrated form or drift into an increasingly fragmented state. Organizations, when viewed as systems, move over time into higher and more productive states or devolve into lower, less organized, and less effective states (Fabum, 1971; Wheatley, 1999). Change allows companies to avoid entropy, the decay that occurs when a system is closed off from its environment and therefore deteriorates. Pascale et al. (2000) state that healthy, complex systems such as multinational organizations need to continually "oscillate to the edges of their boundaries to maintain and grow" (p. 3). The moral directive for postmodern businesses and organizations is, "Learn how to change effectively or die."

Schwartz (1991) observes that "living systems provide a strong model for creating a mental framework for seeing order in the disorder" (p. 21). When one considers chaos a natural part of the change process it can more easily be accepted. However, Pascale et al. (2000) make an important distinction when they note that "the world is not chaotic—it is complex. Chaos is that unlikely occurrence in which patterns cannot be found or interrelationships understood" (p. 6). Complex multinational organizations have many patterns and must be cautiously managed and directed. The skillful global leader must see these patterns early so that intelligent responses can be constructed and true chaos avoided. Jack Welch, former Chairman and CEO of General Electric, illustrates this point when he says that "we can't predict the future, but we can learn to react a lot faster than our adversaries . . . each of GE's initiatives shares a pattern: amplify survival threats and foster disequilibrium to evoke fresh ideas and innovative responses (Schwartz, 1991, p. 28).

Organizations often need both revolution and evolution. Systems thinking, where one views change as a process rather than an event, works best for nonroutine challenges where discontinuous change is the norm. Because work itself has become less sequential, planning needs to incorporate new models of thinking that are inclusive of multiple perspectives and nonlinear cycles of production. This is a shift in how change is conceived, and Pascale et al. (2000)

contend that many organizations fail at change attempts because they are based on the "premise of predictable change" (p. 13). What is required is a revolutionary new way of perceiving change.

Rather than destroying the past to change the future, Ogbor and Williams (2003) introduce the term "creative synthesis," which refers to "a situation where the deliberate retention of important elements of cultural traditions may be serviceable in promoting change and modernization of an organizational system" especially when those characteristics "derive much from the traditional culture in which it is located" (p. 19). On the basis of their study, they found that innovative organizations call on traditional values and new values based on the context and the recognition of the desired outcomes for each behavior. The successful change agent seeks to integrate seemingly opposing values rather than change the essential qualities of either one. Thus, although chaos creates disequilibrium, it is often the seed that helps organizations grow and evolve. Global organizations and their cosmopolitan leaders need to watch the trends and anticipate the future knowing that the greatest potential lies in seeing ahead and responding now.

Strategies for Innovation and Change: Theoretical Frameworks

Theoretical frameworks provide us with mental models that can be useful for planning and implementing change. All change models begin by defining both the current reality and the ideal future state of the organization. This allows change agents to conduct a "gap analysis" and determine what is needed to move from the one to the other (see Figure 8.1).

Stakeholders initially articulate an honest assessment of their current state and then describe the ideal future with as much detail as possible. Trompenaars

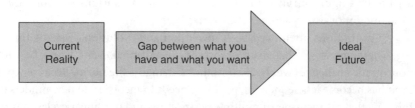

Figure 8.1   Gap Analysis

and Woolliams (2003) note that "the change process is energized by the tension between the two . . . it is not simply the replacement of the existing with the desired" (p. 362).

To illustrate, Asea Brown Bovari (ABB), a multinational company, wanted to incorporate a more team-based approach to improving quality in their manufacturing plant in Florence, South Carolina. A change integration team was established to help lead the effort and was made up of multiple reporting structures within the hierarchy, each representing a different department. They started by asking all the frontline employees to work together to create lists of words that described how they saw their current work environment. These lists were then compared to the senior management team's list. Surprisingly, both lists were very similar and included items such as poor quality, no teamwork, limited trust, no clear objectives, poor training, disorganized, and low morale. The frontline employees and senior managers then separately created lists of their ideal future. Again both lists were similar as they used such words as high trust, teamwork, excellent quality, outstanding customer service, continual learning, and innovation. These lists helped them to envision a collective image of the future. The final and most daunting step was to develop and implement a plan to move from the current reality to the ideal future. This process helped bring to the surface important and unspoken information that aligned the workforce and mobilized them to work together toward making the necessary changes.

LEWIN'S CHANGE MODEL

Kurt Lewin (1952) was one of the first to capture the essence of the change process, and most traditional ways of thinking about change are rooted in his work. He described the process of change as consisting of three stages: (1) unfreezing or creating the motivation to change, (2) changing or developing new responses based on new information, and (3) refreezing or stabilizing and incorporating the changes. According to this way of looking at change, if it is to occur it must be preceded by an alteration of the present stable equilibrium that supports the organizational system. Once that equilibrium has been upset, the system will seek out, process, and use information to achieve new perceptions, attitudes, and behaviors. Last, the adopted changes must be integrated and stabilized if they are to endure. In other words, the organization gets ready for change, implements the change, and then returns to stability as soon as possible.

Lewin's (1952) work on force field analysis further broadened this perspective about change by identifying driving forces (those that move toward a change) and restraining forces (those that inhibit change). Even though these forces imply an adversarial relationship, the value in force field analysis lies in the ability to surface resistance and to embrace it as part of the whole, recognizing the importance of looking at multiple perspectives. Suppressing or removing barriers without acknowledging their existence often increases resistance, resulting in greater entrenchment as individuals take sides on the various controversial issues.

Lewin's model provides a way to strategically address the forces of change and treats change as a manageable event. However, it is designed for more predictable business processes such as manufacturing rather than today's more "uncertain organizational environmental conditions" (Orlikowski & Hofman, 1997, p. 3). Therefore, such a model may be less appropriate for rapid, large-scale change. Still, there seems to be general agreement that the essential assumptions underlying the change sequence are that problems are perceived and such perceptions lead to search activity that results in a choice for or against change (Huse, 1975; Kanter, 1983; Nadler & Tushman, 1989). There is also agreement that rapidly changing environments require that organizations change for continued growth and development (Cleveland, Neuroth, & Plastrik, 1996; Foster, 1986; Meyer & Goes, 1989; Waldrop, 1992).

SOCIAL-TECHNICAL-ADMINISTRATIVE SYSTEMS INTEGRATION MODEL

Large-scale organizational change requires a shift in how the company does business. Often when changes are introduced, people focus on the micro level of change, such as buying new computers or software, rather than the impact of change at multiple levels of the organization. The social-technical-administrative (STA) model ensures that all pertinent organizational systems are included and prepared to support change and ensure an easy, secure transition. For example, in the 1990s the printing department of the American Automobile Association (AAA) experienced a dramatic change with the introduction of new technology. For years, AAA's mapmakers were hired on the basis of their background as artists and historians. They literally drew the maps by hand and updated them daily by sketching changes to show road and traffic patterns. Their work brought a sense of pride, and they were respected for their knowledge and educational levels. They were also rewarded through higher salaries and often a sense of security because these positions were difficult to fill. However, new computer software made these skills obsolete. The technical skills shifted from educated artisans to computer technicians, and the previously high salaries paid to artists with college degrees were no longer needed, as graphic artists were less expensive. The most senior people were those individuals whose skills were now becoming archaic, and as the sense of job security plummeted so did morale. To respond organizationally, AAA had to establish training programs, develop new compensation and benefit policies, and address employee morale issues.

Implementing organizational change can be difficult because it implies a new way of doing things. As the AAA example demonstrates, profound changes can put seemingly secure individuals at risk once the rules have changed (J. Barker, 1992). Consequently, all must be involved and committed to change, and change efforts must be well integrated throughout the organization.

FORMULA FOR CHANGE

The formula for change permits us to see four essential components of change that need to be simultaneously addressed. Beckhard and Harris (1977) are most frequently credited with the original "formula for change," which has been enhanced by others (Dannemiller & Jacobs, 1992) to read: $D \times V \times A \times F > R = C$. *Dissatisfaction* with the current reality multiplied by a *Vision* of the ideal future that is clear and compelling multiplied by concrete *Action* and first steps multiplied by *Follow-up* and follow-through must be greater than *Resistance* in order to produce successful *Change*. If change is to occur, the first four factors must be addressed concurrently, and their joint effect must be greater than the refusal to accept change or challenges to change within the organization. Because of the interdependence of these factors as represented by the multiplication element, if any component is equal to zero, such as a lack of vision or action, then the resulting change will be zero as well.

There are additional complications that can occur if the four factors composing the formula are not managed correctly during the change process. For example, if dissatisfaction with the current organizational state has not adequately surfaced, the organization will experience formal but superficial change with strong, hidden resistance. If the vision is not shared and clearly communicated to all stakeholders, people will easily lose sight of the goal. If concrete first steps are not taken toward active change, efforts become confused and dispersed. If there is no follow-up, such as targeted evaluation used as feedback for corrective action, then there is a loss of momentum and the organization reverts back to the status quo.

The formula for change suggests that an important measure to take is to identify the amount of dissatisfaction within the current state of affairs. There is a strong urge in most organizations to succinctly deal with dissatisfaction. As a result, change efforts rest on the energy created through discussion of hypothetical positive outcomes alone and the desire to alleviate the strongly felt dissatisfaction. This alone will not sustain long-term change because problems frequently emerge during the tactical, day-to-day phases of follow-up and follow-through. Stakeholders and decision-makers must be engaged and committed or change efforts are at risk of losing resources and failing. Unless a clear process is established at the beginning to determine how decisions become policy, and a strategy is in place for how to use the feedback, the results are often less than positive.

DELIBERATE, EMERGENT, AND IMPROVISATIONAL CHANGE

Contemporary scholars generally agree that planning and implementing change are more effective when considered as an ongoing effort to respond to the fluid and ever changing environments in which organizations function (MacGrath & MacMillan, 1995; Mintzberg, 1994). Change can be divided into various types. Mintzberg (1987) distinguishes between *deliberate* (those planned in advance) and *emergent* (those spontaneously arising from local innovation) change strategies. Deliberate change works best when it is well planned and well timed and when change is more orderly, focused, and carefully sequenced. The disadvantage of this type of change can be that input from those on the frontline is lacking and buy-in may be hard to obtain. Emergent change often results from issues that surface that were not anticipated in advance. These are purposefully introduced during the change process because of a need that rises to enhance the original plan. Frequently these suggestions come from the frontline workers without formal supervision and often create engagement and involvement. The disadvantages of emergent change are that it lacks context and is not embedded in the organization's planning and official support structures of budget and resources.

Orlikowski and Hofman (1997) do not see change in organizations as a predefined program but value the addition of an improvisational component to the change model, noting that "using such a model to manage change requires a set of processes and mechanisms to recognize the different types of change as they occur and to respond effectively to them" (p. 4). They recognize change's evolutionary nature and unpredictability. Being flexible and creatively adaptive is particularly important when managing technological change because new applications can evolve out of practical experience.

For example, Rubbermaid teaches its people to let ideas flow out of so-called core competencies. Bud Hellman, who used to run a Rubbermaid subsidiary, was touring one of the company's picnic cooler plants in the late 1980s when he realized he could use its plastic blow-molding technique to make a durable, lightweight, and inexpensive line of office furniture. The result was the WorkManager

System that now accounts for 60 percent of Rubbermaid's furniture division sales. Charles Hassel observes that "if top management hadn't encouraged us to look at processes and technologies elsewhere in the company, none of this would have ever happened" (Dumaine, 1991, p. 59). Today, Rubbermaid also makes small and medium-sized storage sheds that are easy to assemble and suitable to a variety of terrain. Constructive change may be deliberate, emergent, or improvisational depending on the situation and business needs.

In the late 1980s, many U.S. companies were complacent about change, and organizational strategists were frequently encouraging businesses to change for the sake of change. The mantra became, "If it ain't broke, break it!" Despite this frequent encouragement by management consultants and authors (Hammer & Champy, 1993; S. Johnson, 1998; Peters, 1988), many advise caution against radical approaches to creative destruction and unnecessary change (Abrahamsom, 2004; Clampitt, DeKoch, & Cashman, 2000; Gallivan, Hofman, & Orlikowski, 1994; Ogbor & Williams, 2003). Most agree that planned change is more desirable than chaos and that the radical and rigid approaches introduced as "programs of the month" are doomed to fail. Abrahamsom (2004) proposes "the notion of dynamic stability or alternating periods of stability and change in order to exploit the benefits of each and to counter the disadvantages of both in isolation" (p. 2). This balanced approach results in fewer of the unintended consequences seen in the previous decade, when massive restructuring and layoffs were followed by the company's inability to meet production demands. The diversity in today's marketplace requires an even more balanced approach to managing change.

For example, John McGovern, while CEO and president of Campbell Soup Company, saw the need for organizational change. The red-and-white soup cans were calling up memories for fewer and fewer folks. He identified regional and ethnic marketing as the key attitudes he needed in his organization, and divided Campbell into 50 quasi-independent business units, each responsible for its own profit and loss. Defining the top spots in these independent units as his key leverage positions, he placed marketing-oriented leaders in those spots and gave them autonomy. They produced more than 400 new products between the years 1981 and 1985, with lots of regional and ethnic variations (Saporito, 1988). This case illustrates the importance of the people who make up the organization. People in organizations must be open to new ideas and the organization must foster a climate that invites new ideas. Change and innovation "calls for a collection of talents [and] the entire process is fraught with anxiety . . . so that people must have a belief and a commitment, a courage and a persistence that are invaluable to the inevitable vicissitudes that accompany all innovations" (Steele, 1975, p. 20).

Communicating About Changes

Karp (1996) proposes that communicating change can best be envisioned as a two-phase process: (1) presenting the change and (2) working with the resistance that accompanies every change. Both phases require a communication strategy. For many organizations, a communication plan provides a structure for ensuring that everyone involved is receiving important information that is relevant from his or her perspective. Once stakeholder groups have been identified, a communication plan can be useful to keep everyone aligned and involved.

Timing is an important aspect to introducing organizational change. Changes can be introduced too quickly and result in chaos as people react without enough context to understand the business and personal ramifications. Or changes can be announced and not acted on for months, resulting in the buildup of anxiety that contributes to low morale and ultimately less support for the changes themselves. The best strategy is to announce changes as close to the time for active planning and implementation as possible. It can also be helpful to break changes down into more basic elements so that implementation becomes a series of predictable steps that gives greater flexibility and buy-in to those who have to make the changes happen (Karp, 1996). Prahalad (1998), coauthor of *Competing for the Future*, notes that there are many channels for communicating change. He calls attention to convening monthly meetings with top people in the company or bringing middle-level and junior people into the office twice a month and discussing potential changes.

In addition to presenting changes, it's equally important to coordinate changes with an organization's cultural artifacts. Shrivastava (1985) identifies four types of artifacts that reinforce an organization's culture and impact change strategy and execution: (1) myths and sagas, (2) language and metaphors, (3) rituals, ceremonies, and symbols, and (4) behavioral norms. Higgins and Mcallaster (2004) note several examples of how Continental Airlines used artifacts to implement their successful transition from a company on the edge of bankruptcy to a strong, viable business today. One such artifact was the symbolic distribution of a separate paycheck to all employees whenever Continental placed in the top five airline rankings for customer service. Although it would have been more efficient and cost effective to just add this bonus to the employees' paycheck, the distribution of a special payment reinforced the reward for customer service—a core value.

COMMUNICATION STRATEGIES

Researchers have proposed a variety of specific strategies for communicating organizational changes. The most common top-down approaches are

(1) withhold and uphold, (2) spray and pray, (3) tell and sell, (4) identify and reply, and (5) underscore and explore (Clampitt et al., 2000). *Withhold and uphold* is where managers withhold as much information as possible until confronted with questions or rumors. Then they defend the company's position and the planned changes. This is the least effective approach to take. *Spray and pray* provides employees with enormous amounts of information but often without context or opportunities for response. Management hopes employees will be able to sort it out for themselves. *Tell and sell* is where management chooses to persuade employees to support a limited number of specific changes rather than sharing with them all of the changes planned. This approach focuses only on changes that most directly affect employees, assuming that they cannot understand or are not interested in those changes affecting the larger picture. *Identify and reply* is where employees identify key issues of the change plan and management listens and responds to their concerns. *Underscore and explore* is a communication approach that focuses on fundamental issues related to changes and offers employees an opportunity to discuss various possibilities for implementation and adoption. This open, involving approach is probably the most effective because it is engaging and gains commitment to overall changes.

Lionel Richie was significantly changing how we might help the dispossessed and marginalized in the world when he cowrote (with Michael Jackson) and organized the production of the popular song, "We Are the World." He had invited music luminaries to assist in making a record that would raise money for starving people in Africa and needed to clearly articulate his purpose and gain their creative cooperation. Quincy Jones, the producer, included in his invitation to performers a note that said, "Check your ego at the door." The message was clear: the success of the record depended on the cooperation of everyone, not the brilliance of a few. This, likewise, applies to those who wish to embrace change and innovation. Companies must create cultures in which new ideas can thrive and systems that will promote change. A study of corporate innovation practices by the Arthur D. Little consulting firm reveals, however, that U.S. executives' greatest concern about innovation is not a lack of brilliant scientists and engineers but a "dearth of managers who know how to drive the creative process" (Dumaine, 1991, p. 57). Consequently, it is important to examine the role of leadership in the change and innovation process.

Leaders need to understand that during change, productivity often drops, good people leave, teamwork may deteriorate, and morale may decline. Therefore, it is important to manage expectations, increase participation in the change process, reward and recognize those employees promoting the change effort, and continue to communicate information to reduce ambiguity and stress. Additionally, leaders when implementing change should do the following:

- Have compelling reasons for changes and a clear plan for articulating them
- Use opinion leaders with referent power who can shape messages that garner support and commitment
- Build in feedback mechanisms and use multiple methods of communication

LEADERSHIP'S ROLE

Often it is the leader who is responsible for sharing the plan and managing change and innovation. For many, the personal channel of face-to-face communication is the most effective way to give and receive information so that one can ask questions and respond as requested. However, consideration should also be given to the leader's role in the organization, the personal style of the leader, and the group's expectations. Is this announcement of change consistent with previous behavior or does the uniqueness of this announcement send subtle messages about its importance and salience?

The direct supervisor is an important link in the communication of organizational change. As a representative of management, the supervisor serves as a change agent and needs to interpret, align, and provide context for the organization's objectives. Valentino (2004) integrates Bennis's (1989) four competencies of leadership (i.e., creating a vision, communicating the vision, demonstrating trust, and making individual and collective decisions) with Schein's (1996) eight process steps for integrating and transmitting an organization's culture (i.e., create a vision, provide feedback, be a role model, provide training, generate empowerment, create group networks; provide support groups, and align the reward and discipline systems with the new thinking). Her study reveals that all layers of management need to be aligned and clear about the purpose and strategy before messages are constructed and delivered.

Even when changes are planned, there are typical pitfalls that arise in organizations. Managers and consultants involved in change efforts have identified several common problems including (1) change forced from the top down without input from employees, (2) unrealistic expectations, (3) no follow-up to initial actions, (4) inconsistent behavior by senior managers, and (5) poor communications with reasons for the changes never being clearly articulated (Covin & Kilmann, 1990). These pitfalls were evident when one multinational company introduced a large-scale change effort and people who questioned the rationale or spoke up in resistance were told to "get on the bus or get run over by it!" The changes were part of a radical reengineering effort in which new people were brought in as senior managers because the new CEO believed they had "fresh ideas" and were more valuable. This was in direct contradiction to the historic cultural norm of promoting from within. With new top managers, the ideas of former senior people were considered "outdated," where previously they were treated with great respect for their years of loyalty. Even the company ring, given to employees for 25 years of service and which was previously worn with honor and pride, was now felt to be a badge of disgrace and was often removed. After several months of low employee morale and high turnover, the company began to realize that there was a vast amount of knowledge lost that could not be reclaimed by new employees and consequently customer service and quality dramatically suffered. Ironically, their next change program was centered on "service recovery." Change happens best when we seek to preserve an organization's values and culture and reconcile change with continuity (Trompenaars & Woolliams, 2003). This is a critical distinction from the change philosophies that encourage a total break from the past.

In Chapter 3, we discussed four broad representative organizational models identified by Trompenaars and Hampden-Turner (1998): the family, the Eiffel Tower, the guided missile, and the incubator. Each of these organizational cultures will respond to different change strategies. When introducing changes in organizations with a family culture, change is primarily political and is best accomplished by getting key leaders to make charismatic appeals or articulate inspiring goals and visions. Rarely are changes implemented from the bottom up. In companies that exemplify the Eiffel Tower, changes are best implemented by changing the policies and rules themselves. These companies ardently resist change until it becomes inevitable and then require rewriting job descriptions and procedure manuals. This can be very unsettling and dislocating for all involved. In the guided missile culture, changes happen quickly as new targets emerge. Turnover is frequent as new groups are formed and old ones dissolve. It is this culture in which loyalties to one's profession and work are of greater importance than company loyalty. Finally, in the incubator, culture changes are quickly and easily incorporated if members are in alignment with each other.

It is important to create a strategy for how changes will be introduced and presented to the workforce. The first responsibility is for leaders to have a strong business rationale that indicates that changes are necessary. Then a cohesive communication strategy and plan should be developed that takes multiple perspectives into account. Finally, it is essential to find ways to honor the past while changing to the future so that the strengths of the organization are not lost (Odenwald, 1996).

When Carol Hawkins, Vice President of Organizational Effectiveness at Seminole Community College in Sanford, Florida, was faced with the options for implementing a new enterprise resource planning (ERP) system, she used an approach that ensured open participation from the employees. An ERP implementation affects all employees as it changes the computer systems, software, and databases used on a daily basis. She first established a leadership team representing each of 25 departments of the college who then created a decision matrix to define what requirements they needed when selecting new vendors. To build this matrix, they used cross-functional teams and conducted focus-group meetings to hear the specific needs of the users. These teams were then responsible to a constituency of employees to hear their requirements and concerns and then report back to the leadership team. When the requirements were defined and vendors were brought in to conduct sales presentations, all employees in any department could attend the sessions to hear how the new software would directly affect their business, and to ask questions. By the time the vendors were selected, over one-third of the entire college had been involved in discussions or meetings to help determine which software program they would select. This was critical to the successful implementation because each employee would have to actively participate to make it work, and although the overall product would greatly improve his or her ability to do business, it also required adjustment from each person. The thoughtful and inclusive approach made the implementation process less disruptive and saved both time and money in the end. Here a clear plan for the change effort and an inclusive process where input was sought and incorporated into subsequent strategies for change proved successful.

Cross-Cultural Considerations for Implementing Change

In any organization, change is a complex phenomenon affecting human dynamics as individuals adjust to new roles; therefore, when presenting information, change agents need to consider that different cultures may have unique audience expectations. For example, audiences in the United States prefer humor, joking, slogans or catch phrases, action orientation, and youthful presenters full of energy. In contrast, Chinese audiences prefer a humble tone, reserve and patience, older speakers who are respected, and a long-term view. Korean audiences respond best to hard facts, well-dressed and formal speakers, quick solutions, some humor, respect for the audience, and reserve. Arabian audiences expect rhetorical eloquence, clean appearance, direct eye contact, extra talk after the formal presentation, physical proximity, liveliness, and educated speakers with proven abilities. Canadian audiences prefer low-key presentations, technical facts, no ostentation, no hard sell, plenty of context, humor, quick feed-back, and debate. These examples illustrate the wide variety of preferences, but typically each culture presents information on the basis of its own predilections rather than considering its audiences' ideal style (R. Lewis, 1999).

In multicultural organizations, introducing change requires addressing important cultural issues. When communicating across national cultural boundaries, Harris and Moran (1991) suggest emphasizing quality of life in addition to increased efficiency. They further urge promoting cooperation and acknowledging interdependence among all members of the workforce as well as encouraging corporate social responsibility. Finally, they emphasize that Westerners should "encourage work and technology in harmony with nature, rather than conquering it and avoiding environmental/ecological conse-quences" (p. 81). It is important to acknowledge and respect a culture's relevant traditional values such as individual responsibility, personal integrity, regard for other's property, and work ethic.

The importance of cultural patterns and the nuances of integrating changes across cultures are illustrated in Muratbekova-Touron's (2005) case study of a French multinational organization. The influence of France's high-context culture caused frustration for those from low-context cultures as meet-ings seemed to lack organization and focus. The change agents should have provided a clearly articulated message that was reinforced in a written format and incorporated into company policies or mandates. Those from low-context cultures wanted to see a project plan with dates and milestones denoting cur-rent status against a specific timeline. They expected a clear rationale and well defined lines of authority and responsibility. Muratbekova-Touron (2005) specifically noted that the influence of Anglo Saxon values had created a more performance-oriented culture and "the ancient culture [had] to change from just being nice and intelligent" (p. 212).

Concerns regarding decision-making and power distance were cultural fac-tors evidenced in B. Smith and Dodd's (1994) study that contrasted various international differences. They found that their Saudi clients were very con-cerned with status and frequently needed to revisit or review previously made decisions. This was often frustrating to their European counterparts, who were already prepared to move to implementation on key issues. They also found that Saudis preferred face-to-face meetings to confirm messages and decisions and were reluctant to conclude business via teleconference or videoconferences.

In many cultures, one's relationship to time becomes a principal factor when addressing organizational change. For some cultures, it is important to retain the past to preserve a sense of identity. Cultures tend to be sequential or synchronistic regarding change and time. The Western approach is sequential, with scheduled plans, timelines, and benchmarks. Other cultures prefer a more synchronistic approach, in which deadlines are not rigid and may be considered as guidelines, not specific dates. People may arrive late to planned meetings and/or allow themselves to be interrupted by telephone calls or visitors. Belief in a superior plan is often overridden by a desire to allow other ways of accomplishing the goals to emerge. The sequential approach may be seen by some as aggressive and inflexible. The synchronistic approach may be viewed by others as lacking structure and alignment. In both cases, cosmopolitan leaders need to understand that others may resist because of the strategy alone even if the final outcome is desired. Trompenaars and Hampden-Turner (1998) observe that "the wise cross-cultural manager perceives all the ways preferred by different cultures" (p. 140).

Sometimes it takes several attempts to find a strategy for honoring multiple cultural perspectives. The opening of EuroDisney (now called Disneyland Paris) provides an example of these challenges. Many Disney leaders who were successful in the United States initially failed in France because they assumed they could use the same leadership approaches without attempting to incorporate a European approach. Eventually, Disneyland Paris made adjustments that respected the cultural codes of France such as "lower admissions prices, wine with lunch and looser dress codes . . . [and] Disney continues to incorporate a multicultural perspective into its daily operations" (Stanoch, 1994). Today, Disneyland Paris is one of Europe's top vacation destinations. This example illustrates how multiple inputs from a variety of stakeholders can create emergent change as new scenarios are realized.

Also, some cultures have a tendency to resist changes and uncertainty more than others. Hofstede's (1980) research on work values indicated that some cultures have high uncertainty avoidance and as a result believe that uncertainty is best dealt with if everyone behaves according to widely accepted guidelines. This results in slower changes but greater security. Continued research will need to be conducted to reveal whether national cultural values will change over time. Although research emphasizes the stability of cultural values (Adler, 2002; Shenkar, 2001), dramatic and unpredictable outside events could potentially invalidate Hoftede's country dimension index scores. For example, in their study of the new generation of Chinese managers, Ralston, Egri, Stewart, Terpstra, and Kaicheng (1999) found a co-existence of values and a blending of corporate and national perspectives. Their study reported that new managers were "more likely to act independently, while taking risks in the pursuit of profits," although they were "not forsaking their Confucian values" (p. 179).

Cross-cultural concerns when implementing large-scale change may appear to make the process more complicated; however, Trompenaar and Woolliams (2003) remind us that "basic to understanding cultural change is the understanding that culture is a series of rules and methods which a society or organization has evolved to deal with the regular problems that face it [and] while cultures differ markedly in how they approach these dilemmas, they do not differ in a need to make some kind of response" (p. 363). The desire and commitment of the entire workforce to respond collectively to solve business problems is at the heart of successful change efforts. Cross-cultural issues and concerns require that a thoughtful approach be taken to the implementation of changes, but this additional planning makes good business sense.

Taking the Long View: Seeing the Future

Peter Schwartz (1991), author of *The Art of the Long View: Planning for the Future in an Uncertain World,* suggests that thinking about the distant future helps companies make good choices in the present. In global organizations, this requires planning change. Even though taking the long view is counterintuitive for most U.S. business leaders, some are seeing the advantage of this perspective. John Chambers, CEO of Cisco Systems, states, "We decided to become more aggressive as a company and to look at the market more in Internet years, as opposed to calendar years. Things are changing so fast with regard to the Internet that each regular business calendar year equals seven Internet business years" (Chambers, 1998, p. 106). He continues to note that "by exercising skill in planned change, we not only facilitate people's preparation and acceptance of change, but we do it in such a way as to reduce stress and energy waste" (p. 106). Still, James Clark, founder of Silicon Graphics, observes, "We're losing our creative edge. American industry is on the decline because U.S. managers are too concerned about protecting short-term earnings to innovate" (Dumaine, 1991, p. 56). Robert Colton of the National Science Foundation sounds a more hopeful note when he says, "If you look at the absolute numbers, we're still ahead in productivity [and] innovation . . . what we have to do is keep ahead" (Dumaine, 1991, p. 57). James Belasco (1991) would add that "leaders create a new tomorrow [and] tomorrow will not be an extension of today" (p. 50). Scenario planning is an effective approach to generating strategies that can ensure our staying ahead of the rest of the world and creating a new tomorrow.

Current research in change and business strategy has shown that tactical flexibility can be achieved through a scenario planning perspective for long-term competition and performance (Lindgren & Bandhold, 2003). Schwartz (1991) proposes that scenario planning best provides a tool for helping us think about change, uncertainty, and the future. He suggests that scenario planning is similar to the theater in that it is necessary to suspend disbelief long enough to discuss multiple possibilities and multiple pathways to accomplish potential outcomes. This process emerged from military strategies used during World War II and has been used by Royal Dutch Shell since the early 1970s. To incorporate scenario planning throughout the company when dealing with planned change, Arie de Geus, Shell's Planning Coordinator, held "learning conferences" around the world. Those who've incorporated the practice into their corporate strategy suggest that it is not about predicting the future; rather, it is about perceiving futures in the present.

Scenario planning allows global organizations to move away from linear thinking and better understand external changes (Heijden, 2005). It involves imagining what the future will be like, given current trends. Participants scan popular culture and the business economy to identify the potential forces that will shape events. Then they examine those forces, looking for all possible connections that might help them discover the critical uncertainties (Ogilvy & Schwartz, 2002). Scenario planning permits multinational organizations to be proactive to the changing global marketplace and environment.

Summary

Change and innovation are swirling all about, and rigid companies will fail because they will be unable to cope. But this age of kaleidoscopic change can offer unparalleled opportunities. Global organizations can develop strategies that anticipate where tomorrow's greatest changes are likely to occur. In an era when competitive advantage is fleeting, change is constant, and the whole globe is home base, multinational organizations must learn how to address issues related to the impact of change. It is imperative that they adopt strategies that capitalize on their technical and human strengths. Forward-thinking and determined global leaders will accept the idea that change is inevitable and immediate, and will, according to Jard DeVille (1980), "get on with business rather than retrenching and holding out until the last round is fired in a futile last stand" (p. 76).

Unit Four

Entering the Global Marketplace and World Bazaar

There is an unprecedented opportunity as we enter this new millennium to use our unequaled influence wisely and with a generous spirit.

—Jimmy Carter

Human beings draw close to one another by their common nature, but habits and customs keep them apart.

—Confucian saying

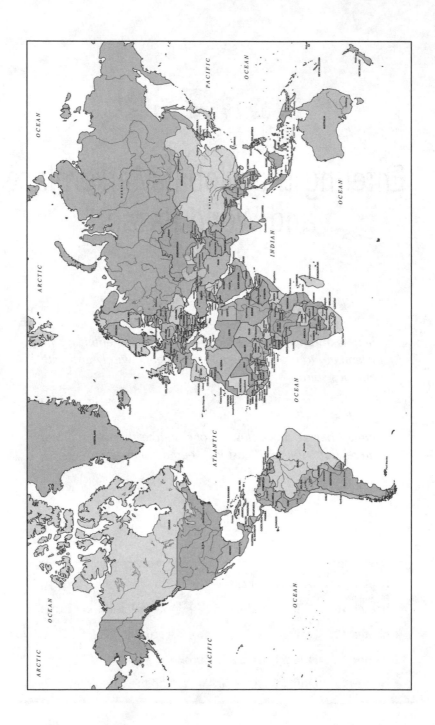

9

Doing Business in North America

Photo by W. V. Schmidt

Photo by W. V. Schmidt

Photo by W. V. Schmidt

N orth America is home to many of the leading financial, commercial, and technology centers of the world. The United States, along with its cultural counterpart, Canada, compete with other global giants such as Japan, China, Great Britain, and the European Union, as well as with almost every other country in the world. The implementation of the North American Free Trade Agreement in 1994 united these two countries and Mexico into the highest volume trade organization in the world. Today the region sets the standard for much of the business practices around the globe.

Geography and Demographics

North America is the world's third-largest continent in area and fourth-largest continent in population (Encarta, 2005). Geographically, the continent comprises the United States, Canada, Mexico, Central America, Greenland, the Caribbean, and a number of islands. Culturally, however, the term "North America" is frequently used to refer to the United States and Canada only. The overlapping histories of these two countries, their tight economic integration, and their geographical closeness blend them together culturally in many respects. Canada is the second-largest country in the world, by area, after Russia; the United States is fourth.

Stretching over 9 million square miles, North America is characterized by a variety of typology and climates. Mountain ranges, including the Rocky Mountains, stretch from the southern part of the United States to northern Canada, as do the Central and Coastal Plains. Although arctic conditions prevail in the far northern part of the continent, the southern tips are mostly tropical or subtropical. The entire continent is surrounded by the Atlantic Ocean on the east and the Pacific Ocean on the west. Terms such as "mainland" or "continental" are used to refer to the 48 contiguous states of the United States (Alaska and Hawaii are the other two states). Additionally, the United States includes the Pacific dependencies of American Samoa, Guam, and the Northern Mariana Islands, and the Atlantic commonwealths of Puerto Rico and the Virgin Islands. A number of islands—Baker Island, Howland Island, Jarvis Island, Johnson Atoll, Kingman Reef, Midway Islands, Navassa Island, Palmyra Atoll, and Wake Island—are uninhabited except for military and U.S. Fish and Wildlife personnel.

The populations of the U.S. and Canada are 290 million and 32 million, respectively (Central Intelligence Agency, 2005a, 2005e). Population growth in Canada during the 1990s and early 2000s has been modest in comparison to the United States. Declining birth rates and an aging population slowed that country's growth to about 4 percent during 1996 and 2001 (Statistics Canada, 2005). Yet the populations of Canada's biggest cities and largest commercial centers are flourishing: Toronto, Montreal, Vancouver, Ottawa, Calgary, and Edmonton all have populations exceeding one million people (Brinkoff, 2005a). Toronto, a major financial center, is the world's 42nd largest city (City Mayors, 2005a), with approximately two and half million people in the city proper, and is home to several major U.S. companies and the Toronto Stock Exchange, one of the largest exchanges in the world. The nation's capital is Ottawa, located in the Province of Ontario, which is the most populated province—over 12 million, or over a third of the country's population (Infoplease, 2005a). The population of the city of Ottawa is approximately that of Washington, DC.

Many of the world's largest cities and financial centers are located in the United States. The 10 largest U.S. cities are home to 125 of the Fortune 500 Companies. Additionally, four U.S. metropolitan areas—New York, Los Angeles, Chicago, and Washington, D.C.—are among the world's 20 most populated urban areas (City Mayors, 2005a). Five of the top 10 busiest airports in the world are located in the United States (Fleming, 2005).

Since the 1990s, population growth in the United States has been concentrated primarily in the Southwest part of the country—namely, California, Arizona, Nevada, and Texas. From 1990 to 1999, five of the country's most rapidly growing metropolitan areas were located in this region (Rubin & Cox, 2001); by 2002, nine of the fastest growing cities were located in three states—Arizona, Nevada, and California, while the populations of Chicago, Philadelphia, and Detroit actually dropped (U.S. Census Bureau, 2003a). The fastest growing states are now Arizona, Nevada, Idaho, and Utah (http://money .cnn.com/2005/12/22/real_estate/fastest_growing_states/index.htm). Among some of the fastest growing mid-sized communities in the country are the "border towns" of South Texas, which are now thriving commercial centers, thanks mostly to NAFTA traffic, 79 percent of which enters through Texas (Rubin & Cox, 2001).

Case Study: The Growing Latin American Population

An increasing Hispanic population represents much of the population growth in the Southwest United States—as well as in other regions. Most of this growth has occurred since 1990, at which time about 9 percent of the country's population was Hispanic (U.S. Census Bureau, 2000). Ten years later, that portion had grown to 12 percent, or approximately 32 million Hispanics in the United States (U.S. Census Bureau, 2000), and by 2003 it had grown to over 37 million (U.S. Census Bureau, 2003b). This population is predominantly Mexicans, followed by Central and South Americans, Puerto Ricans, and Cubans (Therrien & Ramirez, 2001).

Although this growth has happened primarily in historically large centers such as New York, California, and Florida, it has been most pronounced in the southwest United States: nine of the fastest growing Hispanic counties in the country in 2002 were located in three states: Arizona, California, and Nevada (U.S. Census Bureau, 2003a); 51 of the top 100 Hispanic counties in the United States are located in the Southwest (Hispanic Business, 2004). Additionally, the Midwest has seen exponential growth (Kong, 2001) in such states as Iowa, Illinois, Minnesota, and Wisconsin.

Estimates of Hispanic population growth suggest that they will make up as much as 16 percent of the U.S. population by the year 2020 (U.S. Department of Education, 2000), increasing to 25 percent or 100 million people in 2050 (Korzenny, 2000). The number of Hispanics in the workforce is expected to increase by 36 million in 2006 (National Association of Diversity Management, 2000), composing 16% of the total U.S. workforce. Consequently, the purchasing power of Hispanics is expected to reach $1 trillion by the year 2010 (Hispanic Business, 2005c), representing a significant portion of U.S. domestic commerce. Currently, the number of Hispanic-owned businesses is projected to grow by 55 percent by the year 2010, to approximately 3 million (Hispanic Business, 2005a).

The diversity added by an increasing Hispanic population presents many opportunities—and challenges—for the U.S. workforce. Cultural differences (see Chapter 10 for a discussion of U.S.-Hispanic cultural differences) create career obstacles for Hispanics (Educational Testing Service, 1999), particularly in moving up career ladders (Minor, 1999). Hispanics face difficulties in the workplace because of lack of educational attainment (U.S. Census Bureau, 2000), lower salaries (Yzaguirre, 2001), and lack of encouragement, opportunity, and work skills (National Association of Diversity Management, 2000). The increased number of undocumented Mexican nationals working and living in the United States has been a concern of the Bush administration, which has proposed an amnesty program that would allow illegal immigrants to work and live in the United States. Most of these workers would perform unskilled labor—thus the administration claims they are, in fact, taking jobs that many naturalized Americans don't want—but the proposal has evoked a great deal of political controversy. How the U.S. government and workforce handle this issue will determine, in large part, if the population projections hold true in the years to come.

Cultural Themes and Patterns

Canada and the United States share many cultural characteristics, fashioned from their common European roots, much as do Australia and New Zealand. The geographical closeness between the United States and Canada, however, has created a stronger cultural link, especially in border areas such as Detroit-Windsor, Vancouver-Seattle, and Toronto-Buffalo. Populations in these areas live, work, and shop across the border, are exposed to the same print and broadcast media, and have family backgrounds on both sides. Some variations in culture may be found in Northern and Eastern Canada, particularly in Québec, where similarities to French society, history, and law still abound.

In general, however, people in Canada and the United States rank high on Hofstede's individualism scale, low on power orientation and context (Hall, 1976), moderate on masculinity and uncertainty avoidance (ITIM Culture and Management Consultancy, 2005) and are largely monochronic (Van der Boon, 2005). The business societies of both countries place premiums on efficiency, time management, personal success and achievement, freedom of choice, independence, and competition. They value openness and directness in their communication, are egalitarian in their views of individual rights (Matthews, 2005), and place great personal emphasis on "living to work" rather than "working to live."

Although in most regards Canadians and Americans share basic cultural dimensions, there are some distinctive variations between the two mainstream societies. Owing to different beginnings, the United States fought a revolutionary war to gain its independence, whereas Canada negotiated its, and a different sense of individualism and competition thrives in the U.S. culture (Lipset, 1990). The colonial United States, for which complete self-governance was a priority, adopted a less centralized form of government, being "suspicious of monarchies, theocracies, and anything that smacked of big government" (Aldridge, 2005). Canadians' lifestyle is generally less hurried than their southern neighbors' (Riel, 1996), and they tend to place a greater emphasis on privacy than do Americans (ITIM Culture and Management Consultancy, 2005). They often interpret personal questions from relative strangers or remote business associates as inappropriate until a more permanent relationship is established.

The people making up the United States value the ability to (1) control their environment, (2) control their use of time, (3) effect change, (4) compete in a free enterprise system, (5) be actively and assertively involved in their work, (6) work efficiently toward practical ends, and (7) acquire material goods as a reward for hard work (Kohls, 1984). They also practice and enjoy equality and stress the future rather than the past.

The importance of efficiency, success, directness, and individualism in Anglo cultures is evident in many common work-related expressions. These idioms casually point to the socially embedded ethic of work common to the North American continent. Table 9.1 lists a few of these expressions and their generally understood meanings.

Table 9.1   Common Business Expressions Used in North America

Expression	Example of Use	Meaning	Value
Above board	"Our proposal is completely above board."	All of the terms and details are exactly as presented.	Directness
Bottom line	"What's the bottom line?"	What's your final offer?	Directness, Efficiency
Cut to the chase	"Stop wasting time and cut to the chase."	Get to the point.	Directness, Efficiency
Ducks in a row	"Get your ducks in a row before the project is due."	Get organized.	Efficiency, Success
Early bird gets the worm	"Successful people know that the early bird gets the worm."	People who work hard succeed.	Success
Penny for your thoughts	"Give me a penny for your thoughts."	Say what you're thinking, or give an opinion.	Directness
The squeaky wheel gets the grease	"She got promoted. I guess the squeaky wheel gets the grease."	People who speak their minds get what they want.	Individualism
Time is money	"We need to finish now. Time is money."	Getting something done in a timely manner makes a better profit.	Efficiency, Success
Two cents' worth	"I'll offer my two cents' worth."	I will tell you what I think.	Individualism

Because of these characteristics, Americans are often stereotyped as being arrogant, self-focused, rigid-thinking, and overly concerned with material wealth. It is therefore incumbent upon North Americans to refrain from speech that might inadvertently reinforce any of these stereotypes. Openness to new and different points of view is critical as trade agreements across the globe continue to develop and a deeper understanding and acceptance of cultural differences becomes essential.

Social, Economic, and Political Factors

Much of the history and culture of the United States and Canada are similar. Both countries were colonized during the "New World" explorations of the 15th and 16th centuries. The eastern seaboards of both countries were established primarily as English or French commonwealths, whereas Spanish colonizers settled more in the southern part of the continent. Canada declared its independence from Great Britain in 1867, almost a century after the United States declared its emancipation from the English crown.

Despite a great deal of shared history between the two countries, some basic cultural and political differences exist. Although Canada operates as an independent state, it is still technically considered a commonwealth of the United Kingdom, acknowledging the English crown (currently Queen Elizabeth II) as chief of state, as do Australia and New Zealand. However, the Canadian government officially became autonomous with the signing of the Constitution Act of 1982, which completely severed the nation's government from the United Kingdom (Infoplease, 2005b). Canada is governed by a Prime Minister and Parliament and is divided into judicial, executive, and legislative branches similar to those of the United States. Each of Canada's 10 provinces (Alberta, British Columbia, Manitoba, New Brunswick, Newfoundland and Labrador, Nova Scotia, Ontario, Prince Edward Island, Quebec, and Saskatchewan) and three territories (Northwest Territories, Nunavut, and Yukon) have state-level governments, although federalism is stronger in the territories than in the provinces.

Another significant difference between the United States and Canada is the cultural distinctiveness of Québec, where French—Canada's official language besides English—is spoken by 80 percent of the population (World Languages Knowledge Fair, 1999); about 25 percent of Canadians speak French (French Language in Canada, 2005), primarily in Ontario, New Brunswick, and Manitoba. In Québec City, 80 percent of the population speaks French, and local business laws in that city even require that advertising be conducted predominantly in French (D. Brown, 2001). The division between French and English culture also prompted Québec to make two attempts to secede from Canada—once in 1980 and again in 1995—although both attempts narrowly failed (Infoplease, 2005b).

The linguistic distinctiveness of the eastern part of Canada also sets it apart politically and socially from the rest of the country. For example, the legal system of Québec is based on a civil law system, similar to the legal system still practiced in France, whereas the rest of Canada is based on English Common Law, comparable to that of the United States (Central Intelligence Agency, 2005a). Canada is also known for liberal social policies regarding such issues as gay marriage and medical uses of marijuana (Infoplease, 2005b). Their law regarding pharmaceuticals has made it a popular mail-order distribution source of prescriptions for uninsured and senior patients in the United States.

Religion in both the United States and Canada is predominantly Christian; in each country, slightly over 76 percent of the respective population identify themselves as following some branch of Christianity, followed in number by adherents of Judaism, Islam, Buddhism, and Hinduism (Adherents.com 2005; Statistics Canada, 2001). About 43 percent of Canadian Christians and 24 percent of United States Christians are Catholic; the largest Protestant denominations across the continent include Anglican, Southern Baptist, Methodist, Lutheran, Presbyterian, and the United Church of Christ (Adherents.com, 2005; Statistics Canada, 2001). Since 1990, the United States has seen an exponential growth in Pentecostal and Evangelical Churches such as the Assemblies of God (U.S. Census Bureau, 2005). These and other religious affiliations are significant from a consumer standpoint in that many of the beliefs of many of these different religious groups influence practitioners' lifestyle purchases of items related to diet, health care, and alcohol consumption.

North America leads most of the world in per-capita gross domestic product (GDP) and income. Despite economic downturns in early 2000, both countries observed moderate growth, controlled inflation, and relatively low unemployment rates during that time. The United States and Canada account for approximately 30-35 percent of the world's GDP. This combined GDP exceeds that of all other regions in the world, including all of Western Europe (Central Intelligence Agency, 2005c). Projections indicate that these figures will be stable, although China and Eastern Europe are expected to rise significantly through the year 2015.

North America is the home of 821 of the Forbes 2000 list of companies, about 41 percent: 711 are located in the United States, and 67 are located in Canada (Forbes, 2005). Canada has thriving banking and financial service and telecommunications sectors, along with major export sectors of chemicals, timber and wood products, machinery, motor vehicles, metals, crude petroleum, and energy (Central Intelligence Agency, 2005a; U.S. Department of State, 2004).

During the 1980s and most of the 1990s, the United States enjoyed an era of prosperity unprecedented since the period immediately following World War II.

Attributed in part to "Reaganomics" (economic policies named after two-term President Ronald Reagan during the 1980s), the U.S. economy opened jobs and business partnerships for an enterprising Baby-Boom Generation. By the late 1990s and early 2000s, however, a tightening economy that lasted well into the mid-2000s changed the financial nomenclature of the entire North American continent. The failure of the "dotcom" and high-tech industries, followed by a modest worldwide recession, led the way for dramatic layoffs in the U.S. and Canadian job markets. Exacerbated by the impact of the September 11 attacks, poor economic conditions caused many companies to downsize, declare bankruptcy, or reorganize. Devastating hurricanes *Katrina* and *Rita* in 2005 escalated the situation further (MSNBC, 2005), causing major corporations such as General Motors, Ford Motor Co., and Merck to lay off significant portions of their workforces in order to survive (CNNMoney.com, 2005). The housing market, which had boomed in the early 2000s (largely because of record-low interest rates on homes), also began to falter in mid-decade, eliminating thousands of construction jobs in the process. This further contributed to a distressed U.S. economy as interest rates began to rise in the middle and later parts of that year.

As financial leaders in the world, both the United States and Canada boast high-volume national and regional stock markets. Among the largest in the United States are the New York Stock Exchange (the largest in the world), the NASDAQ, the American Stock Exchange, and the Chicago Stock Exchange. There are several stock exchanges in Canada, including the Toronto Stock Exchange, the Canadian Venture Exchange, the Montreal Exchange, NASDAQ-Canada, the Winnipeg Stock Exchange, the NGX (Natural Gas Exchange), and the Winnipeg Commodity Exchange (Rutgers University Libraries, 2005). The Toronto Stock Exchange (TSX) is Canada's largest stock market (and the fourth-largest on the continent), followed by NASDAQ-Canada, the Canadian Venture Exchange, and the Winnipeg Stock Exchange. The TSX Group headquarters, which is also a large holder of equities, is the third-largest financial center in North America.

The exchange rates of the U.S. dollar (USD) and Canadian dollar (CAD) have remained historically stable in relation to each other, even during the economic downturns of the early 2000s. Although the U.S. and Canadian dollars have fluctuated against other leading world currencies, their relationship to each other has remained close (Interactive Currency Table, 2005).

Case Study: The Cost of Terrorism

On September 11, 2001, life in the United States—and across all of the free world—was irrevocably changed. Terrorist attacks on the World Trade Center, the Pentagon, and four commercial airliners took over 3,000 lives and instilled fear through the governments and societies of the world, permeating every aspect of daily life. The aftermath of those attacks had a particular impact on economic matters, both short and long term.

The effects of those attacks were felt almost immediately. The damage and destruction to property was over $18 billion (USD), not to mention almost $1.5 billion in lost revenues resulting from a shutdown of the airline industry for three days (National Center for Policy Analysis, 2002). Even after air travel had been restored, the U.S. airline industry saw a dramatic drop in revenues due to lingering fears about the safety of air travel. This lack of revenue had a devastating impact on major airlines in particular, several of which were already teetering on the brink of bankruptcy. The devastation of these industries trickled down to other service industries, contributing in part to a recession that had already begun earlier in the decade.

But the events of September 11 had a significantly longer effect on the U.S. economy. Shortly after the attacks, several actions by the Bush administration dramatically affected the U.S. economy: the invasion of Afghanistan in 2001—later followed by the invasion and occupation of Iraq in 2003—and the creation of the Department of Homeland Security, a new government agency charged with protecting the country against terrorism, would prove to be costly investments. Additionally, the federal government created the Transportation Security Administration (TSA), which essentially became responsible for maintaining security in every commercial airport across the country. Funding the wars and additional domestic security measures cost well in excess of $200 billion (A. Belasco, 2005). Consequently, the United States began to experience record-breaking federal deficits, quickly consuming the surplus that had been accumulated throughout the 1990s. Projections indicate that if the occupation of Iraq is to continue indefinitely, war costs may reach a half-trillion dollars by the year 2010 (Weisman & Murray, 2005). Despite the distress of the U.S. economy, exacerbated by rising fuel costs and the expense of humanitarian aid following the devastating hurricanes *Katrina* and *Rita* in 2005, favorable conditions are starting to return in the mid 2000s. But the continued expense of maintaining national security—at home and abroad—and its related costs represents a formidable challenge to the country's economic health.

Because of their cultural similarities and geographic closeness, the United States and Canada have a strong trading history. Most of this trade, however, was not liberalized until 1989, at the signing of the U.S.-Canada Free Trade Agreement. Widely unpopular among Canadians, and ignored by many in the U.S., the agreement did not significantly affect trade between the two countries. Moreover, the autonomous characteristic of several Canadian provinces presented legal barriers to free trade (Daniels et al., 2004). It was not until 1994, at the signing of the North American Free Trade Agreement (NAFTA), the signatories of which were the United States, Canada, and Mexico, that more assertive levels of trade developed. Since that time, North America's two largest countries compose the world's largest bilateral trade relationship, represented in 2004 by $445 billion in trade (U.S. Department of State, 2004). The United States is Canada's largest importer. The countries exchange a variety of goods, as shown in Table 9.2.

The establishment of NAFTA, which brought Mexico into trade partnership with Canada and the United States, has been touted as one of the most successful trade integrations in the world. The agreement, which suspended the earlier U.S.-Canada Free Trade Agreement, more than doubled the trade among the three countries from $306 billion in 1993 to $621 billion in 2002 (Office of the U.S. Trade Representative, 2005b). In addition to its primary objective—reducing and eventually eliminating tariffs among the signatory countries—NAFTA offers comprehensive governance over environmental, agricultural, intellectual property, and territorial issues (SICE, 2005).

Although they are faithful trade partners, the United States and Canada have not always agreed on issues of mutual interest. For example, Canada did not support the United States' preemptive military actions in Iraq, although it

Table 9.2   Major U.S. and Canadian Exports and Imports

	Primary Exports	Primary Imports	Primary Trade Partners
United States	Agricultural products, industrial chemicals & supplies, computers & electronics	Agricultural products, industrial supplies, machinery, consumer goods	Canada, China, Mexico, Japan, Germany
Canada	Automobiles & parts, chemicals, energy, wood/ wood products, telecommunications	Motor vehicles, industrial machinery, chemicals, energy	United States, China, Japan, Mexico, UK

has been actively involved in reconstruction efforts in that country. Canada also signed the Kyoto Accord to restrict global pollution, to which the United States was a signatory but did not ratify. Furthermore, global warming in the Arctic Ocean is causing shifts in sea routes, causing potential territorial disputes between the United States and Canada (Terra Daily, 2005). The future political relationship between the two countries depends in part on the new Conservative government elected in the 2005 Canadian special elections that followed the no-confidence vote in then-Prime Minister Paul Martin (Gillies, 2005). Although it is still early, the new Conservative Prime Minister has taken a more cordial stance toward the Bush administration. A mutual interest in increased trade and commercial ventures puts forward the promise of an improved and perhaps a more robust U.S.-Canadian relationship. There has also been increased cooperation in counterterrorist initiatives and securing the U.S.-Canadian borders.

Business Conduct and Characteristics

In a business context, the standards of work in the United States and to a somewhat lesser extent in Canada, can be attributed to the "Protestant (Work) Ethic." The term was applied by Max Weber to refer to a work philosophy that valued "diligence, punctuality, deferment of gratification, and primacy of the work domain" (Hill, 1996, p. 6, citing Rose, 1985). Although the "ethic" developed in Europe prior to New World colonization, its fruition came about as European colonists fled religious suppression from a monarchy-controlled state, and found life in the colonies difficult but liberating. In an effort to build a society that was founded on self-determination and that rewarded hard work with success, New World society emphasized the attainment of needs through a system in which "an individual could be the master of his [her] own fate through hard work" (Hill, 1996, p. 9). This newfound attraction to hard work was one of the key reasons for the Industrial Revolution in the 1900s and led to the commercial domination of the United States throughout most of the 20th century.

Many of these traits are still evident today in U.S. society, even though the basic survival needs of most Americans have long since been met. Thus, today's "ethic" tends to focus on the good life—a nice home, a good education, physical comforts and leisure, social standing, and other rewards for hard work and careful planning. The ethic is still rooted, however, in work, and Americans work more hours per week than do other cultures, including the Japanese, British, and Germans (Greenhouse, 2001). The typical U.S. employee works 350 more hours a year than the typical European, more hours even than the notoriously industrious Japanese, but only 8 percent would prefer fewer hours of work for less pay as compared with 38 percent of Germans, 30 percent of Japanese, and 30 percent of Britons (Reich, 2000). They also are inclined to be self-employed. In 2002, there were almost 23 million small businesses in the United States (United States Small Business Administration, 2005); and curricular programs in entrepreneurship are now an essential component to a comprehensive Business School curriculum (Riel, 1996).

Visitors to North America are amazed and often somewhat distressed at the rapid pace of life and the accompanying emphasis on punctuality and efficiency. Also, because Americans are generally gregarious on first meeting someone, visitors mistakenly interpret this as the beginning of a deep reciprocal friendship, and they may later be disappointed when there is no follow-up. Visitors are usually deeply impressed by the individual freedom and equality Americans enjoy, but are distressed by the directness and brusqueness displayed. Finally, particularly unsettling to many visitors is the American's lack of knowledge of and interest in other cultures. This ethnocentric attitude has developed because of our longstanding geographical isolation and dominant leadership role in world affairs. Today, more effort needs to be given to learning about other cultures and understanding our new role in a global economy.

Emerging Trends

In a rapidly evolving and increasingly globalized environment typical of North America, the list of emerging issues or trends is too comprehensive to imagine. Certainly North America, like every other region in the world, is subject to developments in technology, various domestic and international political issues, health and medical issues, and the threat of terrorism. However, within the continent there are certain issues of particular importance to the Canadian and U.S. economies with which the governments and companies in those countries must cope.

1. *An increasingly aging workforce.* The "Baby Boom" generation—those born approximately between 1945 and 1960—is entering a retirement stage during the first part of the 21st century. Opting for early or modified retirement programs, many of these workers will begin second careers, part-time work, or self-employment, or will otherwise be employed until their 70s or even 80s. Rising concerns about the virility of social security and an overall longer, healthier life span among workers contribute to this demographic. Consequently, the work philosophies, practices, knowledge, and skill levels of

an older generation will mesh with those of a younger crowd. Both parties will have to learn tolerance for, and adaptation to, each other if a successfully integrated workplace is to become commonplace.

2. *Globalization and immigration.* Since the September 11 attacks, there has been a great deal of discussion, particularly in the United States, about immigration practices. This discourse has been fueled in part by the threat that terrorists can gain entry into the country through a third party, such as Mexico. As an objective of President George W. Bush's second term, the creation of an amnesty program allowing undocumented immigrants access to jobs and social benefits in the United States has fallen under fire by many social conservatives in the United States; fears of domestic job loss and a stretched social programs budget have been at the forefront of the resistance. The extent to which immigration policies will allow or discourage future influx from other countries and cultures will determine, in large part, the demographic makeup of the North American workplace, and will influence local job markets and economies accordingly.

3. *An increased corporate and governmental focus on ethics.* The early part of the 2000s witnessed several major business scandals that rocked corporate America. The accounting frauds of Enron and WorldCom and the insider trading of Martha Stewart brought attention to the importance of ethics in big business. Those scandals resulted in monetary losses for employees and shareholders and criminal charges for key officers in those organizations. Consequently, businesses today fall under tighter auditing scrutiny and a higher cost of loss is often factored into prices; most university business programs provide more attention to business ethics. No longer is a person's resume, portfolio, or business plan the key determinant for success—his or her reputation for ethical behavior has become just as paramount.

Summary

Despite the challenges presented by terrorism, a changing workforce, economic shifts, and a more competitive world market, North America still enjoys a position of leadership among developed countries across the world. As its major competitors—China, Japan, and the European Union—assert themselves more in the world market, the United States and Canada will find it necessary to keep pace. The entrepreneurial spirit, dedication to hard work, and ingenuity of the continent's population will keep the two countries at the top of the list.

Resource Guide

Books

Culture, Communication, and People

Kalman, B. (1999). *Canada the culture* (2nd ed.). New York: Crabtree.

Thomas, D. M. (2000). *Canada and the United States: Differences that count* (2nd ed.). Peterborough, NJ: Broadview.

Customs and Business Conduct

Kranc, B., Roman, K., & Kranc, B. (2002). *Living and working in Canada: A practical guide to life in Canada* (2nd ed.). Oxford, UK: How To Books.

Woznick, A., Nolan, J., & Reif, J. (1997). *Canada business.* New York: World Trade Press.

History and Politics

Starowics, M. (2004). *Making history: The remarkable story behind Canada—A people's history.* Toronto: McClelland & Stewart.

Zinn, H. (2003). *A people's history of the United States: 1492–present.* New York: HarperCollins.

International Business and Globalism

Lomborg, B. (2004). *Global crisis, global solutions.* New York: Cambridge University Press.

Wolf, M. (2004). *Why globalization works.* New Haven, CT: Yale University Press.

Web Sites

Canada Business Etiquette (http://www.executiveplanet.com/index.php?title=Canada). Essential business culture guide for the Canadian traveler. It addresses business conduct and characteristics of the culture.

CanadaInfo (http://www.craigmarlatt.com/canada/index.html). CanadaInfo is more than 400 pages of information about Canada—its government, history, facts, people, geography, provinces, and more, including statistics, maps, and photographs and dozens of fact sheets.

Canada International (http://canadainternational.gc.ca/ci/main_menu-en.aspx). Provides information to non-Canadians about doing business, working, studying, and traveling in Canada.

Canada Business (http://canadabusiness.gc.ca/gol/cbec/site.nsf/en/index.html). Key business information by territory or province. Also includes links to associations, company directories, and maps.

Canada's Cultural Gateway (http://culture.ca/canada/english.jsp). Discover quality cultural content and the many festivals and events happening across Canada. Search thousands of select cultural resources regarding the Canadian people, environment, and history.

Industry Canada (http://www.ic.gc.ca). This site is all about social, economic, and political factors affecting Canada. Through its programs, initiatives, and services, Industry Canada is helping to build a dynamic and innovative economy.

North American Industry Classification System (NAICS) (http://www.census.gov/ naics). NAICS was developed jointly by the U.S., Canada, and Mexico to provide new comparability in statistics about business activity across North America.

Strategis (http://strategis.ic.gc.ca/engdoc/main.html). Strategis is Canada's primary business and consumer site.

Statistics Canada (http://www.statcan.ca/start.html). Canada's national statistical agency, providing information on Canadian business, economy, and society.

10

Doing Business in Latin America and the Caribbean

Photo by W. J. Wardrope

Photo by W. J. Wardrope

Photo by W. J. Wardrope

179

L atin America is one of the fastest growing areas in today's global market. Spanning the majority of the Western Hemisphere, the region offers rapidly developing business opportunities for countries across the world. Its growing population, political transformations, monetary reforms, and participation in emerging trade agreements have paved the way for importers and exporters, transnational enterprises, franchises, and foreign investors to expand in practically every industry. Still, deep inequalities of wealth persist in most Latin American and Caribbean countries, with around one-third of the region's people living in poverty. The average per capita income is about $3,600 a year. Life expectancy is 71 years, and infant mortality is 28 per 1,000 births (World Gazetteer, 2005).

Geography and Demographics

The term "Latin America" is used generally to refer to a large region of the Western hemisphere that comprises 13 countries in South America, seven countries in Central America, Mexico, and some 20 countries and island states located throughout the Caribbean (Latin American Network Information Center, 2005). Almost 8 million square miles (Geography of Development, n.d.) are occupied by the area's 5.5 million people (CountryWatch, 2003). The topography and climate are diverse, characterized by tropical regions, deserts, rain forests, rich plains, the Andean Mountains, and frigid conditions in the southern tip of South America. Countries in Latin America are rich in natural resources, enabling them to produce, consume, and export large amounts of minerals, oil, fish, meat, grains, coffee, fruits, vegetables, sugar, wood, clothing, flowers, hydroelectric power, precious metals, chemicals, and various manufactured goods (U.S. Department of State, 2005c). The thousands of coastline miles along both the Atlantic and Pacific oceans offer convenient trade potential to the entire world market. Many port cities exist along each coastline, including Rio de Janeiro, Fortaleza, Valparaiso, Lima, Montevideo, and Trujilo, allowing Latin American businesses to import and export goods around the globe.

Latin America is one of the most densely urbanized areas of the world. Approximately 75 percent of its population resides in large metropolitan areas (Geography of Development, 2005), and the region contains 17 of the largest 100 cities in the world (WorldAtlas, 2005b). The United States has nine such metropolitan areas, most of which are hubs for leading international enterprises.

Spanish, which is spoken by over 351 million people worldwide and accounts for about 7 percent of the entire world's output (Daniels et al., 2004), is the language spoken predominantly in most of Latin America. Portuguese, French, Dutch, and English are the official languages of Brazil, French Guiana, Suriname, and Belize, respectively. A substantial number of Latin Americans also speak various indigenous languages, particularly in Central America and in the northern section of South America. Approximately 5–10 percent of Latin America's population is mestizo (people of European and American Indian descent) or mulatto (people of European and African descent). The average literacy rate for Spanish and Portuguese speakers in Latin American countries is about 95 percent (U.S. Department of State, 2005c). Students graduating from most major universities in Latin America are required to complete several semesters of English, which is spoken widely in many domestic and international corporate offices. Strong European influences are evident in most Central and South American countries, reflected particularly in the literature, architecture, and religious traditions. Historical and cultural ties to Europe have earned Buenos Aires the title "Paris of the Americas" (Glaser & Glaser, 2005) and Uruguay the "Switzerland of South America" (Hudson, 1992); recent economic developments in Chile have earned it the title "Singapore of South America" (Fernando, 2005).

The Caribbean region is a conglomeration of countries, territories, and various political dependencies spread across 7,000 islands in the Atlantic Ocean, close in proximity to North, Central, and South American markets. Originally thought to be a western passage to India (hence the name, "West Indies"), the area was settled by Europeans prior to their coming to the North or South American continents. Today Spanish-, English-, and French-speaking people, many of whom are mulattos, populate the islands.

In addition to the presence of U.S. and European governments in the Caribbean, several islands in the region are part of Latin American countries, including San Andres and Providencia (Colombia), Isle de Bahia and Swan Islands (Honduras), Isla Mujeres and Isla Cozumel (Mexico), and Corn Islands (Nicaragua). The largest commercial cities in the region and their respective populations include Santo Domingo, Dominican Republic (2,900,000); San Juan, Puerto Rico (2,800,000); Habana, Cuba (2,300,000); and Port-au-Prince, Haiti (2,200,000) (Brinkhoff, 2005b).

Cultural Themes and Patterns

Themes are basic orientations that are shared by many or most of the people in a region or country. They are a beginning point for understanding another culture and sometimes form a pattern of behavior. Many customs and norms that are common in Latin American and Caribbean societies are not practiced in mainstream U.S. culture. Recognizing and understanding the cultural nuances of Latin America and the Caribbean are key to establishing, negotiating, and maintaining lasting, profitable business relationships.

Latin Americans tend to be highly relationship oriented. These tendencies are reflected in several important cultural aspects of Latin American culture: (1) *simpatiá* or kindness toward others even in circumstances of conflict (Gomez, 1994), (2) *confianza* or trust and mutual reciprocity between one another (Lange-Churin & Medieta, 2001), (3) *enchufado* or "a man who makes things happen" because of his connectedness (Axtell, 1987, p. 126), (4) *mañana* or things will get done when they get done (Axtell, 1987), and (5) *simpático* or a comfort with Latin ways (Lange-Churin & Medieta, 2001). Outsiders must display comfort with Latin ways before Latins will feel comfortable with them. This means demonstrating a high regard for the well-being of other persons and expressing the same sincerity for the overall relationship. It is important to meet a Latin on his or her terms, and those terms are very simple—your friendship, trust, and forthright candidness.

The cultural characteristics of Latin America can further be understood through Geert Hofstede's (1980) concepts of time, uncertainty avoidance, power, masculinity, and individualism-collectivism. Latin American culture holds a different perception of time than most Anglo-based cultures. The differences between the two general time orientations are best explained by Edward T. Hall's (1959) notion of monochronicity and polychronicity. Monochronicity, which is typical of the United States, reflects a linear and task-focused approach to communication, whereas polychronicity, more commonly found in Latin American countries (Chaney & Martin, 2004), places a higher premium on flexibility. Latin Americans are more spontaneous, use schedules only as guides, and are more accustomed to multitasking than most Anglos. The siesta illustrates this accommodation toward time. Stores, banks, and business offices all close for two or three hours in the early afternoon to permit people a chance to rest and replenish their energy. Latins perceive this as personal time needed to prepare them for the remainder of the day, whereas outsiders often regard this as an inconvenient nuisance and the source of much frustration.

Context refers to the "pattern of physical cues, environmental stimuli, and implicit understanding that convey meaning between two members of the same culture" (Thill & Bovee, 2005, p. 70). Thus, the meaning of words in a social or business setting may depend more on the way in which they were delivered rather than in the word choice itself. Latin American countries tend to be "high-context," meaning that cultural messages are implicit and one needs to read between the lines when interpreting another person's meaning

(Ulijn, O'Hare, Weggerman, Ledlow, & Hall, 2000). For example, to avoid hurting a business associate's feelings, a person may say, "Maybe we'll do business with your firm in the future," which is understood as a polite "no." In the United States, however, such a statement would most likely be taken literally, with one businessperson expecting a future business transaction.

Uncertainty avoidance is the extent to which a culture relies upon and expects ample information to accomplish a task. People in cultures with high levels of uncertainty avoidance, like most of Latin America, feel uncomfortable if they are given vague or incomplete information (Hofstede Chart, 2005) and most likely will seek additional data from another person. An example of uncertainty avoidance might occur when an employee, hesitant to make a mistake, asks a supervisor for more detailed instructions on how to complete a task; a U.S. employee would be more inclined to proceed on the available information without requesting more.

Power orientation refers to the extent to which a culture defers to legitimate authority in familial, societal, and organizational authority structures. Unlike mainstream U.S. culture, Latin American culture is more authoritarian (Lorrain, 1999). Subordinates in Latin American companies do not feel as free to question or challenge authority. They use formal titles more frequently (Clutter & Nieto, 2001), show greater respect to authority figures, and are much more hesitant to complain or even offer suggestions than their Anglo counterparts.

Each society has a perspective about the roles that men and women play. In high-masculine cultures, men tend to hold the positions of power and make the critical decisions. This cultural tendency toward masculinity is found predominantly in Latin America (Hofstede, 1980) and may also coincide with an inclination toward *machismo* (from which the English word "macho" is derived), which prescribes a particular code of behavior for men in their society. Machismo is an attitude that men have toward women and one another. The macho man is aggressive and sometimes insensitive—machismo represents power. Machismo is made up of virility, zest for action, daring, competitiveness, and the will to conquer. In business, a man must demonstrate forcefulness, self-confidence, visible courage, and leadership with a flourish. The machismo concept is implanted early in childhood and is impressed in both sexes (Harris & Moran, 1991). Today the United States tends to be less masculine-oriented than it once was, although elements of traditional male and female roles are still apparent in various aspects of society. Consequently, women may be put off by macho swaggering and flirting. Men may feel uncomfortable with the unflinching and nose-to-nose style of conversation.

Individualism-collectivism refers to the extent to which a culture or subculture emphasizes the well-being of a group over the benefit of an individual.

Whereas in U.S. contexts there is a focus on individual rights and privileges, Latin Americans place more value on social and business groups (Tuleja, 2005). For the most part, Latins' concerns are their family, their personal friends, their business associates or professional colleagues, their political party, and their athletic team. So to reach a Latin, relate everything in those terms. Because of this collectivistic tendency, the abundance of legal protection afforded by U.S. law for individual workers is not as readily present in many Latin American legal systems. However, with continued globalization and as exposure to more individualistic countries occurs, this may change. Venezuela and Colombia have two of the highest collectivism scores in the world (International Hospitality Operations, 2005).

Although there is consistency among most Latin American subcultures with respect to these behavioral standards (see Table 10.1), there is also some variation among different Latin American countries in how these traits are operationalized. Countries closer to the equator, for example, tend to be higher power than those in the "cone" countries of South America—Brazil, Chile, Uruguay, and Argentina. Before generalizing too broadly, a potential business partner

Table 10.1   A Comparison of U.S. and Latin American Cultural Dimensions

Dimension	United States	Latin America
Time Orientation	Monochronistic: people value punctuality	Polychronistic: time is flexible
Context	Low context: Words have literal meaning	High context: words interpreted according to situation and cultural norms
Uncertainty Avoidance	Low avoidance: feel comfortable working with limited information	High avoidance: seek thorough information before making decisions
Power	Low power: feel free to question and challenge authority	High power: defer to authority
Masculinity	Low masculine: men and women are equal in authority	High masculine: men hold authority
Individualism/ Collectivism	Individualistic: Emphasize individuals' rights	Collectivistic: place value on the group's well-being

should thoroughly familiarize himself or herself with the particular aspects of a country's society; just as the United States and Canada are similar in most respects, even they differ on some finer issues of cultural distinctiveness. Failure to show appropriate sensitivity to the nuances of local cultures can offend Latin American partners or associates (Hugenberg, LaCivita, & Lubanovic, 1996).

The instability in many Latin American economies has created a tendency to let chance guide their destiny. Most Latins are convinced that outside forces govern their lives, so they will more readily speculate, risk, and gamble. They are willing to accept the inevitable (Harris & Moran, 1991).

The islands of the Caribbean come closer to the eternal fantasy of an earthly paradise than almost anywhere in the world. Yet, the idyllic landscapes of the Caribbean belie a dramatic and often cruel history. Fought over by colonial powers and vulnerable to natural disasters, these small islands have also been marked by slavery, migration, and a tradition of resistance and rebellion. The people of the Caribbean reflect a powerful mix of influences that has resulted in today's striking cultural diversity and creative self-expression (Nausbaum, 2002).

Historically, the Caribbean has been a New World crossroads, giving the region the distinction of being a coalescence of civilizations with an eclectic synthesis of cultures and a unique worldview. The major ethnic groups of the region, namely the West Indians, Africans, and European peoples, have maintained to varying degrees their ancestral heritage. Articulation of Caribbean culture has been most clearly expressed by the creative ideas that have emanated from the area, especially voiced through its scholars, writers, ideologues, artists, and artistes. Such intellectuals as Sir Arthur Lewis, who won the 1979 Nobel Prize in Economics, or writers and activists like Paul Bogle, Louise Bennett, Marcus Garvey, C.L.R. James, and the 1992 Nobel Prize winning author Derek Walcott have all shared their cultural thinking and ideas with the world. Artists like Enriquillo Amiama, Janis Rankin, Cynthia Hatfield, Phyllis Biddle, Juan Fernando Chaon, and Mario Enrique Mendez Matos have presented through watercolor, oil, and mixed media the colorful cultures of the Caribbean. The tropical rhythms of the region have been globally conveyed through the reggae music of Bob Marley and by the Mighty Sparrow or Dr. Slinger Francisco, known as "The Calypso King of the World." The Creole languages are perhaps one of the more clearly identifiable cultural forms to have emerged in the Caribbean area, explicitly preserving African, European, and Asian ideas and words in the common, everyday, popular expression (Mintz & Price, 1985; Welcome to the Caribbean, 2005).

Before the arrival of Christopher Columbus in the Caribbean, the Taino-Arawak-Carib Indians peopled the region. Following numerous confrontations with the Europeans, these indigenous societies were wiped out and the

Caribbean was colonized by European powers. More recently, the United States has played an influential role in the region. As a result of this particular history, the political traditions of the Caribbean are varied and mirror those of the former and present colonizing powers. The English-speaking Caribbean has adopted the British pattern of a parliament. The Dominican Republic adheres to the Spanish American pattern of a president. Cuba has implemented a revolutionary communist system. Puerto Rico as part of the United States follows that pattern. Suriname and the Dutch Caribbean operate a system consistent with the Netherlands. The political systems of Martinique and Guadeloupe are an integral part of French political arrangements (Richardson et al., 1992). The Caribbean, therefore, is a very diverse region of people and politics. The single most important explanation for this diversity is the variety of colonial history and related influence.

Social, Economic, and Political Factors

Before the 1980s, Latin America was not poised to be a major player in the world market. Social and political unrest, chronic inflation rates, and high cascading taxes in many Latin American countries prevented regional businesses from competing with the larger markets such as the United States and Europe. Nations like Chile, Argentina, and Uruguay, which now enjoy fully democratic governments, suffered under dictatorships and tight government control of their economies through most of the 1960s, 1970s, and 1980s, restricting both domestic and international business environments. It was not until the latter part of the 20th century that many Latin American countries returned to, or implemented for the first time, democratic governments. Currently, most Latin American countries have political and economic mechanisms that allow and even encourage foreign businesses to flourish within and between their respective borders.

These reforms have caused Latin America to quickly emerge as a serious competitor in an increasingly globalized market. Since 1990, the influx of U.S. foreign direct investment (FDI) into Latin America increased exponentially, surpassing worldwide FDI to the Asia-Pacific, African, or Middle East Regions (U.S. Department of Commerce, 2003). Total foreign direct investment into Latin American countries almost doubled from 1995 to 1998, most of which went to Brazil, Mexico, Argentina, Chile, Colombia, and Venezuela (Economic Commission for Latin America and the Caribbean, 1999); by 1998, five of the top 10 countries receiving foreign direct investment were Latin American (U.N. Economic and Social Commission for Asia and the Pacific, 2005). The United States is Latin America's largest trading partner, representing 16.9 percent of total U.S. exports in 1993 and constituting over 21 percent of total U.S. exports in 2000 (Council of State Governments, 2001). The United States is Colombia's principal trading partner and Venezuela's primary importer (U.S. Department of State, 2005b). Over 170,000 U.S. citizens reside in South America, and over half a million U.S. tourists visit the continent each year for business and recreation (per U.S. Department of State statistics). Worldwide exports to Latin America "far outpaced the other regions of the world in terms of their rate of increase between 1993 and 2000" (Council of State Governments, 2001, p. 15).

In general, Latin America's trade is divided equitably among the United States, the European Union, Asia, and other Latin American countries. Twelve Latin American countries—Mexico, Brazil, Venezuela, Colombia, Dominican Republic, Argentina, Chile, Costa Rica, Honduras, Guatemala, El Salvador, and Peru—were among the United States' top 50 trade partners for the period of 1991–2000 (Council of State Governments, 2001). Eleven of these countries had triple-digit growth rates during the 1990s. During the early 2000s, inflation rates in Argentina, Brazil, and Mexico, the "big three economies" of Latin America, remained stable; these countries accounted for 74 percent of the region's GDP in 2003. Brazil and Mexico are the 8th and 11th largest economies in the world, respectively (S. Anderson & Cavanaugh, 2000). Although FDI into the region has dropped since 2000, it went from $14 billion in 1991 to $61 billion in 1998 (U.N. Economic and Social Commission for Asia and the Pacific, 2005), an increase of over 400 percent. The growth rate of Latin America peaked in 2003, dropping off in response to the economic problems suffered by many of its trade partners, including the United States.

Today the region boasts emerging economies, with rapidly developing fiscal and commercial policies. Mexico and Brazil have GDPs surpassing those of most European nations. Additionally, Chile and Uruguay now each have progressive bilateral trade agreements with the United States; the presence of multinational companies in the region is evidenced by the many U.S. fast-food chains such as Dunkin Donuts, Pizza Hut, Subway, Kentucky Fried Chicken, and McDonald's, the latter of which was named among the best companies to work for in Latin America in 2005 (Hispanic Business, 2005b; Central Intelligence Agency, 2005c). Domestic companies such as Embraer, the Brazilian jet manufacturer that supplies commercial aircraft for several U.S.-based carriers, are recognized industry leaders, and many Latin American companies are listed on world stock exchanges. Companies in Latin America that bear the suffix "S.A." (Sociedad Anomia) are roughly the equivalent of incorporated entities in the United States that bear the designation "Inc."

Despite the considerable economic activity that has recently occurred in Latin America, it is difficult to generalize the economy of the region as a whole because of the variation in economic and political conditions across all countries. For example, extreme inflation rates in Haiti (39 percent) and in

187

Venezuela (31 percent) skew the region's modest rates of 7.8 percent. Unemployment rates that are relatively low in certain countries (3.7 percent in Cuba; 3 percent in Guatemala) are much higher in other countries (22 percent in Saint Vincent and Grenadines, 13.4 percent in Peru, and 14.5 percent in Panama) (Economic Commission for Latin American and the Caribbean, 2006). The mean economic indicators suggest, however, that the region as a whole is strong.

Trade and Economic Integration

Latin America has a long history of efforts, many of them only marginally successful, to establish regional economic integration. Unsuccessful economic policies, political turmoil, and lack of administrative infrastructure within the region limited the success of these efforts. Through a series of measures, including deregulation and economic integration, the region has made some progress in establishing itself as a strong trading entity. Table 10.2 shows a brief history of the integration process.

One of the first attempts to integrate the economies of Latin America was the Latin American Free Trade Association (LAFTA), created in 1960 with the Treaty of Montevideo. Not entirely successful, LAFTA was replaced with the 1980 Treaty of Montevideo, which created the Latin American Integration Association (ALADI), with the same 11 countries (International Labour Office, 2004; Lima, 1997; SICE, 2002). It was not until several years later, however, that a significant trade agreement was established. MERCOSUR (Common Market of the South) was developed as a result of the Treaties of Asunsciön and Ouro Preto in 1991 and 1994, respectively (Mercosur in Brief, 1999). This agreement was designed to reduce and eventually eliminate tariffs on goods exchanged between member countries, to fix a common external tariff, to coordinate macroeconomic policies within member countries, and to strengthen the overall integration process (SICE, 2002). The composition of this trade agreement, similar to that of the European Union but lacking in supranational structure (EU & Mercosur, 2000), joined the member countries into a structure of economic cooperation representing over $1 trillion in GDP and $52 billion in U.S. foreign direct investment (EU & Mercosur, 2000). As an outgrowth of the Latin American Integration Association (1980–1982) and the Andean Group (1969–1973), MERCOSUR emerged at about the same time as the Free Trade Area of the Americas (FTAA) in 1994 and the North American Free Trade Agreement (NAFTA) in 1994. Today MERCOSUR struggles to hold a vital posture in the world market but remains the third-largest trading bloc in the world after NAFTA

Table 10.2   A History of Economic Integration in Latin America

Agreement	Year	Countries
Latin American Free Trade Association	1960	Argentina, Bolivia, Brazil, Chile, Colombia, Ecuador, Mexico, Paraguay, Peru, Uruguay, Venezuela
Central American Common Market	1960	Guatemala, Honduras, Nicaragua, El Salvador, Costa Rica
Andean	1969	Bolivia, Chile, Colombia, Ecuador, Peru
CARICOM (Common Market of the Caribbean)	1973	Antigua & Barbuda, Bahamas, Barbados, Belize, Dominica, Grenada, Guyana, Haiti, Jamaica, Montserrat, St. Kitts & Nevis, St. Lucia, Suriname, St. Vincent & Grenadines, Trinidad & Tobago
Latin American Integration Association	1980	Argentina, Bolivia, Brazil, Chile, Colombia, Ecuador, Mexico, Paraguay, Peru, Uruguay, Venezuela
MERCOSUR	1991	Argentina, Brazil, Paraguay, Uruguay (with Chile and Bolivia as Associate Members)
NAFTA	1994	Canada, Mexico, United States
South American Community of Nations	2004	Bolivia, Colombia, Ecuador, Peru, Venezuela, Argentina, Brazil, Paraguay, Uruguay, Chile, Guyana, Suriname
DR-CAFTA (Central American Free Trade Association)	2005	Guatemala, Honduras, Nicaragua, El Salvador, Costa Rica, Dominican Republic, United States
Free Trade Area of the Americas	pending	All democratic countries in the Western Hemisphere

and the EU. Its common tariffs account for 85 percent of all traded goods within the region (Daniels & Radebaugh, 2001). MERCOSUR is the fourth-largest economic entity in the world after the EU, the United States and Japan (Mercosur, 2005). In the 2000s MERCOSUR countries and Andean Group countries are negotiating through the Cuzco Declaration an effort to create a large trading bloc encompassing the entire South American continent. The Central American Free Trade agreement, signed by U.S. President George W. Bush in 2004, was approved by the U.S. Congress in 2005 as CAFTA-DR after the Dominican Republic joined.

Another regional agreement that even more significantly influenced trade in the Western Hemisphere was NAFTA, which created a free-trade zone among the United States, Canada, and Mexico. The agreement, signed in 1992 and implemented in 1994, was an outgrowth of two previous bilateral trade agreements between the United States and Canada, and between Canada and Mexico, respectively. In addition to the gradual elimination of tariffs among member countries, the agreement provided for (1) sanitary and environmental standards; (2) protection against import surges; (3) special phase-out processes for certain agricultural products, such as dairy, orange juice, and sugar; (4) the "Rule of Origin," which provided that products come from within the three member countries or be significantly altered with products developed within those countries; and (5) the "De Minimus Rule," which allowed no more than 7 percent of any product to be produced in a nonmember country (U.S. Department of Agriculture, 2006).

Initially, NAFTA proved problematic for Mexico. In addition to experiencing a decidedly uneven balance of trade with the United States, Mexico also reeled from the domino effects of the Asian Financial Crisis (see Chapter 11) and a sharp devaluation of the peso. The latter has been referred to as the "Mexican Peso Crisis." As the balance of trade began to even out in the late 1990s, however, NAFTA began to strengthen the Mexican economy. All tariffs are to be completely eliminated by 2008.

Case Study: The Mexican Peso Crisis

This well-known financial disaster, also known as the "Mexican Tequila Crisis of 1995," had a rippling effect on economies throughout Latin America. During the late 1980s and early 1990s, Mexico experienced a capital surge after aggressively seeking and infusing foreign capital into its market, then losing a large portion of that capital following the devaluation of the peso in 1994 and the loss of investor confidence. To compensate for the depletion of capital, the Mexican Bank issued a large amount of tesobonos, or short-term notes, which fell due the following year. Unable to pay those investors who chose not to renew their notes, the government was forced to seek international aid to bail it out (Arner, 1996).

Investors in many other countries, especially Argentina and Brazil, felt the impact of Mexico's actions. Followed shortly by the Asian Financial Crisis in

1997 (see Chapter 11), countries with struggling economies undertook measures to compensate. For example, two of Brazil's reforms of the 1990s—the Fiscal Responsibility Law and the Plano Real—helped to stabilize that country's economy. The former set standards for public accounting practices, limited public debt, and relaxed trade barriers (Brazilian Fiscal Responsibility Law, 2000); the latter "pegged" the country's currency, the real, to the U.S. dollar (Janse, 2005). Brazil's GDP now exceeds $1 trillion (Economic Commission for Latin America and the Caribbean, 2006). Argentina, for a short time, dollarized, temporarily stabilizing its financial problems. Argentina still struggles to maintain a steady economy, although the tumultuous extremes of previous decades have not been repeated.

More recently, however, Latin America has become more involved in integration with the United States. In December 2002, the United States Congress granted President George W. Bush Trade Promotion Authority, a "fast-track" ability to establish bilateral trade agreements with individual countries in the Western Hemisphere. This authority gave the U.S. president the power to quickly create a trade agreement with another country without extensive involvement of the two houses of Congress. The intention was to create the Free Trade Area of the Americas (FTAA), which would eventually eliminate trade barriers among all participating countries in the Western Hemisphere, creating a trade zone with a GDP of over $10 trillion (Council of the Americas, 2003). It was this initiative that expedited the negotiations with Chile, which had been negotiating with the United States for several years for such an agreement without success and which became the first country in the hemisphere to actually establish a bilateral trade agreement with the United States under FTAA provisions. Uruguay completed a similar agreement in late 2004 that should soon go into effect provided that certain disputed issues can be successfully negotiated, and Peru is currently negotiating such an agreement. The FTAA dialogue has occurred through a series of meetings attended by leaders of 34 countries in the Western Hemisphere. These began in 1994 with transnational summits (Summit of the Americas, 2005) held in Miami, Santiago, and Quebec City and continued through a series of Ministerial Meetings in the United States, Colombia, Brazil, Costa Rica, Canada, Argentina, and Ecuador from 1994 to 2004 (Antecedents, 2005; Council of the Americas, 2003; Summit of the Americas, 2005). Upon completion of negotiations, virtually the entire Western Hemisphere and its almost one billion people will be part of the largest trading bloc in the world.

The Central American Free Trade agreement (DR-CAFTA) emerged shortly after "fast track" trade authority was given to President Bush in 2002. The initial agreements established a trade zone between the United States and five Central American countries—Costa Rica, El Salvador, Guatemala, Honduras, and Nicaragua—and began in May 2004 (Washington Office on

Latin America, 2004). Congressional approval of CAFTA-DR in 2005 has opened up trade in most key sectors of goods and services and eliminated some tariffs on products within the member countries. It also ensures enforcement of antidumping measures and the protection of intellectual property rights. The agreement, modeled after NAFTA, is an important step in establishing a hemisphere-wide trade zone under the FTAA and should create new opportunities within manufacturing, agriculture, textiles, and other industries, as it will eventually reduce tariffs on 80 percent of goods and services exported from the United States to Central America and the Dominican Republic (Office of the United States Trade Representative, 2005a).

Money in Latin American countries has responded sometimes dramatically to chronic problems in Latin America, namely hyperinflation and political turmoil. To stabilize the value of their currencies, some countries turned to the U.S. dollar as a solution. Many countries, such as Argentina and Ecuador, "dollarized" their currencies, making the Argentine peso equal to the U.S. dollar; Ecuador's currency was eliminated and replaced with the U.S. dollar; and merchants in the country accepted either currency, although they actually favored the dollar. Other countries such as Brazil "pegged" their currencies to the U.S. dollar, meaning the value changed in conjunction with the variations experienced by the U.S. dollar. Although many economists in the region feared that replacing a country's historical currency would have a deteriorating effect on the country's cultural identity (Beim & Bulmer-Thomas, 2003), the efforts, at least in the short term, proved to be helpful, especially for Ecuador, which reduced its inflation rate dramatically (Bamrud, 2001).

The economic conditions in Latin America are generally favorable for domestic and international investment, albeit with some caution. Those countries with the strongest commitment to democracy typically offer the "safest bet" for business. However, all economic indicators as well as political events should be considered carefully before a company or individual considers expanding to or investing in any country.

The Caribbean is considered an attractive area for foreign investment and international business. The people are honest, hospitable, and hardworking, and the societies are for the most part stable and safe with a rather laid-back lifestyle. By per capita income measures, Caribbean economies are classified as middle-income countries, with the exception of Guyana and Haiti, which are decidedly low-income countries. However, Caribbean economies are much less advanced than other middle-income countries like Brazil, Chile, and Mexico (Welcome to the Caribbean, 2005).

The infrastructure is modern in most of the countries of the region, and these countries also offer affordable and well-trained labor forces. Add to that the close proximity of this region to North and South America and the special trading arrangements they enjoy with the United States, Canada, the European Union, and such countries as Venezuela, Colombia, and Mexico and you have a region that is situated well for doing international business. Moreover, many of the countries are currently in the process of privatizing state-owned enterprises, including their telecommunications services, and are looking for business in nontraditional sectors of their economies (Atkins, 1998).

Sugar, bananas, and oil are among the commodities that continue to play a role in the economic life of the region. Apparel and textiles from the Dominican Republic, Jamaica, and Haiti should increase with the recent passage of the Caribbean Basin Trade Enhancement Act. Caribbean-based businesses have access to loan and grant capital through a variety of local and international sources, including the Caribbean Development Bank (CDB), the Inter-American Development Bank (IDB), the Multilateral Investment Facility (MIF), and the European Investment Bank (EIB). The capitalist system of production is still the overarching economic culture in the region (Barker & McGregor, 2003).

Presently tourism is replacing agriculture, and the islands of the Caribbean are facing the challenge of economic survival while still maintaining their distinctive identities. The impact of tourism is tremendous in the Caribbean, and it seems only destined to grow with cheap airfares and travel channels vigorously promoting the region, its splendid climate, and many recreational amenities. Although some voice reservation about the cultural and ecological impact of this invasion, others argue that the material benefits imparted to the island economies are real, needed, and benign. Each island's cultural identity is a dynamic asset that can be preserved but not totally protected from change with civic planning and an eye toward promoting local traditions. In this way, tourism and local identity might possibly evolve together (Wagenheim, 2004).

There is willingness in the Caribbean to embrace change, and the area has actively pursued economic integration. The Caribbean Community and Common Market (CARICOM) represents a significant effort of economic integration in the Western Hemisphere. The primary initiative went into effect in 1965 with the Agreement at Dickenson Bay, which established the Caribbean Free Trade Association (CARIFTA). Originally intended to lay a foundation for a customs union, CARIFTA was initially signed by three countries but wasn't fully implemented until 1968 when five other countries gained entry into the agreement. By the early 1970s, more member countries had joined CARIFTA, creating an impetus to change the structure of the agreement to a common market. At the 1973 Treaty of Chaguaramas, CARIFTA became CARICOM. Today the body serves not only as a force of economic integration within the region, but also as an important tool in coordinating the development of social and political policy (CARICOM, 2006) as well as serving as a critical link to the rest of the Western Hemisphere. As of 2005, CARICOM has 15 full members and five associate members across the Caribbean region. In this new era of economic liberalization, the Caribbean is committed to creating diverse and truly competitive economies. These efforts at integration are strengthening the economic outlook for the Caribbean, but caution should still be exercised given the many challenges still facing the area. Individual investors and multinational organizations must carefully analyze the specific islands they plan to enter because social, political, and technological issues can vary.

Business Conduct and Characteristics

Business conduct and characteristics will vary somewhat from country to country; therefore, we will present certain generalizations that can safely be made regarding business etiquette in Latin America and the Caribbean. Understanding the culture and the people as well as the economic and political background of Latin America and the Caribbean is clearly a prerequisite to conducting business. However, global managers must also be open to new business practices and behaviors.

TITLES

Because Latin America is generally considered to be a high-power area, using appropriate titles when first meeting associates is essential. Unless they hold a specialized title such as *Doctor/Doctora* or *Professor/Professora*, men should be addressed as *Señor* and women as *Señora*. Moreover, most people in Latin America use their mothers' surnames in their formal names but should not be addressed as such. For example, Señor Roberto Morales Gonzales should be called *Señor Morales*, because Gonzales is most likely his mother's name. Once an initial relationship has been established, your Latin American counterpart will probably ask to be addressed by his or her first name. It is also customary to be polite, but not overly talkative, to an executive's secretary or to a housekeeper; any request a guest makes should be channeled through the office manager or the *señora* of the household.

ATTIRE

Dress in Latin America, especially in business contexts, is generally very formal. In most South American cities, it is not generally acceptable to wear shorts unless one is at a beach or swimming pool. In the cooler climates of Chile, Argentina, and Southern Brazil, men generally wear suits, ties, and sweater vests and women wear blouses, sweaters, jackets, and dresses. Because of the heat, countries closer to the equator tend to be less formal in attire, although they are still very conservative by U.S. standards. Colors and styles for men— and to a lesser extent for women—should be "business conservative" at all times (Devine & Braganti, 2000).

In the Caribbean, dress is very casual and informal. Comfortable warm-weather clothing is acceptable in most areas.

TIME

Whereas U.S. business people tend to focus on one task at a time and place great emphasis on punctuality and efficiency, Latin Americans generally feel more comfortable building relationships slowly, focusing at first more on establishing personal friendships (Devine & Braganti, 2000; Kras, 1994; Ober, 2001). They also are less concerned about punctuality, although a visitor to the region should always show up for meetings on time.

The Caribbean also tends to be very flexible and informal regarding time. However, although punctuality is not closely adhered to in the region, prior appointments with business clients or associates are advisable.

CONVERSATIONAL TABOOS

Selecting appropriate topics for casual conversations is crucial to starting a positive relationship with Latin Americans. Although people in the United States frequently argue politics, doing so with a Chilean, an Argentine, or a Venezuelan may create an uncomfortable situation because of unpleasant pasts or current events in their countries' memories. Discussing sensitive social issues, especially those related to religion or ethnic groups, should be avoided. Stereotypical allusions to Brazil as a "jungle" or a "land of carnival" are also generally offensive. Ethnocentric references to the United States as "America" are considered particularly distasteful because most people in Central and South America also consider themselves to be Americans. Brazilians are also insulted when labeled as "Hispanic." The international business traveler should discuss sports, food, literature, music, and art until a comfortable relationship with the future business associate is established.

Likewise, in the Caribbean it is acceptable to discuss the economy, art, sports, or the weather, but it is advisable to avoid local politics, religion, and other controversial subjects. The topic of race should particularly be avoided.

BUSINESS MEETINGS AND DECISION-MAKING

Most Latins favor long deliberations before engaging in business. Inquiring about the well-being of family members or discussing hobbies and interests are also expected as a precursor to building a business relationship. The U.S. method of conducting business first or jumping to the bottom line may seem cold, impersonal, and even suspicious.

GREETINGS, BUSINESS ETIQUETTE, AND COURTESIES

Latin Americans tend to be more tactile (Gudykunst, 1998) than people in the United States, touching each other more during greetings. Men typically engage in longer handshakes and often embrace; women may kiss each other on the cheek, and men may even kiss women in a similar fashion. Latins will stand very close when talking, and moving away could be considered an insult.

It is customary in most Latin American countries to bring a gift to a host or potential client. Types of acceptable gifts vary by country. Usually a fine wine or elegant drink, a gift that can be appreciated by everybody in the home, or even gifts for children are considered appropriate.

Many important social and professional events are centered on lunch or dinner, each of which may be multicourse and over two hours long, with conversational intervals between courses. In many Latin American countries, dinner may not begin until 8 or 9 o'clock and is preceded by drinks and followed by coffee. Lunch, which is eaten late in the afternoon (2 or 3 o'clock), may last well over an hour (Noble & Lascam, 1991). Being impatient may damage a potential business relationship, so travelers should be well versed on the local dining and entertainment norms before ever stepping on a plane.

Emerging Trends

Given the rapidly expanding economy of Latin America, there are several issues that will likely have a dramatic effect on international business. Some of the most likely developments involve the following:

1. *The effects of e-commerce.* The increasing availability of the Internet has exacerbated Latin America's presence in the world market; there are more than 47 million Spanish-speaking consumers online, as well as 19 million speakers of Portuguese (Business News America, 2002). These figures are only expected to grow. Latin American–based e-commerce has increased 30 times since its $6.8 billion in 2002 and will continue to play an influential role in the

economy (Global Reach, 2002). This open floodgate of electronically conducted business will be a boon to almost every industry in Latin America, especially those related to marketing, communications, and business services.

2. *The continued emergence of free trade in the Western Hemisphere and beyond.* As the goals of the FTAA are reached across the United States and Latin America, greater opportunities will exist for importing and exporting and for moving jobs across borders. Related travel opportunities for business will increase, resulting in extended opportunities for the transportation, food, leisure, and hotel industries. CARICOM will extend these same benefits to the Caribbean area.

3. *The melding of culture and language across borders.* As a result of continued trade, travel, and collaboration between the United States and Latin America, each respective culture will undoubtedly assimilate parts of the other. Just as English continues to become more common in corporate circles of Latin America, the need for U.S. business professionals to learn Spanish and Portuguese will increase. Also, with the sharing of products and services, cultures will incorporate various aspects of the other, reflected by such expressions as "Tex-Mex," or "Spanglish," which are common in the U.S. Southwest and northern Mexico.

Summary

Like the rest of the world, the United States is beginning to realize the business potential offered by Latin America and the Caribbean. No longer considered a land of jungles, fiestas, and coffee plantations, Latin America is making a niche for its natural resources, its available workforce, and its relatively newfound political and economic freedom. As it continues to forge its place in the world market and as trade liberalization continues to sweep the Western Hemisphere, Latin America will be a new Mecca for goods and services for prudent entrepreneurs in every country.

Likewise, the Caribbean is being perceived as more than an island paradise. It too is emerging as an area with considerable international business potential. Although tourism is its growing industry, the Caribbean does have considerable resources that creative entrepreneurs and multinational organizations can tap into. Despite these encouraging signs, substantial challenges still remain. The achievements of the past decade have not created enough economic development to reduce poverty and income inequality or to resolve the area's health and education problems. However, as it further integrates itself with the global economy and attracts more investors, the Caribbean will be better able to deal with the many social and political issues that hinder its full development.

Resource Guide

Books

Culture, Communication, and People

Clawson, D. L. (2003). *Latin America and the Caribbean: Lands and peoples* (3rd ed). New York: McGraw-Hill.

Crouch, N. (2004). *Mexicans and Americans: Cracking the cultural code*. London: Nicholas Brealey.

Wiarda, H. (2003). *The soul of Latin America: The cultural and political tradition*. New Haven, CT: Yale University Press.

Customs and Business Conduct

Becker, T. (2004). *Doing business in the new Latin America: A guide to cultures, practices, and opportunities*. New York: Praeger.

Deaton, G. L. (2003). *The guide to Mexico for business* (11th ed.). Mexico City: American Chamber of Commerce of Mexico.

Hillman, R. S., & D'Agostino, T. J. (2003). *Understanding the contemporary Caribbean*. Boulder, CO: Lynne Rienner.

History and Politics

Garreton, M. A. (2003). *Latin America in the twenty-first century: Toward a new sociopolitical matrix*. Miami, FL: University of Miami North/South Center Press.

Henke, H., & Reno, F. (2003). *Modern political culture in the Caribbean*. Jamaica: University of West Indies Press.

Maingot, A. P., & Lozano, W. (2004). *The United States and the Caribbean: Transforming hegemony and sovereignty*. New York: Routledge.

Pastor, R. (2001). *Exiting the whirlpool: U.S. foreign policy toward Latin America and the Caribbean* (2nd ed.). Oakland, CA: Westview.

Tulchin, J. S., & Garland, A. M. (2000). *Social development in Latin America: The politics of reform*. Boulder, CO: Lynne Rienner.

Tulchin, J. S., & Selee, A. D. (2002). *Mexico's politics and society in transition*. Boulder, CO: Lynne Rienner.

Winn, P. (1999). *Americas: The changing face of Latin America and the Caribbean*. Los Angeles: University of California Press.

International Business and Globalism

Davidow, J. (2004). *The U.S. and Mexico: The bear and the porcupine*. Princeton, NJ: Markus Wiener.

Gwynne, B., Kay, C., & Gwynne, R. N. (2004). *Latin America transformed: Globalization and modernity* (2nd ed.). Edmonton, Canada: Arnold.

Martinez-Vergne, T., & Knight, F. W. (2005). *Contemporary Caribbean cultures and societies in a global context.* Jamaica: University of West Indies Press.

Roberts, J. T., & Thanos, N. D. (2003). *Trouble in paradise: Globalization and environmental crisis in Latin America.* New York: Routledge.

Tirado de Alonso, I. (2002). *Caribbean Economies in the twenty-first century.* Gainesville: University Press of Florida.

Weaver, F. S. (2000). *Latin America in the world economy: Mercantile colonialism to global capitalism.* Oakland, CA: Westview.

Trends and Challenges

Black, J. K. (2005). *Latin America: Its problems and its promise* (4th ed.). Oakland, CA: Westview.

Rich, P. G. (2000). *Latin America: Its future in the global economy.* New York: Palgrave.

Stark, J. (2001). *The challenge of change in Latin America and the Caribbean.* Miami, FL: University of Miami Press.

Web Sites

Association of American Chambers of Commerce in Latin America (http://www.aaccla.org). The Association of American Chambers of Commerce in Latin America (AACCLA) is a leading advocate of increased trade and investment between the United States and Latin America and the Caribbean. The site addresses social, economic, and political factors.

Caribseek Search Engine (http://www.caribseek.com). A Caribbean search engine that addresses social, economic, and political factors. It provides country directories and other useful links.

Latin America Business Link (http://www.labl.com). An international business portal addressing business conduct and characteristics in Latin America.

Latin America Network Information Center (http://lanic.utexas.edu). Provides excellent links to countries and addresses the economy, education, government, humanities, the Internet and computing, media and communications, science, society and culture, and sustainable development. The mission of this Web site is to facilitate research and academic endeavors to schools, teachers, and students as well as private and public sector professionals.

Mexico Business Opportunities and Legal Framework (http://www.mexico-trade.com/table.html). This guide alerts those who approach the Mexican market about business conduct, and the existing legal and regulatory framework.

MexOnline (http://www.mexonline.com). A broad collection of resources including accommodations, activities, business, city guides, culture, food, history, holidays, maps, demographics, the environment, health, science, social information, weather, and climate.

Organization of Eastern Caribbean States (http://www.oecs.org). This is an excellent Caribbean news resource. The OECS is now a nine-member grouping comprising Antigua and Barbuda, Commonwealth of Dominica, Grenada, Montserrat,

St. Kitts and Nevis, St. Lucia, and St. Vincent and the Grenadines. Anguilla and the British Virgin Islands are associate members of the OECS.

Znet. Latin American Watch (http://www.zmag.org/LAM/latamwat.cfm). This site allows you to browse or search 1,000 archived articles pertaining to economics, politics, history, and media regarding any specific Latin American country.

11

Doing Business in East Asia and the Pacific Rim

Photo by K. Phillip Taylor

Photo by K. Phillip Taylor

Photo by K. Phillip Taylor

his chapter focuses mainly on the countries composing the western edge of the Pacific Rim, namely Australia and East Asia. This is an area that includes some of the world's most diverse populations and economies. According to the World Bank, East Asia and the Pacific Rim include the developing countries of Indonesia, Malaysia, Philippines, and Thailand; the transitional economies of China and Vietnam; the newly industrialized economies of South Korea, Taiwan, and Singapore; and the mature industrialized economies of Japan, Australia, and New Zealand. It is difficult to generalize about these markets because historical, cultural, and economic differences can mask the realities of the marketplace and varied human conditions (C. Craig, 1993). Therefore, we specifically examine China, which is by some measures the second largest economy in the world and a transitional economy that is changing the value systems and the economic well being of its neighbors. We also examine Japan as another special case study because it has an aggressive history with its neighbors and a strong nationalist sentiment. Finally, because cultural factors are important in the formation of living conditions and economic growth, we study the cultural values of Asia that have led to risky behaviors and the Asian financial crisis. East Asia and the Pacific Rim are very much a part of the total global economy.

Geography and Demographics

The eastern portion of the Eurasian land mass could be thought of as a sub-continent in itself that slopes downward to the east and south from the great uplifted massif of Tibet. From Tibet (which is an autonomous region within the People's Republic of China) and from the parallel mountain ranges that lie just to its east emerge many of the great and famous rivers of China and Southeast Asia, including the Huang He (Yellow River), the Yangtze, and the Mekong. China's western region includes not only Tibet but also the autonomous region of Xinjiang and the provinces of Qinghai and Gansu. Lofty mountains and vast deserts dominate all these areas, whereas the eastern half of China is both humid and less mountainous. The north central region of China, through which the Yellow River flows, also receives relatively little rainfall and has for millennia been plagued by occasional droughts. This area is thought of as the cradle of Chinese civilization because it was here that the earliest dynasties emerged (Murowchick, 1994). China, which is about the same size as the United States, is also similar to the United States in that it includes a variety of energy, mineral, and other natural resources.

Vietnam, which borders China on the south, was a part of the Chinese empire for about 1,000 years. The Vietnamese view their successful rebellion from the Chinese as an indication of their love of independence, and they view their history in general as a series of struggles against powerful invaders, including the Chinese, the Mongols, the French, the Japanese, and the United States. Its climate is largely tropical and subtropical.

The climates of Korea and Japan are similar to neighboring regions of northeastern China (which in turn is similar to the northeastern United States), with some ameliorating effects in Japan due to the influence of the surrounding oceans. Summers in Japan, however, can be surprisingly humid, reminding some visitors of the summer climates of Miami or New Orleans.

The total population of China (including the People's Republic and the Republic of China or Taiwan), Japan, Korea (North and South), Vietnam, and Australia is over 1.5 billion, or roughly one-fourth of the world's entire population. The giant among these Pacific Rim nations is China, whose current population of 1.3 billion accounts for over 80 percent of the Pacific Rim's total. China's great size, combined with its rapidly developing economy, makes it a power to be reckoned with in the 21st century (Atlas of the World, 2004).

China is also the most ethnically diverse of the western Pacific Rim countries. When picturing the people of China, most observers think automatically of the Han people, the majority population whose name is derived from the Han dynasty, a contemporary of the Roman Empire. The Han people dominate China today and have done so since the fall of the Qing dynasty in 1911, a dynasty whose rulers were Manchus, not Han Chinese. Mao Zedong, Deng Xiaoping, Jiang Zemin, and Hu Jintao, the four most prominent leaders of the People's Republic, have all been Han Chinese. So are those Chinese who have made an impression in the West, including Bruce Lee, Jackie Chan, and Yao Ming.

The Han Chinese, accounting for about 1.2 billion of China's population, are themselves diverse. The largest group consists of the Mandarin speakers who populate northern, northeastern, and central China. But also significant are the Cantonese who live mainly in Hong Kong and Guangdong province. Other significant Han Chinese groups are the Hakka and the Min, who are the majority population of Taiwan, where they are often referred to as Taiwanese. These various Han groups are distinguished most importantly by the forms of Chinese they speak. All of these so-called dialects of Chinese are mutually unintelligible. In other words, a Mandarin speaker from Beijing cannot understand the Cantonese spoken by a Hong Kong Chinese, who, in turn, cannot understand the Taiwanese spoken by someone from Taibei. The two forces that hold the Han Chinese together are their use of a character-based writing system (which allows them to read and understand each other even when they cannot do so by talking) and a powerful pride in China as an enduring civilization.

The non-Han Chinese on the mainland are divided into 55 ethnic groups or nationalities, according to the government of the People's Republic. The best known of these are the Mongols, the Manchus, the Tibetans, and the Uighurs. Within the latter two groups some resistance against Han domination has occurred, and the Beijing government is extremely sensitive about the issue of ethnic relations with them. Because the Uighurs are Muslims, a few of their anti-Han members have made their way to Afghanistan where they have been trained under the auspices of al-Qaeda. The southwestern provinces of Yunnan and Guangxi are home to dozens of other ethnic minorities, some of whom overlap the borders of Vietnam, Laos, and other Southeast Asian countries. Some of the better known groups from this extremely varied area are the Zhuang, Miao, and Dai (Harrell, 2001).

Where China is marked by ethnic diversity, Japan is characterized by homogeneity. The vast majority of the Japanese speak more or less the same language (with certain definite regional dialect variations) and identify themselves as descendants of an ancestry dating back thousands of years. The very small minority populations are the Ryukyu Islanders (including the Okinawans), the Ainu of the extreme north, and the immigrant populations of Korean and Chinese. There is also a group of Japanese known as the burakumin that has traditionally suffered discrimination from the majority population (Hendry, 2003).

Korea is even more ethnically homogeneous than Japan, with the main distinctions today being those stemming from the isolation between north and south that began as World War II ended. The northern half of the Korean peninsula is occupied by the isolated Democratic People's Republic of Korea, currently ruled by the dictator Kim Jong-il. The south is known as the Republic of Korea and has been ruled by democratically elected leaders since the late 1980s.

Vietnam, unified after a long, bitter war against first the French and then the United States, is dominated by a single majority population. Like China, Vietnam has a large number of mountain-based minority groups; indeed, some of the same groups found in southwestern China also live in the mountains of Vietnam.

Australia and New Zealand consist of a majority population that is of European and English-speaking descent, and each also has some non-English-speaking immigrant minorities as well as native minority groups. The Aborigines reside in Australia and the Polynesian Maori in New Zealand.

Cultural Themes and Patterns

Although Australia and New Zealand are island cultures with their own distinct cultural features, they closely resemble North America and Western Europe, and we do not closely study them here. Instead, we consider in more detail the cultural themes and patterns of Asia proper. A mistake Westerners often make regarding the people of East Asia is to overemphasize their similarities. Japan, for example, is as culturally different from China as Finland is from Greece. Yet, being aware of cultural diversity should not blind us to broadly shared themes.

One underlying theme applicable to China, Japan, Vietnam, and the Koreas is that of the Confucian family ideal. In any society, East or West, the family occupies a place of honor and is a powerful shaper of ordinary lives. But a feature of the Confucian-influenced family that differentiates East Asia from the West is the emphasis on hierarchy that favors the old over the young and males over females. This hierarchical pattern is also reflected in the wider society. No modern East Asian country has been led by anyone younger than fifty years of age, nor by a woman of any age. Large corporations tend to be similarly dominated at their highest levels by men of late middle age or older. However, these biases favoring age and favoring males are not written in stone, and in an energized economy like that of China, it is quite within the realm of possibility that a young Bill Gates or even a "Belinda" Gates may rise to prominence in the near future.

In East Asia, family loyalty is supported by real behavior. For example, adolescent children who are university-bound expect much more input from their parents on what universities and what majors to select than do their Western counterparts. And, a university graduate's first job often comes by virtue of parental activation of social connections or what in China is called *guanxi*. In general, there is a strong expectation that one's relatives will extend themselves on one's behalf.

Another feature distinguishing the East Asian family systems is the deeply rooted sense that religion itself is largely a matter of tending to family interests. It has long been thought in these societies that ancestors continue to oversee the behavior of their descendants and that they can actually have an effect on their descendants' lives. Although this notion has been strongly discouraged in communist-dominated societies, it continues to live on, particularly among those of modest education.

This Confucian family-focused religion is supplemented and in some ways contradicted by other religious traditions such as Buddhism, Daoism, and Shinto. Catholicism established a strong foothold in Vietnam during the French colonial era, and both Catholic and Protestant churches have made significant inroads among South Koreans. The People's Republic of China is also seeing an increase in the number of Christian converts, a somewhat surprising development given the long Chinese tradition of seeing Christian missionaries as instruments of imperialism.

These and other lesser religions serve to provide adherents with a sense of spiritual purpose that is not strictly confined to family interests and, in the case of Buddhism, to offer practical rituals for dealing with the deaths of family members. East Asia differs from the West in that most people do not divide themselves into mutually exclusive religious groupings but rather approach religious ideologies as a kind of spiritual smorgasbord. It is typical, for example, for East Asians to visit temples of various different religions throughout their lives without feeling a need to commit entirely to a single religion.

Other Confucian-based values that have an impact on the economies of East Asia are its emphasis on the value of education and its glorification of harmony and *ren* or "human-heartedness." Harmony and human-heartedness (sometimes translated as benevolence) help shape interpersonal and intercultural relationships as well as the way business is done in East Asia.

Case Study: How Cultural Factors Contributed to the 1997 Asian Economic Crisis

In July 1997, the Asian economic crisis burst to life when Thailand could not maintain its currency exchange rate. The crisis spread throughout Asia with a profound impact on local and global economies (Roubini, 1999). South Korea, Thailand, Indonesia, Malaysia, and the Philippines (hereafter referred to as "crisis Asia"), previously areas of unprecedented and sustained growth, were hit hardest. Within several months, the flight of foreign investment, declining currency values, crashing stock markets, large layoffs, contracting GDPs, bank closures and consolidations, and rising prices of staples afflicted the region severely. Furthermore, the area experienced an overall rise in lending rates, inflation, debt repayment problems, and cutbacks on mega projects.

Joel Kotkin, senior fellow at the Institute for Public Policy at Pepperdine University, believes that culture forms a basis for most of what happens in economic progress and that a "cultural virus" shapes most of what societies do in politics, economics, and other areas and how they do it (M. Lewis, 1998). This supports an emerging body of literature pointing toward such cultural factors as collectivism, authoritarianism, and power distance as the antecedent conditions that produced the Asian economic crisis. Asian values had brought Asian countries to the major leagues of the global economy, but their failure to adopt Western norms in transparency and democracy issues prevented them from avoiding certain pitfalls (Gardels, 1998). Singapore Senior Minister Lee Kuan Yew and others have observed that Asian governments and the business community had taken on a type of "hubris" and lack of humility uncharacteristic of Asians (Hitchcock, 1998).

COLLECTIVISM

Cultures differ in their members' orientation towards the group and the individual. A 1994 Center for Strategic and International Studies survey of 100 respected observers of Southeast Asia revealed that Asians rate orderly society, group harmony, and respect for authority as high priorities. Although the Asian ideals of hard work, respect for learning, collectivism, and lack of individualism brought them unparalleled growth, many analysts now believe that these same cultural factors led to the abuses of collusion, lack of transparency, poor banking practices, and corruption that precipitated large weaknesses in many of these countries' economies and continue to forestall recovery (Hitchcock, 1998). The cultural phenomenon of a collective, familistic, and *quanxi* (personal connections) form of capitalism allowed government and business collusion, corruption, and competition-thwarting to exist (Gardels, 1998). Zaman (1998) asserts that even the International Monetary Fund (IMF) failed to warn the world financial markets about Asia's impending collapse to "assure continued cooperation and working relations with the governments concerned" (p. 38).

Walker (1998) points out that the modern business practice of debt protection, liquidation, and bankruptcy so commonly utilized in the West were largely unused in Asia because reconstruction and compromise better conform to Confucian tradition. According to Hitchcock (1998), the Asian collectivist practice of indirectness and avoiding public embarrassments led to the moral hazard of bailouts that contributed to the lack of market correction that precipitated the crash. This, combined with the cultural practice of "special" relationships among favored clients for rewarding contracts and a lack of oversight (Hitchcock, 1998), precluded the public from asking for transparency even when faced with overwhelming evidence of mismanagement, corruption, and years of insolvency. Perhaps liberalization in transparency practices would have led to stabilization because market correction would have occurred sooner, avoiding such a large boom and bust cycle. This is a concept that former Japanese Prime Minister Kiichi Miyazawa has been recommending for his country.

AUTHORITARIANISM

To say that Asian culture is heavily devoted to strong authority (government, corporate, familial, or societal) is an understatement. On the surface, the belief in an elite ruling power provides for a measure of certainty and security. On the other hand, this respect for an "elite" ruler ensures that even outrageous allegations against entrenched interests go unheeded. Sicherman (1998) suggests that the often-touted "Asian model" is an exaggeration of a benevolent autocracy characterized by a modern "free" economy and that such governments are not strong enough to compel sacrifice for necessary market corrections nor popular enough to inspire sacrifice voluntarily. This situation led to a reckless and irresponsible pursuit of profits and piled risks onto an already fragile structure that increased the external vulnerability of crisis Asia (Zhou, 1998).

The financial bubble grew, and each newly funded project became another step in a giant Ponzi scheme (Alon & Kellerman, 1999; Krugman, 1998). To a large degree, this financial bubble was hidden from the eyes of investors and regulators. The authoritarian governments in Asia had no interest in revealing the structural weaknesses in their economies. Prior to the economic crisis, dire predictions and warnings of financial turmoil often brought accusations of promoting disharmony and seditious attempts at destabilization. Malaysian Prime Minister Mahatir bin Mohammed's jailing of Deputy Prime Minister and Finance Minister Anwar Ibrahim in 1998 for sedition and sexual perversion is a prime example. When charges of nepotism and cronyism against Dr. Mahatir began to surface at the ruling party's general assembly, he told delegates "those who raise issues that may destabilize the party must be accountable for their actions" (Be Responsible, 1998, p. 1). Authoritarian societies, at least on the surface, appear stable because the authoritarians rarely permit challenges to their perception of events.

When the economies started to fail, denial and efforts to find scapegoats became dominant public themes, whether or not anyone outside these countries believed even the most outrageous claims. First, the Thais "blamed Americans upset with Thai policy toward Cambodia; the Koreans blamed Westerners who feared they could not compete with Koreans; the Malaysian Prime Minister blamed Jews" (M. Lewis, 1998, p. 36). Dr. Mahatir blamed "rogue speculators," and many Asian governments accused Western nations of trying to buy Asian assets at "bargain" rates (Roubini, 1999).

Serious reform efforts rarely succeed in authoritarian administrations. Paternalistic, familial, and authoritarian governments tend to control the information about conditions leading up to and after a crisis, and this jeopardizes efforts at correction. Cultures that prize authoritarianism in a belief that the leaders will provide for the people may have to realize that, as Gardels (1998) advocated, adopting Western norms of democracy in the form of individual responsibility, transparency, and accountability may have to be part of economic reform. Francis Fukuyama (1998), professor of public policy at George Mason University, observes that "in the absence of adequate feedback mechanisms and institutional controls on state power, it ends up being a matter of luck whether authoritarian institutions are turned toward the single-minded pursuit of investment and growth or become vehicles for padding the bank accounts of the politicians in charge" (p. 24).

POWER DISTANCE

Power distance is the extent to which members of a culture adhere to unequal distributions of power and the amount of respect accorded people's positions and status in a hierarchy. Power distance is an extension of the indirect communication style favored by Asians and accounts for the lack of transparency throughout the years leading up to the economic crisis. When state banks ran out of money to lend, government ministers, state bank officers, well-connected business executives, and top loan officers encouraged risky short-term external borrowing—the very damaging practice that started the currency collapses. The lack of confrontation led to 10 years of face-value government assurances until July 2, 1997, when the Central Bank of Thailand admitted publicly that they were insolvent because of unpaid loans.

Culturally, there could not have been any public or private challenge. Too much respect for hierarchy had led to a critical lack of transparency just when Asia needed it most. Government officials and business people throughout Asia have continually stated that Asian values brought them incredible economic progress over the years, yet another set of values (absolute trust in leaders, tolerance of corruption, and lack of confrontation) encouraged risky antecedent conditions that led to the economic crisis. According to Meuhring (1998), some of the solutions to Asian economic woes include economic practices such as new codes of conduct governing fiscal transparency from the G-7 and the IMF.

The causes of the Asian economic crisis were economic (too much growth too fast, too much unsecured credit, too many unworthy ventures and leaders) and cultural (too much confidence in the leaders' grand visions, too little investigation of people and institutions that needed scrutiny, and too much insistence on group harmony by the leaders). This economic cataclysm has spurred deep philosophical introspection that should encourage Asian countries to forge economies that are less prone to a wild roller coaster ride so that they can enjoy a lengthy boom without this spectacular and devastating bust. Although there is no lack of educated leaders and population who should be insisting on change, Zhou (1998) reiterates that Asian values and mores are products of thousands of years and cannot be expected to change quickly and drastically. Walter Russel Mead (1998), senior fellow at the Council on Foreign Relations, notes that in the old days a handshake, customs, and family relationships were strong enough to build a modern social safety net; however, "when modern cities spring up, you need courts of law, unions, and government oversight" (p. 38).

Social, Economic, and Political Factors

Personal relationships, sensitivity to others, trust, and connections characterize East Asia. This emphasis on relationships and the dignity of the person is evidenced in the Asian interest in maintaining "face." Face is not an entirely alien concept for Westerners. What differentiates China, Japan, and other Confucian-influenced countries from the West is the principle that makes sensitivity to the other person's dignity so acute that sometimes obvious truths are disregarded in favor of polite fictions. For example, there is a general reluctance to say "no" to a direct request. Rather, one is told, "That might not be convenient," which should be interpreted as a definite "no" couched in face-saving terms. "Telling it like it is" is not valued in Asia the way it is in many U.S. contexts (R. Moore, 1988).

A business deal is not a marriage proposal, but in East Asia, the best business deals are thought to be based (like good marriages) on well-established foundations of mutual understanding and trust. For this reason, patience is a powerful virtue in doing business in Asia. The long-term cultivation of good relations between investors and entrepreneurs is the norm, and it is advisable to nurture relationships before signing any agreements. A corollary of the Asian idea that the human connection supersedes in importance the pragmatic one is the idea that the best business relations are built on trust and trust takes time to develop.

Along with the idea of simple practical matters being best embedded in complex human relationships is the idea that getting anything important done requires a connection with someone in a key position. In China, this is reflected in the widely used term guanxi, which literally means "connection" (Gold, Guthrie, & Wank, 2002). The connections themselves can be natural, as through relatives or old college classmates, or they can be the result of intentional cultivation as when gifts and services are offered to someone whose influence or help is sought (L. Young, 1994). Guanxi networks are those in which individuals respond readily to people with whom they have developed some kind of relationship, while sometimes disregarding the needs of those with whom no such relationship has been established. Guanxi can easily evolve into simple corruption, a problem that plagues China, Vietnam, and to a lesser extent, Japan and South Korea. The governments of China and other Asian countries occasionally pursue anticorruption campaigns when illegal favor trading has gotten seriously and disruptively out of hand.

The political systems of the Western Pacific are extraordinarily diverse. Australia and New Zealand have a system of government that combines the parliamentary features of the United Kingdom with the federalism of the United States and Canada. As in the other English-speaking democracies, their governments tend to be broadly pro-business, seeing the promotion of commerce as the key to prosperity.

The democracies of Japan and South Korea are in some ways similar to those of Western nations. Japan differs from the Western model in that political parties and factions, allied with specific economic interests and segments of the bureaucracy, tend to be unusually stable. The Liberal Democratic Party (LDP), for example, has enjoyed almost 50 years of uninterrupted power. This is partly due to the family-based model of strong group loyalty and respect for seniors, both of which ensure that shifts in personnel are relatively rare. Thus, a tightly woven, loyalty-based pyramid of power in the LDP parallels similar structures in the bureaucracies it controls and the corporate networks it serves and on whom it relies for funds (Hendry, 2003). The stability and generally business-friendly world that "Japan, Inc." has created has proven its worth given the decades of prosperity it has yielded. Japan, between 1955 and 1990, illustrated the tremendous power of an economy organized around the principles of loyalty and seniority. Since 1990, the Japanese have learned the limits to the benefits of such a "personalized" economic system.

South Korea, with an elected president and National Assembly, has followed Japan into the liberal democratic world, albeit somewhat belatedly. Where Japan had an essentially democratic system in place immediately following the end of the American Occupation in 1950, South Korea continued as a dictatorship until the late 1980s. Today, as one of East Asia's rising economic powers, it resembles its longtime rival Japan and has followed Japan's political, economic, and technological lead.

Father and son dictators, Kim Il-song and Kim Jong-il, have ruled North Korea since the end of World War II. It is so impoverished and inaccessible to the West that it is of little interest to those seeking economic opportunities. This may change in the near future if South Korea's efforts at developing a stronger relationship with the North prove fruitful.

China is politically the most dramatic and problematic country in East Asia. Following a long civil war between two dictatorial camps, the Communists under Mao Zedong and the Nationalists under Chiang Kai-shek, the People's Republic was declared in Beijing on October 1, 1949, and the Nationalists fled to the island province of Taiwan where they established the Republic of China. Today the People's Republic of China (PRC) and the Republic of China (ROC) stand in opposition to each other across the Taiwan Straits.

The Republic of China, commonly referred to as Taiwan, has gradually evolved a relatively democratic system of government similar to that of South Korea. As a conservative dictatorship, Taiwan had always supported commercial and technological ventures, and it has for decades enjoyed a level of prosperity unusual in this part of the world.

The People's Republic of China has been intensely hostile to capitalism and consequently prohibited the development of China's resources for the better part of three decades. Since the death of the communist dictator Mao

Zedong in 1976, China has opened itself to trade, investment, technological innovation, and various forms of international cooperation. The result is the looming power that is China today, a nation virtually assured of becoming the world's largest economy within the next few decades.

A major problem confronting China is its continuing resistance to openness and freedom of expression typical of more liberal societies. The current ruling party, which continues to call itself the Chinese Communist Party, is in fact free of any Marxist ideology. It governs a population that remains docile only insofar as prosperity continues to grow. In fact, this has been described as the "deal" that China's "communist" rulers have made with the populace—in exchange for stability and increasing prosperity, the public will accept the rule of a self-serving and undemocratic government (Alon, 2003a, 2003b).

Hong Kong remains a unique geopolitical entity, following its return to China in 1997. It had been a British colony since the 19th century, and under the colonial authorities it managed to develop a level of prosperity rivaling that of the much larger island of Taiwan. Its proximity to China and the advantages of travel for its citizens afforded by its connection to the British government gave Hong Kong the leverage required to establish itself as a remarkable economic engine. Although smaller than a typical U.S. county, Hong Kong became a center of shipping, banking, and manufacturing that no city in China proper could rival. Although the government of the PRC sees Shanghai as superseding Hong Kong as a center of finance, Hong Kong will continue to be a regional force to be reckoned with. According to the treaty of 1997, Hong Kong is supposed to be allowed to run its own internal affairs with minimal interference from Beijing until 2047.

Vietnam has followed a path that resembles the PRC just as South Korea followed a path blazed by Japan. In 1986, after years of communist-controlled economic stagnation, Vietnam threw off its doctrinaire Marxist program in favor of *doi-moi* or broad economic reform. The result has been a burst of economic activity and a general improvement in living standards that promises to trend upward in the future. As in China, however, Vietnam's government has not been as friendly to liberal democratic reform as it has been to economic reform, and clashes between the rising expectations of its citizens and the rigidity of the governing authorities can be expected in the future as well (Chang, 2001).

Business Conduct and Characteristics

Professional attire is essential for formal business gatherings in Asian countries. For social gatherings and entertaining, it is recommended that you dress conservatively and let your Asian counterparts set the tone. At the first meeting, a few phrases of greeting in the native language will be greatly appreciated by the local people. Although business meetings may be conducted in English, the key decision-makers of the hosting organization may not have sufficient foreign language skills or they may prefer to communicate in the native language. So, instead of relying on a translator provided by the host, it is highly desirable to have someone on your side with ample language and cultural knowledge of the hosting country. Before departing or immediately upon arrival, have your business cards translated into the native language on the reverse side and make sure you bring plenty of them. Your official title and decision-making authority should be clearly stated. When attending business meetings, punctuality is expected. At the initial gathering, business cards should be given and received with both hands in a manner that the person receiving it can read the card without turning it.

A polite handshake and a slight bow are the greeting customs in Asian countries. Unlike expressive and straightforward Westerners, Chinese, Japanese, and Koreans pride themselves on holding their emotions inside. It is extremely rare to see people embrace in public. In East Asian countries, family name traditionally precedes the given name. However, some people will switch the order of their names when dealing with Westerners. To avoid confusion, it is always advisable to ask how to address someone. People with formal titles should be addressed accordingly along with family names. Although many Asian nations have experienced some degree of democratic reform in corporate culture, most Asians still have a high regard for rank and seniority, and the highest ranking members of the company will always be introduced first.

Dining and entertaining are a major part of business culture in Asian countries. When initiating business dealings, one should plan for a series of meetings, dinners, and conversations to build trust and reinforce good feelings. Deals are often reached over a meal. Because Asians place a great emphasis on formality, it is best to wait for the host to gesture where you should sit and be prepared to make a short speech and exchange toasts. Several rounds of liquor toasts are not uncommon at business banquets, and one needs to be careful to retain control of the situation. During informal conversations, try to avoid sensitive issues such as politics, religion, and human rights as well as questions of a strictly personal nature.

In Asian business culture, gift exchange signifies the establishment of a relationship. Therefore, gifts of reasonable value are considered a normal part of business interactions. Expensive gifts should be avoided. They not only create significant obligations but may also be violations of anticorruption legislation of the hosting country. Appropriate gifts would be representative of your company or your city and country. Be certain to indicate that the gifts are only a small token of appreciation for your host's business assistance during your visit.

A closer examination of Japanese firms further reveals the special cultural context and complex relational structure that characterizes business conduct and distinguishes it from Western organizations (Bhappu, 2000; Nishiyama, 1999). For example, decision-making processes are quite different in Japanese organizations. According to the Japanese philosophy of *ringiseido,* participative decision-making utilizing opinions from multiple levels of management is preferred (Ala & Cordeiro, 1999). The *ringi* decision-making process stimulates group harmony and conformity, enforces group compliance, and creates a sense of hierarchy and loyalty to the group. The Japanese system also focuses on long-term strategies and emphasizes human resource investment. It balances shareholders' value with that of other stakeholders of the organization, such as employees, banks, suppliers, and customers (Kono & Clegg, 2001). Although some authors contend that Japanese and Western approaches are converging (Simeon, 2001), others maintain that important differences continue to exist despite some recent changes (Kono & Clegg, 2001).

Today Asians are holding their breath over Japan and China because, as they go, oftentimes so goes much of Asia. The relationship between China and Japan is multidimensional and requires an examination that cuts across the economic, political, and social spectrums. The following case study examines the dynamics of Sino-Japanese economic and sociopolitical engagements in a global context.

Case Study: The Sino-Japanese Struggle—Who Will Trump Asia?

China is a sleeping giant. Let her lie and sleep for when she awakens the world will tremble.

–Napoleon Bonaparte

Napoleon's visionary statement about China resounds nearly two centuries later. The sleeping dragon has awakened and is jockeying for position in the global political economy. This requires that Japan come to grips with this new global reality and China's willingness to develop cooperative bilateral relations.

After decades of astonishing economic growth during the Cold War period, Japan has taken pride in being an economic miracle and has become the second largest economy in the world. According to Professor Toshihiko Kinoshita of Waseda University, "Japan's glorious decades from the 1960s to the 1980s have been followed by a lost decade from the 1990s to 2002 during which time China rose to economic prominence" (Kinoshita, 2006). Still, according to the GDP measured in current market exchange rates, Japan's economy is more than triple the size of China's. "Japan remains a 1st ranked Sumo, a real Yokosuna," says Kevin Newman (2006), senior manager with Nathan Associates, Inc., who has previously worked with the Japanese Ministry of Home Affairs, the World Bank, the UN, and other international development agencies. He adds that, although battered by 15 years of deflation and economic stagnation, Japan is recovering, and an economic map of its per capita wealth, global investment, and value-added goods demonstrates its present and future competitive strength. Indeed, Japan trumps China in its per capita income using market exchange rates as well as purchasing power. And despite China's tenfold larger population, Japan's total foreign reserves are more than double those of China.

Of course, the growing Chinese economic prowess looms large in the global arena. Although Japan is the second-largest economy on the basis of GDP, China's economic size in terms of GDP measured by purchasing power parity (PPP) is much larger than that of Japan, and second only to the United States. China's population is about 10 times larger than that of Japan, and the top 10 percent of the population in China earn approximately $14,519 per person in PPP terms, which is on par with industrialized countries. China also has a substantially higher growth rate in real domestic demand, a much lower cost of labor, and foreign investment inflows that no other in the world rivals, including the United States. For businesses, the size of the market coupled with its robust growth rate means higher per capita disposable income and larger markets, and an inexpensive labor force and investment inflows create a fertile environment for production.

Still, according to Professor Kinoshita, "Japan can co-prosper with China since the two countries have different cost structures and complementary industries and products" (Kinoshita, 2006). Japan is the third-largest market (following the United States and Hong Kong) for Chinese goods and services, accounting for 14.9 percent of China's total exports. Conversely, China buys more from Japan than any other country, about 18.1 percent of its total imports. According to Shane Frecklington (2006), manager of the American Chamber of Commerce in Shanghai, Japan is the second largest investor in China, with 8 percent of total investment. For China, foreign direct investments in general contribute 20 percent of the GDP, 50 percent of total exports, 10 percent of urban workforce, and 16 percent of taxes collected. China and Japan share a symbiotic relationship as well as a common economic space. If one country falters, the other will be adversely affected. If one prospers, the other can piggyback. Moreover, both countries face similar problems for which they can seek joint solutions—both countries are in the process of deregulating and liberalizing sectors of their respective economies and both need to overhaul their banking systems. The two economies also have complementary needs. Whereas the Japanese economy is sluggish, the Chinese one is overheating; whereas the Japanese are experiencing asset price deflation, the Chinese are experiencing asset price inflation. China and Japan can potentially benefit from multilayered cooperation and take advantage of long-term opportunities through a mutual partnership.

Although the prospects for economic relations between China and Japan are promising, these connections are threatened by increasing political conflicts. Japan's actions during World War II and in particular the Nanjing Massacre (1937–1938) have never been adequately addressed by the Japanese leadership. Frequent visits by the political elite of Japan to the Yasukuni war museum understandably anger the Chinese who have not forgotten or forgiven the Japanese for their harsh occupation of China and victimization of the Chinese people. The bitter past and the present indignation confirm for the Chinese that Japan refuses to renounce its militarist past.

China, however, can carry some of the blame for the contentious political environment that threatens their bilateral relationship. The ominous political tension between China and Taiwan, the United States, and its neighbors (including Australia) may force Japan to take sides and to jeopardize the economic relations thus far built. China's figures on defense spending are believed to be understated, fast rising, and comparable to Japan's. But Japan can only use its military for collective self-defense. Recent U.S. overtures to Japan by the Bush administration could be aimed at turning Japan into a military ally, similar to Britain, by allowing Japan to revise its constitution for a more activist role. The Chinese in the meantime are posturing in the South China Sea, making occasional naval incursions into Japan's waters, and building oil-drilling platforms dangerously close to Japanese territory.

However, not everyone is convinced that China will remain the economic superpower everybody takes for granted. According to Kevin Newman (2006), "China is simply an amalgamation of provinces, hinterlands, and different ethnic groups that now must be forged to achieve national economic integration. Dissent and regional rivalries will increasingly become rife, if not causing major disruptions. China cannot pollute unabated and discriminate with a heavy-hand forever." He continues to note that China's history is marked by "arrogance, belligerence, and then dramatic downfalls." Gordon G. Chang's (2001) book, *The Coming Collapse of China*, echoes some of the same arguments. Among Chang's arguments are that people are discontented, the state-owned enterprises are dying, information is not controllable, industrial policies reward the inept, Chinese banks are failing, WTO accession will trigger collapse, and ideology and politics restrain progress.

An unstable China is very worrisome. Given the threats and opportunities that China poses, how should Japan respond? According to Kim Beng Phar (2006), from the Asian Center for Media Studies at Kuala Lumpur, China and Japan should promote dialogue across and between governments, think tanks, universities, cultural organizations, companies, tourism agencies, nongovernmental organizations, religious organizations, and media organizations. Also, a sincere apology for the Nanjing Massacre would be an example of the needed diplomacy to release the tensions. The Japanese people, government, and businesses must face the reality and enigma that is China. Engaging China productively requires internal assessment, willingness to change, and behaviors that will encourage China to cooperate using relationships, diplomacy, patience, and restraint.

Summary

Five hundred years ago, the world's center of trade began moving from the Mediterranean to the Atlantic. Today it is shifting from the Atlantic to the Pacific. The countries constituting East Asia and the Pacific Rim will significantly influence, both culturally and economically, the 21st century, and successful global organizations will have to fashion their mission and strategies to service this geographic area.

East Asia and the Pacific Rim demonstrate the complexity and multidimensional aspects of culture. Global managers will have to be aware of the important distinctions that exist between the people of this region and understand the assumptions that influence business practice and relationships. The countries that make up this region of the world have evolved very differently, and each holds a unique place in our global marketplace. Moreover, the emerging importance of this area is evidenced in the impact of the Asian economic crisis on the global economy. The old saying, "East is East, and West is West, and never the twain shall meet" must be revised for the new millennium.

Resource Guide

Books

Culture, Communication, and People

Craig, T. J. (2000). *Japan pop: Inside the world of Japanese popular culture.* New York: M. E. Sharpe.

Leibo, S. A. (2004). *East, Southeast Asia, and the Western Pacific.* Harpers Ferry, WV: Stryker-Post Publication.

Varley, H. P., & Varley, P. (2000). *Japanese culture.* Honolulu: University of Hawaii Press.

Customs and Business Conduct

Amber, T., & Witzel, M. (2004). *Doing business in China* (2nd ed.). New York: Routledge/Curzon.

Blackwell, C. (1998). *Negotiating China: Case studies and strategies.* Sydney, Australia: Allen & Unwin.

Brannen, C. (2002). *Going to Japan on business: Protocol, strategies, and language for the corporate traveler* (3rd ed.). Berkeley, CA: Stone Bridge.

Brannen, C., & Wilen, T. (1993). *Doing business with Japanese men: A woman's handbook.* Berkeley, CA: Stone Bridge.

Chan, J. (2003). *China streetsmart: What you must know to be effective and profitable in China.* New York: Prentice Hall.

Chee, H., & West, C. (2005). *Myths about doing business in China.* New York: Palgrave Macmillan.

Haley, G. T., Haley, U. C. V., & Tan, C. T. (2004). *The Chinese Tao of business: The logic of successful business strategy.* New York: Wiley.

Hampshire, D. (2005). *Living and working in Australia: A survival handbook* (3rd ed.). London, UK: Survival Book.

Lee, C. (2003). *Cowboys and dragons: Shattering cultural myths to advance Chinese/American business.* Chicago: Dearborn Trade.

Nishiyama, K. (1999). *Doing business with Japan: Successful strategies for intercultural communication.* Honolulu: University of Hawaii Press.

Norton, J., & Shibusawa, T. (2001). *Living in Japan: A guide to living, working, and traveling in Japan.* North Clarendon, VT: Tuttle.

Seligman, S. D. (1999). *Chinese business etiquette: A guide to protocol, manners, and culture in the People's Republic of China.* New York: Warner Books.

Sieff, J. D. (2003). *A practical guide to living in Japan: Everything you need to know to successfully settle in.* Berkeley, CA: Stone Bridge.

Stuttard, J. B. (2000). *The new silk road: Secrets of business success in China today.* New York: Wiley.

Tannen, D., & Yamada, H. (2002). *Different games, different rules: Why Americans and Japanese misunderstand each other.* New York: Oxford University Press.

Yan, R., & Liberthal, K. (2004). *Harvard Business Review on doing business in China.* Cambridge: Harvard Business School Press.

History and Politics

Fewsmith, J., & Kirby, W. (2001). *China since Tiananmen.* New York: Cambridge University Press.

Gomez, E. T. (2001). *Political business in East Asia.* New York: Routledge.

Jansen, M. B. (2002). *The making of modern Japan.* Cambridge, MA: Belknap.

Osborne, M. (2005). *Southeast Asia: An introductory history.* Sydney, Australia: Allen & Unwin.

Owen, N. G. (2004). *The emergence of modern Southeast Asia: A new history.* Honolulu: University of Hawaii Press.

Spence, J. D. (2001). *The search for modern China*. New York: W. W. Norton.

Wang, H., & Huters, T. (2003). *China's new order: Society, politics, and economy in transition*. Cambridge: Harvard University Press.

International Business and Globalism

Lim, R. (2003). *The geopolitics of East Asia*. New York: Routledge/Curzon.

Neher, C. D., & Neher, C. (2000). *Southeast Asia: Crossroads of the world*. Dekalb, IL: Northern Illinois University Press.

Shenkar, O. (2004). *The Chinese century: The rising Chinese economy and its impact on the global economy, the balance of power, and your job*. Philadelphia, PA: Wharton School Publishing.

Studwell, J. (2003). *The China dream: The quest for the last great untapped market on earth*. New York: Grove.

Sull, D. N., & Wang, Y. (2005). *Modern China: What Western managers can learn from trailblazing Chinese entrepreneurs*. Cambridge: Harvard Business School Press.

Zweig, D. (2002). *Internationalizing China: Domestic interests and global linkages*. Ithaca, NY: Cornell University Press.

Trends and Challenges

Fishman, T. C. (2005). *China, Inc.: How the rise of the next superpower challenges America and the world*. New York: Scribner.

Prestowitz, C. (2005). *Three billion new capitalists: The great shift of wealth and power to the East*. New York: Basic Books.

Web Sites

Country Profiles (http://news.bbc.co.uk/2/hi/country_profiles). This British Broadcasting Corporation site provides full profiles of countries including an instant guide to history, politics, and economic background.

Export.gov (http://www.export.gov). This U.S. Government site provides online trade resources and one-on-one assistance for your international business—whether you're just starting or expanding your global sales.

globalEDGE (http://globaledge.msu.edu/ibrd/CountryList.asp). This Michigan State University site provides current information on the business climate, news, history, political structure, economic landscape, and relevant statistical data in a region and country-specific format, covering 196 countries.

International Statistical Sources (http://www.ssb.no/english/-links/international.html). Excellent resource for all forms of international statistics for all countries: economy, education, foreign trade, health, social conditions and services, industrial activities, labor market, natural resources, and the environment.

PricewaterhouseCoopers Countries Online (http://www.pwc.com/gx/eng/main/countriesonline/index.html). Provides basic information on international business, the environment, geography and history, transport and communications, climate and population, political, economic, and social culture.

12

Doing Business in Europe

Photo by W. V. Schmidt

Photo by K. Phillip Taylor

Photo by W. V. Schmidt

E urope is one of the oldest and most culturally diverse business regions of the world. Centuries of political and social change across the region have produced 54 existing countries on the continent today (U.S. Department of State, 2005b), a greater number of countries than any other single continent in the world. Europe's cultural, political, linguistic, and economic influences, both historical and contemporary, have shaped the face of commerce in societies across the globe.

Geography and Demographics

Europe is the sixth largest continent in the world. It comprises some 3,837,000 square miles, significantly smaller than Asia's 17 million square miles and Africa's 11 million square miles (WorldAtlas, 2005a). Within this area are some of the most densely populated nations of the world, with a combined population of over 727 million people (WorldAtlas, 2005a). The continent itself is geographically connected to Asia, separated by the Ural Mountains in central Russia. Consequently, the area in Far Eastern Europe and Far Western Asia is referred to as "Eurasia," much of which is Russian Siberia. The rest of Europe, except the British Isles (the United Kingdom and Ireland) and Iceland, is termed "continental Europe." Although Turkey and Greece may be considered part of Europe, the respective cultures of those countries are distinctive from the rest of the continent.

While the landmass of Europe is small compared to that of other continents, the land is rich in political and cultural variety. In fact, Europe is more easily characterized by its historical and cultural demarcations than by its geographic features. In general, the continent can be classified into four general regions:

1. *Northern Europe* includes the Scandinavian countries of Norway, Sweden, Finland, Denmark, and Iceland, traditionally referred to as the "Nordic" countries.

2. *Southern Europe* comprises the Mediterranean countries of Italy, Greece, Turkey, Cyprus, Malta, Spain, and Portugal, the latter two of which constitute the Iberian Peninsula.

3. *Eastern Europe*, much of which was part of the former U.S.S.R., includes the largest number of countries, such as Ukraine, Hungary, Poland, and the Czech Republic.

4. *Western Europe* refers to the countries of France, Germany, Switzerland, Belgium, the Netherlands, the United Kingdom, and others. The term "Western Europe" may also refer to those countries whose democratic governments stood

in contrast to the substantial part of Eastern Europe that became communist-controlled throughout the mid and late 20th century (EuropeEtravel, 2005).

Although at one point in history London and Paris were considered to be the cultural and commercial capitals of the Western world, today many other cosmopolitan areas rival these two cities across the region. Other major European cities include Liverpool, England; Istanbul and Ankara, Turkey; St. Petersburg, Russia; Essen, Germany; Naples, Italy; and Kiev, Ukraine.

Social, Economic, and Political Factors

Much of Europe, especially the "Eastern Bloc" countries including the former Soviet Union, underwent radical change during the 20th century. Most of this transformation occurred during two periods: the first in the years prior to and during World War II when fascism replaced democracy in a significant portion of Europe and after the division of Germany; then again in the late 1980s and early 1990s when communism collapsed and the Soviet Union was dissolved. Probably the most remarkable and significant year of this latter period was 1989, when the wall dividing Berlin came down, symbolically eliminating the barrier between the free world and communist rule in that city and in Eastern Europe. Currently Berlin, like many of the former Soviet-occupied cities in the region, is one of the largest and most progressive industrialized cities on the continent.

Today most European governments identify themselves as representative republics or democracies, exercising division of power between judicial, legislative, and executive branches of government. Several of the larger European countries, including the United Kingdom, Denmark, Norway, the Netherlands, Spain, and Sweden, have remained constitutional monarchies. A prime minister governs these countries but they still retain hereditary royalty as chiefs of state, such as Queen Elizabeth II of Great Britain and King Juan Carlos and Queen Sophia of Spain. Most European countries operate under civil law or codified legal systems, which make international business difficult from the common law practices of the United States (Daniels et al., 2004).

The United Kingdom, Denmark, Estonia, Finland, Iceland, Ireland, the Netherlands, and Switzerland as well as Belgium, France, Germany, Italy, Norway, Poland, Portugal, and Spain are considered free or mostly free of government intervention (Index of Economic Freedom, 2005). However, businesses in other European countries face tighter restriction from their respective governments, although they still may draw considerable foreign direct investment or other types of international business. Turkey, Russia, and Romania as well as Tajikistan, Uzbekistan, Turkmenistan, Serbia, and Montenegro are considered mostly unfree or repressed (Index of Economic Freedom, 2005).

The dispersion of personal income varies greatly across Europe. The World Bank labels as "high income" or "upper-middle-income" the economies of 32 countries, mostly in Northern and Western Europe, whereas 17 countries, primarily in Eastern Europe, are considered "lower-middle-income" or "low income" (World Bank, 2005a). Five countries—Germany, France, the United Kingdom, Italy, and Spain—rank in the top 10 largest economies in the world (Anderson & Cavanaugh, 2000). These powerhouses are surpassed only by the top two world economies—the United States and Japan.

With the exception of Russia, all of the top-producing countries are located in Western and Northern Europe. These two regions have also held the lengthiest record of democratic governments and free economies, whereas the newer democracies in eastern and southern parts of the continent have not enjoyed as much time to develop their economies. The inflation and unemployment rates in these regions are typically much higher than those of the western and northern nations.

Trade and Economic Integration

By far the most substantial effort in European economic integration is the European Union. The creation of the now 25-member customs union began a few years after World War II, fueled in part by the threat of communism and other political turmoil in the world (Rempel, 1995). It began with the European Coal and Steel Community, established in 1951, with six Western European countries—Belgium, West Germany, Luxembourg, France, Italy, and the Netherlands—and was limited to the coordination of the coal and steel industries only. In 1957, the European Atomic Energy Commission and the European Economic Commission (collectively referred to as the Treaties of Paris and Rome, respectively [Europa, 2005]) emerged, a primary objective of which was to remove trade barriers across the continent. A decade later, in 1967, all three commissions combined, setting the stage for what today is the European Union. The current EU body was established in 1992 at the Treaty of Masstricht.

Today, it is the political and commercial organization of over 453 million people (7 percent of the world's population) (Eurostat, 2004) and has a GDP exceeding $13 trillion (Central Intelligence Agency, 2005b). Its trade relations expand to the Western Hemisphere where it maintains bilateral trade agreements with Chile and Mercosur (Common Market of the South). Although commanding a position of great strength in both hemispheres, the EU countries have somewhat low per capita GDPs—less than those of their major competitors, Canada, the United States, and Japan (Eurostat, 2004).

The structure of the EU is complex. It consists of five major assemblies—the European Commission, the European Parliament, the Council of the European Union, the Court of Justice, and the Court of Auditors (Europa, 2005b). The first three of these bodies acts as a check-and-balance system for creating and implementing EU policy and law; the last two monitor and apply EU law in various aspects of the organization's operation. Numerous other committees and groups under each of these five primary organizations are responsible for various workings of the EU. Two significant treaties since the creation of the European Union—the Treaty of Amsterdam and the Treaty of Nice—served as instruments for developing and protecting citizenship rights, foreign policy, environmental protection, international property rights, and other important legal and political issues (SCADPlus, 2005).

In addition to the EU, there are several other regional associations in existence today, most of them among former Eastern Bloc countries, which have facilitated economic integration. The European Free Trade Area, formed in 1960 by four countries—Iceland, Liechtenstein, Norway, and Switzerland—has agreements with 21 countries and trade bodies, including Israel, Jordan, Chile, and Egypt, and serves as a "bridge" organization with the EU, forming "The 28" (EFTA, 2005). Other European organizations facilitating trade include the Central Europe Free Trade Area, the Commonwealth of Independent States, the Black Sea Economic Cooperation, New Independent States, the GUUAM (Georgia, Ukraine, Uzbekistan, Azerbaijan, Moldova) trade organization, and the Eurasian Economic Community, to name a few. Most of these organizations have six to ten members, mainly from the former Eastern Bloc countries.

The European Union and the Euro

Soon after its inception in 2001, the European Union's Euro (EUR) became Europe's largest currency. The new currency was a result of several steps of economic integration across Europe over four decades, starting with the European Payments Union in 1950, which began a journey to the present structure of the European Union. The Euro is now the only currency used in 12 of the European Union's member countries, plus several non-EU countries such as Monaco, the Holy See (the Vatican), Andorra, Kosovo, and Montenegro. Other EU countries, including the United Kingdom, Slovakia, and Denmark, still use their own currencies, sometimes in conjunction with the Euro.

In most EU countries, however, the original currencies are obsolete, including the Netherlands guilder, the Greek drachma, the Italian lira, the Finnish markka, the Portuguese escudo, the French franc, the German deutschmark, the Luxembourgish franc, the Irish pound, the Belgian franc, the Austrian schilling, and the Spanish peseta (Interactive Currency Table, 2005; Europa, 2005a). Other major currencies of Europe still remaining include the British pound (GBP), the Russian Federation ruble (RUB), the Swiss franc (CHF), and the Danish kroner (DKK). The U.S. dollar (USD) has fluctuated somewhat since 2000, but the greatest fluctuations have been against the Euro (EUR), which has increased in value as its usage has become more widespread within Europe and the world. Exchange rates between the U.S. dollar and the British pound have been generally stable during this period.

The currencies of many islands and former French commonwealths are called "francs." On the exchange market, these currencies may be designated by the symbols XPF, XOF, GNF, or XAF. Other francs, such as the Belgian franc, are obsolete and no longer traded as official currency. Also, several countries have currencies that are spelled very similarly, such as the Danish kroner (DKK), the Icelandic kronur (ISK), the Norwegian kronor (NOK), the Estonian krooni (EEK), the Slovakian koruny (SKK), the Swedish kronor (SEK), and the Czech Republic korany (CZK). Any transactions involving these currencies should be checked carefully to confirm their proper monetary designation.

Case Study: The Russian Federation

Perhaps no other country in the world has undergone as much transformation in the 20th century as the Russian Federation, formerly recognized as the Union of Soviet Socialist Republics (USSR). The most spacious country in the world and the only nation to occupy two continents, Russia has a history that is replete with political, economic, and social upheaval that has garnered world attention. After centuries of monarchy, including some historically notable figures such as Catherine the Great, Peter the Great, and the Alexanders, Russia became the USSR in 1922 after the overthrow of Nicholas II and the rise of Vladimir Lenin. The next 60 years of communist leadership witnessed harsh life under the ruthless rule of men such as Josef Stalin. During this time, the USSR expanded its territory by occupying much of Eastern Europe, including Hungary, Poland, Romania, East Germany, Albania, and Czechoslovakia (now The Czech Republic and Slovakia). Together these countries became known as the "Eastern Bloc," although members of these nations now do not necessarily prefer to consider themselves as "Eastern Europeans" but rather as culturally distinctive ethnic groups.

The people of the USSR and Eastern Bloc countries experienced decades of economic and humanitarian hardships under communist rule and through the horrors of World War II (the USSR fought with the United States, France, and Great Britain against Nazism). Following the war, the country entered into what was known as the "Cold War" with the United States and Western Europe. During this period, each side amassed nuclear arsenals large enough to obliterate the other. Political and social exchange with the USSR became highly inhibited, resulting in Winston Churchill's reference to the USSR and much of Eastern Europe as being behind an "Iron Curtain." Most of the Western world, particularly the United States, did not enjoy commercial or cultural relations with the Soviets and came close to war on several occasions. Thus, the USSR did not offer accessible or favorable business opportunities to most of the free world.

In the 1980s, Soviet leader Mikhail Gorbachev began a series of political and social reforms that instigated a movement toward economic and political freedom. In 1991, two years after the fall of the Berlin Wall, the USSR collapsed, becoming the Russian Federation. At that time, Eastern Bloc countries were liberated from communist rule and began their own individual journeys to a democratic way of life. Many of these countries, particularly Poland, Hungary, Ukraine, and the Czech Republic, now are substantial regional and international business centers. The Russian Federation, with a population of approximately half that of the United States, now enjoys its second decade as a democratic government, although human rights and distribution of powers are still developing (U.S. Department of State, 2005a). The Federation is considered a "mostly unfree" country (Heritage Foundation, 2005), even though its economy has grown robustly since the late 1990s (Central Intelligence Agency, 2005d).

Business Conduct and Characteristics

Like many other regions of the world, Europe is often mistakenly stereotyped as homogeneous. Nothing could be further from the truth. References to European "culture" as a whole are misnomers—many Europeans don't consider themselves to be conventional or typical (EuropeETravel, 2005). Current European societies can be classified by a variety of factors, such as language, religion, political ideology, and history. Even within the borders of most countries, there is much diversity. However, there is a great deal of commonality across the continent, much of which is due to the widespread influence of the Roman Empire, which at one time occupied the bulk of the Western civilized world. This influence accounts for the widespread acceptance of Christianity throughout most of the continent and explains the groupings of languages, which to a large measure follow along political demarcations in Europe.

LANGUAGES

Several principal language groups, primarily from Indo-European linguistic roots, are found regionally. Nordic languages are spoken in Northern Europe; Germanic and Latin languages are spoken in Western Europe; Baltic-Slavic languages are spoken in Eastern and Central Europe; non-Indo-European languages such as Hungarian and Turkish are spoken elsewhere.

Although each of these language clusters is unique, many of them bear commonalities with other clusters. English, for example, belongs to the family of Germanic languages, yet it shares a significant portion of its linguistic characteristics with the Latin or Romance languages such as French and Spanish. The diversity of language in current-day Europe is also demonstrated by the fact that most Europeans are multilingual. English is taught in the schools in most countries and is the most popular second language in Europe, followed by German, French, Italian, and Spanish (Europa, 2005c).

Yet, European languages do not necessarily follow political boundaries. Parts of Switzerland, for example, speak German, whereas other areas of that country speak French or Italian predominantly. Several languages are spoken across Spain, including Basque, which is not a derivative of Latin at all. Moreover, numerous dialects are spoken in Germany, with the differences being significant enough that residents have difficulty understanding each other. There are also significant differences between continental French and Canadian French, between Iberian Spanish and Latin American Spanish, and between Iberian Portuguese and Brazilian Portuguese. The main variations lie primarily in the formation of idioms—region-specific expressions that defy literal translation—and in pronunciation.

HOFSTEDE'S CULTURAL DIMENSIONS

Patterns are also found relative to Hofstede's cultural dimensions of power, uncertainty avoidance, context, individualism, masculinity, and time orientation. As Table 12.1 indicates, Nordic countries tend to be low-power, low-masculine, and strongly individualistic. Western and Southern countries tend to be high-power and high-masculine. Eastern countries are typically more collectivistic and polychronic (McSweeney, 2005).

RELIGIOUS INFLUENCE

Europe is home to all major world religions. Like its languages, the continent's many religions are region-concentrated. For example, Roman Catholicism is predominant in Western Europe, particularly France, Spain, Portugal, and

Table 12.1   Cultural Dimensions of European Countries

High Power	**Low Power**
France, Turkey, Belgium, Slovenia, Croatia, Russia	Denmark, Sweden, Great Britain, Finland, Switzerland
High Context	**Low Context**
France, Spain, Portugal	Germany, Sweden, Norway
High Uncertainty Avoidance	**Low Uncertainty Avoidance**
Greece, Portugal, Belgium, France, Spain	Sweden, Denmark, Great Britain, Ireland, Norway
High Masculine	**Low Masculine**
Austria, Italy, Switzerland, Germany	Scandinavia, Great Britain, France
Individualistic	**Collectivistic**
Great Britain, Netherlands, Italy, Denmark, Belgium, Finland, France	Portugal, Greece, Turkey
Monochronic	**Polychronic**
Greece, Hungary, Baltic States, Germany	Russia, Poland, Romania

SOURCE: Kiriakos, 2005; Country Characteristics, 2005; Hofstede's Dimensions, 2005; Varner & Beamer, 2005.

Italy; Orthodoxy is prevalent in Russia and Eastern Europe; Protestantism is found mainly in Northern Europe and Germany; and Islam is practiced widely in Turkey and in several Eastern European countries.

The religion of European associates should be considered when conducting business. Issues include dietary laws, use of alcohol, matters of hygiene, male-female relationships, respect for calendars and respective Holy Days, attire, and religious symbolism and references. For example, whereas wine is almost always a part of lunch or dinner in France, alcohol may not be appropriate—or even illegal—in communities that are largely Muslim. As a rule, religion or religious issues (as well as political issues) should not be topics of casual conversation, at least until a solid business relationship between people of different cultures has been established.

WORK HOURS AND BUSINESS ATTIRE

Each country and region has its own unique cultural norms regarding work hours and business attire. For example, many businesses in Spain close for an extended lunch break, allowing workers to take siestas (naps) before resuming work at 3:00 or 4:00 in the afternoon. They may also take one to two hour breakfast breaks shortly after reporting to work in the morning (Graff, 2004). The business hours in Northern Italy generally differ from those of Southern Italy, as the northern Italians are more concerned about punctuality and attire than are their southern counterparts. However, in most of Europe, conservatism and modesty in attire should be observed. It is considered inappropriate, for example, in many European contexts to wear shorts unless one is at the beach or participating in sporting activities. Good taste in apparel is considered important in such business cultures as France, Italy, and Spain (International Business Etiquette and Manners, 2005a, 2005c, 2005d) and may influence a potential business partner's initial perception of an international traveler. The business environments of most Western European countries are quite formal, whereas Northern and Eastern European countries tend to be less strict about business attire (International Business Etiquette and Manners, 2005a, 2005b). Wearing an expensive, well-tailored suit is preferable in France or Spain, whereas a neatly pressed shirt without a tie would work just as well in Slovakia or the Czech Republic. When in doubt, err on the side of conservatism or ask your host for suggestions on dress or about other cultural norms.

EATING

Eating "European style" is to be expected across the continent. European-style eating calls for certain protocol (e.g., the fork should not be switched from left hand to right and both hands should be visible while eating). Also, most Europeans regard dining as a "social activity to be enjoyed" (Flippo, 1999) and that is not to be rushed. In Europe, meals constitute a standard part of business negotiations to a much greater extent than they do in the United States. In some cultures, business is actually discussed over meals; in others, meals are used only as a means of getting to know a potential business partner. The evening meal in most European countries is served quite late by U.S. standards, usually not until 9:00 p.m. or even later. Like lunch, dinner is typically a multicourse meal and eaten over a period of one to two hours. Wine or other alcoholic drinks are usually served in moderation before, during, and/or after meals, and food portions are generally smaller than in the United States.

COMMUNICATION

Interaction patterns differ significantly across Europe. What may be considered polite in one country might be considered inappropriate in a neighboring country. Even within the confines of a single country—Italy, for example, where

Southern cities are less formal than their Northern counterparts—customs may be different. German business culture tends to be very formal, with a high regard for privacy, chain of command, great attention to detail (Flippo, 1999), and punctuality (International Business Etiquette and Manners, 2005b). French culture values politeness and quiet conversation, yet allows for a certain degree of argumentativeness when negotiating (International Business Etiquette and Manners, 2005a), and a foreign businessperson should not construe this behavior as negative. In France as well as in Italy it is considered rude to ask a stranger about his or her profession. Instead, most Europeans expect that their guests will be able to discuss less private issues, such as art, travel, or sports.

Many Europeans are not comfortable being on a first-name basis with a new business associate at the initial meeting. The initial contact should be formal, respectful, and courteous. Touching and kissing are also standard fare in many European business contacts. Men may offer kisses to women, women may kiss each other, and men may engage in extended handshakes or hugs when greeting each other. Refusal to participate in these rituals may be interpreted as untrustworthy or insensitive. Moreover, Americans are considered to be pushy by many Europeans—not always an undeserved stereotype—thus, spending more time getting to know your European business partner may be more conducive to establishing effective business relationships. It is also helpful to be familiar with polite forms of address and expressions used in written or spoken business (Constantino & Gambella, 2000; Pearce, 2005). Although being fluent is preferred, using or trying to use the local language may go a long way toward building a rapport in face-to-face, written, or electronic correspondence. Table 12.2 shows some common courtesy expressions and terms for the major language groups of Europe.

As noted above, it is customary in French correspondence to use the person's title and name ("Monsieur Gilbond") as the opening of a letter, instead of using an equivalent of the English "Dear" (Webster's, 2004). In Italian, "dear" literally is "caro" but would hardly be appropriate in a business letter from an international professional. Many online translation services will offer a direct translation such as "Dear" to "Caro," but a literal linguistic translation is not always culturally correct. Spaniards typically use their mother's maiden names in written presentation. For example, in the written title Sr. Antonio Galvez Rodruigo, Rodruigo would be his mother's maiden name, which would appear on correspondence, but he would be addressed as "Sr. Galvez." To make sure you use names correctly, closely observe how that person signs his or her name in business correspondence.

Lack of fluency in a second language and a failure to understand the linguistic nuances of another culture can be problematic as well as a barrier to successful business negotiations. Consider, for example, how slight differences in verbal or numerical symbols can change the entire meaning of an important document or other form of communication.

Most Europeans reverse the U.S. pattern used to denote numerical values. The United States uses the designation $3,400.00 to represent three thousand, four hundred dollars. In France, Italy, or Germany, the same value would typically be depicted as $3.400,00. It is therefore important when preparing correspondence or documents to write out exact amounts in parentheses. For example, "We agree to pay $4,300 (four thousand, three hundred U.S. dollars) for your consultation."

Europeans also invert the numbers representing day and month from what people in the United States normally do. Where 5/11/07 would be understood as May 11, 2007, in the United States, such a designation would be understood to mean November 5, 2007, in European cities. Therefore, it is advisable to use the actual name of the month to avoid confusion. Decimal points are also frequently used to separate day and month rather than a forward slash—05.11.07. Furthermore, a 24-hour clock is used to designate time in many parts of Europe. This is the same system used by the U.S. military, where 6:30 p.m. becomes 18:30.

Even within the same language there can be considerable potential for misunderstanding. English spoken in Great Britain differs in many of its terms for everyday items (e.g., "lift" for "elevator" or "rubber" for "eraser"), and these extend to business concepts (Business English, 2005). A few examples are depicted in Table 12.3.

Table 12.2 Courtesy Language Expressions

English	French	Spanish	Italian	German
Mr.	Monsieur	Señor	Signore	Herr
Ms.	Madame	Señora	Signora	Frau
"Dear" (Letter Salutation)	Use title only Monsier/ Madame	Estimado/ Estimada	Egregio Signore/ Gentile Signora	Sehr geehrte
Please	s'il vous plait	por favor	per favore	bitte
Thank you	merci	gracias	grazie	danke
Closing (Letter)	Use title only	Atentamente	saluti	mit freundlichem gruß

Table 12.3   American-British English Differences

American English	British English
Annual stockholders meeting	Annual general meeting
Chief Executive Officer (CEO)	Managing Director (MD)
Common stock	Ordinary stock
Deductible	Excess
Inc. (Incorporated)	Ltd. (Limited)
Labor union	Trade union
Mutual funds	Unit trusts
Resume	Curriculum vita
Sales tax	Value-added tax
Stock dividend or stock split	Bonus or capitalization issue
Treasury bonds	Gilt-edged stock

SOURCE: http://www.english club.com/business-english/vocabulary_ft-ukus.htm; WWlib-Notes on American English, retrieved Dec. 8 2006 from:http://www.sclt.wlv.ac.uk/~jphb/american.html; UK Corporate Actions (SSN) Glossary, retrieved Dec. 8, 2006 from http://www.exchange-data.com/products/ssn_gloss.aspx.

In general, Canadian English resembles the language spoken in the United States; Australian and New Zealand English are more similar to the language spoken in the United Kingdom. International business travelers or investors should always consult an attorney or a solicitor or barrister in London for linguistic help even if the country speaks the "same" language as their own. It should also be noted that communities bordering other countries, such as the Lugano region of Switzerland where Italian is the predominant language, often use their neighbor's main language as their official form of communication.

Emerging Trends

The diversity of historical Europe and the dynamic quality of contemporary Europe make that continent an exciting theater of business and growth. Along with such potential, however, there are some challenges that must be considered when planning business ventures. Among these challenges are the following:

1. *The sustained growth of the European Union.* When the earliest forms of economic integration in Europe began in the 1950s, only a handful of countries, most of them concentrated in Western Europe, participated. At that time, the combined GDP was not substantial from an international standpoint, and the future of a larger, more politically powerful entity was still in question. Today, that small growth has transformed itself into one of the largest and most powerful economic forces on the planet. With that growth come various difficulties, such as the expansion of its infrastructure, the coordination of its extended monetary, legal, environmental, and social processes among its member countries, and the relationship between the EU and non-EU countries such as the United States and Japan.

2. *The changing demographics of Europe.* Europe is a culturally heterogeneous continent and is becoming more so with continued globalization and the development of democracies. Specifically, its population is aging, more Europeans are receiving higher education (Ulaga, 2005), and more younger Europeans now speak English (Europa, 2005c). Taken together, these changes have equipped European entrepreneurs to pursue greater international business opportunities. The influence of religion is also changing the face of the continent, represented in part by significant changes in the Roman Catholic Church and by the increasing Muslim population. As new and different ways of thinking about business permeate the various societies, changes in practice are bound to follow.

3. *The impact of global terrorism on Europe's economy.* Unfortunately, no continent or nation is spared the horrors of terrorism. Since the bombing of the World Trade Center in New York on September 11, 2001, the economic impact of terrorism has been a concern secondary to safety but significant in its ramifications for economic systems. Although many European countries have long histories of domestic terrorism that predate September 11, since that fateful day, several European countries have felt its impact directly or indirectly. For example, terrorists struck Spain in 2003 and London in 2005, raising the economic burden of maintaining security for their citizens. The added cost of security has affected nearly every industry in the world; these expenses ultimately are passed down to the most fundamental level of the economic process—the consumer. These costs must be considered when making proposals, setting prices, and budgeting for travel.

Summary

A multinational organization or international business can make one of two very serious mistakes when initiating business with European associates. The first mistake would be to stereotype people as "Europeans" by assuming the whole population shares the same attitudes, history, and business practices. The other mistake would be to assume that, because globalization and technology have introduced Europeans to American styles of behavior, they expect to be treated the same as Americans. Therefore, careful attention must be given not only to institutional, structural, and operational differences but also to intercultural factors.

Resource Guide

Books

Culture, Communication, and People

Ellington, L. (2004). *Eastern Europe: An introduction to the people, lands, and culture.* Santa Barbara, CA: ABC-CLIO.

Lane, J., & Erssen, S. (1999). *Politics and society in Western Europe* (4th ed.). Thousand Oaks, CA: Sage.

Customs and Business Conduct

Sabbath, A. M. (1999). *International business etiquette: Europe.* Franklin Lakes, NJ: Career Press.

Sears, W. H., & Tamulionyte-Lentz, A. (2001). *Succeeding in business in Central and Eastern Europe: A guide to cultures, markets, and practices.* Oxford, UK: Butterworth-Heinemann.

History and Politics

Bideleux, R., & Jefferies, I. (1998). *A history of Eastern Europe: Crisis and challenge.* New York: Routledge.

Mannin, M. (1999). *Pushing back the boundaries: The European Union and Central and Eastern Europe.* Manchester, UK: Manchester University Press.

International Business and Globalism

Kelemen, M., & Kostera, M. (2002). *Critical management research in Eastern Europe: Managing the transition.* New York: Palgrave Macmillan.

Schimmelfennig, F., & Sedelmeier, U. (2005). *The Europeanization of Central and Eastern Europe.* Ithaca, NY: Cornell University Press.

Trends and Challenges

Gros, D., & Steinhern, A. (2004). *Economic transition in Central and Eastern Europe: Planting the seeds* (2nd ed.). New York: Cambridge University Press.

Orenstein, M. A. (2001). *Out of the red: Building capitalism and democracy in postcommunist Europe*. Ann Arbor: University of Michigan Press.

Pinder, D. (1992). *Western Europe: Challenge and change*. London: Pinter.

Web sites

Directory of Internet Resources on Central and Eastern Europe and Russia (http://www.ssees.ac.uk/dirctory.htm). Extensive links on all subjects by country.

Euro Pages (http://www.europages.net). Addresses business conduct and cultural characteristics. A directory of businesses throughout Europe.

Britannia: UK Travel & British History (http://www.britannia.com). Over 6,000 pages of British travel and history information.

BusinessEurope.com (http://www.businesseurope.com). Trusted source of news and analysis for small and medium sized business.

EU Business (http://www.eubusiness.com). Europe's leading independent online business news and information service about the European Union.

Database CE (http://www.databasece.com). Dedicated to economic research covering Central and Eastern Europe with a special focus on labor costs and earnings.

Rustocks.com (http://www.rustocks.com). Informative guide to Russian financial markets, privatization events, and major stock indices.

Eurochambres (http://www.eurochambres.be). The Association of European Chambers of Commerce and Industry represents a network of 2,000 regional and local Chambers with over 18 million member enterprises in Europe.

Europa: Your Europe (http://ec.europa.eu/youreurope/nav/en/business/index.html). Provides you with practical information on your rights and opportunities in running your business in the EU and its internal market by bringing together data, information, and useful links to other sources of information.

13

Doing Business in Africa and the Middle East

Photo by S. J. Wolff

Photo by S. J. Wolff

Photo by S. J. Wolff

When the drumbeat changes, so must the dance.

This simple Swahili proverb should be the mantra for every company or multinational organization conducting business with people from other cultures. Foreign managers and CEOs should hang it on the wall of their offices and read it every morning to remind them that business practices in host countries may be quite different from what they are accustomed to. Local employees of multinational firms should also realize that they will be confronted with new conventions and expectations. In order for mutual international business ventures to succeed, all parties must be creative in finding ways to build on their similarities while accommodating their differences. By learning the new dance, they will be able to turn daunting challenges into promising opportunities.

Geography and Demographics

It is fitting—perhaps even inevitable—that the opening proverb originated in Africa, the second largest of the world's continents, comprising more than 50 countries and where more than a thousand different languages are spoken. Here the drumbeat changes constantly. To know any one country is not to know Africa, because of the wide variety of ethnic groups living within each country. Language, customs, arts and crafts, traditional stories, way of life, and religion will vary, sometimes greatly, in each one.

Africa covers 20.3 percent of the total land area on earth and is the only continent that equally spans the equator. It is separated from Europe by the Mediterranean Sea and is joined to Asia by the Isthmus of Suez. From the most northerly point, Cape Blanc, Morocco, to the most southerly point, Cape Agulhas, South Africa, is approximately 5,000 miles. From the most westerly point, Cape Verde, to the most easterly point, Ras Hafun, Somalia, is approximately 4,600 miles. The mean elevation of the continent is approximately 2,000 feet with the characteristic features of moderately elevated tablelands interspersed with higher mountain peaks and ranges and equatorial rainforests. Africa is divided into six geographic regions (see Table 13.1). The coastal plains include mangrove swamps and the deltas of the Congo and Nile rivers, the largest and longest, respectively. The north and west African plains contain the world's largest desert, the Sahara, the highest peak in Africa, Mount Kilimanjaro, and the equatorial rainforests of the Congo basin. The high southern and eastern plateaus include the South African svelte and the

Kalahari Desert. Africa also consists of several island nations, the largest being Madagascar. Africa is divided into six regions and covers six time zones (Central Intelligence Agency, 2005f).

Africa lies almost entirely within the tropics and therefore does not show excessive variations of temperature. In the extreme north and south, the climate is warm and temperate. In the high Atlas mountain range, snow falls and the climate is alpine. Monsoons from the Indian Ocean are regularly felt on the eastern coast, whereas the countries that border the desert regions are exposed to very dry winds called siroccos. The equatorial zone experiences two main rainy seasons. Consequently, the African climate is quite variable (WordIQ, 2004).

Demographically, Africa can be divided into North Africa and sub-Saharan Africa. Because Northern Africa is almost entirely Muslim, it tends to have more in common both linguistically and culturally with the Middle East than with sub-Saharan Africa. Therefore, unless otherwise noted, the term "Africa" will refer to sub-Saharan Africa and the designation "Middle East" will include Northern Africa. The current population of sub-Saharan Africa is about 715 million and is

Table 13.1   The Six Geographic Regions of Africa

I. Western Africa	Benin, Burkina Faso, Côte d'Ivoire, Gabon, Gambia, Ghana, Guinea, Guinea-Bissau, Liberia, Mali, Mauritania, Niger, Nigeria, Senegal, Sierra Leone, and Togo
II. Central Africa	Angola, Burundi, Cameroon, Chad, Congo, Central African Republic, Democratic Republic of the Congo, Equatorial Guinea, Rwanda, Uganda, and Zambia
III. Northern Africa	Algeria, Egypt, Libya, Morocco, Sudan, and Tunisia
IV. Eastern Africa	Djibouti, Eritrea, Ethiopia, Kenya, Malawi, Somalia, and Tanzania
V. Southern Africa	Botswana, Lesotho, Mozambique, Namibia, South Africa, Swaziland, and Zimbabwe
VI. African Islands	Cape Verde, Comoros, Madagascar, Mauritius, São Tomé e Príncipe, and the Seychelles

expected to reach 1.6 billion by 2050 (Population Resource Center, 2002). It remained largely unknown to the Western world until the early European voyages of discovery and Europe's subsequent colonization of most of the African continent in the 19th century (Munro, 1995). Since World War II the great majority of its inhabitants have struggled to move beyond the constraining effects of colonialism, tribalism, and poverty. Although most of the countries have regained their independence, they still struggle with political and economic instability. From an economic perspective and with the exception of South Africa, it is largely the Third World of developing nations. Widespread disease, especially AIDS, and food shortages caused by war, corruption, draught, and a population growth of 3 percent annually—10 times that of Europe—exacerbate its problems (Haber, North, & Weingast, 2003). Most African economies rely heavily on tourism and agricultural exports such as coffee, cocoa, tea, and sisal. Africa may not be as mysterious today, but it is still largely unknown and misunderstood. What most of the world is aware of are the horror stories of draught and famine, the struggles with apartheid, and the political unrest, civil wars, and corruption. Overlooked are the immense resources and natural beauty of Africa as well as the warmth, generosity, and hardworking ways of the African people.

The Middle East, although significantly smaller geographically than Africa with 5,600,000 square miles, is nonetheless nearly as culturally diverse (Encarta online). The majority of the roughly 444,000,000 people living in the 21 countries of the Middle East and North Africa are Arabs, whose ancestors began migrating from the Arabian Peninsula in the fifth and sixth centuries A.D. (World Statistics, 2005). Other major ethnic groups include the Turks, Persians, Kurds, and Jews. Arabic is naturally the predominant language in the Middle East, but Turkish, Persian, Kurdish, and Modern Hebrew are also spoken. The countries included in the geopolitical/cultural term "Middle East," often referred to as MENA (Middle East North Africa), are Bahrain, Iran, Iraq, Israel, Jordan, Kuwait, Lebanon, Oman, Palestine (Gaza Strip and West Bank), Qatar, Saudi Arabia, Syria, Turkey, the United Arab Emirates, and Yemen, as well as the North African countries of Algeria, Egypt, Libya, Morocco, Sudan, and Tunisia (Oracle ThinkQuest Library, 2005).

The great ancient civilizations of the Middle East have had a profound impact on the development of world history. Alphabets, codes of civilized conduct, and major trading cities all began here, as did Judaism, Christianity, and Islam. Today, more than 90 percent of the population of the Middle East are Muslims, about 4 percent are Christians, and 2 percent are Jews. The Middle Eastern countries are for the most part state controlled, and their economy is heavily dependent on oil exports (the region holds about 70 percent of the world's oil reserves). For the most part, the Middle East remains largely underdeveloped (Encarta online).

In Africa and the Middle East, cultural themes and patterns tend to remain static; when change does occur, it comes about very slowly. On the other hand, economic and political climates change frequently and sometimes radically.

Cultural Themes and Patterns

Conducting business in Africa and the Middle East carries a rich and colorful tradition. For at least 20 centuries, a highly profitable and, for the most part, peaceful trade has connected these two areas. The ancient Greek merchant Periplus recorded this relationship between East Africa and the Middle East as far back as the first century A.D., and trade has continued uninterrupted to this day (*Periplus of the Erythraean Sea*). Nothing is more symbolic of this business than the camel and the dhow, cargo carriers over land and water, respectively, since ancient times. The camel was the chief vessel of trade between North and West Africa and the Middle East well into the 20th century, whereas the dhow was used primarily between East and Southern Africa and the Middle East (Gilbert & Currey, 2004; Shiller, 1999). But neither of them is merely a sentimental image of the past. Both the camel and the dhow are still used today, unchanged in design or function. Camel markets continue to thrive, with sturdy pack camels fetching upwards of $1,000. Similarly, the graceful dhow has not completely given way to the vast flotilla of modern container-carrying super ships that have largely replaced it (A–Z of Camels, 1996). The fact that both the camel and the dhow continue to be important business assets testifies to the fascinating blend of modern technology and age-old methods prevalent in Africa and the Middle East and gives one a clue as to the importance of tradition in these regions. The past is very much a part of the present. Therefore, a basic understanding of the history and culture of each area is essential in order for outsiders to successfully do business here.

Culture, Language, and Religion

Africa and the Middle East are high-context cultures. In the communication process, much of the meaning is not from the words but is internalized in the person. Meaning comes from the environment and is looked for in the relationship between the ideas expressed in the communication process. High-context cultures tend to be more human oriented than low-context cultures.

Although the two regions we are examining are diverse, there does exist a sociolinguistic tie between Africa and the Middle East. For centuries, Arabic has been used in trade with Swahili-speaking Bantu people (more than two-thirds of the African population is Bantu speaking). The Swahili language was heavily influenced by early Arab traders and includes many Arabic words in its vocabulary (Kromer, 2004). Although in both areas European languages are widely spoken and may even be the *lingua franca,* the indigenous language remains a socially important and binding influence. Language has the powerful ability to bind, however loosely, peoples of diverse cultures. The common tongue of Swahili links peoples of different African tribes and nations. A prime example of this is the East African Community (EAC), which was established in the wake of independence in 1967. The primary purpose of this organization was to promote free trade between the nations of Kenya, Tanzania, and Uganda. The major commonality among the three countries was language. Although the EAC objective of doing business among the three countries was deemed a success, it lasted only 10 years. The collapse was due to political differences (Institute for Security Studies, 2005). In 1999, talks were reopened among these three nations to reestablish the trading bloc with a move toward a free market. This officially became a reality on January 1, 2005 (East African Trade Accord Launched, 2005). The three nations considered inviting Rwanda, another Swahili-speaking nation, to join the agreement but eventually decided against it for political reasons.

The bond of the Arabic language is perhaps the most significant of any language. In fact, the only defining feature of being Arab is the language. Any person who adopts the Arabic language is considered an Arab regardless of religious orientation or nationality (Nydell, 1987). According to the *Qur'an,* Arabic is the only language for understanding the Muslim religion, which to some extent regulates business practices (specifically in the matter of loans, interest, and inheritance). Consequently, a working knowledge of Arabic or Swahili is important to reducing the complexity of conducting business in these regions. But learning basic grammar and vocabulary is not enough.

Language is an important part of relationship, and *how* it is used can be just as important as knowing the correct words and their arrangement. For example, a typical Western business approach is to efficiently say what you mean. How something is said is often far less important than the fact that it gets to the point and can be clearly understood. This is not the case in most African societies. One young American who was fluent in Swahili learned this early in his African career, when he went to see his host supervisor on a matter of great importance. After a brief greeting, he immediately dealt with the matter at hand. The African supervisor listened politely for a few moments and then interrupted, saying: "Jambo! How are you? How is your family? Did you sleep well? Have you any news from your parents back home? I am fine, my wife is fine, my children are fine. However, my she-goat is quite ill and I am concerned. Oh, I must tell you, my son is . . ." The supervisor then said to the

American, "That is how we greet people in Africa. Now you can tell me what it is you want." Language is perceived as a bridge to building relationships.

Likewise, the use of language carries considerable significance in the Middle East. What Westerner who is not familiar with Arabic can possibly understand the power of the repetitious words that come from the minaret? Middle East scholar Kenneth Craig (1964) compares language usage in the West and Middle East when he observes that "ours, surely, is an age that more than any other multiplies words [and] uses them in great quantity [unlike] the two-score words of the muezzin . . . in which Islam summons itself to its faith and practice. In them the Muslim is confronted with his own vocation, while the listening outsider learns what shapes and makes Islam" (p. vii). The Council for Advancement of Arab-British Understanding (2005) notes that "one should not underestimate the significance of the Arabic language . . . the mother tongue of some 150 million Arabs [and] seen by all Muslims as sacred." In fact, Arabic is so revered by Muslims that often the sound is more important than the meaning.

Religion is of paramount importance in both Africa and the Middle East. Its consequence cannot be overstated. One has only to pay attention to current world affairs to see the dominant impact religion has on the lives of people in these two regions. Although Islam is by far the predominant religion of North Africa and the Middle East, it plays a lesser role in sub-Saharan Africa, where both Christianity and Islam are widely represented and growing significantly. African Traditional Religion also continues to affect the lives of many (Barrett, 1982). But whatever the faith might be, it is an important factor in a person's life.

Religion in Western countries is primarily a private matter and rarely influences the flow of commerce. Because a separation of church and state is practiced in the United States as well as in other Western countries, their commercial sector is not in the habit of studying how religion might affect the conduct of business. However, religion plays a central role in African societies and cultures, and to ignore this aspect could easily doom an otherwise promising venture to failure. Religion seeps into each and every aspect of life in African society. In fact, the religious beliefs and practices are so encompassing that it would be impossible to separate them from other dimensions of African society and culture. All across Africa, faith is openly expressed. Prayer is not confined to the church or mosque, but one might expect the invocation of God when entering a business meeting or before making a major financial decision. Therefore, to understand Africa, including its social, economic, and political facets, one has to appreciate and respect the importance religion plays in the lives of its people (Tillia, 2003). Bishop Phillip Baji (2004), a former professor of African Traditional Religion at St. Mark's Anglican School of Theology in Dar es Salaam, Tanzania, observes that "a study of these religious systems is . . . a study of the peoples themselves in all the complexities of traditional and modern life."

In the Middle East, people are just as consumed by faith as their African brothers and sisters, if not more so. The primary reason for this is that a vast majority of the people are Muslims, and Islam is not a theoretical ideology but rather a total, comprehensive way of life. Islamic law encompasses a Muslim's duties to God (worshipping, fasting, pilgrimage) and duties to one's fellow man (family, commercial and criminal laws). John Esposito (1980) notes that the "Islamic tradition provides a normative system in which religion is integral to all areas of Muslim life—law, politics, education, business and the family" (p. ix).

The *Qur'an* and the *Hadith,* or Examples of the Prophet, are the two major sources explaining daily life for Muslims. It is to the *Qur'an* and shar'ia, or Islamic law, that Muslims look for almost all matters of prayer, conduct, and daily living, from clothing and food to education, finances, dating, marriage, family, and employment. A number of these precepts also apply to foreigners or sojourners, so it is important to have a basic understanding of them. If one cannot find an answer to one of life's dilemmas in the *Qur'an,* then one looks to what the Prophet Muhammad said or did. In popular Islam, the Prophet can be even more influential than the *Qur'an.* Muslims will "allow attacks on Allah . . . but to malign Muhammad will provoke from even the most liberal sections of the community a fanaticism of blazing vehemence" (Barakat, 1993, p. 65). Any company that wishes to conduct business in the Middle East would do well to heed the esteem in which Muhammad is held and consider the dictates and the influence of local religions when developing their policies and practices. An awareness of religion will help ensure success as companies enter the Middle Eastern and African marketplaces.

Social, Economic, and Political Factors

Despite having 70 percent of all proven oil reserves and producing 40 percent of the world's oil, North Africa and the Middle East remain a highly traditional and much underdeveloped region caught in the midst of conflict and change. Sub-Saharan Africa successfully gained independence from its colonial rulers, only to experience political and economic instability due largely to the educational deprivation of the masses and the failure to adequately develop personnel for the needed infrastructure. The clash of ancient tradition with postmodern influences requires an understanding of certain social, economic, and political factors.

IMPORTANCE OF FAMILY AND RELATIONSHIP

An ancient proverb says, "Each Arab has one thousand close relatives." Relationship in both Africa and the Middle East is very important. In fact, family and relationship is a high moral value (Pearson-Roden, 2005). The basic unit of African and Middle Eastern society is the family, which includes the nuclear family and the extended family. The African or Arab will place relationship before almost anything else; therefore, how one conducts business and deals with employees and co-workers is extremely important. If an African or Arab senses that you care about them and their culture, they will work for you or with you; if not, they likely will not. Consequently, how something is said can be even more important than what is said. Once while traveling in my car in Kenya with several of my African colleagues, we ran out of gas and were stranded in the middle of nowhere. It took many inconvenient hours to procure some gas, and thus we arrived for our meeting quite late. When asked why we were late, my colleagues explained that "the vehicle, its petrol was finished." They could not blame me, as that would have betrayed our relationship. Moreover, in most African cultures it is considered rude to give an answer that people do not want to hear. Thus, a person may give you the answer that he or she thinks you want, but which may not necessarily be correct—relationship can be even more important than accuracy.

When speaking of relationship in Africa and the Middle East, one must be aware that both are very nonconfrontational cultures. They seek the least conflict possible (Almaney & Alwar, 1982). This cannot be overemphasized, as the Western business style is often candid, direct, and blunt. This frank, straightforward approach will backfire in African and Arabian cultures where humility and sensitivity are highly valued, especially when someone's dignity is at issue (Axtell, 1987).

ROLE OF WOMEN

The traditional role of women in Africa has changed dramatically in the past 20 years. For example, the Evangelical Lutheran Church in Tanzania, which is the largest Protestant denomination in the country, began ordaining women into the ministry as early as 1990. The far more conservative Anglican Church in Tanzania followed a few years later, putting these church bodies ahead of many churches in the United States and Western countries. In most parts of Africa, women can be seen holding high positions in government offices, on the police force, in the army, in education, and in private business.

However, men and women have entirely dissimilar roles in Middle Eastern societies where the *Qur'an* notes that men and women are different and therefore should perform different tasks. On the extreme side of the continuum, in Saudi Arabia and Iran women are subordinate to men and require their husbands' permission to seek employment or to travel. However, Syria and Morocco are more moderate and tend to reflect Western mores. It is fairly accurate to say that women are the caregivers of the family and men the breadwinners. Thus, the men handle public life while the women take care of home life, which means that much of Middle Eastern business is male dominated. However, this does not necessarily mean that there is no place for women in the business world. As Arab women are becoming more educated they are beginning, albeit slowly, to fill important roles and positions in the public domain (Stovall, 2000). Still, a company anticipating posting a woman in the region should consider doing so only after consulting with knowledgeable people or by invitation of the government or a national partner company.

CHALLENGE OF HIV/AIDS

Tragically, almost any discussion on sub-Saharan Africa will eventually have to address HIV/AIDS and its devastating impact on all aspects of life. It destroys the social fabric of humanity, takes an astonishing economic toll, and is a hot button politically. According to the World Health Organization's (WHO) report on sub-Saharan Africa, over 25 million people are HIV/AIDS infected and approximately three million die each year. Almost a third of the deaths in South Africa are caused by HIV/AIDS (Aids Kills One in Three in SA, 2005). Even these alarming statistics can be deceptively low as the HIV/AIDS infected rate can climb to as high as 25 percent of the adult population of some countries, such as South Africa (World Health Organization Update, 2004). With these disturbing numbers, doing business in such an environment can be both personally and organizationally risky. HIV/AIDS affects a company's bottom line because it must constantly recruit new employees, as well-trained employees are lost to the disease. Health care costs for employees are constantly rising. And, depending on the country, a company may have to bear the cost of burial. This can be significant because most Africans are buried in their ancestral homes and the bodies must somehow be transported to these remote locations. These costs are insignificant in comparison to the emotional impact on employee moral and worker productivity that even one death has on the entire business. To assist businesses, the United States Agency for International Development (USAID) has developed and distributed some very useful information for international companies operating in an HIV/AIDS environment (USAID, 2003).

The impact of HIV/AIDS is far less significant in the Middle East, where the infection rate is less than one half million with 24,000 annual deaths (World Health Organization Update, 2004). Consequently, it is not a major business consideration.

GOVERNMENTAL REGULATIONS

All African and Middle Eastern countries have laws that require some form of license. The requirements for a license to do business vary from country to country and will depend on a variety of factors, including the nature of the business, the duration of the involvement, and the kind of transactions. For example, in Ethiopia, utilities, banking, insurance, and a host of other service and trade industries are either controlled by the government or reserved for only domestic investors (U.S. Foreign and Commercial Service, 2005a). In Africa, each government has its own unique regulations for doing business, whereas in the Middle East Islamic law or shar'ia controls how one must conduct business. In Saudi Arabia, for example, employment contracts must be written in Arabic if they are to be considered binding (Prescott, 2005). Still, a long history of successful Western-Arab business partnerships proves that Western companies can flourish in an Islamic environment if they pay attention to the social and cultural aspects of the region.

WIDESPREAD CORRUPTION

A popular saying in Tanzania is "corruption in Africa means you get paid for a bridge that you never build!" Sadly for Africa, corruption is one of the greatest obstacles to doing business. A Sudanese man living in Australia commented to the BBC, "The day when corruption is stopped in Africa will be the very day that we shall wave goodbye to poverty, wars, AIDS, and crime" (How Deep Is Corruption in Africa?, 2004). He understands that corruption not only seems eternal but also pervades every aspect of life in Africa. From the few dollars slipped to the customs official to help expedite one's entry into the country, to the fabulous Swiss chalets owned by ex-presidents, there is an assumption that nothing will ever get done without something changing hands. Corruption is so integral to some societies that Swahili speakers call it *chai* or tea. Because tea is the national drink and no one could get through the day without it, the assumption is that no one will pass the day without corruption either. The long history of dealing with corrupt officials has made foreign businesses especially vulnerable.

However, for over a decade there have been calls, both internally and externally, for more transparency in how governments and businesses conduct themselves. The response has been mixed, but some positive signs are emerging. People seem less willing to tolerate corruption. Groups such as Transparency International are mounting pressure on African governments to clean up their act, and they are forcing companies that do business in Africa to play by the rules as well. They have developed "integrity pacts" whereby local industries as well as international companies and multinational organizations agree to adopt a common standard against bribery with heavy penalties being administered to those who violate the pact (Eigen, 2005). Another positive sign is that Western countries are increasingly linking aid to good governance and in particular to efforts to tackle corruption (Gidley-Kitchen, 2005). Today Africa is definitely a less corrupt place, and it is possible to do business there without being entangled in the endless cycle of corruption. However, there is still considerable room for improvement.

Corruption is also prevalent in the Middle East; one only has to recall the very recent "food for oil" program to realize this. The International Anti-Corruption Conference (IACC) identified the leading areas of corruption in the Middle East to be abuses of public positions, nepotism, facilitation of permits and tax cuts for unqualified individuals based on personal relations, and abuses of public properties (Shauabi, 1999). As in Africa, there are some positive steps being taken against corruption, and conducting business there without becoming involved in corruption can be accomplished.

WEAK INFRASTRUCTURE

International companies can expect to find dramatic differences between Western infrastructures and those in Africa and parts of the Middle East. Companies face difficulties rarely found in the Western business world, from inadequate road systems to frequent periods without water and power. For example, the World Bank estimates that a company starting a business in Tanzania can expect up to a 54-day delay in getting an electrical connection and will average 67.2 days of electrical outages per year, and in Eritrea companies experience up to 80 days of water failure per year. In Kenya, it can take nearly 100 days to obtain a telephone line (World Bank, 2005b). This deficiency in the telecommunications infrastructure is one of the most important economic concerns in Africa's development. Currently there is a wide disparity between regions, and some countries have a more developed telecommunications infrastructure than others. The introduction of foreign strategic investors has made modernization and expansion of a telecommunications infrastructure a priority, with developmental plans calling for growth rates of more than 20 percent per year (Africa Infrastructure, 2004).

Infrastructure is far less problematic in the Middle East than in Africa. Still, although the infrastructure may work better in the Middle East, it will be different from most Western systems. Islamic law and strict governmental regulations can create some problems and difficulties.

POLITICAL UNREST

Few countries in sub-Saharan Africa meet the criteria for a free nation set by Freedom House, a New York-based human rights organization. Instead, elitist military and political leaders who have little affinity for the people or their progress have replaced the former colonial rulers. The Organization for African Unity (OAU) remains more a hope than an effective force today. But, with the help of Western countries working through the United Nations, efforts are being made to democratize the region and restore political stability. Many of these newly reformed institutions are still in their developmental stage, which means that foreign investors may be confronted with conflicting regulations and incorrect information. Therefore, it is important to seek professional advice from the host country regarding licensing requirements and the conduct of business. Political favoritism, however, still remains an obstacle to foreign investors.

The Middle East is a region in the midst of profound political transition. A few privileged families or fundamentalist religious leaders have traditionally held political power. Although this still characterizes much of the region, there are growing efforts to democratize the area. The introduction of some democratic reforms and the controversial presence of the United States in Afghanistan and Iraq currently illustrate these efforts (Nafie, 2005).

Cross-cultural sensitivity and cooperation are especially important when dealing with these traditional cultures because they already feel threatened by the promotion of Western values and its empowerment of the individual through access to information. Insensitivity can seriously impede the incorporation of these societies into the globalized system. In his book *The Lexus and the Olive Tree*, Thomas Friedman (2000) explains that "for traditional societies . . . the collective, the group, is much more important than the individual, and empowering the individual is equated with dividing the society. So 'globalizing' for them . . . means changing the relationship of the individual to his state and community in a way that they feel is socially disintegrating" (p. 341). Perhaps Western managers working in Africa and the Middle East can succeed where politicians are failing. If they show respect for these value systems by learning about and working constructively with them, people in the host countries will feel less threatened and will in turn be more willing to make adjustments in dealing with foreign investors. Together they can help bring about the reforms necessary to overcome economic operational modes in the region which "seem

249

to embody the very definition of anti-globalization" (p. 20) such as high tariffs, restrictions on foreign investment, state control of information and industries, and distrust of Western practices (Houry, 2001). By becoming more culturally knowledgeable and interculturally astute, expatriate managers will be less frustrated and more successful in overcoming potential obstacles. This will translate into greater success also for their African and Middle Eastern business partners as they assume competitive roles in the global marketplace.

Business Conduct and Characteristics

Business customs in Africa and the Middle East vary from country to country; therefore, we will not attempt to provide a comprehensive list of all of them. Instead, we will present certain generalizations that can safely be made regarding these two regions as well as focus on some specific characteristics to illustrate the kinds of differences in business practices that can be expected. Although it is indispensable for expatriate managers to learn as much as possible about the host country, their most important tools will be an open mind and an attitude that is accepting of other ways of doing business.

APPROPRIATE DRESS

In all of Africa and the Middle East, modest dress in all public places is expected for both men and women. Mini skirts, sleeveless dresses, tank tops, and shorts would not be considered appropriate.

Dress codes for Arab women in the Middle East can be quite strict and may even be regulated by law, as is the case in countries such as Saudi Arabia, which applies *hijab,* a severe practice of a woman being covered from head to toe at all times in public. *Hijab* does not apply to Western businesswomen or spouses living in these countries, but depending on the country, they may be required to wear Western clothes that cover neck, shoulders, and all of the leg. One should always check with the country's embassy or consulate about the specific requirements.

WORK WEEK

The workweek in sub-Saharan Africa basically conforms to that of Western countries. However, in Muslim countries the workweek is from Saturday through Wednesday because Friday is the day of Islamic worship. Moreover, because Muslims are called to pray five times a day—at sunrise, noon, afternoon, sunset, and evening—many businesses close for a half hour at these times. Some people go to the mosque to pray; others pray at home or in the office. Meetings and appointments must be scheduled around these prayer times, and people at prayer should not be interrupted. The day of worship in Israel is Saturday, so the workweek is from Sunday through Thursday and sometimes Friday morning.

Religious holidays must also be taken into consideration. For example, during the month of Ramadan, which is the ninth month of the Islamic calendar, Muslims fast from dawn until dusk. Business activity slows down during this time and as a courtesy non-Muslims should refrain from eating or drinking in the presence of Muslims.

TIME

Anyone doing business in Africa must take into account the difference in the attitude towards time. There is such a thing as "African time," which differs from Western time. A popular African saying is "Americans have the watches but we have the time." The implication is that Americans or Europeans run around looking at their watches trying to get from place to place, whereas Africans measure their activities more slowly. Consequently, being a little late or even being habitually late is not considered a major offense to an African. Some African cultures, specifically Swahili-speaking people, also use what is called "Biblical time," whereby the clock starts at 7:00 a.m. instead of 1:00 a.m. This can prove quite confusing unless one asks in advance for clarification. In Africa, time is flexible, not rigid and segmented. People come first. Anyone in a hurry is viewed with suspicion and distrust.

Attitudes toward time in the Middle East also tend to be more relaxed. People want to sit and talk and get to know the other person before discussing business. Time is not seen as a limited commodity. What cannot be done today can always be accomplished tomorrow if God wills it. This sense of time is changing among modern Arab business leaders as they move beyond the culture of their tribal, nomadic past.

BUSINESS MEETINGS AND DECISION-MAKING

Business decisions are often made by consensus in Africa. This can take a very long time and can cause Westerners considerable frustration, but it is important to remember that Africans are a communal people who do not consider it a waste of time to discuss problems until everyone agrees. If pressured and hurried to make business decisions, an African suspects cheating and chicanery. One American businessman recounts that during his 10 years on the board of directors of a major oil company in Africa nothing was ever put to a vote. The

Swahili word *baraza* means "assembly" and is based on the concept that each person at a meeting has wisdom and therefore must speak. This philosophy of decision-making further confirms the high value that Africans place on relationship. Because getting to know their business partners is important to them, Ugandans begin meetings with conversations about each other's backgrounds and families. In some countries, the use of first names is the norm, whereas in others this level of familiarity takes longer and people are more reserved and formal. As a legacy of colonialism, English, French, and Portuguese are commonly spoken in respective areas of Africa, and in some countries they are the official languages of government and business.

Because Arab organizations are typically flat, with all employees having equal access to the chief operating officer, meetings in the Middle East may seem chaotic, with people entering the room unannounced to discuss their own issues while others are taking phone calls. To a Western businessperson, such conduct is considered confusing, inefficient, poorly organized, and a waste of precious time. Decisions are made slowly, in part because of a fondness for negotiating, which is rooted in Arab tradition, and in part because of bureaucratic formalities. Because business is based on relationship building and trust, early meetings focus on getting to know the other person. In a culture that places more value on someone's word than on a written agreement and often relegates written contracts to the status of memorandums rather than binding agreements, establishing a person's trust and honor is a prerequisite for doing business together. Still, this too often leaves Western executives and managers confused and believing that no work is being accomplished. However, Arabs have always operated this way and know exactly what is transpiring and with whom. Although English is widely used in business in the Middle East, one should not assume that meetings will be conducted in English. In Morocco, for example, they are generally conducted in French. It is advisable to find out in advance which language will be used so that interpreters can be arranged if necessary (U.S. Foreign and Commercial Service, 2005b).

Trust and confidence are essential elements needed for successful enterprise in both Africa and the Middle East. Friendship comes first.

GREETINGS, BUSINESS ETIQUETTE, AND COURTESIES

Greetings are important to Africans, and the same greeting may be repeated several times. Handshaking is very common when greeting someone. Women and other subordinates will sometimes offer both hands as a sign of respect. In some areas, the handshake is finished with a snap of the fingers. Africans are always courteous and hospitable. They are gregarious and not afraid to show their emotions or display body language. However, in some African cultures eye contact is considered disrespectful or even defiant; consequently, these Africans may avert their eyes during conversations, particularly with strangers. Age is important in Africa. It is believed that the older one gets, the wiser one becomes, thus age is an asset. Respect for elders is an essential part of African cultures. Professional titles are widely used and visitors are addressed by their title and last name. Although gifts are not necessary when meeting someone for the first time, it would still be considered appropriate to give a small gift as a token of friendship. A product of your country, an engraved ballpoint pen, or candy would be welcome. Don't bring flowers except when expressing condolences.

In the Middle East, elaborate and ritualized forms of greetings and leave takings are common. The handshake is a common way to greet others; however, kissing on the cheeks is also commonplace when men greet other men or when women greet other women. Business cards are essential and are usually presented upon the first meeting. Business cards should be presented with English on one side and Arabic on the other. Arabs will stand very close when talking and Westerners should not back away even if they feel uncomfortable. Also, eye contact, considered a mark of trust and truthfulness, can be intense between men, but between men and women it should be only fleeting. During a meeting, it is fine to ask about a man's "family" but never specifically about his wife or daughters until a level of friendship has been established. Although titles are not in general use on the Arabian Peninsula except for royal families, ministers, and high-level military officers, Arabs are very status and rank conscious and care must be taken to pay deference to those who are more senior. A meeting concludes with an offer of coffee or tea. Middle Easterners consider coffee or tea to be more than a beverage: it is the ultimate sign of hospitality and cordiality in a region where graciousness is a way of life. It is important to note that this system of hospitality is based on mutuality and must be returned in due course. It is also important to consider gestures and body language. Be careful of hand gestures. The right hand is for public matters and the left hand for private. Shaking hands, giving and receiving gifts, and eating must be done with the right hand because the left hand is considered unclean. Also, one should never sit with the soles of the shoes or bottoms of the feet displayed towards someone since this is considered rude and disrespectful. In the Middle East, mutual respect is expected at all times. Touching or kissing someone from the opposite sex in public is considered bad taste or even obscene, but it is common to see people of the same sex holding hands as a sign of friendship. Much more bodily contact is made between Arab men than between Western men. Even during conversations, tapping a person gently or resting a hand on the other's shoulder or knee is not uncommon. We should note that the ritual of burping after a big meal is no longer considered acceptable in polite circles. Gift giving is not compulsory, but fountain pens make excellent gifts given the grace and flow of the Arab alphabet. Avoid gifts of liquor and other items prohibited by Islam. Also, be careful not to admire one of your host's possessions too warmly or he may insist on giving it to you, and you may be forced to accept rather than offend.

The cultural nuances discussed here should serve as a springboard for learning more about the specific countries comprising Africa and the Middle East. We hope that they will also prompt potential foreign business representatives to take a closer look at their own cultures and recognize learned habits and expectations that may hinder their efforts in doing business with people in these regions. Such awareness will be the key to developing long-lasting, mutually productive business relationships in this globalized world.

Emerging Trends

The global power configuration has changed significantly in the past few years, and such changes are bound to be reflected in the global marketplace. Although the effects of many of the changes are difficult to define and impossible to predict, there are some emerging trends that are distinct and apply to both Africa and the Middle East.

POLITICAL REFORM

Political reform appears to be dawning in Africa and the Middle East. Current debate by civil society activists calls for democracy, and promises of change by leaders in both regions suggest that democratization may finally be underway. The elections in Zimbabwe and Iraq and the new moves towards peace in the Middle East are all encouraging signs (Africa Can Jump-Start Its Own Revival, 2005).

Democracy is being embraced in sub-Saharan Africa as never before. There is a growing intolerance of human rights abuses as evidenced by Africa's response to the developments in the Democratic Republic of the Congo (Zaire), the Great Lakes area, and the Republic of Congo.

Most African governments realize that a good and stable government is necessary if their country is going to compete for global investments (Callisto, 1998). They understand that political reform will contribute to economic growth and foreign investment.

The Middle East also recognizes the need for political reform in order to bolster international business. Houry (2001) notes that "most [Middle Eastern and North African] MENA states have recognized the inadequacies of the old economy and have begun to venture into liberal economic territory with added emphasis on the private sector, freer trade, fiscal responsibility, foreign invest-ment, and a persistent, yet cautious, incorporation of information technology" (p. 14). A positive sign is Egyptian President Mubarak's call for parliament to amend Article 76 of the constitution to allow for direct multicandidate elec-tions. This has started fundamental governmental changes that will bring political parties into the national decision-making process (Hawthorne, 2004). But political reform will not come easily. Witness the municipal elections in Saudi Arabia—the first in 40 years—which will not transfer any real power to the people, and where the only female candidate (and one of the first women in Saudi history to run for public office) had to withdraw her candidacy when the government banned women from voting or running for office. Still, it is an important start given the considerable resistance toward democratic reforms by the ruling families (Bakhurji, 2005). Currently, however, only Israel is considered a "free" country by Freedom House standards. Jordan, Kuwait, Morocco, and Bahrain are rated "partly free" (Freedom House, 2005). But, given the forces for change, a new order or paradigm is in the process of emerg-ing. No one yet knows what its final characteristics will be.

TECHNOLOGICAL EXPANSION

Africa and the Middle East have lagged far behind the rest of the world in basic technology. However, in recent years computers, the Internet, e-mail, cellular tele-phones, and satellite television have been introduced into these areas at an encouraging rate. Computer programmers are working with linguists to make computers more accessible to Africans who do not know the key languages of cyberspace. A search engine in Swahili is already available from Google, and Microsoft is developing a Swahili version of its Windows software (African Business Pages, 2005). Developments such as these have the potential to bring technology to even the remotest areas and can greatly enhance business opportu-nities. There are already search engines, software, and Web sites in Arabic. Sometimes, especially in Africa where infrastructure is often a hindrance, modern computer technology is bound to meet primitive functional technology. In Tanzania, thousands of Burundian refugees are learning computer skills in a com-puter lab that uses cow manure to provide the electricity to run the computers (D. Lewis, 2003). This is not just an interesting anecdote; it shows how a business that is willing to be creative and uses available resources can adapt to adverse con-ditions. As the computer swiftly moves into Africa and the Middle East, interna-tional business is bound to benefit because the infrastructure for computers will already be in place and there will also be potential employees with computer skills.

Cellular phones are also making a dramatic difference in doing business in Africa and the Middle East. Telecommunication problems have long been a business hindrance. With the rapid advance of cellular phones, that impediment is quickly disappearing (Clark, 2005).

The technological advance that will most likely have the greatest impact on Africa and the Middle East is satellite television. Until very recently, the populations in both regions were limited to government-sponsored and government-censored programs. With the rapid spread of satellite technology, this has changed dramatically. Most African and Arab countries now have up to 150 channels to choose from (The World Through Their Eyes, 2005). In African and Middle Eastern countries where lack of democracy has often impeded foreign business investment, the exposure to satellite television is opening the door to further political reform and more representative government, which will in turn benefit the business climate.

Summary

International businesses can adapt to Africa and the Middle East, where the cultural drumbeats are vastly different from their own and require them to learn the ever-changing steps to the dance. The countries of Africa and the Middle East are also changing the way they dance in response to the demands and opportunities of globalization. They have recognized that the old ways of government and business will not work in securing for themselves competitive positions in the world marketplace, and they have begun to make some political and economic reforms. The fact that this is happening in a part of the world where governments have historically resisted such reforms as a threat to their hold on power testifies not only to the strength of the globalizing forces but also to the people's keen desire to not be left behind. However, the huge problems of population control, HIV/AIDS, environmental protection, and cultural preservation need to be addressed just as aggressively as company policy if the ultimate goal of globalization is to improve the global standard of living.

The old stereotypes held by Westerners about Africa and the Middle East are counterproductive to globalization and international business. They are condescending and hinder doing business in these two regions. The countries that constitute Africa and the Middle East are not simply collections of poverty-stricken villages filled with downtrodden people living quaint lives, but are also home to modern cities, great architecture, emerging technology, and a highly ambitious, dedicated, and educated people. The aspirations and achievements of these countries must be honored and respected in order for true communication and cooperation to take place.

Global managers must appreciate both the potential of Africa's human and natural resources and the struggles of its Third World nations seeking to move beyond the effects of colonialism. Joint ventures will do much to contribute to the development of the area and its people if all parties can work to create an atmosphere of nonjudgmental acceptance. Likewise, in the Middle East, Western educational, technical, and financial expertise is needed to develop a modern infrastructure. This can only occur if Pan American, European, and Asian representatives are sensitive to the Islamic renaissance underway and respect Muslim tradition as it struggles to integrate with the political, economic, and social realities of a postmodern world.

Today, Africa and the Middle East are experiencing a transitional change that can advance international business and liberate the creativity of their people. If the tools of this transformation are thoughtfully employed in ways that are culturally validating, the potential is there for governments and business to succeed in developing Africa and the Middle East into competitive forces in the world market.

Resource Guide

Books

Culture, Communication, and People

Fisher, A., & Beckwith, C. (2004). *Faces of Africa*. Washington, DC: National Geographic.

Lewis, B. (2001). *The multiple identities of the Middle East*. New York: Schocken.

Taschen, A. (2004). *Inside Africa*. Koeln, Germany: Taschen.

Customs and Business Conduct

Foster, D. (2002). *Global etiquette guide to Africa and the Middle East*. New York: Wiley.

Hughes, R., & Laredo, J. (2002). *Living and working in the Middle East*. Berkeley, CA: Survival Books.

Nadozie, E. (1998). *African culture and American business in Africa: How to strategically manage cultural difference in African business*. Kirksville, MO: Afrimax.

History and Politics

Nugent, P. (2004). *Africa since independence: A comparative history*. New York: Palgrave Macmillan.

Reader, J. (1999). *Africa: The biography of the continent*. New York: Vintage.

Roskin, M. G., & Coyle, J. J. (2003). *Politics of the Middle East: Cultures and conflicts*. New York: Prentice Hall.

International Business and Globalism

Cheru, F. (2002). *African renaissance: Roadmaps to the challenge of globalization.* London: Zed Books.

Fawcett, L. (2005). *International relations of the Middle East.* New York: Oxford University Press.

Schaebler, B., Stenberg, L., Schabler, B., & Mottahedeh, R. M. (2004). *Globalization and the Muslim world: Culture, religion, and modernity.* Syracuse, NY: Syracuse University Press.

Trends and Challenges: Africa

Ayittey, G. B. N. (2005). *Africa unchained: The blueprint for Africa's future.* New York: Palgrave Macmillan.

French, H. (2004). *A continent for the taking: The tragedy and hope of Africa.* New York: Knopf.

Satloff, R. B., & Clowson, P. (2001). *Navigating through turbulence: America and the Middle East in a new century.* Washington, DC Washington Institute for Near East Policy.

Web Sites

The Africa Guide (http://www.africaguide.com). Examines the countries of Africa and presents relevant cultural and business information.

The Civilized Explorer (http://www.cieux.com/trinfo0.html). The Civilized Explorer Travel Information Page contains links to resources for the world traveler, whether for business or for pleasure.

The Nations Online Project (http://www.nationsonline.org/oneworld). This site is a portal of gateways to the countries and cultures of the world, a reference directory, and a destination guide. Excellent country links.

U.S. Department of State-Background Notes (http://www.state.gov/r/pa/ei/bgn). Contains information on all the countries with which the United States has relations and includes facts on the country's land, people, history, government, political conditions, and economy.

Worldbiz.com (http://www.worldbiz.com). Offers information on international business practices, international business protocol, international etiquette, cross-cultural communication, negotiating tactics, and country-specific data.

Epilogue

Breaking Free and the Road Ahead

In the children's fable *Chicken Little*, we were warned that the sky was falling and no one listened. Today, although the sky isn't falling, the Iron Curtain has fallen and previously rigid economic blocs have cracked, resulting in a global economy and increasingly seamless trading environment. Still, many are not noticing these changes affecting developed and developing countries alike. Accepting the challenges of globalization will permit us to reap its benefits. In a globalized world, there will be priceless opportunities for those who understand the new rules, position themselves well, and take personal responsibility for the future.

Globalization allows diverse resources to be massed on complex problems. The focus in business is on flattening, empowering, networking, and the resulting consequences of our actions. Communication is what will matter in the future. The trends that follow form the basis of the image of the future presented here.

Trends Shaping the Global Marketplace

Worldwide competition for new ideas. In the future, the most important factors in economic competition become (1) the availability of ideas, namely sophisticated research and development; (2) the availability of a trained and capable workforce; and (3) organizations that are designed to adapt. Given the enormity of the world's problems and the need for imaginative, creative thinking, there will be a growing cooperation among researchers in many parts of the world and a tightening of the linkages between research and development. Moreover, the importance of a long-term strategy will supplant our decades of short-term thinking. Global organizations will have to learn the art of creativity and invention. Alvin Toffler (1990), in *PowerShift*, states that an "innovation imperative" will be essential and "what counts for each nation in the long run are products of mind-work" (p. 165). The people who will gain the most value in this new global economy are the imaginative, creative workers; the dreamers and visionaries who take pleasure in discovery and actively seek out new possibilities. And this creation of options will be a shared activity involving mutual learning that combines knowledge of what's possible with knowledge about what's needed. Robert Reich (2000) observes that "great ideas are the new currency of the realm . . . the creation of new possibilities [will be] all-consuming" (pp. 53, 55).

Changing, mobile, educated workforce. Success in higher education has become the new social mobility indicator, replacing, at least to some extent, inherited wealth as the important determinant of one's career opportunities. To be sure, inherited wealth can buy and furnish education, but education will be a prerequisite to achievement in a global marketplace. Thus, there will be a social demand for educational credentials driven by social mobility considerations. The consequence of this need for credentials is that the demand for access to higher education will continue, and as levels of education and training in labor markets rise, employers will prefer better educated employees. Therefore, the global workforce of the future will be even more mobile as corporations reach across borders to find the skills they need. The combination of a globalized workforce and global corporations means that managers and employees must be able to work effectively with more and more people of differing cultures, customs, values, beliefs, and practices.

Additionally, as technology flattens the world and the workforce becomes increasingly more mobile and better educated, entrepreneurship will become a driving force for future economic opportunity. Entrepreneurs will play a central role in the world economy. A healthy economy is never in tidy equilibrium; it's continuously wracked by invention and change. Innovation will occur most readily when entrepreneurs are rewarded for their brave efforts to try something new. The world economy cannot progress without the creative destruction wrought by entrepreneurial activity. With the old walls of business tumbling, entrepreneurs can more easily enter the global game. They can ask questions, thoughtfully listen, carefully watch behavioral cues, and, on these bases, imagine what will be most appealing or useful and bring it to the world bazaar.

New technologies in communication and information. The current transformation of inter- and intra-organizational communication is bound to accelerate as media richness increases and the need for faster decision-making modifies managerial tasks. Moreover, greater use of information technology and programmed robotics could have repercussions for the workforce—namely, the possibility of far fewer routine jobs (except for in-person services) and the increasing sophistication of technology operation and analytical white-collar work. However, it is not the new technology that will dictate the characteristics and quality of work life; the technology will be impartially applied, as it is today. Decisions to centralize or decentralize, to delegate or not, to control or not, will be determined by the need for innovation, the pressure of competition, the impetus of new cultural values, and the need to accommodate the aspirations of an increasingly credentialed and educated workforce.

New understanding of organizations. Robert Reich (2000) declares that "the world is in the midst of another great opening: the Age of the Terrific Deal" (p. 15). Competitive strength will turn on being better, faster, and cheaper than rivals. This will require organizations to consider alternative structures and ways of working with people. The theoretical concepts of organizations are already showing signs of shifting from hierarchical to somewhat more egalitarian models as the culture of world politics shifts away from authoritarian to more democratic ideas. The concept of organizational boundaries will be altered as multinational organizations take a more holistic view of their roles and responsibilities. Moreover, the values of a multicultural, educated population will eventually span the world as new technologies are used to achieve a better life at work and at play. In such a climate, collaborative and quality issues take on greater importance, and organizations will have to be concerned with real creativity and effectiveness. Those responsible organizations that provide quality products and service will survive and thrive; those that do not will wither and die.

Institution of social, political, and cultural change. Learning and adapting to change and the introduction of innovations do not take place automatically. However, globalization is instituting widespread social, political, and cultural change. All around the globe countries are experiencing social and political reform resulting in significant cultural change. The increased democratization has contributed to an equality in the workplace that has transformed cultural views. Moreover, the countries constituting East Asia and the Pacific Rim will significantly influence, both culturally and economically, the organizations of the future. Successful multinational organizations will have to include in their vision, mission, and strategies the servicing of this geographic area. Thus, cross-cultural interactions, adaptability, and intercultural training become necessary and ever more important. Globalization will be the major cause for change well into the 21st century, and we need to be willing to take the first steps toward understanding one another. Henri Nouwen (1996), in *Bread for the Journey,* observes that "we become neighbors when we are willing to cross the road for one another . . . there is a lot of road crossing to do . . . but if we could cross the road once in a while and pay attention to what is happening on the other side, we might indeed become neighbors" (p. 315).

Work Habits for the Global Marketplace

Career choices and opportunities are in flux, and we jeopardize our future if we cling to old assumptions and expectations about how careers should operate. Organizations will keep reshaping themselves, shifting and flexing to fit a rapidly changing world. That's the *only* way they can hope to survive in this fiercely competitive global economy. Look for them to restructure, outsource, downsize, subcontract, and form new alliances. Taking care of your career in this environment means managing perpetual motion. The following guidelines, however, can help you meet the challenges presented during this era of globalization.

1. *Accept ambiguity and uncertainty.* A rapidly changing world deals ruthlessly with individuals and organizations that don't change, and people are coming to respect that fact. Take personal responsibility for adapting to change. Instead of being a drag on change initiatives—one of the resistors who cause delay—be open minded and develop a reputation as one who pushes the change process along. Be a catalyst for change and regeneration.

2. *Reflect and deliberate before acting.* As complex multinational organizations involve themselves in multicultural projects, the need for careful, mindful appraisal and judgment becomes important. Global leaders will need to possess the personal resolve and willingness to "push the pause button" before acting or reacting and consider the implications or consequences of their actions. Often, problems are created and difficulties unnecessarily escalated because of a thoughtless disregard of cultural sensitivities and values. Multinational organizations are accelerating the worldwide exchange of innovations and ideas; therefore, it is essential that we pause long enough to responsibly think through the unfolding possibilities and scenarios rather than mindlessly acting in haste. Prudent patience, common sense, good judgment, and a fascination with people will be valued business virtues.

3. *Be creative and hardworking.* All problems present themselves to the mind as threats of failure. Only people who are unwilling to be intimidated by the prospect of failure and who are determined to succeed no matter what effort is required have a chance to succeed. Creative people are willing to make

the necessary commitment. Part of creative people's industriousness is due to their ability to be thoroughly absorbed in a problem and to give it their undivided attention. But it is due, as well, to their competitiveness, which is unlike most people's in that it is not directed toward other people, but toward ideas. They take the challenge of ideas personally. It is this quality that Thomas Edison had in mind when he said, "Genius is 99 percent perspiration and 1 percent inspiration," and George Bernard Shaw recognized when he explained, "When I was a young man I observed that 9 out of 10 things I did were failures. I didn't want to be a failure, so I did 10 times more work."

4. *Be dynamic, daring, and resourceful.* Keep your curiosity burning, or at least rekindle it. Like little children with building blocks, play with ideas, arranging them in new combinations, looking at them from different perspectives. Thinking should be an adventure; go about it with openness to experience. Resourcefulness is the ability to act effectively and conceptualize the approach that solves the problem—even when the problem stymies others, and even when the resources at hand are meager. This ability is not measured by IQ tests, but is a willingness to take risks and try, try, and try again.

5. *Take personal responsibility for continuing your education and managing your career.* Lifelong learning is the only way to remain competitive in the global job market. You should invest in your own growth, development, and self-renewal. Continuous improvement—the Japanese call it *kaizen*—offers some of the best insurance for both your career and the organization. It keeps you reaching and stretching to outdo yesterday.

6. *Invent the future instead of trying to redesign the past.* The best way to predict the future is to invent it. This suggests that the best way to know what's coming is to put yourself in charge of creating the situation you want. Be purposeful. Look at what's needed now, and set about doing it. One of the keys to being successful in your efforts is to anticipate how you can rise to the occasion. Instead of changing with the times, make a habit of changing just a little ahead of the times. Be a "searcher for the new new thing . . . the person . . . who does not seriously want to sink back into any chair . . . who prefers not to get too comfortable" (Lewis, 2000, p. 15). The "new new thing" is an idea that will change the world and is poised to be taken seriously in the global marketplace.

Tomorrow will be different, and it behooves us to contribute to its invention. We need to be prepared for the enormous social, political, and economic transformations that are taking place, including the evolution of new international, multicultural organizations joined together in mutual worldwide ventures. And we need to be willing to adopt new attitudes and behavioral postures as part of a continual learning process that will let us become resourceful and responsible "citizens of the world." Pluralism on a global scale is the reality with which we must learn to cope constructively. Astronauts uniformly confirm that, from the distance of outer space, this blue orb is small, and one realizes we are one human race. We are different human beings but one human race. This is the delicate balance facing global leaders and confronting international business—to understand the differences and recognize the unity. There are unlimited international opportunities to build, explore, and bring about immeasurable results.

References

The A–Z of camels. (1996). *Arab News* on Arab Net. Retrieved June 8, 2004, from http://www.arab.net/camels

Abelson, R. (1976). Script processing in attitude formation and decision making. In J. Carroll & J. Payne (Eds.), *Cognition and social behavior* (pp. 33–46). Hillsdale, NJ: Lawrence Erlbaum.

Abrahamson, E. (2004). Managing change in a world of excessive change: Counter-balancing creative destruction and creative recombination. *Ivey Business Journal Online, 68* (January/February), 1–8.

Ackbar, A. (1997). *Hong Kong cultures and the politics of disappearance.* Minneapolis, MN: University of Minnesota Press.

Adherents.com (2005). Retrieved December 12, 2005, from http://www.adherents.com

Adler, N. (2002). *International dimensions of organizational behavior.* Cincinnati, OH: South-Western.

Adler, P. S. (1975). The transition experience: An alternative view of culture shock. *Journal of Humanistic Psychology, 15,* 13–23.

Adler, P. S. (1987). Beyond cultural identity: Reflections on cultural and multicultural man. In L. Samovar & R. Porter (Eds.), *Intercultural communication: A reader* (4th ed.). Bellmont, CA: Wadsworth, 389–405.

Adler, R. B., Rosenfeld, L. B., & Proctor, R. F. (2004). *Interplay: The process of interpersonal communication.* New York: Oxford University Press.

Africa Business Pages. (2005). The market for computers in Africa. Retrieved March 11, 2005, from http://www.africa-business.com/features/computers.html

Africa can jump-start its own revival. (2005, March 20). *International Herald Tribune,* p. 6.

Africa infrastructure. (2004). Retrieved March 9, 2005, from http://www.marketresearch.com

Ahuja, M. K., & Carley, K. M. (1998). Network structure in virtual organizations. *Journal of Computer-Mediated Communication, 3,* 1–35.

Ahuja, M. K., & Carley, K. M. (1999). Network structure in virtual organizations. *Organization Science, 10,* 741–757.

Aids Kills One in Three in SA. (2005). *BBC News Online.* Retrieved May 16, 2005, from http://news.bbc.co.uk/2/hi/africa/4558367.stm

Ala, M., & Cordeiro, W. P. (1999). Can we learn management techniques from the Japanese ringi process? *Business Forum, 24,* 22–23.

Aldridge, M. G. (2005). What is the basis of American culture? What is it that intercultural communication students cannot afford to miss about the American culture? New Mexico Independence Research Institute. Retrieved November 27, 2005, from http://www.zianet.com/NMIRI/am_culture.htm

Alldregde, M., & Nilan, K. (2000). 3M's leadership competency model: An internally developed solution. *Human Resource Management Journal, 39,* 133–145.

Allen, I. (1990). *Unkind words.* New York: Bergin and Garvey.

Allen, T. (1967). Communications in the research and development laboratory. *Technology Review,* Oct./Nov., 30–36.

Allport, G. W. (1954). *The nature of prejudice.* New York: MacMillan.

Allwood, J., & Schroeder, R. (2000). Intercultural communication in a virtual environment. *Intercultural Communication, 4.* Retrieved on September 14, 2004, from http://www.immi.se/intercultural

Almaney, A. J., & Alwar, A. J. (1982). *Communicating with Arabs: A handbook for the business executive.* Prospect Heights, IL: Waveland.

Alon, I. (Ed.). (2003a). *Chinese culture, organizational behavior, and international business management.* Westport, CT: Praeger.

Alon, I. (Ed.) (2003b). *Chinese economic transition and international marketing strategy.* Westport, CT: Praeger.

Alon, I., & Kellerman, E. (1999). Meltdown in Southeast Asia: Internal antecedents in the 1997 Asian economic crisis. *Multinational Business Review, 7,* 1–12.

Altman, I., & Taylor, D. (1973). *Social penetration: The development of interpersonal relationships.* New York: Holt.

Ancona, D. G., & Caldwell, D. F. (1992). Demography and design: Predictors of new product team performance. *Organization Science, 3,* 321–341.

Andersen, P. (1998). *Nonverbal communication: Forms and functions.* New York: McGraw-Hill.

Anderson, R., Baxter, L. A., & Cissna, K. N. (2003). *Dialogue: Theorizing differences in communication studies.* Thousands Oaks, CA: Sage.

Anderson, S., & Cavanaugh, J. (2000). Report on the top 2000 corporations. Institute for Policy Studies. Retrieved May 4, 2005, from http://www.corporations.org/system/top100html

Andres, H. P. (2002). A comparison of face-to-face and virtual software development teams. *Team Performance Management, 8,* 39–48.

Antecedents of the FTAA Process. (2005). Retrieved January 7, 2005, from http://www.ftaa-alca.org/view_e.asp

Appadwal, A. (1996). *Modernity at large: Cultural dimensions of globalization.* Minneapolis, MN: University of Minnesota Press.

Applegate, L. (1995, August). In search of new organization model for the 1990s: Lessons from the field. Academy of Management Annual Meeting Best Paper Proceedings.

Arner, D. W. (1996). The Mexican Peso crisis: Implications for the regulation of financial markets. *Essays in International Financial & Economic Law, 4*(October). Retrieved June 1, 2005, from http://iibf.law.smu.edu/arner.pdf

Atkins, G. P. (1998). *Latin America and the Caribbean in the international system* (4th ed.). Oakland, CA: Westview.

Atlas of the World. (2004). Twelfth edition. London: Oxford University Press.

Auer, P. (1995). The pragmatics of code-switching: A sequential approach. In L. Milroy & P. Muysken (Eds.), *One speaker, two languages, cross-disciplinary perspectives* (pp. 115–135). Cambridge, UK: Cambridge University Press.

Auer, P. (1998). *Code-switching in conversation: Language, interaction and identity.* London, UK: Routledge.

Axtell, R. E. (1987). *Dos and taboos around the world: A guide to international behavior.* New York: Wiley.

Bacharach, S. B., & Lawler, E. J. (1980). *Power and politics in organizations.* San Francisco: Jossey-Bass.

Baji, P. E. (2004). Anglican Bishop, District of Korogwe, Tanzania. Interview on October 17, 2004.

Baker, J. R. (2005, April 24). Japan's fortunes slipped as nation failed to adapt. *Orlando Sentinel,* p. G4.

Bakhurji, N. (2005, March 9). NPR radio interview, *Talk of the Nation.*

Bamrud, J. (2001). Latin America: To dollarize or not? Retrieved January 8, 2005, from http://www.latinbusinesschronicle.com/app/article.aspx?id=212

Bandura, A. (1986). *Social foundations of action and thought: A social cognitive view.* Englewood Cliffs, NJ: Prentice Hall.

Bantz, C. R. (1993). Cultural diversity and group dynamics: Managing differences in cross-cultural team research. *Journal of Applied Communication Research, 21,* 1–20.

Barakat, H. (1993). *The Arab world.* Berkeley: University of California Press.

Barber, B. (1992, March). Jihad vs. McWorld. *Atlantic Monthly,* 53–63.

Barczak, G., & McDonough, E. F. (2003). Leading global product development teams. *Research Technology Management, 46,* 14–26.

Barker, D., & McGregor, D. (2003). *Resources, planning, and environmental management and the changing Caribbean.* Jamaica: University of West Indies Press.

Barker, J. (1992). *Discovering the new paradigms of success: Future's edge.* New York: William Morrow and Company.

Barnlund, D. (1968). *Interpersonal communication: Survey and studies.* New York: Houghton Mifflin.

Barrett, D. B. (Ed.). (1982). *World Christian encyclopedia.* Nairobi: Oxford University Press, 136–171.

Baugh, S.G., & Graen, G. B. (1997). Effects of team gender and racial composition on perceptions of team performance in cross-functional teams. *Group & Organization Management, 22,* 366–383.

Baxter, L. A. (1992). Interpersonal communication as dialogue: A response to the social approaches forum. *Communication Theory, 2,* 329–342.

Baxter, L. A., & Montgomery, B. M. (1996). *Relating: Dialogues and dialectics.* New York: Guilford.

Baxter, L. A., & Montgomery, B. M. (1997). Rethinking communication in personal relationships from a dialectical perspective. In S. Duck (Ed.), *A handbook of personal relationships* (2nd ed.) (pp. 325–349). New York: Wiley.

Baxter, L. A., & Simon, E. P. (1993). Relationship maintenance strategies and dialectical contradictions in personal relationships. *Journal of Social and Personal Relationships, 10,* 225–242.

Bazerman, M. H., & Neale, M. A. (1992). *Negotiating rationally.* New York: Free Press.

Be responsible, Umno delegates told (HL). (1998, June 18). *The New Straits Times,* pp. 1, 34–38.

Beckhard, R., & Harris, R. T. (1977). *Organizational transitions: Managing complex change.* Reading, MA: Addison-Wesley.

Beebe, L. M., & Giles, H. (1984). Speech accommodation theories: A discussion in terms of second-language acquisition. *International Journal of the Sociology of Language, 46,* 5–32.

Beebe, S., & Masterson, J. (1982). *Communicating in small groups.* Glenview, IL: Scott, Foreman.

Begley, S. (2002, August 26). New ABCs of branding—Branding names pack punch one letter at a time. *The Wall Street Journal,* p. B1.

Beim, D., & Bulmer-Thomas, V. (2003). United States of Latin America? Retrieved March 20, 2003, from http://www.financewise.com/public/edit/latin/latrisk/latr-currenciesp.htm

Belasco, A. (2005). *CRS Report for Congress: The cost of operations in Iraq, Afghanistan, and enhanced security.* Washington, DC: Library of Congress Congressional Research Service.

Belasco, J. (1991) *Teaching the elephant to dance.* New York: Plume.

Bell, C., & Harari, O. (2000). *Beep! Beep! Competing in the age of the Road Runner.* New York: Warner Books.

Bell, R. (1987). Social involvement. In J. McCrosky & J. Daly (Eds.), *Personality and interpersonal communication* (pp. 195–242). Beverly Hills, CA: Sage.

Bellah, R., Madsen, R., Sullivan, W., Swindler, A., & Tipton, S. (1985). *Habits of the heart.* Berkeley: University of California Press.

Benge, R. C. (1972). *Communication and identity.* London: Clive Bingley.

Bennett, J. M. (1977). Transition shock. In N. Jain (Ed.), *International and intercultural communication annual* (Vol. IV) (pp. 45–52). Falls Church, VA: Speech Communication Association.

Bennett, J. M. (1979). Overcoming the golden rule: Sympathy and empathy. In D. Nimmo (Ed.), *Communication yearbook, 3* (pp. 407–422). New Brunswick, NJ: Transaction.

Bennett, J. M. (1986). Modes of cross-cultural training: Conceptualizing cross-cultural training as education. *International Journal of Intercultural Relations, 10,* 117–134.

Bennis, W. (1989). *Why leaders can't lead.* San Francisco: Jossey-Bass.

Benveniste, G. (1994). *The twenty-first century organization.* San Francisco: Jossey-Bass.

Berger, C., & Bradac, J. (1982). *Language and social knowledge.* London: Edward Arnold.

Berger, C., & Calabrese, R. (1975). Some explorations in initial interaction and beyond. *Human Communication Research, 1,* 99–112.

Berger, C., Gardner, R., Parks, M., Schulman, L., & Miller, G. (1976). Interpersonal epistemology and interpersonal communication. In G. Miller (Ed.), *Explorations in interpersonal communication* (pp. 122–144). Beverly Hills, CA: Sage.

Bernstein, B. (1966). Elaborated and restricted codes: An outline. *Sociological Inquiry, 36,* 254–261.

Bernstein, B. (1971). *Class, codes, and control: Theoretical studies toward a sociology of language.* London, UK: Routledge & Kegan Paul.

Bernstein, B. (2000). *Pedagogy, symbolic control and identity: Theory, research, critique.* Lanham, MD: Rowman & Littlefield.

Berry, J. (1990). Psychology of acculturation. In R. Brislin (Ed.), *Applied cross-cultural psychology* (pp. 232–253). Newbury Park, CA: Sage.

Beyerlein, M., & Johnson, D. (1994). *Theories of self-managing work teams.* Stamford, CT: JAI Press.

Bhagwati, J. (2004). *In defense of globalization.* New York: Oxford University Press.

Bhappu, A. D. (2000). The Japanese family: An institutional logic for Japanese corporate networks and Japanese management. *Academy of Management Review, 25,* 409–415.

Bidgoli, J. (1996). A new productivity tool for the 90's: Group support systems. *Journal of Systems Management. 47,* 56–62.

Bikson, T., & Eveland, J. D. (1990). The interplay of work group structures and computer support. In J. Galegher, R. Kraut, & C. Egido (Eds.), *Intellectual teamwork: Social and technological foundations of cooperative work* (pp. 243–290). Hillsdale, NJ: Lawrence Erlbaum.

Birdwhistell, R. (1955). Background to kinesics. *ETC, 13,* 10–18.

Birdwhistell, R. (1970). *Kinesics and context.* Philadelphia: University of Pennsylvania Press.

Black, J., & Gregersen, H. (1991). Antecedents to cross-cultural adjustment for expatriates in Pacific Rim assignments. *Human Relations, 44,* 497–515.

Blake, R. R., & Mouton, S. (1964). *The managerial grid: Key orientations for achieving production through people.* Houston, TX: Gulf Publishing.

Bloodworth, J. (2005). Manager, General Services Department Printing, Graphics and Map Design, The World Bank, Washington, DC. Interview by S. S. Easton, March 29.

Boekestijn, C. (1988). Intercultural migration and the development of personal identity. *International Journal of Intercultural Relations, 12,* 83–105.

Bordia, P. (1997). Face-to-face versus computer-mediated communication: A synthesis of experimental literature. *Journal of Business Communication, 34,* 99–119.

Borisoff, D., & Victor, D. A. (1989). *Conflict management: A communication skills approach.* Englewood Cliffs, NJ: Prentice Hall.

Bormann, E. G. (1972). Fantasy and rhetorical vision: The rhetorical criticism of social reality. *Quarterly Journal of Speech, 58,* 396–407.

Bormann, E. G. (1982). Fantasy and rhetorical vision: Ten years later. *Quarterly Journal of Speech, 68,* 1–28.

Bormann, E. G. (1985). *The force of fantasy: Restoring the American dream.* Carbondale: Southern Illinois University Press.

Bormann, E. G. (1990). *Small group communication: Theory and practice* (3rd ed.). New York: Harper & Row.

Bormann, E. G., Cragan, J. F., & Shields, D. C. (1996). An expansion of the rhetorical vision component of the symbolic convergence theory: The Cold War paradigm case. *Communication Monographs, 63,* 1–28.

Bosrock, M. M. (1994). *Put your best foot forward*. St. Paul, MN: International Education Systems.

Brabant, S., Palmer, C., & Grambling, R. (1990). Returning home. *International Journal of Intercultural Relations, 14,* 387–404.

Bradburn, N. (1969). *The structure of psychological well-being.* Chicago: Aldine.

Branden, N. (1997). Self-esteem in the information age. In F. Hesselbein, M. Goldsmith, & R. Beckhard (Eds.), *The organization of the future* (pp. 221–229). San Francisco: Jossey-Bass.

Brazilian Fiscal Responsibility Law. (2000). Retrieved May 5, 2005, from http://www1 .worldbank.org/publicsector/pe/budgetlaws/BRLRFEnglish.pdf

Brett, J. M. (2001). *Negotiating globally.* San Francisco: Jossey-Bass.

Brim, O., & Wheeler, S. (1966). *Socialization through the life cycle.* New York: Doubleday.

Brinkhoff, T. (2005a). Canada – City population. Retrieved November 25, 2005, from http://www.citypopulation.de/Canada.html

Brinkhoff, T. (2005b). Principal agglomerations of the world. Retrieved April 3, 2005, from http://www.citypopulation.de/World.html

Brislin, R. W. (1981). *Cross-cultural encounters: Face-to-face interaction.* New York: Pergamon.

Brislin, R. W. (1993). *Understanding culture's influence on behavior.* Orlando: Harcourt Brace College Publishers.

Brislin, R. W., & Yoshida, T. (1994). *Intercultural communication training.* Thousand Oaks, CA: Sage.

Brown, C. T., Yelsmer, P., & Keller, P. W. (1981). Communication-conflict predispositions: Development of a theory and an instrument. *Human Relations, 34,* 103–117.

Brown, D. L. (2001, April 8). Quebec law on French signs makes some people gag 'Tongue Troopers' protect culture, supporters say. *The Washington Post.* Retrieved November 4, 2005, from http://www.janda.org/b20/News%20articles/Language %20law

Brown, L. D. (1983). *Managing conflict at organizational interfaces.* Reading, MA: Addison-Wesley.

Brown, P., & Levinson, S. (1987). *Politeness: Some universals in language use.* Cambridge: Cambridge University Press.

Brummett, B. (1994). *Rhetoric in popular culture.* New York: St. Martin's.

Buckman, R. H. (1997). Lions and tigers and bears: Following the road from command and control to knowledge sharing. Retrieved May 8, 2005, from http://www .knowldge-nurture.com/web/bulabdoc.nsf/0/5478fdad627ffa7086256ab50075 7089/$FILE/LIONS.pdf

Buckman, R. H. (2000). Knowledge sharing and innovation. Speech given to a group of business leaders. Retrieved May 8, 2005, from http://www.knowledge-nurture.com

Burgoon, J. K. (1994). Nonverbal signals. In M. L. Knapp & G. R. Miller (Eds.), *Handbook of interpersonal communication* (pp. 253–255). Thousand Oaks, CA: Sage.

Burgoon, J., Berger, C., & Waldron, B. (2000). Mindfulness and interpersonal communication. *Journal of Social Issues, 56,* 105–128.

Burgoon, J. K., Buller, D. B., Hale, J. L., & deTurck, M. A. (1984). Relational messages associated with nonverbal behaviors. *Human Communication Research, 10,* 351–378.

Burgoon, J. K., & Hale, J. L. (1984). The fundamental topoi of relational communication. *Communication Monographs, 51,* 193–214.

Burgoon, J. K., & Hale, J. L. (1988). Nonverbal expectancy violations: Model elaboration and application. *Communication Monographs, 55,* 58–79.

Burgoon, J. K., & Langer, E. J. (1996). Language fallacies, and mindlessness-mindfulness in social interaction. In B. R. Burleson (Ed.), *Communication Yearbook 18* (pp. 105–132). Thousand Oaks, CA: Sage, 105–132.

Burgoon, J. K., Stern, L. A., & Dillman, L. (1995). *Interpersonal adaptation: Dyadic interaction patterns.* New York: Cambridge University Press.

Burleson, B., & Caplan, S. (1998). Cognitive complexity. In J. McCroskey, J. Daly, & M. Martin (Eds.), *Communication and personality: Trait perspectives* (pp. 223–286). Cresskill, NJ: Hampton.

Burleson, B., & Waltman, M. S. (1988). Cognitive complexity: Using the role category questionnaire measure. In C. Tardy (Ed.), *A handbook for the study of human communication* (pp. 1–35). Norwood, NJ: Ablex.

Bush, R., & Folger, J. P. (1994). *The promise of mediation.* San Francisco: Jossey-Bass.

Business English. (2005). British and American financial terms. Retrieved July 10, 2005, from http://www.englishclub.com/business-english/vocabulary_ft-ukus.htm

Business News America. (2002, July 11). World Cup drew Brazilians to the net. Retrieved April 3, 2005, from http://www.bnamericas.com

Cady, S. H., & Valentine, J. (1999). Team innovation and perceptions of considerations: What difference does diversity make? *Small Group Research, 30,* 730–750.

Callisto, M. (1998, March 13). Why passionate hope is rising again in East Africa. *The East African,* p. A1.

Camillus, J. (1993). Crafting the competitive corporation: Management systems for future organizations. In P. Lorange, B. Chakravarhy, J. Roos, & A. Van De Ven (Eds.), *Implementing strategic process: Change, learning, and cooperation* (pp. 313–328). Oxford, UK: Blackwell.

Canary, D. J., & Cupach, W. R. (1988). Relational and episodic characteristics associated with conflict tactics. *Journal of Social and Personal Relationships, 5,* 305–322.

Cappel, J. J., & Windsor, J. C. (2000). Ethical decision making: A comparison of computer-supported and face-to-face group. *Journal of Business Ethics, 28,* 95–107.

Carbaugh, D. (1990). Intercultural communication. In D. Carbaugh (Ed.), *Cultural communication and intercultural contact* (pp. 91–116). Hillsdale, NJ: Lawrence Erlbaum.

Carbaugh, D. (1995). The ethnographic communication theory of Philipsen and associates. In D. Cushman & B. Kovacic (Eds.), *Watershed research traditions in communication theory* (pp. 241–265). Albany: State University of New York.

CARICOM. (2006). History of the Caribbean Community (CARICOM). Retrieved April 3, 2005, from http://www.caricom.org/jsp/community/history.jsp?menu=community

Carroll, J. B. (1956). *Language, thought, and reality: Selected writings of Benjamin Lee Whorf.* New York: Wiley.

Casmir, F. (1999). Foundations for the study of intercultural communication based on a third-culture building model. *International Journal of Intercultural Relations, 23*, 91–116.

Central Intelligence Agency. (2005a). World Factbook: Canada. Retrieved September 21, 2006, from https://www.cia.gov/cia/publications/factbook/geos/ca.html

Central Intelligence Agency. (2005b). World Factbook: European Union. Retrieved September 21, 2006, from https://www.cia.gov/cia/publications/factbook/geos/ee.html

Central Intelligence Agency. (2005c). World Factbook: Rank order – GDP, inflation rate, unemployment rate, real growth rate. Retrieved December 23, 2005, from https://www.cia.gov/cia/publications/factbook/docs/rankorderguide.html

Central Intelligence Agency. (2005d). World Factbook: Russia. Retrieved December 23, 2005, from https://www.cia.gov/cia/publications/factbook/geos/rs.html

Central Intelligence Agency. (2005e). World Factbook: United States. November 25, 2005, from https://www.cia.gov/cia/publications/factbook/geos/us.html

Central Intelligence Agency. (2005f). World Factbook: World. Retrieved June 13, 2004, from https://www.cia.gov/cia/publications/factbook/geos/xx.html

Chambers, J. (1998). An interview with John Chambers. In J. Kurtzman (Ed.) *Thought leaders* (pp. 23–47). San Francisco: Jossey-Bass.

Chaney, L. H., & Martin, J. S. (2004). *Intercultural business communication* (3rd ed.). Upper Saddle River, NJ: Pearson Prentice Hall.

Chang, G. G. (2001). *The coming collapse of China.* New York: Random House.

Chen, G., & Ma, R. (2001). *Chinese conflict management and resolution.* Stamford, CT: Ablex.

Chinese Culture Connection. (1987). Chinese values and the search for culture-free dimensions of culture. *Journal of Cross-Cultural Psychology, 18*, 143–164.

Chollet, D. (2005, April 24). Rice takes State where no one has gone before. *Orlando Sentinel,* pp. G1, G5.

Chua, A. (2003). *World on fire.* New York: Doubleday.

Church, A. (1982). Sojourner adjustment. *Psychological Bulletin, 24*, 949–960.

City Mayors. (2005a). The world's largest urban areas. Retrieved November 11, 2005, from http://www.citymayors.com/features/urban_areas1.html

City Mayors. (2005b). U.S. Sunshine cities grow fastest while Detroit loses top ten place. Retrieved November 26, 2005, from: http://www.citymayors.com/statistics/us_cities_population.html

Clampitt, P. G., DeKoch, R. J., & Cashman, T. (2000). A strategy for communicating about uncertainty. *Academy of Management Executive, 14*, 41–57.

Clark, A. (2005, March 28). The final frontier. *Newsweek, p. 6.*

Clarke, C. C., & Lipp, G. D. (1998). Conflict resolution for contrasting cultures. *Training & Development,* February, 21–33.

Cleveland, J., Neuroth, J., & Plastrik, N. (1996). *Welcome to the edge of chaos.* Lansing, MI: On Purpose Associates.

Clutter, A. W., & Nieto, R. D. (2001). *FactSheet: Understanding the Hispanic culture.* Athens, OH: The Ohio State University. Retrieved April 9, 2004, from http://ohioline.osu.edu/hyg-fact/5000/5237.html

CNNMoney.com. (2005, December 19). A pink slip in your stocking? Companies used to avoid holiday layoffs, but a rash of job cuts shows that's no longer the case. Retrieved December 23, 2005, from http://money.cnn.com/2005/12/19/news/economy/jobs_holiday_layoffs/index.htm?section

Collier, M. J. (1998). Reaching cultural identity: Reconciling interpretive and postcolonial perspectives. In D. Tanno & A. Gonzalez (Eds.), *Communication and identity across cultures* (pp. 122–147). Thousand Oaks, CA: Sage.

Collier, M. J., & Thomas, M. (1988). Cultural identity: An interpretive perspective. In Y. Y. Kim & W. Gudykunst (Eds.), *Theories in intercultural communication* (pp. 99–122). Newbury Park, CA: Sage.

Collins, J., & Porras, J. (1994). *Built to last.* New York: Harper Business.

Conrad, C., & Poole, M. S. (2002). *Strategic organizational communication in a global economy* (5th ed.). Fort Worth, TX: Harcourt College Publishers.

Constantino, M., & Gambella, L. (2000). *The Italian way: Aspects of behavior, attitudes, and customs of the Italians.* New York: McGraw-Hill.

Copeland, L., & Griggs, L. (1985). *Going international: How to make friends and deal effectively in the global marketplace.* New York: New American Library.

Cordoba, J. (2004, December 24). To fix Venezuela, ex-guerrillas want to make 'new man.' *The Wall Street Journal,* front page.

Council for Advancement of Arab-British Understanding. (2005). Educational Briefings. The Importance of Arabic. Retrieved February 11, 2005, from http://www.caabu.org/education/arabic-briefing.html

Council of State Governments. (2001). Forging new trade relationships: Latin America and the Southern Legislative Conference states. Atlanta, GA: The Council of State Governments, Southern Office.

Council of the Americas. (2003). Free Trade Area of the Americas (FTAA). Retrieved May 23, 2003, from http://www.americas-society.org/coa/advocacy/ftaa.html

CountryWatch. (2003). Retrieved January 8, 2005, from http://www.countrywatch.com

Covin, T. J., & Kilmann, R. H. (1990). Participant perceptions of positive and negative influences on large-scale change. *Group and Organizational Studies, 15,* 244–248.

Cox, T. H., Lobel, A. A., & McLeod, P. L. (1991). Effects of ethnic group cultural differences on cooperative versus competitive behavior on a group task. *Academy of Management Journal, 34,* 827–847.

Craig, C. (1993). *Hunting with the tigers: Doing business with Hong Kong, Indonesia, South Korea, Malaysia, the Philippines, Singapore, Taiwan, Thailand, and Vietnam.* San Francisco: Pfeiffer and Company.

Craig, K. (1964). *The call of the minaret.* New York: Oxford University Press.

Crocker, J., Major, B., & Steele, C. (1998). Social stigma. In D. Gilbert, S. Fiske, & G. Lindsey (Eds.), *Handbook of social psychology* (4th ed., Vol. 2, pp. 210–217). New York: McGraw-Hill.

Cronen, V., Chen, V., & Pearce, W. B. (1988). Coordinated management of meaning: A critical theory. In Y. Y. Kim & W. Gudykunst (Eds.), *Theories in intercultural communication* (pp. 30–55). Newbury Park, CA: Sage.

Cronen, V., & Pearce, W. B. (1981). Logical force in interpersonal communication: A new concept of the "necessity" in social behavior. *Communication, 6,* 5–67.

Cronen, V., Pearce, W. B., & Harris, L. (1979). The logic of the coordinated management of meaning. *Communication Education, 28,* 22–38.

Cronen, V., Pearce, W. B., & Harris, L. M. (1982). The coordinated management of meaning: A theory of communication. In F. E. X. Dance (Ed.), *Human communication theory* (pp. 61–89). New York: Harper & Row.

Crookes, D., & Thomas, I. (1998). Problem solving and culture—exploring some stereotypes. *The Journal of Management Development, 17,* 583–590.

Csikszentmihalyi, M. (1990). *Flow: The psychology of optimal experiences.* New York: Harper & Row.

Daft, R., & Becker, S. (1978). *The innovative organization.* New York: Elsevier North-Holland.

Daniels, J. D., & Radebaugh, L. H. (2001). *International business: Environments and operations* (9th ed.). Upper Saddle River, NJ: Prentice Hall.

Daniels, J. D., Radebaugh, L. H., & Sullivan, D. P. (2004). *International business: Environments and operations* (10th ed.). Upper Saddle River, NJ: Pearson Prentice Hall.

Dannemiller, K. D., & Jacobs, R. W. (1992). Changing the way organizations change: A revolution of common sense. *The Journal of Applied Behavioral Science, 28,* 480–498.

Davitz, J. (1964). *The communication of emotional meaning.* New York: McGraw-Hill.

Delia, J., O'Keefe, B. J., & O'Keefe, D. J. (1982). The constructivist approach to communication. In F. E. X. Dance (Ed.), *Human communication theory* (pp. 147–191). New York: Harper and Row.

DeSanctis, G. B., & Jackson, B. M. (1994). Coordination of information technology management: Team-based structures and computer-based communication systems. *Journal of Management Information Systems, 10,* 85–110.

DeSaussure, F. (1960). *Course in general linguistics.* London, UK: Peter Owen.

Deutsch, M. (1973). Conflicts: Productive and destructive. In F. E. Jandt (Ed.), *Conflict resolution through communication* (pp. 155–167). New York: Harper and Row.

Deutsch, S., & Won, G. (1963). Some factors in the adjustment of foreign nationals. *Journal of Social Issues, 19,* 115–122.

DeVille, J. (1980, February). Let's learn better ways to cope with social change. *Training,* pp. 72–80.

Devine, E., & Braganti, N. L. (2000). *The traveler's guide to Latin American customs & manners.* New York: St. Martin's Griffin.

Devine, P., Evett, S., & Vasquez-Suson, K. (1996). Exploring the interpersonal dynamics of intergroup contact. In R. Sorrentino & E. Higgins (Eds.), *Handbook of motivation and cognition* (Vol. 3) (pp. 423–464). New York: Guilford.

Dimitrius, J., & Mazzarella, M. C. (1999). *Reading people: How to understand people and predict their behavior—anytime, anyplace.* New York: Ballantine.

Dodd, C. (1998). *Dynamics of intercultural communication* (5th ed.). Boston: McGraw-Hill.

Dooley, R. (2003). Four cultures, one company: Achieving corporate excellence through working cultural complexity (part 1).*Organization Development Journal, 21,* 56–67.

Drucker, P. F. (1994, November). The age of social transformation. *The Atlantic Monthly* online. Retrieved November 29, 2005, from http://www.theatlantic.com

Drucker, P. F. (1997). Toward the new organization. In F. Hesselbein, M. Goldsmith, & R. Beckhard (Eds.), *The organization of the future* (pp. 1–5). San Francisco: Jossey-Bass.

Dubrovsky, V. Kiesler, S., & Sethna, B. (1991). The equalization phenomenon: Status effects in computer-mediated and face-to-face decision making groups. *Human Computer Interaction, 6,* 119–146.

Duck, S., & Barnes, M. K. (1992). Disagreeing about agreement: Reconciling differences about similarity. *Communication Monographs, 59,* 199–208.

Duffy, K. G., Grosch, J. W., & Olczak, P. V. (1991). *Community mediation.* San Francisco: Jossey-Bass.

Dumaine, B. (1991, December 2). Closing the innovation gap. *Fortune,* 55–65.

Dyal, J., & Dyal, R. (1981). Acculturation, stress and coping. *International Journal of Intercultural Relations, 5,* 301–328.

Earley, C., & Mosakowski, E. (2000). Creating hybrid team cultures: An empirical test of transnational team functioning. *Academy of Management Journal, 43,* 26–49.

East African trade accord launched. (2005, January 1). *BBC News, World Edition.* Retrieved January 12, 2005, from http://news.bbc.co.uk/2/hi/africa/4139635.stm

Economic Commission for Latin America and the Caribbean. (1999). Characteristics of Foreign Direct Investment (FDI) in Latin America. Retrieved January 8, 2005, from http://magnet.undp.org/new/pdf/PDFscomplete/ECLAC2.pdf#search=' FDI%20Latin%20America%20Investment%20Foreign

Economic Commission for Latin America and the Caribbean. (2006). Economic survey of Latin America and the Caribbean 2005-2006. Retrieved September 21, 2006, from http://www.eclac.cl/cgibin/getProd.asp?xml=/publicaciones/xml/3/26143/ P26143.xml&xsl=/de/tpl-i/p9f.xsl&base=/tpl/top-bottom.xslt

Edelman, J., & Crain, M. B. (1993). *The Tao of negotiation.* New York: Harper & Row.

Educational Testing Service. (1999). ETS/HACU Study: Bridging the Hispanic education/ employment gap. Retrieved July 17, 2001, from http://www.ets.org/portal/site/ ets/menuitem.3a88fea28f42ada7c6ce5a10c3921509/vgnextoid=85b65784623f4010 VgnVCM10000022f95910RCRD

EFTA Surveillance Authority. (2005). European Free Trade Association. Retrieved July 25, 2005, from http://www.eftasurv.int/

Eigen, P. (2005, March 1). Kibaki must keep fighting corruption, bribe by bribe! [Nairobi] *Daily Nation.* Retrieved March 15, 2005, from http://www.nation-media.com/eastafrican/15032004/Opinion/Opinion1503200421.html

Eisenberg, E. M., & Riley, P. (2001). Organizational culture. In F. M. Jablin & L. L. Putnam (Eds.), *The new handbook of organizational communication: Advances in theory, research, and methods* (pp. 291–322). Thousand Oaks, CA: Sage.

Ekman, P. (2004). *Emotions revealed: Recognizing faces and feelings to improve communication and emotional life.* Phoenix, AZ: Nite Owl Books.

Ekman, P., & Friesen, W. (1969). The repertoire of nonverbal behavior: Categories, origins, usage, and coding. *Semiotica, 1,* 49–98.

Ekman, P., Friesen, W., & Ellsworth, P. (1971). *The face and emotion.* New York: Pergamon.

Ellinor, L., & Gerard, G. (1998). *Dialogue.* New York: Wiley.

Ellis, C. (2005). Global Downstream Coordination Office Senior Advisor. Personal interview by S.S. Easton, March 27.

Encarta. (n.d.). Middle East. Retrieved February 6, 2005, from http://encarta.msn.-com/encyclopedia_7615792982/Middle_East.html

Encarta. (2005). North America. Retrieved November 26, 2005, from http://uk.encarta.msn.com/encyclopedia_761562468/North_America.html

Engholm, C. (1991). *When business east meets business west.* New York: Wiley.

Esposito, J. L. (1980). *Islam and development.* Syracuse, NY: Syracuse University Press.

EU & Mercosur. (2000). Europa—The European Commission. Retrieved April 9, 2004, from http://europa.ed.int

Europa. (2005a). The Euro: Our currency. Retrieved July 6, 2005, from http://europa.eu.int/euro/entry.html

Europa. (2005b). European Union institutions and other bodies. Retrieved July 3, 2005, from http://europa.eu

Europa. (2005c). Languages of Europe. Retrieved July 6, 2005, from http://ec.europa.eu/education/policies/lang/languages/index_en.html

EuropeETravel.com. (2005b). Eastern Europe Map. Retrieved July 3, 2005, from http://europeetravel.com/maps/eastern-europe-map.htm

Eurostat. (2004). Yearbook. Retrieved July 3, 2005, from http://epp.eurostat.ec.europa.eu/portal/page?_pageid=1334,49092079,1334_49092421&_dad=portal&_schema=PORTAL

Fabum, D. (1971). *Dimensions of change.* Beverly Hills, CA: Glencoe.

Feather, N. (1990). Bridging the gap between values and action. In E. Higgins & R. Sorrentino (Eds.), *Handbook of motivation and cognition* (Vol. 2, pp. 55–65). New York: Guilford.

Feather, N. (1995). Values, valences, and choice. *Journal of Personality and Social Psychology, 68,* 1135–1151.

Featherstone, J. (2002, April 1). International migration: Work flows. *Financial Times Expatriate,* 5–17.

Feldman, R. S. (1991). *Fundamentals of nonverbal behavior.* New York: Cambridge University Press.

Fernandez, D., Carlson, D., Stepina, L., & Nicholson, J. (1997). Hofstsede's country classification 25 years later. *Journal of Social Psychology, 137,* 43–54.

Fernando, A. (2005). Chile: Singapore of South America. *Government Activity-International Pages* (Brief Article). Retrieved April 9, 2004, from http://www.findarticles.com

Ferraro, G. P. (1990). *The cultural dimension of international business.* Upper Saddle River, NJ: Prentice Hall.

Fisher, G. (1980). *International negotiation.* Yarmouth, ME: Intercultural Press.

Fisher, G. (1997). *Mindsets* (2nd ed.). Yarmouth, ME: Intercultural Press.

Fisher, R., & Ury, W. (1991). *Getting to yes* (2nd ed.). New York: Penguin.

Fiske, D., & Maddi, S. (1961). *Functions of varied experiences.* Homewood, IL: Dorsey.

Fiske, J. (1989). *Understanding popular culture.* New York: Routledge.

Fleming, A. (2005). Info about the world's busiest airports. About Air Travel. Retrieved Nov. 26, 2005, from http://airtravel.about.com/od/airports/a/bigarpts.htm

Flippo, H. (1999). *The German way: Aspects of behavior, attitudes, and customs in the German-speaking world.* Lincolnwood, IL: NTC/Contemporary Publishing Group.

Fogg, R. W. (1985). Dealing with conflict: A repertoire of creative peaceful approaches. *Journal of Conflict Resolution, 29,* 330–358.

Folger, J. P., Poole, M. S., & Stutman, R. K. (1993). *Working through conflict* (2nd ed.). New York: HarperCollins.

Forbes. (2005). The Forbes Global 2000: A World of big companies. Retrieved December 17, 2005, from http://www.forbes.com/2005/03/30/05f2000land.html

Forteza , J. H., & Neilson, G. L. (1999). Multinationals in the next decade: Blueprint, flow & soul, *Strategy & Business, 16* (Third Quarter), 13–27.

Fortner, R. S. (1993). *International communication: History, conflict, and control of the global metropolis.* Belmont, CA: Wadsworth.

Foster, R. (1986). *Innovation.* New York: Summit.

Frecklington, S. (2006). Interview by Ilan Alon, January 25, 2006.

Freedom House. (2005). Freedom in the world. Retrieved March 19, 2005, from http://www.freedomhouse.org/template.cfm?page=129&year=2005

French Language in Canada. (2005). Retrieved November 4, 2005, from http.//langage.ifrance.com/quebec/quebpage.htm

Friedman, T. (2000). *The Lexus and the olive tree: Understanding globalization.* New York: Anchor.

Friedman, T. (2005). *The world is flat: A brief history of the 21st century.* New York: Farrar, Straus, & Giroux.

Froggatt, C. C. (2001). *Work naked: Eight essential principles for peak performance in the virtual workplace.* San Francisco: Jossey-Bass.

Fukuyama, F. (1998). Asian values and the Asian crisis. *Commentary, 105,* 23–28.

Fulk, J. (1993). Social construction of communication technology. *Academy of Management Journal, 36,* 921–950.

Fulk, J., & Collin-Jarvis, L. (2001). Wired meetings: Technological mediation of organizational gatherings. In F. M. Jablin & L. L. Putnam (Eds.), *The new handbook of organizational communication: Advances in theory, research, and methods* (pp. 624–654). Thousand Oaks, CA: Sage.

Furnham, A., & Ribchester, T. (1995). Tolerance of ambiguity: A review of the concept, its measurement and applications. *Current Psychology, 14,* 179–199.

Galbraith, J. R. (1997). The reconfigurable organization. In F. Hesselbein, M. Goldsmith, & R. Beckhard (Eds.), *The organization of the future* (pp. 87–108). San Francisco: Jossey-Bass.

Gallivan, M. J., Hofman, J. D., & Orlikowski, W. J. (1994). Implementing radical change: Gradual versus rapid pace. *Proceedings of the Fifteenth International Conference on*

Information Systems, Vancouver, British Columbia, Canada, December 14-17, 325–339. New York: Society for Information Management.

Gardels, N. (1998). *Global fusion: Asian ideals and Anglo-Saxon norms.* Washington, DC: Center for Democratic Institutions.

Gardner, G. (1962). Cross-cultural communication. *Journal of Social Psychology, 58,* 241–256.

Gardner, L., & Stough, C. (2002). Examining the relationship between leadership and emotional intelligence in senior level managers. *Leadership & Organizational Development Journal, 23,* 68–78.

Gass, S., & Varonis, E. (1985). Variations in native speaker speech modification on non-native speakers. *Studies in Second Language Acquisition, 7,* 37–58.

Geertz, C. (1973). *The interpretation of cultures.* New York: Basic.

Geography of Development. (n.d.) Latin America. Retrieved January 8, 2005, from http://www-scf.usc.edu/~yucekus/march19-lecture7.html

George, A. M. (2003). Teaching culture: The challenges and opportunities of international public relations. *Business Communication Quarterly, 66,* 97–113.

Georgi-Findlay, B. (2002). Americanization and globalization. In A. Satzger & G. Poncini (Eds.), *International perspectives on business communication: From past approaches to future trends* (pp. 3–16). New York: Peter Lang.

Gerbner, G., Gross, L., Morgan, M., & Signorielli, N. (1980). The "mainstreaming" of America. *Journal of Communication, 30,* 10–29.

Gergen, K. (1991). *The saturated self: Dilemmas of identity in contemporary life.* New York: HarperCollins-Basic Books.

Gersick, C. J. (1988). Time and transition in work teams: Toward a new model of group development. *Academy of Management Journal, 31,* 9–41.

Gidley-Kitchen, V. (2005, February 11). Is corruption getting worse in Africa? *BBC News Online.* Retrieved March 1, 2005, from http://news.bbc.co.uk/2/hi/africa/4254845.stm

Gilbert, E., & Currey, J. (2004). *Dhows and the colonial economy of Zanzibar, 1860–1970.* Columbus: University of Ohio Press.

Giles, H. (1973). Communication effectiveness as a function of accented speech. *Communication Monographs, 40,* 330–331.

Giles, H., Henwood, K., Coupland, N., Harriman, J., & Coupland, J. (1992a). Language attitudes and cognitive mediation, *Human Communication Research, 18,* 500–527.

Giles, H., Mulac, A., Bradac, J. J., & Johnson, P. (1987). Speech accommodation theory: The first decade and beyond. In M. L. McLaughlin (Ed.), *Communication Yearbook 10* (pp. 13–48). Newbury Park, CA: Sage.

Giles, H., Mulac, A., Bradac, J. J., & Smith, P. J. (1992b). Speech accommodation. In W. B. Gudykunst & Y. Y. Kim (Eds.), *Readings on communicating with strangers* (pp. 257–271). New York: McGraw-Hill.

Gillies, R. (2005, November 28). Canadian government falls on no-confidence. Retrieved December 4, 2005, from http://www.breitbart.com/news/2005/11/28/D8E5QI500.html

Glaser, W., & Glaser, C. (2005). Buenos Aires: Paris of the Americas. Global travel writers' syndicate. Retrieved April 9, 2005, from http://www.globaltravelwriters.com

Global Reach. (2002). Retrieved January 8, 2005, from http://www.globalreach.biz

Goffman, E. (1959). *The presentation of self in everyday life*. New York: Doubleday Anchor.

Goffman, E. (1967). *Interaction ritual: Essays on face-to-face behavior*. New York: Doubleday Anchor.

Gold, T., Guthrie, D., & Wank, D. (2002). *Social connections in China: Institutions, culture, and the changing nature of guanxi*. London: Cambridge University Press.

Goldhaber, G. (1993). *Organizational communication* (6th ed.). Dubuque, IA: Brown & Benchmark.

Goldman, S., Nagel, R., & Preiss, K. (1995). *Agile competitors and virtual organizations: Strategies for enriching the customer*. New York: Van Nostrand Reinhold.

Goleman, D. (1998). What makes a leader? *Harvard Business Review, 76*, 93–102.

Gomez, M. J. (1994). Latinos/Latinas at work: Cultural considerations. *The Public Manager, 23*, 31–38.

Gongloff, M. (2003, March 13). U.S. jobs jumping ship. *CNN Money*. Retrieved May 3, 2005, from http://cnnmoney.printthis.clickability.com/pt/cpt?action=cpt&expire=&urlID=5686054&fb=Y&partnerID=2200

Goto, S. G. (1997). Majority and minority perspectives on cross cultural interactions. In C. S. Granrose & S. Oskamp (Eds.), *Cross cultural work groups* (pp. 90–112). Thousand Oaks, CA: Sage.

Grabowski, M., & Roberts, K. H. (1998). Risk mitigation in virtual organizations. *Journal of Computer-Mediated Communication, 3*. Retrieved November 7, 2004, from http://www.ascusc.org/jcmc/vol3/issue4/grabowski.html

Graff, M. L. (2004). *Culture shock: A guide to customs and etiquette (Spain)*. Portland, OR: Graphic Arts Center Publishing Company.

Greenhouse, S. (2001, September 1). Report shows Americans have more "labor days." *New York Times*. Retrieved December 21, 2005, from http://www.contemporaryfamilies.org/subtemplate.php?t=discussion&ext=change50

Griffin, E. (2003). *A first look at communication* (5th ed.). New York: McGraw-Hill.

Griffith, T. L., & Neale, M. A. (2001). Information processing in traditional, hybrid, and virtual teams: From nascent knowledge to transactive memory. *Research in Organizational Behavior, 23*, 379–421.

Gudykunst, W. B. (1988). Uncertainty and anxiety. In Y. Y. Kim & W. B. Gudykunst (Eds.), *Intercultural communication theory* (pp. 183–205). Newbury Park, CA: Sage.

Gudykunst, W. B. (1991). *Bridging differences*. Newbury Park, CA: Sage.

Gudykunst, W. B. (1995). Anxiety/uncertainty management (AUM) theory. In R. Wiseman (Ed.), *Intercultural communication theory* (pp. 8–58). Thousand Oaks, CA: Sage.

Gudykunst, W. B. (1998). Individualistic and collectivistic perspectives on communication: An introduction. *International Journal of Intercultural Relations, 22*, 107–134.

Gudykunst, W. B., & Hammer, M. (1988). The influence of social identity and intimacy of interethnic relationships on uncertainty reduction processes. *Human Communication Research, 14*, 569–601.

Gudykunst, W. B., & Kim, Y. Y. (2003). *Communicating with strangers* (4th ed.). New York: McGraw-Hill.

Gudykunst, W. B., & Nishida, T. (1989). Theoretical perspectives for studying intercultural communication. In M. K. Asante & W. B. Gudykunst (Eds.), *Handbook of international and intercultural communication* (pp. 17–46). Newbury Park, CA: Sage.

Gudykunst, W. B., Nishida, T., & Chua, E. (1986). Uncertainty reduction in Japanese-North American dyads. *Communication Research Reports, 3,* 39–46.

Gudykunst, W. B., Nishida, T., & Chua, E. (1987). Perceptions of social penetration in Japanese-North American dyads. *International Journal of Intercultural Relations, 11,* 171–190.

Gudykunst, W. B., & Ting-Toomey, S. (1988). *Culture and interpersonal communication.* Newbury Park, CA: Sage.

Gullahorn, J. T., & Gullahorn, J. E. (1963). An extension of the U-curve hypothesis. *Journal of Social Issues, 19,* 33–47.

Haber, S., North, D. C., & Weingast, B. R. (2003, July 30). If economists are so smart, why is Africa so poor? *The Wall Street Journal,* p. A12.

Hage, J. (1974). *Communication and organizational control: Cybernetics in health and welfare settings.* New York: Wiley.

Hall, E. T. (1959). *The silent language.* Garden City, NY: Doubleday.

Hall, E. T. (1976). *Beyond culture.* New York: Anchor/Doubleday.

Hall, E. T., & Hall, M. R. (1987). *Hidden differences—doing business with the Japanese.* Garden City, NY: Anchor/Doubleday.

Hall, E. T., & Hall, M. R. (1990). *Understanding cultural differences.* Yarmouth, ME: Intercultural Press.

Hall, J. (1986). *Conflict management survey: A survey of one's characteristic reaction to and handling of conflicts between himself and others.* Conroe, TX: Teleometrics International.

Hamilton, C., & Parker, C. (1997). *Communicating for results* (5th ed.). Belmont, CA: Wadsworth.

Hammer, M., & Champy, J. (1993). *Reengineering the corporation: A manifesto for business revolution.* New York: HarperCollins.

Hammer, M., Gudykunst, W., & Wiseman, R. (1978). Dimensions of intercultural effectiveness. *International Journal of Intercultural Relations, 2,* 382–393.

Hampden-Turner, C., & Trompenaars, F. (2002). *Building cross-cultural competence: How to create wealth from conflicting values.* London: Yale University Press.

Handy, C. (1995). *The age of paradox.* Boston: Harvard Business School Press.

Handy, C. (1998). An interview with Charles Handy. In J. Kurtzman (Ed.), *Thought leaders* (pp. 4–16). San Francisco: Jossey-Bass.

Harmon, W. (1988). *Global mind change.* Indianapolis: Knowledge Systems, Inc.

Harms, S. L. (1961). Listener judgments of status cues in speech. *Quarterly Journal of Speech, 47,* 164–168.

Harrell, S. (2001). *Ways of being ethnic in Southwest China.* Seattle: University of Washington Press.

Harris, P. R., & Moran, R. T. (1991). *Managing cultural differences* (3rd ed.). Houston: Gulf Publishing.

Harrison, R. (1972). Nonverbal behavior: An approach to human communication. In R. Budd & B. Ruben (Eds.), *Approaches to human communication* (pp. 65–72). New York: Spartan Books.

Hart, R. P., & Burks, D. M. (1972). Rhetorical sensitivity and social interaction. *Speech Monographs, 39,* 75–91.

Hart, R. P., Carlson, R. E., & Eadie, W. F. (1980). Attitudes toward communication and the assessment of rhetorical sensitivity. *Communication Monographs, 47,* 1–22.

Harvey, M. G. (1985, Spring). The executive family: An overlooked variable in international assignments. *Columbia Journal of World Business,* p. 84–92.

Hawthorne, A. (2004, October). Political reform in the Arab world: A new ferment. (Carnegie Paper No. 52.) Retrieved March 28, 2005, from http://www.carnegie endowment.org/publications/index.cfm

Haythornthwaite, C., Wellman, B., & Garton, L. (1998). Work and community via computer-mediated communication. In J. Gakenbach (Eds.), *Psychology of the Internet* (pp. 199–226). San Diego, CA: Academic Press.

Hecht, M. (1978). The conceptualization of communication satisfaction. *Human Communication Research, 4,* 253–264.

Heijden, K. (2005). *Scenarios: The art of strategic conversation* (2nd ed.). New York: Wiley.

Heitler, S. M. (1990). *From conflict to resolution.* New York: Norton.

Held, D., & McGrew, A. (2000). The great globalization debate: An introduction. In D. Held & A. McGrew (Eds.), *The global transformations reader: An introduction to the globalization debate* (pp. 1–46). Malden, MA: Polity Press.

Henderson, D. R. (2005, October 11). The great game. *The Wall Street Journal,* p. A16.

Hendry, J. (2003). *Understanding Japanese society* (3rd ed.). London: Routledge.

Heritage, J. (1989). Current developments in conversation analysis. In D. Roger & P. Bull (Eds.), *Conversation: An interdisciplinary perspective* (pp. 211–247). Clevedon, UK: Multilingual Matters.

Heritage Foundation. (2005). Index of economic freedom. Countries. Retrieved July 8, 2005, from http://www.heritage.org/research/features/index/countries.cfm

Herskovits, M. (1955). *Cultural anthropology.* New York: Knopf.

Herskovits, M. (1973). *Cultural relativism.* New York: Random House.

Heslin, R., & Alper, T. (1983). Touch: A bonding gesture. In J. M. Wiemann & R. P. Harrison (Eds.), *Nonverbal interaction* (pp. 47–75). Beverly Hills, CA: Sage.

Higgins, J. M., & Mcallaster, C. (2004). If you want strategic change, don't forget to change your cultural artifacts. *Journal of Change Management, 4,* 63–73.

Hill, R. B. (1996). Historical context of the work ethic. Retrieved December 18, 2005, from http://www.coe.uga.edu/~rhill/workethic/hist.htm

Hilton, C. (1992). International business communication: The place of English. *Journal of Business Communication, 29,* 253–265.

Hiltz, S. R., Johnson, K., & Turoff, M. (1986). Experiments in group decision making: Communication process and outcome in face-to-face versus computerized conferences. *Human Communication Research, 13,* 225–252.

Hiltz, S. R., Johnson, K., & Turoff, M. (1991). Group decision support: The effects of designated human leaders and statistical feedback in computer conferences. *Journal of Management Information Systems, 8,* 81–108.

Hime, J. S. (1980). *Conflict and conflict management.* Athens, GA: University of Georgia Press.

Hinds, P., & Kiesler, S. (1995). Communication across boundaries: Work, structure, and use of communication technologies in large organizations. *Organization Science, 6,* 373–393.

Hispanic Business. (2004). Top 100 counties by Hispanic population – Web exclusive. Retrieved December 3, 2005, from http://www.hispanicbusiness.com/news/news byid.asp?id=18492

Hispanic Business (2005a). Hispanic-owned businesses: Growth projections, 2004-2010. Retrieved December 3, 2005, from: https://secure.hbinc.com/product/view .asp?id=143

Hispanic Business. (2005b). McDonald's named amongst best companies to work for in Latin America. Retrieved June 1, 2005, from http://www.hispanic business.com/news/newsbyid.asp?id=22880

Hispanic Business. (2005c). U.S. Hispanic purchasing power: 1978-2010. Retrieved December 3, 2005, from https://secure.hbinc.com/product/view.asp?id=85

Hitchcock, D. I. (1998, April 9). Asian crisis is cultural as well as economic. *Christian Science Monitor,* p. 19.

Hobman, E. V., Bordia, P., & Gallois, C. (2004). Perceived dissimilarity and work group involvement: The moderating effects of group openness to diversity. *Group & Organization Management, 29,* 560–587.

Hofstede Chart. (2005). Dimensions by cluster. Retrieved May 5, 2005, from http://geert-hofstede.international-business-center.com

Hofstede, G. (1979). Value systems in forty countries. In L. Eckenberger, W. Lonner, & Pootinga (Eds.), *Cross-cultural contributions to psychology* (pp. 25–38). Lisse, Netherlands: Swets and Zeitlinger.

Hofstede, G. (1980). *Culture's consequences: International differences in work-related values.* Beverly Hills, CA: Sage.

Hofstede, G. (1983). Dimensions of national cultures in fifty countries and three regions. In J. Deregowski, S. Dzuirawiee, & R. Amis (Eds.), *Explications in cross-cultural psychology* (pp. 335–355). Lisse, Netherlands: Swets and Zeitlinger.

Hofstede, G. (1991). *Cultures and organizations.* London: McGraw-Hill.

Hofstede, G. (1998). *Masculinity and femininity.* Thousand Oaks, CA: Sage.

Hofstede, G. (2001). *Culture's consequences: Comparing values, behaviors, institutions, and organizations across nations* (2nd ed.). Thousand Oaks, CA: Sage.

Hollingshead, A. B. (1996). Information suppression and status persistence in group decision making. *Human Communication Research. 23,* 193–219.

Houry, E. (2001). Globalization: Opportunities and challenges for the Middle East. Paper presented at the International Studies Association Conference, Hong Kong, July 26–28. Retrieved March 29, 2005, from http://www.isanet.org/archive/houry.txt

House, R. J., Hanges, P. J., Javidan, M., Dorfman, P. W., & Gupta V. (2004). *Culture, leadership, and organizations.* Thousand Oaks, CA: Sage.

How deep is corruption in Africa? (2004, June 18). *BBC News Online.* Retrieved March 2, 2005, from http://news.bbc.co.uk/2/hi/africa/3819027.stm

Howell, W. S. (1982). *The empathic communicator.* Belmont, CA: Wadsworth.

Hoyle, R., Pinkley, R., & Insko, C. (1989). Perceptions of social behavior. *Personality and Social Psychology Bulletin, 15,* 365–376.

Hubbert, K., Gudykunst, W., & Guerrero, S. (1999). Intergroup communication over time. *International Journal of Intercultural Relations, 23,* 13–46.

Hudson, R. (1992). Uruguay country study & guide. Retrieved April 4, 2005, from http://www.reference.allrefer.com/country-guide-study/uruguay11.html

Hugenberg, L. W., LaCivita, R. M., & Lubanovic, A. M. (1996). International business and training: Preparing for the global economy. *The Journal of Business Communication, 33,* 205–222.

Hui, C. H., & Triandis, H. C. (1986). Individualism-collectivism: A study of cross-cultural researchers. *Journal of Cross-Cultural Psychology, 17,* 225–248.

Hurn, B. J., & Jenkins, M. (2000). International peer group development. *Industrial and Commercial Training, 32,* 128–131.

Huse, E. (1975). *Organizational development and change.* New York: West Publishing.

Hwang, J., Chase, L., & Kelly, C. (1980). An intercultural examination of communication competence. *Communication, 9,* 70–79.

Infoplease. (2005a). Population by provinces and territories. Retrieved December 11, 2005, from http://www.infoplease.com/ipa/A0107390.html

Infoplease (2005b). Canada. Retrieved December 11, 2005, from http://www.infoplease.com/ipa/A0107386.html

Institute for Security Studies. (2005). Profile: East African Community (EAC). Retrieved January 13, 2005, from http://www.iss.co.za/AF/RegOrg/unity_to_union/pdfs/eac/EACoverview.pdf

Interactive Currency Table. (2005). Retrieved November 27, 2005, from http://www.xe.com/ict

International Business Etiquette and Manners. (2005a). France. Retrieved July 10, 2005, from http://www.cyborlink.com/besite/france.htm

International Business Etiquette and Manners. (2005b). Germany. Retrieved July 10, 2005, from http://www.cyborlink.com/besite/germany.htm

International Business Etiquette and Manners. (2005c). Italy. Retrieved July 22, 2005, from http://www.cyborlink.com/besite/italy.htm

International Business Etiquette and Manners. (2005d). Spain. Retrieved July 22, 2005, from http://www.cyborlink.com/besite/spain.html

International Energy Outlook (2004). Shares of world gross domestic product by selected countries and regions. Retrieved November 27, 2005, from http://web.lexisnexis.com.vortex2.ucok.edu:2050statuniv/document?_m=9ebOd7388 a09623

International Hospitality Operations. (2005). Lesson4-2-1: Valuing cultural diversity. Retrieved March 19, 2002 from http://jan.ucc.nau.edu/~caj4/ha390/class/dimensions/diversity/lesson4-2-1.html

International Labour Office. (2004). Southern Common Market, MERCOSUR. Retrieved January 8, 2005, from http://www.itcilo.it/english/actrav/telearn/global/ilo/blokit/mercosur.htm

International Monetary Fund. (2005). Home page. Retrieved February 4, 2005, from http://www.imf.org

Isenhart, M. W., & Spangle, M. (2000). *Collaborative approaches to resolving conflict.* Thousand Oaks, CA: Sage.

ITIM Culture and Management Consultancy. (2005). Geert Hofstede cultural dimensions: Canada. Retrieved November 27, 2005, from http://www.geert-hofstede .com/hofstede_canada.shtml

Janis, I. (1971). *Stress and frustration.* New York: Harcourt, Brace, Jovanovich.

Janse, G. (2005). Plano Real. Retrieved May 5, 2005, from http://www.brazilnow .info

Jarvenpaa, S. L., & Leidner, D. E. (1998). Communication and trust in global virtual teams. *Journal of Computer Mediated Communication, 3,* Retrieved November 4, 2004, from http://www.ascusc.org/jcmc/vol3/issue4/jarvenpaa.html

Jarvenpaa, S. L., & Leidner, D. E. (1999). Communication and trust in global virtual teams. *Organization Science, 10,* 791–815.

Jia, W., Lu, X., & Heisey, D. D. (2002). *Chinese communication theory and research: Reflections, new frontiers, and new directions.* Stamford, CT: Ablex.

Johnson, J., & Sarason, I. (1978). Life stress, depression and anxiety. *Journal of Psychosomatic Research, 22,* 205–208.

Johnson, S. (1998). *Who moved my cheese?* New York: Penguin Putnam.

Kanter, R. M. (1983). *The change masters.* New York: Simon & Schuster.

Kao, J. (1998). An interview with John Kao. In J. Kurtzman (Ed.), *Thought leaders* (pp. 52–65). San Francisco: Jossey-Bass.

Karp, H. B. (1996). *The change leader: Using a gestalt approach with work groups.* San Francisco: Jossey-Bass.

Kealey, D. J. (1989). A study of cross-cultural effectiveness: Theoretical issues, practical applications. *International Journal of Intercultural Relations, 13,* 387–428.

Kearney, A. T. (2004). *Globalization index.* Washington, DC: Carnegie Endowment for International Peace.

Keesing, R. (1974). Theories of culture. *Annual Review of Anthropology, 3,* 73–97.

Kellett, P. M., & Dalton, D. G. (2001). *Managing conflict in a negotiated world.* Thousand Oaks, CA: Sage.

Kelley, E. (2001). Keys to effective virtual global teams. *The Academy of Management Executive, 15,* 132–133.

Kelley, H. H., & Thibaut, J. W. (1978). *Interpersonal relationships.* New York: Wiley.

Keyton, J. (2005). *Communication and organizational culture: A key to understanding work experiences.* Thousand Oaks: Sage.

Kim, U. (1994). Individualism and collectivism: Conceptual clarification and elaboration. In U. Kim, H. Triandis, C. Kagitcibsi, S. Choi, & G. Yoon (Eds.), *Individualism-collectivism* (pp. 19–40). Thousand Oaks, CA: Sage.

Kim, Y. Y. (1979). Communication patterns of foreign immigrants in the process of acculturation. *Human Communication Research, 4,* 66–77.

Kim, Y. Y. (1980). *Psychological, social, and cultural adjustment of Indochinese refugees.* Vol. IV of Indochinese refugees in the State of Illinois (5 vols.). Chicago: Travelers Aid Society of Metropolitan Chicago.

Kim, Y. Y. (1988). *Communication and cross-cultural adaptation: An integrative theory.* Clevedon, England: Multilingual Matters.

Kim, Y. Y. (1991). Intercultural communication competence. In S. Ting-Toomey & F. Korzenny (Eds.), *Cross-cultural interpersonal communication* (pp. 261–291). Newbury Park, CA: Sage.

Kim. Y. Y. (1995). Cross-cultural adaptation. In R. Wiseman (Ed.), *Intercultural communication theory* (pp. 170–193). Thousand Oaks, CA: Sage.

Kim, Y. Y. (2001). *Becoming intercultural: An integrative theory of communication and cross-cultural adaptation.* Thousand Oaks, CA: Sage.

Kim, Y. Y., Lujan, P., & Dixon, L. (1998). "I can walk both ways": Identity integration of American Indians in Oklahoma. *Human Communication Research, 25,* 252–274.

Kim, Y. Y., & Ruben, B. D. (1988). Intercultural transformation: A systems approach. In Y. Y. Kim & W. B. Gudykunst (Eds.), *Theories in intercultural communication* (pp. 299–322). Newbury Park, CA: Sage.

Kinoshita, T. (2006). Interview by Ilan Alon, January 10, 2006.

Kirchmeyer, C., & Cohen, A. (1992). Multicultural groups: Their performance and reactions with constructive conflict. *Group and Organization Management, 17,* 153–170.

Kirkman, B. L, Rosen, B., Tesluk, P. E., & Gibson, C. B. (2004). The impact of team empowerment on virtual team performance: The moderating role of face-to-face interaction. *Academy of Management Journal, 47,* 175–192.

Kirkman, B. L., Tesluk, P. E., & Rosen, B. (2004). The impact of demographic heterogeneity and team leader-team member fit on team empowerment and effectiveness. *Group & Organization Management, 29,* 334–368.

Kirton, M. J. (1987). Adaptors and innovators: Cognitive style and personality. In S. G. Isaksen (Ed.), *Frontiers of creativity research* (pp. 282–304). Buffalo, NY: Bearly.

Kleinjans, E. (1972). Opening remarks at a conference on world communication held at the East-West Center, Honolulu, HI. In W. B. Gudykunst & Y. Y. Kim (Eds.). *Communicating with strangers* (4th ed.). New York: McGraw-Hill.

Klopf, D. W. (1991). *Intercultural encounters.* Englewood, CO: Morton.

Kluckhohn, F., & Strodtbeck, F. (1961). *Variations in value orientations.* New York: Row, Peterson.

Knapp, M. L. (1980). *Essentials of nonverbal communication.* New York: Holt, Rinehart & Winston.

Knapp, M. L., & Hall, J. A. (2001). *Nonverbal communication in human interaction* (5th ed.). Belmont, CA: Wadsworth.

Koester, J., & Olebe, M. (1988). The behavioral assessment scale for intercultural communication effectiveness. *International Journal of Intercultural Relations, 12,* 233–246.

Kohls, L. R. (1984). *Values Americans live by.* Washington, DC: Meridian House International.

Kohn, A. (1976). *The case against competition.* Boston: Houghton Mifflin.

Kolb, D. (1994). *When talk works.* San Francisco: Jossey-Bass.

Kong, D. (2001, July 16). Report shows Hispanic opportunity gaps. Retrieved July 16, 2001, from http://www.freerepublic.com/forum/a3b52664f1c27.htm

Kono, T., & Clegg, S. (2001). *Trends in Japanese management: Continuing strengths, current problems, and changing priorities.* New York: Palgrave.

Korzenny, F. (2000). Hispanic business challenges and opportunities for the new millennium. *Hispanic Business Journal* (online). Retrieved July 16, 2001, from http://www.cheskin.com/think/articles/fkhisbj0100.html

Korzybski, A. (1948). *Science and sanity: An introduction to nonaristotelian systems and general semantics.* Garden City, NY: Country Life Publishing.

Kotabe, M., & Aulakh, P. S. (2002). International business research: From functional to issue-based focus. In M. Kotabe & P. S. Aulakh, (Eds.), *Emerging issues in international business* (pp. 1–11). Northampton, MA: E. Elgar.

Kouzes, J. M., & Posner, B. Z. (1993). *Credibility.* San Francisco: Jossey-Bass.

Krackhardt, D., & Hanson, J. (1993). Informal networks: The company behind the chart. *Harvard Business Review, 71,* 104–111.

Kraft, C. (1978). Worldview in intercultural communication. In F. Casmir (Ed.), *International and intercultural communication* (pp. 14–28). Washington, DC: University Press of America.

Kramer, E. (1963). Judgment of personal characteristics and emotions from nonverbal properties. *Psychology Bulletin, 60,* 408–420.

Kras, E. (1994). *Modernizing Mexican management style.* Las Cruces, NM: Editts.

Kristof, A. L., Brown, K. G., Sims, H. P., & Smith, K. A. (1995). The virtual team: A case study and inductive model. In M. M. Beyerlein, D. A. Johnson, & S. T. Beyerlean (Eds.). *Advances in interdisciplinary studies of work teams: Knowledge work in teams* (vol. 2, pp. 229–253). Greenwich, CT: JAI Press.

Kromer, E. (2004). Bantu. Retrieved June 8, 2004, from http://www.mnsu.edu/emuseum/cultural/oldworld/africa/bantu.html

Krugman, P. (1998). Saving Asia: It's time to get radical. *Fortune, 138,* 74–80.

Kumar, K., Subramanian, R., & Nonis, S. A. (1991). Cultural diversity's impact on group processes and performance: Comparing culturally homogeneous and culturally diverse work groups engaged in problem solving tasks. Proceedings of Southern Management Association, Annual Conference, 332–336.

LaGaipa, J. J. (1987). In R. Burnett, P. McGee, & D. Clarke (Eds.), *Accounting for relationships* (pp. 134–157). London: Methuen.

Lamb, J. (2005). Executive Development Manager, Entertainment Company. Interview by S. S. Easton, April 16.

Landis, D., & Brislin, R. (1983). *Handbook of intercultural training* (Vol. I–III). New York: Pergamon.

Lange-Churin, P., & Medieta, E. (2001). *Latin America and postmodernity: A contemporary reader.* New York: Humanity Books.

Langer, E. J. (1978). Rethinking the role of thought in social interaction. In J. Harvey, W. Ickes, & R. Kidd (Eds.), *New directions in attribution research* (Vol. 2, pp. 35–58). Hillsdale, NJ: Lawrence Erlbaum.

Langer, E. J. (1989a). *Mindfulness.* Reading, MA: Addison-Wesley.

Langer, E. J. (1989b). Minding matters: The consequences of mindlessness-mindfulness. In L. Berkowitz (Ed.), *Advances in experimental social psychology* (Vol. 22, pp. 137–173). San Diego: Academic Press.

Langer, E. J. (1997). *The power of mindful learning.* Reading, MA: Addison-Wesley.

Latin American Network Information Center. (2005). Countries in Latin America and the Caribbean. Retrieved January 7, 2005, from http://www.lanic.utexas.edu/subject/countries

Lawrence, P. R., & Lorsch, J. W. (1967). *Organization and environment: Managing differentiation and integration.* Homewood, IL: Irwin.

Leathers, D. G. (1976). *Nonverbal communication systems.* Boston: Allyn & Bacon.

Leathers, D. G. (1986). *Successful nonverbal communication: Principles and applications.* New York: Macmillan.

Levine, R., Locke, C., Searls, D., & Weinberger, D. (2000). *The cluetrain manifesto.* Cambridge, MA: Perseus.

Lewin, K. (1952). Group decision and social change. In E. Newcombe & R. Harley (Eds.) *Readings in social psychology* (pp. 459–473). New York: Henry Holt.

Lewis, D. (2003, June 3). Cow pats fuel computers. *BBC News Online.* Retrieved March 11, 2005, from http://news.bbc.co.uk/2/hi/technology/2957488.stm

Lewis, M. (1998, May 31). The biggest going out of business sale. *The New York Times Magazine,* pp. 37–41, 53, 58–64, 68–69.

Lewis, M. (2000). *The new new thing.* New York: Norton.

Lewis, R. D. (1999). *Cross cultural communication: A visual approach.* Hampshire, UK: Transcreen.

Lewis, R. D. (2000). *When cultures collide: Managing successfully across cultures.* London: Nicholas Brealey.

Lima, P. C. L. (1997). *Mercosur and NAFTA: Trends of trade.* Washington, DC: The George Washington University Institute of Brazilian Business and Public Management Issues – IBI. Retrieved January 8, 2005, from http://www.gwu.edu/~ibi/minerva/Spring1997/Paula.Lopes.Lima/Paula.Lopes.Lima.html

Lindgren, M., & Bandhold, H. (2003). *Scenario planning: The link between future and strategy.* New York: Palgrave Macmillan.

Ling, S. C. (1990).The effects of group cultural composition and cultural attitudes on performance. Unpublished doctoral dissertation, University of Western Ontario, Canada.

Lipnack, J., & Stamps, J. (1997). *Virtual teams: Reaching across space, time, and organizations with technology.* New York: Wiley.

Lippmann, W. (1922). *Public opinion.* New York: Macmillan.

Lipset, S. M. (1990). *Continental divide: The values and institutions of the United States and Canada.* New York: Routledge.

Littlejohn, S.W. (2002). *Theories of human communication* (7th ed.). Belmont, CA: Wadsworth/Thomson Learning.

Littlejohn, S. W., & Domenici, K. (2001). *Engaging communication in conflict.* Thousand Oaks, CA: Sage.

Littlejohn, S., & Jabusch, D. (1982). Communication competence: Model and application. *Journal of Applied Communication Research, 10*, 29–37.

Lorrain, J. (1999). Modernity and identity: Cultural change in Latin America. In R. N. Gwynne & C. Kay (Eds.), *Latin America transformed: Globalization and modernity* (pp. 140–164). London: Arnold.

Lustig, M. W., & Koester, J. (2003). *Intercultural competence: Interpersonal communication across cultures* (4th ed.). Boston: Allyn & Bacon.

Lysgaard, S. (1955). Adjustment in a foreign society: Norwegian Fulbright grantees visiting the United States. *International Social Science Bulletin, 7*, 45–51.

MacGrath, R. G., & MacMillan, I. C. (1995). Discovery-driven planning. *Harvard Business Review, 72*, 44–54.

Makihara, M. (1998). An interview with Minoru Makihara. In J. Kurtzman (Ed.), *Thought leaders* (pp. 16–27). San Francisco: Jossey-Bass.

Mann, H. Siegler, M., & Osmond, H. (1972). Four types of time and four ways of perceiving time. *Psychology Today, 3*, 76–84.

March, J. G., & Savon, G. (1984). Gossip, information, and decision making. In L. Sproull & P. D. Larkey (Eds.), *Advances in information processing in organizations* (vol. 1, pp. 95–108). Greenwich, CT: JAI.

Marquardt, M. J., & Horvath, L. (2001). *Global teams: How top multinationals span boundaries and cultures with high-speed teamwork.* Palo Alto, CA: Davies-Black.

Martin, H. H., & Colburn, W. (1972). *Communication and consensus.* New York: Harcourt Brace Jovanovich.

Martin, J. N., & Nakayama, T. K. (2001). *Experiencing intercultural communication: An introduction.* Mountain View, CA: Mayfield.

Martin, J. N., & Nakayama, T. K. (2003). *Intercultural communication in contexts.* Boston: McGraw-Hill.

Martin, P., & Widgren, J. (2002). International migration: Facing the challenge. *Population Bulletin, 57*, 1–43.

Martins, L. L., Gilson, L. L., & Maynard, M. T. (2004). Virtual teams: What do we know and where do we go from here? *Journal of Management, 30*, 805–835.

Marwell, G., & Schmitt, D. R. (1967). Dimensions of compliance-gaining behavior: An empirical analysis. *Sociometry, 30*, 350–364.

Matthews, D. (2005). Business culture in Canada and the US: Convergence or divergence? *The Americanist, 2*. Retrieved December 22, 2005, from http://www.the americanist.com/journal/july05/july05-2.html

Matveev, A. V., & Nelson, P. E. (2004). Cross cultural competence and multicultural team performance: Perceptions of American and Russian managers. *International Journal of Cross Cultural Management, 4*, 253–271.

Maznevski, M. L. (1994). Understanding our differences: Performance in decision-making groups with diverse members. *Human Relations, 47*, 531–552.

Maznevski, M. L., & Chudoba, K. M. (2000). Bridging space over time: Global virtual team dynamics and effectiveness. *Organization Science, 11,* 473–492.

Maznevski, M. L., & DiStefano, J. J. (2000). Global leaders are team players: Developing global leaders through members on global teams. *Human Resource Management, 39,* 195–208.

Maznevski, M. L., & Peterson, M. F. (1997). Societal values, social interpretation, and multinational teams. In C. S. Granrose & S. Oskamp, (Eds.), *Cross cultural work groups* (pp. 61–89). The Claremont Symposium on Applied Social Psychology. Thousand Oaks, CA: Sage.

McCarthy, J. (2004). *The Forrester report.* In J. E. Hilsenrath, Behind outsourcing debates: Surprisingly few hard numbers. *The Wall Street Journal,* April 12, 2004, p. A1.

McCollom, M. (1990). Group formation: Boundaries, formation, and decision making. In L. Sproull & P. D. Larkey (Eds.), *Advances in information processing in organizations* (pp. 34–48). Greenwich, CT: JAI Press.

McDaniel, E. R. (2000). Japanese nonverbal communication: A reflection of cultural themes in Japan. In L. A. Samovar & R. E. Porter (Eds.) *Intercultural communication: A reader* (9th ed., pp. 312–324). Belmont, CA: Wadsworth.

McDaniel, E. R., & Quasha, S. (2000). The communicative aspects of doing business in Japan. In L. A. Samovar & R. E. Porter (Eds.), *Intercultural communication: A reader* (9th ed., pp. 270–279). Belmont, CA: Wadsworth.

McDonough, E. F., & Cedrone, D. (2000). Meeting the challenge of global team management. *Research Technology Management, 43,* 12–18.

McDonough, E. F., & Kahn, K. B. (1996). Using "hard" and "soft" technologies for global new product development. *R & D Management, 26,* 241–253.

McDonough, E. F., & Kahn, K. B. (1997). Using "hard" and "soft" technologies for global new product development. *IEEE Engineering Management Review 25,* 66–75.

McDonough, E. F., Kahn, K. B., & Barczak, G. (2001). An investigation of the use of global, virtual, and collocated new product development teams. *The Journal of Product Innovation Management, 18,* 110–120.

McLeod, P. L., & Lobel, S. A. (1992). The effects of ethnic diversity on idea generation in small groups. Paper presented at the Academy of Management meeting, Las Vegas, Nevada.

McLuhan, M. (1962). *The Gutenberg galaxy.* New York: New American Library.

McLuhan, M., & Fiore, Q. (1968). *War and peace in the global village.* New York: Touchstone.

McSweeney, B. (2002). Hofstede's model of national cultural differences and their consequences: A triumph of faith—A failure of analysis. *Human Relations, 55,* 89–118. Retrieved April 12, 2005, from http://geert-hofstede.international-business-center.com/mcsweeney.shtml

McSweeney, B. (2005). Cultural dimensions. The International Business Center. Retrieved April 10, 2005, from http://geert-hofstede.international-business-center.com/mcsweeney.shtml

Mead, W. R. (1998, May 31). Asia devalued. *The New York Times Magazine,* pp. 38–39.

Meek, T. (1999, November/December). The evolution of information technology at Buckman Laboratories. *Knowledge Management Review,* pp. 11–21.

Mehrabian, A. (1968). Communication without words. *Psychology Today, 2,* 53.

Mehrabian, A. (1971). *Silent messages.* Belmont, CA: Wadsworth.

Mercosur. (2005). General remarks on Mercosul. (English version). Retrieved May 5, 2005, from http://www.mercosul.gov/br/textos/?Key=127

Mercosur in Brief. (1999). U.S. Government Document. Retrieved January 7, 2005, from http://www.mac.doc.gov/ola/mercosur

Merritt, A. (2000). Culture in the cockpit: Do Hofstede's dimensions replicate? *Journal of Cross-Cultural Psychology, 31,* 283–301.

Meuhring, K. (1998, September). The fire next time. *Institutional Investor,* p. 74.

Meyer, A. D., & Goes, J. B. (1989). Organizational assimilation of innovations: A multi-level contextual analysis. *Academy of Management Journal, 31,* 897–923.

Miles, R., & Snow, C. (1992). Causes of failure in network organizations. *California Management Review, 28,* 62–73.

Miller, D. (1990). *The Icarus Paradox: How exceptional companies bring about their own downfall.* New York: Harper Business.

Miller, G. R., Boster, F., Roloff, M., & Siebold, D. (1977). Compliance-gaining message strategies: A typology and some findings concerning effects of situational differences. *Communication Monographs, 44,* 37–51.

Miller, G., & Steinberg, M. (1975). *Between people.* Chicago: Science Research Associates.

Minor, T. L. (1999). Minority MBAs rate and provide insights on diversity. Hispanic Employment Program. Retrieved July 16, 2001, from http://67.59.159.189/hepm/mba_diversity.htm

Mintz, S. W., & Price, S. (1985). *Caribbean contours.* Baltimore: Johns Hopkins University Press.

Mintzberg, H. (1987). *Strategy concept I: Five Ps for strategy, Strategy concept II: Another look at why organizations need strategies.* Boston: Harvard University Press.

Mintzberg, H. (1989). Organizational design: Fashion or fit? *Harvard Business Review, 59,* 103–115.

Mintzberg, H. (1994). The fall and rise of strategic planning. *Harvard Business Review, 72,* 44–54.

Montgomery, B. M. (1992). Communication as the interface between couples and culture. In S. Deetz (Ed.), *Human Communication Yearbook 15* (pp. 475–507). Newbury Park, CA: Sage.

Montgomery, B. M. (1993). Relationship maintenance versus relationship change: A dialectical dilemma. *Journal of Social and Personal Relationships, 10,* 205–224.

Montgomery, B. M., & Baxter, L. A. (1998). *Dialectical approaches to studying personal relationships.* Mahwah, NJ: Lawrence Erlbaum.

Montoya-Weiss, M. M., Massey, A. P., & Song, M. (2001). Getting it together: Temporal coordination and conflict management in global virtual teams. *Academy of Management Journal, 44,* 1251–1262.

Moore, C. W. (1996). *The mediation process.* San Francisco: Jossey-Bass.

Moore, R. (1988). Face and networks in urban Hong Kong. *City and Society, 2,* 50–59.

Moran, R. T., & Riesenberger, J. R. (1997). *The global challenge: Building the new worldwide enterprise.* London: McGraw-Hill.

Moreland, R. (1985). Social categorization and the assimilation of "new" group members. *Journal of Personality and Social Psychology, 48,* 1173–1190.

MSNBC.com. (2005, September 10). Katrina may cost as much as four years of war. Retrieved December 22, 2005, from http://www.msnbc.msn.com/id/9281409

Muldoon, C. W. (1996). *The heart of conflict.* New York: Putnam.

Munro, D. (1995). *The Oxford dictionary of the world.* Oxford: Oxford University Press, 10–11.

Muratbekova-Touron, M. (2005). Permanence and change: Case study of changes in organizational culture at a multinational company. *Journal of Change Management, 5,* 207–219.

Murowchick, R. (1994). *Cradles of civilization: China.* Norman: University of Oklahoma Press.

Murphy, J. (2005). Professor, University of Perth, Australia. Interview by S. S. Easton, May 2.

Nadler, D. A., & Tushman, M. L. (1989). Organizational frame bending: Principles for managing reorientation. *Academy of Management Executive, 3,* 194–203.

Nafie, I. (2005, March 9). Turning point in reform. *Al-Ahram, 732.* Retrieved March 28, 2005, from http://weekly.ahram.org.eg/2005/732/op1.htm

Naisbitt, J., & Aburdene, P. (1985). *Re-inventing the corporation: Transforming your job and your company for the new information society.* New York: Warner.

National Association of Diversity Management. (2000). Human resources: Workforce trends in the 21st century. Retrieved July 16, 2001, from http://www.nadm.org/hr.html

National Center for Policy Analysis. (2002, May 15). The cost of terrorism. *Daily Policy Digest.* Retrieved December 17, 2005, from http://www.ncpa.org/iss/ter/2002/pd051502f.html

Nausbaum, D. (2002). *Caribbean: The islands.* Jamaica: Caribbean.

Nerbonne, G. P. (1967). The identification of speaker characteristics on the basis of aural cues. Unpublished PhD dissertation, Michigan State University.

Newman, K. (2006). Interview by Ilan Alon, January 20, 2006.

Ng, E. S. W., & Tung, R. L. (1998). Ethnocultural diversity and organizational effectiveness: A field study. *The International Journal of Human Resource Management, 9,* 980–995.

Nierenberg, G. I. (1973). *Intercultural competence: Interpersonal communication across cultures.* Boston: Allyn & Bacon.

Nierenberg, G. I., & Calero, H. H. (1974). *The power of words.* New York: Pocket Books.

Nishiyama, K. (1999). *Doing business in Japan: Successful strategies for intercultural communication.* Honolulu: University of Hawaii Press.

Noble, J., & Lascam, J. (1991). *The Hispanic way.* Lincolnwood, IL: Passport Books.

Nora, J., Rogers, C., & Stramy, R. (1986). *Transforming the workplace.* Princeton, NJ: Princeton Research Press.

Norton, R. W. (1978). Foundation of a communicator style construct. *Human Communication Research, 4*, 99–112.

Nouwen, H. J. M. (1996). *Bread for the journey.* San Francisco: HarperCollins.

Nydell, M. K. (1987). *Understanding Arabs—A guide for Westerners.* Yarmouth, ME: Intercultural Press.

Ober, S. (2001). *Contemporary business communication* (4th ed.). Boston, MA: Houghton Mifflin.

Oberg, K. (1960). Culture shock and the problems of adjustment to new cultural environments. *Practical Anthropology, 7*, 170–179.

O'Brian, C. (1993). Communicating in a brave new world. *PR Florida*, pp. 8–9.

O'Connell, L. (1990, May 30). Some people see wristwatches as mental handcuffs. *The Orlando Sentinel*, pp. E1, E3.

Odenwald, S. B. (1996). *Global solutions for teams: Moving from collision to collaboration.* Chicago: Irwin Professional Publishing.

Oetzel, J., & Ting-Toomey, S. (2003). Face concerns in interpersonal conflict: A cross-cultural empirical test of the face-negotiation theory. *Communication Research, 30*, 599–624.

Oetzel, J., & Ting-Toomey, S. (2006). *The Sage handbook of conflict communication.* Thousand Oaks, CA: Sage.

Oetzel, J., Ting-Toomey, S., Masumoto, T., Yokochi, Y., Pan, X., Takai, J., & Wilcox, R. (2001). Face and facework in conflict: A cross-cultural comparison of China, Germany, Japan, and the United States. *Communication Monographs, 68*, 235–258.

Office of the United States Trade Representative. (2005a). Free trade with Central America and the Dominican Republic. Retrieved January 8, 2005, from http://ustr.gov/assets/Trade_Agreements/Bilateral/CAFTA/Briefing_Book/asset_upload_file152_7179.pdf

Office of the United States Trade Representative. (2005b). North American Free Trade Agreement. Retrieved December 12, 2005, from http://www.ustr.gov/Trade_Agreements/Regional/NAFTA/Section_Index.html

Ogbor, J. O., & Williams, J. (2003). The cross-cultural transfer of management practices: The case for creative synthesis. *Cross Cultural Management, 10*, 3–23.

Ogden, C. K., & Richards, I. A. (1923). *The meaning of meaning: A study of the influence of language upon thought and of the science of symbolism.* New York: Harcourt Brace and World.

Ogilvy, J. A., & Schwartz, P. (2002). *Creating better futures: Scenario planning as a tool for a better tomorrow.* New York: Oxford University Press.

O'Keefe, B. (1988). The logic of message design: Individual differences in reasoning about communication. *Communication Monographs, 55*, 80–103.

O'Keefe, B. (1996). Variation, adaptation, and functional explanation in the study of message design. In G. Philipsen & T. Albrecht (Eds.), *Developing communication theories* (pp. 85–118). Albany: State University of New York Press.

Olsen, M. (1978). *The process of social organization* (2nd ed.). New York: Holt, Rinehart, and Winston.

Operario, D., & Fiske, S. (2001). Stereotypes: Content, structures, processes and context. In R. Brown & S. Gaertner (Eds.), *Intergroup processes* (pp. 147–169). Oxford, UK: Blackwell.

Oracle ThinkQuest Library. (2005). Retrieved February 2, 2005, from http://www.thinkquest.org/library/

Orasanu, J., Fisher, U., & Davison, J. (1997). Cross-cultural barriers to effective communication in aviation. In C. S. Granrose & S. Oskamp (Eds.), *Cross cultural work groups*. The Claremont Symposium on Applied Social Psychology (pp. 134–157). Thousand Oaks, CA: Sage.

Orlikowski, W. J., & Hofman, D. J. (1997). An improvisational model of change management: The case of groupware technologies. Retrieved November 21, 2005, from http://www.ida.liu.se/~TDEI36/documents/CCSWP191.html

Ornstein, S. (1989). The hidden influence of office design. *Academy of Management Executive, 3,* 144–147.

Oudenhoven, J. (2001). Do organizations reflect national cultures? *International Journal of Intercultural Relations, 25,* 89–107.

Owens, D. A., Neale, M. A., & Sutton, R. I. (2000). Technologies of status management: Status dynamics in email communications. In M. A. Neale, E. A. Mannix, & T. L. Griffith (Eds.), *Research on groups and teams* (Vol. 3, pp. 205–230). Greenwich, CT: JAI Press.

Palmer, B., Walls, M., Burgess, Z., & Stough, C. (2001). Emotional intelligence and effective leadership. *Leadership & Organization Journal, 22,* 5–11.

Parker, R. E. (2003). Distinguishing characteristics of virtual groups. In R. Hirokawa, R. Cathcart, L. Samovar, & L. Henman (Eds.), *Small group communication theory and practice* (8th ed., pp. 17–27). Los Angeles: Roxbury.

Parsons, T. (1951). *The social system.* Glencoe, IL: Free Press.

Parsons, T., & Shils, E. (1951). *Toward a general theory of action.* Cambridge, MA: Harvard University Press.

Pascale, R. T., Millemann, M., & Gioja, L. (2000). *Surfing the edge of chaos: The laws of nature and the new laws of business.* New York: Three Rivers Press.

Pearce, F. (2005). International addresses and salutations. Retrieved July 25, 2005, from http://www.bspage.com/address.html

Pearce, W. B. (1989). *Communication and the human condition.* Carbondale, Southern Illinois University Press.

Pearce, W. B., & Cronen, V. (1980). *Communication, action, and meaning: The creation of social realities.* New York: Praeger.

Pearce, W. B., & Pearce, K. A. (2000). Extending the theory of the coordinated management of meaning (CMM) through a community dialogue process. *Communication Theory, 10,* 405–423.

Pearson-Roden, K. (2005). Arab culture. Retrieved April 2, 2005, from http://www.mnsu.edu/emuseum/cultural/oldworld/middle_east/arabculture.html

Peck, M. S. (1987). *The different drum: Community making and peace.* New York: Simon & Schuster.

Peck, M. S. (1993). *A world waiting to be born: Civility rediscovered.* New York: Bantam.

Pelto, P. (1968, April). The difference between "tight" and "loose" societies. *Transactions,* pp. 37–40.

Periplus of the Erythraean Sea, A Greek merchant's guide to the Red Sea and Indian Ocean. From Oracle ThinkQuest. Retrieved February 2, 2005, from http://www .thinkquest.org/library/

Peters, T. J. (1988). *Thriving on chaos: Handbook for a management revolution.* New York: HarperCollins.

Peters, T. J. (1992). *Liberation management.* New York: Fawcett Columbine.

Phar, K. B. (2006). Interview by Ilan Alon, January 5, 2006.

Philipsen, G. (1975). Speaking 'like a man' in Teamsterville: Culture patterns of role enactment in an urban neighborhood. *Quarterly Journal of Speech, 61,* 13–22.

Philipsen, G. (1976). Places for speaking in Teamsterville. *Quarterly Journal of Speech, 62,* 15–72.

Philipsen, G. (1989). An ethnographic approach to communication studies. In F. Dervin, L. Gossberg, B. J. O'Keefe, & E. Wartella (Eds.), *Rethinking communication: Paradigm exemplars* (pp. 258–268). Newbury Park, CA: Sage.

Philipsen, G. (1992). *Speaking culturally: Explorations in social communication.* Albany: State University of New York Press.

Philipsen, G. (1997). A theory of speech codes. In G. Philipsen & T. Albrecht (Eds.), *Developing communication theory* (pp. 119–156). Albany: State University of New York Press.

Philipsen, G. (2001). Cultural communication. In W. B. Gudykunst & B. Mody (Eds.), *Handbook of international and intercultural communication* (2nd ed., pp. 13–43). Thousand Oaks, CA: Sage.

Planalp, S., Rutherford, D., & Honeycutt, J. (1988). Events that increase uncertainty in relationships. *Human Communication Research, 14,* 516–547.

Pleydell-Bouverie, J. (1991, July). To what extent have telecommunications created the "global village"? *Geographical, 63,* 6–11.

Pondy, L. R. (1967). Organizational conflict: Concepts and models. *Administrative Science Quarterly, 12,* 296–320.

Poole-Robb, S., & Bailey, A. (2002). *Risky business: Corruption, fraud, terrorism and other threats to global business.* London: Kogan Page.

Population Resource Center. (2002). Executive summary: Unmet need for contraception in the 21st century: Sub-Saharan Africa. Retrieved February 2, 2005, from http://www.prcdc.org/summaries/unmetneedafrica/unmetneedafrica.html

Pothukuchi, V., Damanpour, F., Choi, J., Chen C. C., & Park, S. H. (2002). National and organizational culture differences and international joint venture performance. *Journal of International Business Studies, 33,* 243–265.

Poyatos, F. (2002). *Nonverbal communication across disciplines* (Vols. 1–3). Amsterdam/ Philadelphia: John Benjamins.

Prahalad, C. K. (1998). An interview with C. K. Prahalad. In J. Kurtzman (Ed.), *Thought leaders* (pp. 40–51). San Francisco: Jossey-Bass.

Prescott, L. (2005). Country specific information . . . Saudi Arabia. Retrieved March 10, 2005, from http://www.prospects.ac.uk/downloads/countryProfiles/Saudi_Arabia.pdf

Pruitt, D. G. (1981). *Negotiation behavior.* Orlando, FL: Academic Press.

Putnam, L. L. (1988). Communication and interpersonal conflicts in organizations, *Management Communication Quarterly, 1,* 293–312.

Putnam, L. L., & Folger, J. P. (1988). Communication, conflict, and dispute resolution: The study of interaction and the development of conflict theory. *Communication Research, 15,* 349–359.

Putnam, L. L., & Poole, S. (1987). Conflict and negotiation. In F. Jablin, L. Putnam, K. Roberts, & L. Porter (Eds.). *Handbook of organizational communication: An interdisciplinary perspective* (pp. 549–599). Newbury Park, CA: Sage.

Quisumbing, M. (1982). *Life events, social support and personality: Their impact upon Filipino psychological adjustment.* Unpublished doctoral dissertation, University of Chicago.

Ralston, D. A., Egri, C. P., Stewart, S., Terpstra, R. H., & Kaicheng, Y. (1999). Doing business in the 21st century with new generation of Chinese managers: A study of generational shifts in work values in China. *Journal of International Business Studies, 24,* 249–275.

Rapoport, A. (1967). Strategy and conscience. In F. Matson & A. Montagu (Eds.), *The human dialogue: Perspectives on communication* (pp. 79–96). New York: Free Press.

Rawlins, W. K. (1992). *Friendship matters: Communication dialectics and the life course.* New York: Aldine de Gruyter.

Readding, W. C. (1972). *Communication within the organization.* New York: Industrial Communication Council.

Reich, R. B. (2000). *The future of success.* New York: Alfred A. Knopf.

Remland, M. (1981). Developing leadership skills in nonverbal communication: A situational perspective. *Journal of Business Communication, 3,* 17–29.

Rempel, G. (1995). European unification. Western New England College. Retrieved July 12, 2005, from http://mars.wnec.edu/~grempel/courses/wc2/lectures/eurunion .html

Richards, Z., & Hewstone, M. (2001). Subtyping and subgrouping. *Personality and Social Psychology Review, 5,* 52–73.

Richardson, B. C., Taylor, P., Agnew, J., Dixon, C., Gregory, P., & Lee, R. (1992). *The Caribbean in the wider world, 1492-1992.* New York: Cambridge University Press.

Riel, B. (1996). Profiles in culture—a snapshot look at the Canadian people. *Relocation Journal & Real Estate News.* Retrieved December 22, 2005, from http://www .relojournal.com/nov96/culture.htm

Roberto, M. A. (2004). Strategic decision-making processes: Beyond the efficiency-consensus trade-off. *Group & Organization Management, 29,* 625–658.

Rogler, L. H, Cooney, R. S., & Ortiz, V. (1980). Intergenerational change in ethnic identity in Puerto Rican family. *International Migration Review, 14,* 193–214.

Rose, M. (1985). *Reworking the work ethic: Economic values and socio-cultural politics.* London: Schocken.

Rossant, J., Cohn, L., Ewing, J. Matlack, C., Reed, S., Reinhardt, A., et al. (2004, October 25). Europe's hot growth companies: They're boosting economies—and creating jobs. *Business Week Online.* Retrieved December 29, 2004, from http://www .businessweek.com/magazine/content/04_43/b3905401.htm

Roubini, N. (1999, January 29). Chronology of the Asian currency crisis and its global contagion. *NYU Asian Crisis Compilation*, p. 2.

Rubin, T. A., & Cox, W. (2001). *The road ahead: Innovations for better Texas transportation*. San Antonio: Texas Public Policy Foundation.

Ruhly, S. (1982). Intercultural communication. In S. Ruhly (Ed.), *MODCOM: Modules in speech communication* (pp. 1–48). Palo Alto, CA: Science Research Associates.

Rummel, R. (1976). *Understanding conflict and war* (Vol. 2). Beverly Hills, CA: Sage.

Ruscher, J. (2001). *Prejudiced communication*. New York: Guilford.

Rutgers University Libraries. (2005). Stock and commodity exchanges. Retrieved November 27, 2005, from http://www.libraries.rutgers.edu/rul/rr_gateway/research_guides/busi/stocks.shtml

Samovar, L. A., Porter, R. E., & McDaniel, E. R. (2006). *Communication between cultures* (6th ed.). Belmont, CA: Wadsworth.

Sampson, G. P. (2003). Overview. In G. P. Sampson (Ed.), *The role of the World Trade Organization in global governance* (pp. 1–8). New York: United Nations Press.

Sapir, E. (1921). *Language: An introduction to the study of speech*, New York: Harcourt, Brace, & World.

Saporito, B. (1988, May 9). The fly in Campbell's soup. *Fortune*, pp. 67–70.

Sarbaugh-Thompson, M., & Feldman, M. S. (1998). Electronic mail and organizational communication: Does saying "Hi" really matter? *Organizational Science, 9*, 685–698.

SCADPlus. (2005). The Amsterdam Treaty: A comprehensive guide. Retrieved July 25, 2005, from http://europa.eu.int/scadplus/leg/en/s50000.htm

Schein, E. (1996). Three cultures of management: The key to organizational learning. *Sloan Management Review, 38*, 9–28.

Schelling, T. C. (1960). *The strategy of conflict*. Oxford: Oxford University Press.

Schmidt, J. B., Montoya-Weiss, M. M., & Massey, A. P. (2001). New product development decision making effectiveness: Comparing individuals, face-to-face teams, and virtual teams. *Decision Sciences, 32*, 575–600.

Schmidt, W. V., & Conaway, R. N. (1999). *Results-oriented interviewing: Principles, practices, and procedures*. Boston: Allyn & Bacon.

Schmidt, W. V., & Dorsey M. E. (1986). Office design: The spatial dimension of organizational communication and reflector of communication climate. In S. Bruno (Ed.), *Perspectives in Business Communication* (pp. 25–37). Proceedings of the annual meeting of the Association of Business Communication-SW. Houston, TX: University of Houston-Clear Lake.

Schmidt, W. V., & Gardner, G. H. (1995). *Business and professional communication: Managing information in an information age*. Cincinnati, OH: South-Western.

Schwartz, P. (1991). *The art of the long view: Planning for the future in an uncertain world*. New York: Doubleday.

Schwartz, S. H. (1994). Beyond individualism/collectivism: New cultural dimensions of values. In U. Kim, H. C. Triandis, C. Kagitcibasi, S. C. Choi, & G. Voon (Eds.), *Individualism and collectivism: Theories, methods, and applications* (pp. 85–119). London: Sage.

Scott, R. (2003). Creating virtual learning environments is much closer than we think. *Computer Graphics, 37,* 26–26.

Searle, W., & Ward, C. (1990). The prediction of psychological and sociocultural adjustment during cross-cultural transitions. *International Journal of Intercultural Relations, 14,* 485–506.

Semlak, W. D. (1982). *Conflict resolving communication: A skill development approach.* Prospect Heights, IL: Waveland.

Shailor, J. (1994). *Empowerment in dispute mediation: A critical analysis of communication.* Westport, CT: Praeger.

Shauabi, A. (1999, October). Elements of corruption in the Middle East and North Africa. Retrieved March 1, 2005, from http://ww1.transparency.org/iacc/9th_iacc/papers/day1/ws5/dnld/d1ws5_ashuaibi.pdf

Shenkar, O. (2001). Cultural distance revisited: Towards a more rigorous conceptualization and measurement of cultural differences. *Journal of International Business Studies, 32,* 519–536.

Shiller, K. (1999). The camel market of Darawar. Retrieved March 21, 2004, from http://www.salon.com/wlust/feature/1999/03/cov_21feature2.html

Shin, S. (1998). An Interview with Stan Shin. In J. Kurtzman (Ed.), *Thought leaders* (pp. 84–93). San Francisco, CA: Jossey-Bass.

Shome, R., & Hegde, R. S. (2002). Culture, communication, and the challenge of globalization. *Critical Studies in Media Communication, 19*(2), 172–189.

Shrivastava, P. (1985). Integrating strategy formulation with organizational culture. *Journal of Business Strategy,* Winter, 103–111.

SICE. (2002). Southern Common Market (Mercosur) Agreement. Retrieved January 8, 2005, from http://www.itcilo.it/cnglish/actrav/telearn/global/ilo/blokit/mercoa.htm

SICE. (2005). OAS Overview of the North American Free Trade Agreement. Retrieved December 18, 2005, from http://www.sice.oas.org/summary/nafta/nafta1.asp

Sicherman, H. (1998). *The Asian panic, round two.* Washington, DC: Foreign Policy Research Institute.

Simeon, R. (2001). Top team characteristics and the business strategies of Japanese firms. *Corporate Governance, 1,* 4–13.

Singhal, A., & Nagao, M. (1993). Assertiveness as communication competence. *Asian Journal of Communication, 3,* 1–18.

Sivanathan, N., & Fekken, G. C. (2002). Emotional intelligence, moral reasoning, and transformational leadership. *Leadership & Organization Development Journal, 23,* 198–204.

Smith, A. G. (1966). *Communication and culture.* New York: Holt, Rinehart and Winston.

Smith, B., & Dodd, B. (1994). Consultancy reflections on the impact of groupware. *Industrial and Commercial Training, 26,* 26–33.

Smith, E. (1994). Social identity and social emotions. In D. Mackie & D. Hamilton (Eds.), *Affect, cognition, and stereotyping* (pp. 50–74). New York: Academic Press.

Snyder, M., & Haugen, J. (1995). Why does behavioral confirmation occur? *Personality and Social Psychology Bulletin, 21,* 963–974.

Sole, D., & Edmondson, A. (2002). Situated knowledge and learning in dispersed teams. *British Journal of Management, 13,* 517–534.

Spangle, M. L., & Isenhart, M. W. (2002). *Negotiation: Communication for diverse settings.* Thousand Oaks, CA: Sage.

Spitzberg, B. (1988). Communication competence: Measure of perceived effectiveness. In C. H. Tardy (Ed.), *A handbook for the study of human communication* (pp. 67–195). Norwood, NJ: Ablex.

Spitzberg, B. (1991). An examination of trait measures of interpersonal competence. *Communication Reports, 4,* 22–29.

Spitzberg, B. (2000). A model of intercultural communication competence. In L. A. Samovar & R. E. Porter (Eds.), *Intercultural communication: A reader* (9th ed., pp. 375–387). Belmont, CA: Wadsworth.

Spitzberg, B., & Cupach, W. (1984). *Interpersonal communication competence.* Beverly Hills, CA: Sage.

Sproull, L., & Kessler, S. (1986). Reducing social context cues: Electronic mail in organizational communication. *Management Science, 32,* 1492–1512.

Stanoch, P. P. (1994). When cultures clash. Retrieved November 28, 2005, from http://www.windowontheworldinc.com/pps_8.html

Statistics Canada. (2001). Retrieved December 18, 2005, from http://www12.statcan.ca/english/census01/Products/Analytic

Statistics Canada. (2005). Canada's 2001 population: Growth rates and trends. Retrieved November 4, 2005, from http://geodepot.statcan.ca/Diss/Highlights/Page2/Page2_e.cfm

Steele, L. W. (1975). *Innovation in big business.* New York: America Elsevier.

Steil, L. K., & Bommelje, R. K. (2004). *Listening leaders: The ten golden rules to listen, lead, and succeed.* Edina, MN: Beaver's Pond Press.

Stephan, W., & Stephan, C. (1985). Intergroup anxiety. *Journal of Social Issues, 41,* 157–166.

Stiglitz, J. (2003). *Globalization and its discontents.* New York: Norton.

Stimpson, C. R. (1994, 16 March). A conversation, not a monologue. *Chronicle of Higher Education,* p. B1.

Stohl, C. (2001). Globalizing organizational communication. In F. M. Jablin & L. L. Putnam (Eds.), *The new handbook of organizational communication: Advances in theory, research, and methods* (pp. 323–375). Thousand Oaks, CA: Sage.

Stovall, H. (2000, October). Arab commercial law—into the future. Retrieved February 18, 2004, from http://www.stovall-law.com/new-01.htm

Straub, D., & Karahanna, E. (1998). Knowledge worker communication and recipient availability: Toward a task closure explanation of media choice. *Organization Science, 9,* 160–175.

Straus, S. G. (1996). Getting a clue: The effects of communication media and information distribution on participation and performance in computer-mediated and face-to-face groups. *Small Groups Research, 27,* 115–142.

Straus, S. G., & McGrath, J. E. (1994). Does the medium matter: The interaction of task type and technology on group performance in computer-mediated reactions. *Journal of Applied Psychology, 79,* 87–97.

Sullivan, D. (1996). Organization structure in multinational corporations. In M. Warner (Ed.), *International encyclopedia of business and management* (pp. 3573–3597). London: Routledge.

Summit of the Americas. (2005). Summit of the Americas Information Network. Retrieved January 8, 2005, from http://www.summit-americas.org

Surowiecki, J. (2004, July 4). The wisdom of the crowd. *Orlando Sentinel,* pp. G1, G4.

Szapocznik, J., & Kurtines, W. (1980). Acculturation, biculturalism and adjustment of Cuban Americans. In A. Padilla (Ed.), *Acculturation* (pp. 113–130). Boulder, CO: Westview.

Szapocznik, J., Kurtines, W., & Fernandez, T. (1980). Bicultural involvement and adjustment of Hispanic-Americans. *International Journal of Intercultural Relations, 4,* 353–365.

Taft, R. (1977). Coping with unfamiliar cultures. In N. Warren (Ed.), *Studies in cross-cultural psychology* (Vol. I, pp. 125–133). New York: Academic Press.

Taylor, D., & Altman, I. (1975). Self-disclosure as a function of reward-cost outcomes. *Sociometry, 38,* 18–31.

Taylor, D., & Altman, I. (1987). Communication in interpersonal relationships: Social penetration processes. In M. Roloff & G. Miller (Eds.), *New directions in communication research* (pp. 257–277). Newbury Park, CA: Sage.

Terpstra, V., & David, K. (1985). *The cultural environment of international business.* Cincinnati, OH: South-Western.

Terpstra, V., & Kenneth, D. (1992). *The cultural environment of international business.* Cincinnati, OH: South-Western.

Terra Daily. (2005, December 1). Melting ice risks Canada-US Territorial dispute. Retrieved December 4, 2005, from http://www.terradaily.com/reports/Melting_ Arctic_Ice_Risks_Canada_US_Territorial_Dispute.html

Therrien, M., & Ramirez, R. R. (2001). The Hispanic population in the United States: Population characteristics. Retrieved March 25, 2001, from http://latinoculture .aboutcom/culture/lationoculture/library/extra/blcensus2000a.htm

Thill, J. V., & Bovee, C. L. (2005). *Excellence in business communication* (6th ed.). Upper Saddle River, NJ: Pearson Prentice Hall.

Thompson, L. L. (1998). *The mind and heart of the negotiator.* Upper Saddle River, NJ: Prentice Hall.

Tillia, C. (2003, December). Understanding and preserving African religions. *Nubian Voyage.* Retrieved December 12, 2004, from http://www.nubianvoyage.com/ DECEMBER_Article3.html

Tinder, G. (1980). *Community.* Baton Rouge: Louisiana State University Press.

Ting-Toomey, S. (1985). Toward a theory of conflict and culture. In W. Gudykunst, L. Stewart, & S. Ting-Toomey (Eds.). *Communication, culture, and organizational processes* (pp. 71–86). Beverly Hills, CA: Sage.

Ting-Toomey, S. (1988). Intercultural conflict styles: A face-negotiation theory. In Y. Y. Kim & W. Gudykunst (Eds.), *Theories in intercultural communication* (pp. 213–235). Newbury Park, CA: Sage.

Ting-Toomey, S., & Chung, L. C. (2005). *Understanding intercultural communication.* Los Angeles, Roxbury.

Ting-Toomey, S., & Oetzel J. G. (2001). *Managing intercultural conflict effectively.* Thousand Oaks, CA: Sage.

Toffler, A. (1970). *Future shock.* New York: Random House.

Toffler, A. (1990). *PowerShift.* New York: Bantam.

Townsend, A. M., DeMarie, S. M., & Hendrickson, A. R. (1996). Are you ready for virtual teams? *HR Magazine, 41,* 122–126.

Triandis, H. C. (1972). *The analysis of subjective culture.* New York: Wiley.

Triandis, H. C. (1984). A theoretical framework for the more efficient construction of cultural assimilators. *International Journal of International Relations, 8,* 301–330.

Triandis, H. C. (1988). Collectivism vs. individualism. In G. Verma & C. Bagley (Eds.), *Cross-cultural studies of personality, attitudes, and cognition* (pp. 60–95). London: Macmillan.

Triandis, H. C. (1990). Cross-cultural studies of individualism-collectivism. In J. Berman (Ed.), *Nebraska symposium on motivation* (Vol. 37, pp. 1–14). Lincoln: University of Nebraska Press.

Triandis, H. C. (1994). *Culture and social behavior.* New York: McGraw-Hill.

Triandis, H. C. (1995). *Individualism-collectivism.* Boulder, CO: Westview.

Triandis, H. C., & Singelis, T. M. (1998). Training to recognize individual differences in collectivism and individualism with culture. *International Journal of Intercultural Relations, 22,* 35–47.

Trifonovitch, G. (1977). Culture learning/culture teaching. *Educational Perspectives, 16,* 18–22.

Trompenaars, F., & Hampden-Turner, C. (1998). *Riding the waves of culture: Understanding diversity in global business* (2nd ed.). New York: McGraw-Hill.

Trompenaars, F., & Wooliiams, P. (2003). A new framework for managing change across cultures. *Journal of Change Management, 3,* 361–375.

Tuleja, E. A. (2005). Intercultural communication for business. In J. S. O'Rourke (Ed.), *Managerial communication series* (pp. 33–47). Mason, OH: Thompson-Southwestern.

Tung, R. L. (1981). Selection and training of personnel for overseas assignments. *Columbia Journal of World Business,* Spring, 68–78.

Tung, R. L. (1997). International and intranational diversity. In C. S. Granrose & S. Oskamp (Eds.), *Cross cultural work groups* (pp. 163–185). The Claremont Symposium on Applied Social Psychology. Thousand Oaks, CA: Sage.

Tung, R. L., & Miller, E. L. (1990). Managing in the twenty-first century: The need for global orientation. *Management International Review, 30,* 5–18.

Turner, J. H. (1988). *A theory of social interaction.* Stanford, CA: Stanford University Press.

Turoff, M., Hiltz, R., Bahgat, N. F., & Rama, A. R. (1993). Distributed group support systems. *MIS Quarterly, 17,* 399–417.

Ulaga, W. (1999). The Euro-consumer: Fiction or reality. Retrieved July 9, 2005, from http://cibs.tamu.edu/syllabi/ulaga10/index.htm

Ulijn, J., O'Hair, D., Weggerman, M., Ledlow, G., & Hall, H. T. (2000). Innovation, corporate strategy, and cultural context: What is the mission for international business communication? *The Journal of Business Communication, 37,* 293–316.

U.N. Economic and Social Commission for Asia and the Pacific. (2005). Foreign Direct Investment in Latin America: Current trends and future prospects. Retrieved January 8, 2005, from http://www.unescap.org/tid/publications/chap5_2069.pdf

United States Small Business Administration. (2005). Small business statistics. Retrieved December 18, 2005, from http://www.sba.gov/aboutsba/sbastats.html

U.S. Census Bureau. (2000). U.S. statistics in brief—population and vital statistics. Retrieved November 25, 2005, from http://www.census.gov/compendia/statab/

U.S. Census Bureau. (2003a). Large suburban cities in west are fastest-growing, census bureau reports. United States Department of Commerce News, July 10. Retrieved November 4, 2005, from http://www.census.gov/Press-Release/www/2003/cb03-106.html

U.S. Census Bureau. (2003b). Population by sex, age, Hispanic origin, and race. Retrieved December 3, 2005, from http://www.census.gov/population/socdemo/hispanic/ppl-165/tab01-1.txt

U.S. Census Bureau. (2005). Statistical Abstract of the United States: 2004–2005. Retrieved December 12, 2005, from http://www.census.gov/prod/2004pubs/04statab/pop.pdf

U.S.-Central America Free Trade Agreement. (2005). Retrieved January 9, 2005, from http://www.ustr.gov/Document_Library/Fact_Sheets/2004/Free_Trade_With_Central_America.html

U.S. Department of Agriculture. (2006). Fact Sheet: North American Free Trade Agreement. Retrieved September 10, 2006, from http://www.fas.usda.gov/info/factsheets/NAFTA.asp

U.S. Department of Commerce. (2003). U.S. direct investment abroad. Retrieved January 8, 2005, from https://bea.gov/bea/di/usdinc/inc_03.htm

U.S. Department of Education. (2000). Office of Minority Impact Hispanic Outreach Initiative. State of the Hispanic community. Retrieved July 16, 2001, from http://www.hr.doe.gov/OMEI/hispchal.html

U.S. Department of State. (2004). Dependencies and areas of special sovereignty. Retrieved December 11, 2005, from http://www.state.gov/s/inr/rls/10543.htm

U.S. Department of State. (2005a). Background notes: Russia. Retrieved July 3, 2005, from http://www.state.gov/r/pa/ei/bgn/3183

U.S. Department of State. (2005b). Countries and other areas. Retrieved July 3, 2005, from http://www.state.gov/p/eur/ci/

U.S. Department of State. (2005c). Country notes. Retrieved January 8, 2005, from http://www.state.gov/countries

U.S. Foreign and Commercial Service. (2005a). Commercial guide to Ethiopia. Retrieved March 11, 2005, from http://export.gov/mrktresearch/index.asp

U.S. Foreign and Commercial Service. (2005b). Commercial guide to Morocco. Retrieved March 11, 2005, from http://export.gov/mrktresearch/index.asp

USAID. (2003). HIV/AIDS and business in Africa. Retrieved January 20, 2005, from http://www.dec.org/pdf_docs/PNACX782.pdf

Valentino, C. L. (2004). The role of middle managers in the transmission and integration of organizational culture. *Journal of Healthcare Management, 49,* 393–375.

Van der Boon, M. (2005). Tempus fugit (time flees). Europublic. Retrieved December 22, 2005 from http://www.globaltmc.com/Articles%20html/temp.fugit.html

Varner, I. (2002). From the President of the Association for Business Communication. In A. Satzger & G. Ponicini (Eds.), *International perspectives on business communication: From past approaches to future trends* (pp. ix–x). New York: Peter Lang.

Varner, I., & Beamer, L. (2005). *Intercultural communication in the global workplace* (3rd ed.). Boston: McGraw-Hill Irwin.

Wade, C., & Jarvis, C. (1987). *Psychology.* New York: Harper and Row.

Wagenheim, K. (2004). Caribbean update including Central America. *Caribbean UPDATE.* Retrieved June 15, 2004, from http://www.caribbeanupdate.org

Waldrop, M. (1992). *Complexity.* New York: Simon & Schuster.

Walker, S. (1998, May 4). Debt "culture", Asian insolvency regimes feel strain; diversity bankruptcy systems in the region are suddenly forced to deal with a huge debt crisis. *National Law Journal, 20,* p. C3.

Wallace, P. (1999). *The psychology of the Internet.* Cambridge, UK: Cambridge University Press.

Walsh, J. E. (1973). *Intercultural education in the community of man.* Honolulu: University of Hawaii Press.

Walsh, J. E. (1979). *Humanistic culture learning.* Honolulu: University of Hawaii press.

Walther, J. B. (1994). Anticipated ongoing interaction versus channel effects on relational communication in computer-mediated interaction. *Human Communication Research, 20,* 473–501

Ward, C., Okura, Y., Kennedy, A., & Kojima, T. (1998). The U-curve on trial. *International Journal of Intercultural Relations, 22,* 277–291.

Washington Office on Latin America. (2004). U.S.-Central American Free Trade Agreement. What is CAFTA? Retrieved January 7, 2005, from http://www.wola.org/economic/cafta.htm

Watson, R. T., Pitt, L. F., Cunningham, C., & Nel, D. (1993). User satisfaction and service quality of the IS department: Closing the gaps. *Journal of Information Technology, 8,* 257–265.

Watson, W. E., Kuman, K., & Michaelson, L. K. (1993). Cultural diversity's impact on interaction process and performance: Comparing homogeneous and diverse task groups. *Academy of Management Journal, 36,* 590–602.

Watzlawick, P., Beavin, J., & Jackson, D. (1967). *The pragmatics of human communication.* New York: Norton.

Webster's New World Concise French Dictionary. (2004). Indianapolis, IN: Chambers Harrap.

Weeks, D. (1994). *The eight essential steps to conflict resolution.* New York: G. P. Putnam's Sons.

Wegner, D., & Vallacher, R. (1977). *Implicit psychology.* New York: Oxford University Press.

Weick, K. (1979). *The social psychology of organizing* (2nd ed.). Reading, MA: Addison-Wesley.

Weick, K. (1989). Organizing improvisation: 20 years of organizing. *Communication Studies, 40,* 241–248.

Weick, K. (2001). *Making sense of the organization.* Malden, MA: Blackwell.

Weick, K., & Van Orden, P. (1990). Organizing on a global scale: A research and teaching agenda. *Human Resource Management, 29*, 49–61.

Weiman, J., & Daly, J. (1990). Communicating strategically: Strategies in interpersonal communication. Hillsdale, NJ: Lawrence Erlbaum.

Weisman, J., & Murray, S. (2005, May 11). Senate passes spending bill: war's cost: $200 billion-plus. *Washington Post,* p. A17.

Welcome to the Caribbean. (2005). Retrieved May 15, 2005, from http://www.welcome tothecaribbean.com/culture.html

West, J. (1993). Ethnography and ideology: The politics of cultural representation. *Western Journal of Communication, 57,* 209–220.

Wheatley, M. J. (1999). *Leadership and the new science: Discovering order in a chaotic world.* New York: Berrett-Koehler.

Wheelen, T. L., & Hunger, J. D. (1998). *Strategic management and business policy* (5th ed.). Reading, MA: Addison-Wesley.

Whorf, B. L. (1956). *Language, thought, and reality.* Cambridge: MIT Press.

Wiemann, J., & Bradac, J. (1989). Metatheoretical issues in the study of communication competence. In B. Dervin (Ed.), *Progress in communication science* (Vol. 9, pp. 194–214). Norwood, NJ: Ablex.

Wiener, N. (1967). *The human use of human beings.* New York: Avon.

Williams, M. R., & Cooper, M. D. (1992). *Power persuasion* (3rd ed.). Greenwood, IA: Educational Video Group.

Williams, R. M. (1947). *The reduction of intergroup tensions.* New York: Social Science Research Council.

Williams, R. (1983). *Keywords: A vocabulary of culture and society* (rev. ed.). New York: Oxford University Press.

Wilmot, W. W., & Hocker, J. L. (2001). *Interpersonal conflict* (6th ed.). New York: McGraw-Hill.

Wilson, S. R., & Waltman, M. S. (1988). Assessing the Putnam-Wilson organizational communication conflict instrument (OCCI). *Management Communication Quarterly, 1,* 368–388.

Winchester, S. (1998). *The professor and the madman: A tale of murder, insanity, and the making of the Oxford English Dictionary.* New York: HarperCollins.

Winchester, S. (2005). *A crack in the edge of the world.* New York: HarperCollins.

Wolff, M. (2004). *Why globalization works.* Cambridge: Yale University Press.

WordIQ. (2004). Definition of Africa. Retrieved June 6, 2004, from http://www.wordiq .com/definition/Africa

WorldAtlas.com. (2005a). Europe; Asia; Africa. Retrieved June 21, 2005, from http:// worldatlas.com

WordAtlas.com. (2005b). Largest cities of the world – by population. Retrieved January 8, 2005, from http://worldatlas.com/citypops.htm

World Bank. (2005a). Data & Statistics: Country classification. Retrieved July 7, 2005, from http://www.worldbank.org/data/countryclass/classgroups.html

World Bank. (2005b). Infrastructure. Retrieved March 9, 2005, from http://rru.world bank.org/InvestmentClimate/ExploreTopics/Infrastructure.aspx

World Gazetteer. (2005). Retrieved May 17, 2005, from http://www.worldgazetteer.com/

World Health Organization Update. (2004, December). Retrieved January 21, 2005, from http://w3whosea.org/en/Section10/Section18/Section348.html

World Languages Knowledge Fair. (1999). French language distribution. Retrieved November 25, 2005 from http://www.lerc.educ.ubc.ca/LERC/courses/489/worldlang/french/frenchlanguagedistribution.html

World Statistics. (2005). Retrieved February 6, 2005, from http://www.internet worldstats.com/stats.htm

The world through their eyes. (2005, February 26). *The Economist*, p. 21.

Yarborough, E., & Wilmot, W. W. (1995). *Artful mediation: Constructive conflict at work.* Boulder, CO: Cairns.

Young, L. W. L. (1994). *Crosstalk and culture in Sino-American communication.* London: Cambridge University Press.

Young, M. H. (1998). The wide-awake club. *People Management, 4,* 46-49.

Yum, J. O. (1982). Communication diversity and information acquisition among Korean immigrants in Hawaii. *Human Communication Research, 10,* 459–469.

Yum, J. O. (1988). Locus of control and communication patterns of immigrants. In Y. Y. Kim & W. Gudykunst (Eds.), *Cross-cultural adaptation* (pp. 80–95). Newbury Park, CA: Sage.

Yzaguirre, R. (2001). Hispanic child outcomes continue to be pressing issues for the nation. Retrieved March 25, 2001, from http://www.nclr.org/content/news/detail/2195

Zack, M. H. (1993). Interactivity and communication mode choice in ongoing management groups. *Information Systems Research, 4,* 207–239.

Zaman, M. R. (1998, Fall). The causes and consequences of the 1997 crisis in financial markets of East Asia. *The Journal of Global Business,* pp. 37–43.

Zhou, D. R. (1998). Charting the course at the edges of the economic storm. *Pacific Forum CSIS,* PacNet no. 41. Retrieved September 20, 2006, from http://www.csis.org/media/csis/pubs/pac9841.pdf

Index

About the Authors

Dr. Roger N. Conaway is a professor of communication at The University of Texas at Tyler, where he teaches intercultural communication, organizational communication, and freedom of speech. Previously, he has taught at Central Missouri State University. Roger is a past president of the Southwest Regional Association for Business Communication and vice president of the Association for Business Communication. He has presented over 30 professional papers at international, national, and regional conferences and conducted workshops in the areas of interviewing and intercultural diversity. In 2002, he received with William J. Wardrope the Irwin-McGraw-Hill Distinguished Paper Award from the Federation of Business Disciplines. In 1992, he was nominated by the faculty of The University of Texas at Tyler for the Minnie Stevens Piper Professor Outstanding Teaching award. Roger travels frequently and conducts research internationally.

Dr. Conaway received a B.S. and an M.A. from Stephen F. Austin Sate University, and a Ph.D. in communication from Bowling Green State University.

Dr. Susan S. Easton is an assistant professor of organizational communication at Rollins College/Hamilton Holt School, Winter Park, Florida, where she teaches courses in organizational communication, group dynamics, and professional consulting. She has incorporated creative teaching methodologies while using on-line distance learning techniques to increase students' knowledge and use of relevant technical skills. Sue is First Vice-president for the Florida Communication Association and an active member of the National Communication Association, the Association for Business Communication, and the Society for Training and Development. Additionally, Easton & Associates has been a respected organizational development consulting network since 1988 specializing in innovative workforces including virtual environments and self-directed work teams. As president, Sue's client base includes such Fortune 500 companies as General Electric, Nike, Lockheed Martin, Walt

Disney World, PricewaterhouseCoopers, and Hyatt Hotels. Moreover, she has consulted to such not-for-profit organizations as Hospice of America, the City of Tallahassee, and the University of Hawaii. In 2003, she received the Walter E. Barden Award for Excellence and Innovation in Teaching from Rollins College, and in 2006 she received the Arthur Vining Davis Award for outstanding teaching and distinguished scholarship.

Dr. Easton received a B.A. degree from the State University of New York, the M.A. in education and human resource development from Syracuse University, and a Ph.D. in educational foundations and policy studies from Florida State University.

Dr. Wallace V. Schmidt is professor of organizational communication at Rollins College/Hamilton Holt School, Winter Park, Florida, where he teaches courses in communication theory, organizational communication, and intercultural communication. Previously, he has taught at Hofstra University, Texas Tech University, and The University of Texas at Tyler. Wally is a past president of the Florida Communication Association and an active member of the National Communication Association, Association for Business Communication, and American Society for Training and Development. He has presented professional papers at international, national, regional, and state conferences and conducted a variety of business workshops. He was awarded the FCA Scholar of the Year in 2004 and is currently editor of *The Florida Communication Journal*. Wally received the Walter E. Barden Award for Excellence and Innovation in Teaching from Rollins College in 1992 and again in 2005.

Dr. Schmidt received a BA degree, *cum laude,* from Midland Lutheran College in speech and communication, the MA in communication from the University of Nebraska, and a PhD in organizational communication from New York University.

William J. Wardrope is associate professor and chair of general business in the College of Business Administration at the University of Central Oklahoma, Edmond, Oklahoma, where he teaches courses in business communication and international business. Previously, he has taught at Baruch College, Stephen F. Austin State University, Texas State University—San Marcos, and the University of Central Oklahoma. William is a past president of the Southwest Regional Association for Business Communication and has been editor of the proceedings for the Association for Business Communication–Southwestern United States and served on the editorial board of *The Communication Teacher*. He has published widely in refereed journals and proceedings and has presented over 100 papers at professional conferences addressing business and international business issues. He has lectured at la Academia de Guerra de Chile, Valparaiso, Chile. William is an active member of the National Communication Association, the Association for Business Communication, the National Business Education

Association, and the American Society for Training and Development. In 1999, he received the Outstanding Business Communication Teacher Award from the Association for Business Communication–Southwestern United States and in 2004 the Outstanding Researcher Award.

Dr. Wardrope received a B.A. degree from the University of Central Oklahoma in speech, the M.A. in organizational communication from Oklahoma State University, and a Ph.D. in communication studies from the University of Nebraska.